We finally reached volume 20. I want to thank all of you for your support! Here's a song to express my appreciation.

"Hungry Hungry Hungry I'm Hungry—Da—nda Dandandan... ♪"

– Takeshi Konomi

## About Takeshi Konomi

Takeshi Konomi exploded onto the manga scene with the incredible **THE PRINCE OF TENNIS**. His refined art style and sleek character designs proved popular with **Weekly Shonen Jump** readers, and **THE PRINCE OF TENNIS** became the number one sports manga in Japan almost overnight. Its cast of fascinating male tennis players attracted legions of female readers even though it was originally intended to be a boys' comic. The manga continues to be a success in Japan and has inspired a hit anime series, as well as several video games and mountains of merchandise.

**THE PRINCE OF TENNIS**
**VOL. 20**
**The SHONEN JUMP Manga Edition**

**STORY AND ART BY**
**TAKESHI KONOMI**

Translation/Joe Yamazaki
Consultant/Michelle Pangilinan
Touch-up Art & Lettering/Vanessa Satone
Design/Sam Elzway
Editor/Joel Enos

Editor in Chief, Books/Alvin Lu
Editor in Chief, Magazines/Marc Weidenbaum
VP of Publishing Licensing/Rika Inouye
VP of Sales/Gonzalo Ferreyra
Sr. VP of Marketing/Liza Coppola
Publisher/Hyoe Narita

Printed in the U.S.A.

Published by VIZ Media, LLC
P.O. Box 77010
San Francisco, CA 94107

SHONEN JUMP Manga Edition
10 9 8 7 6 5 4 3 2
First printing, July 2007
Second printing, October 2007

PARENTAL ADVISORY
THE PRINCE OF TENNIS
is rated A and is suitable
for readers of all ages.
ratings.viz.com

THE WORLD'S
MOST POPULAR MANGA

# VOL. 20
## Seishun vs. Rokkaku

**Story & Art by**
**Takeshi Konomi**

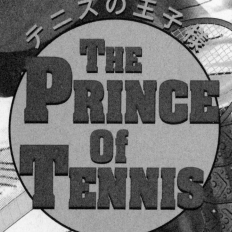

テニスの王子

# THE PRINCE OF TENNIS

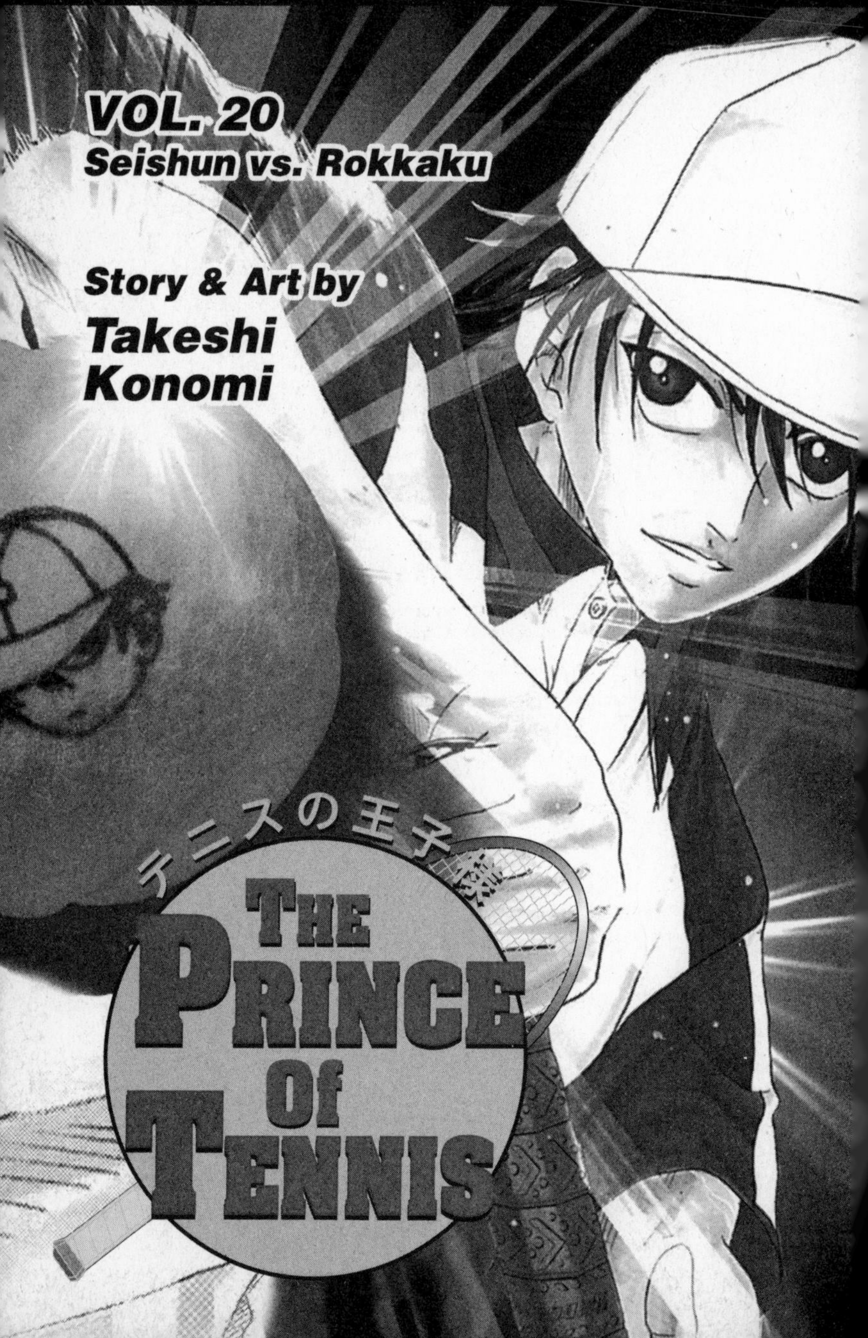

# ENNIS CLUB

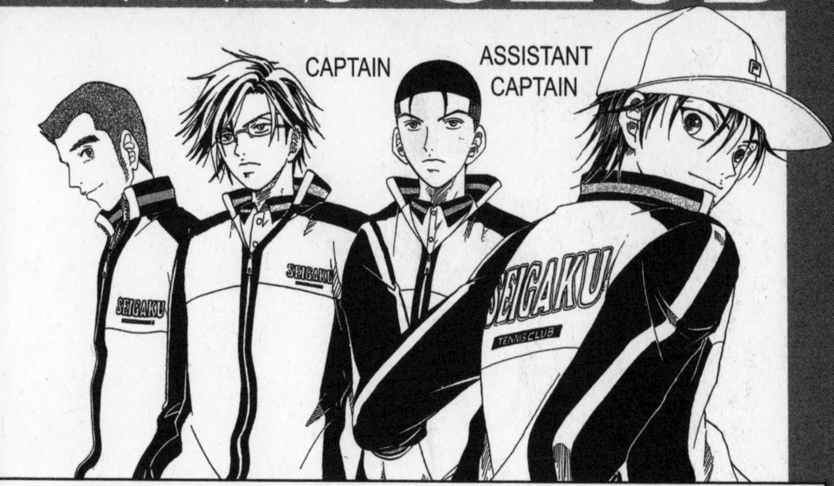

CAPTAIN
ASSISTANT CAPTAIN


● TAKASHI KAWAMURA ● KUNIMITSU TEZUKA ● SHUICHIRO OISHI ● RYOMA ECHIZEN ●

# STORY & CHARACTERS

Seishun Academy student Ryoma Echizen is a tennis prodigy with wins in four consecutive U.S. Junior tournaments under his belt. Then he became a starter as a 7th grader and led his team to the District Preliminaries! Despite a few mishaps, Seishun won the District Prelims and City Tournament, and even earned a ticket to the Kanto Tournament.

Now the Kanto Tournament is underway. Seishun's first round opponent is last year's Nationals runner-up — Hyotei Academy!

With Kunimitsu's surprising loss and Taka's no-contest, there is no winner after the completion of all five matches. But with Ryoma's victory in the 6th match, Seishun advances to the 2nd round. Kunimitsu, who injured his shoulder during his match, heads to Kyushu for treatment. With him gone, Seishun's team bond grows stronger. They defeat powerhouse Midoriyama to make it to the final four, getting them to the long-awaited Nationals!

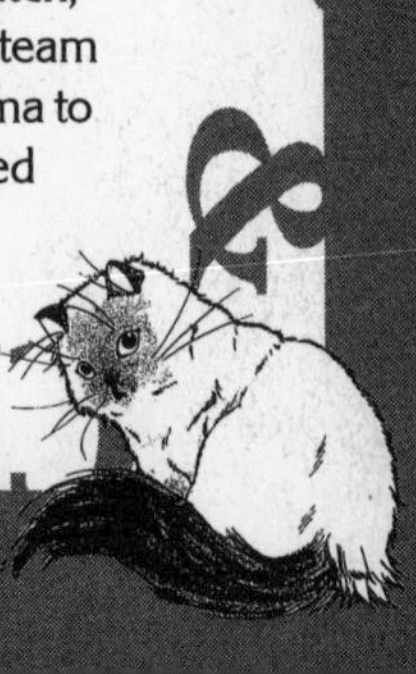

# SEIGAKU T

• KAORU KAIDO • TAKESHI MOMOSHIRO • SADAHARU INUI • EIJI KIKUMARU • SHUSUKE FUJI •

OJI

ROKKAKU JUNIOR HIGH
SCHOOL TENNIS COACH

SUMIRE RYUZAKI

SEISHUN ACADEMY
TENNIS COACH

THE PRINCE OF TENNIS

KOJIRO SAEKI

ROKKAKU

HARUKAZE KUROBANE

ROKKAKU

HIKARU AMANE

ROKKAKU

SAKUNO RYUZAKI

SEISHUN ACADEMY
TENNIS TEAM

KENTARO AOI

ROKKAKU

MAREHIKO ITSUKI

ROKKAKU

# CONTENTS
### Vol. 20
### Seishun vs. Rokkaku

| 5th Match — No. 1 Singles | 4th Match — No. 2 Singles | 3rd Match — No. 3 Singles | 2nd Match — No. 1 Doubles | | 1st Match — No. 2 Doubles | |
|---|---|---|---|---|---|---|
| KIPPEI TACHIBANA (9th Grade) Blood Type O | AKIRA KAMIO (8th Grade) Blood Type O | SHINJI IBU (8th Grade) Blood Type AB | MASAYA SAKURAI (8th Grade) Blood Type O | TETSU ISHIDA (8th Grade) Blood Type O | TATSUNORI MORI (8th Grade) Blood Type A | KYOSUKE UCHIMURA (8th Grade) Blood Type B |

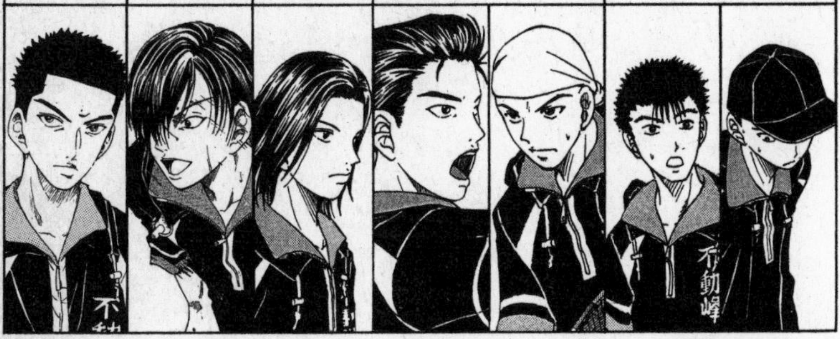
不動峰

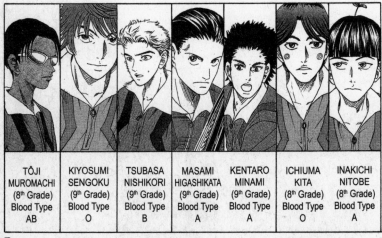

# GENIUS 168: THE MAN WITH THE LONG RACKET

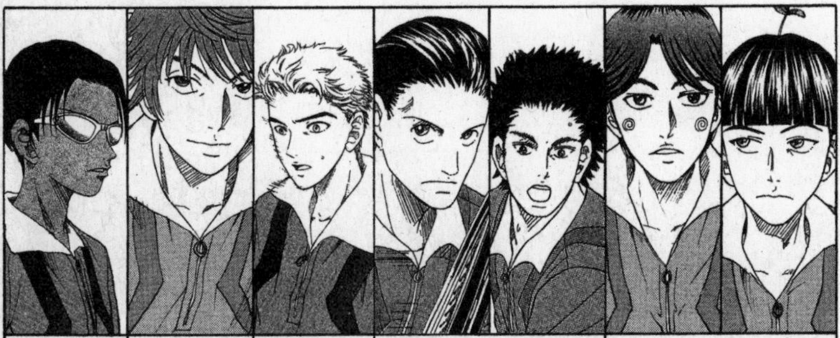

| | | | | | | |
|---|---|---|---|---|---|---|
| TÔJI MUROMACHI (8th Grade) Blood Type AB | KIYOSUMI SENGOKU (9th Grade) Blood Type O | TSUBASA NISHIKORI (9th Grade) Blood Type B | MASAMI HIGASHIKATA (9th Grade) Blood Type A | KENTARO MINAMI (9th Grade) Blood Type A | ICHIUMA KITA (8th Grade) Blood Type O | INAKICHI NITOBE (8th Grade) Blood Type A |

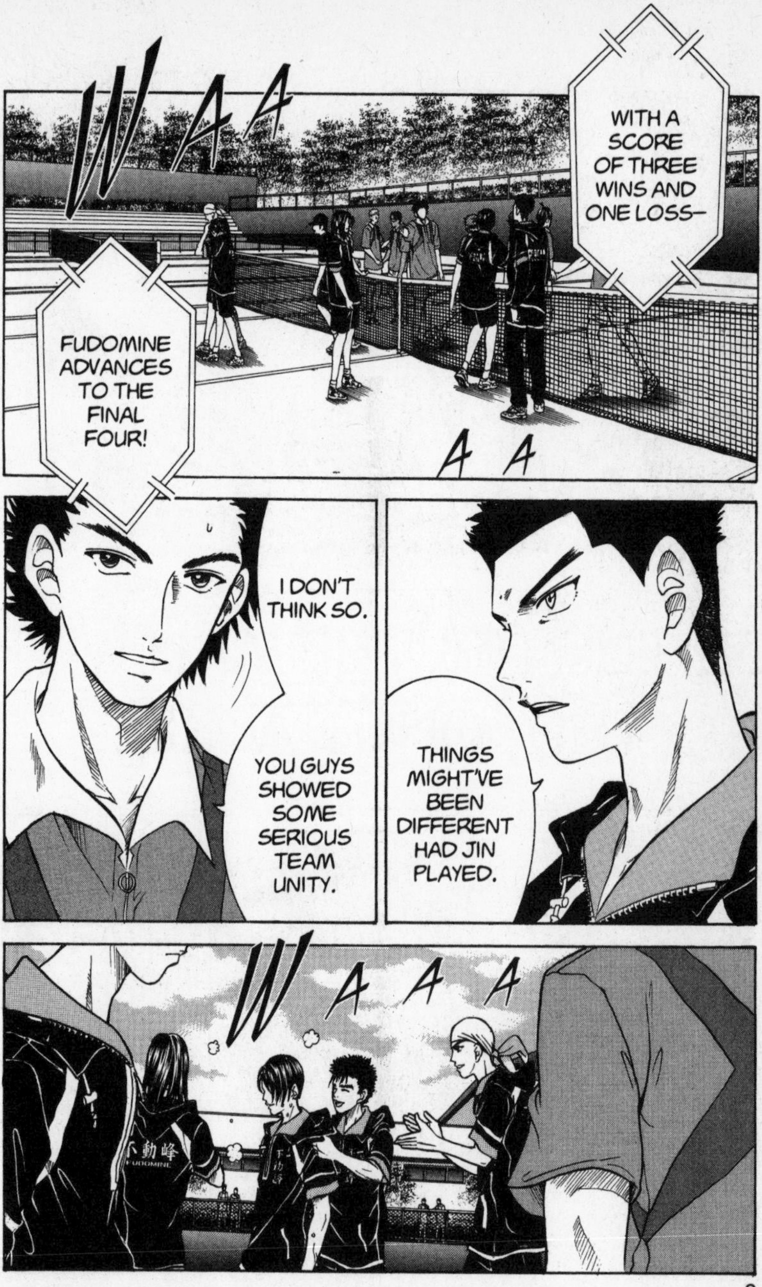

WITH A SCORE OF THREE WINS AND ONE LOSS—
WAA
FUDOMINE ADVANCES TO THE FINAL FOUR!
AA
THINGS MIGHT'VE BEEN DIFFERENT HAD JIN PLAYED.
I DON'T THINK SO.
YOU GUYS SHOWED SOME SERIOUS TEAM UNITY.
WAAA

READ THIS WAY

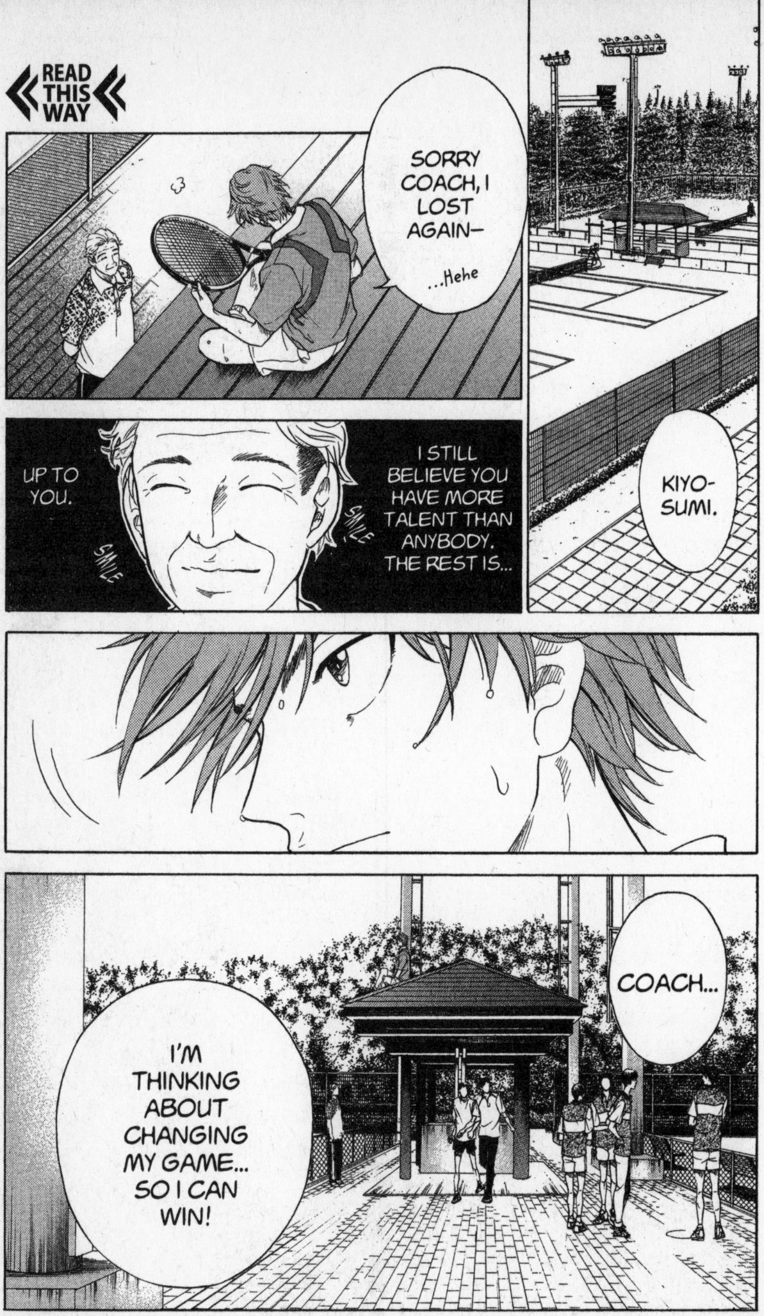

KIYO-SUMI.
SORRY COACH, I LOST AGAIN—
...Hehe
I STILL BELIEVE YOU HAVE MORE TALENT THAN ANYBODY. THE REST IS...
SMILE
SMILE
UP TO YOU.
COACH...
I'M THINKING ABOUT CHANGING MY GAME... SO I CAN WIN!

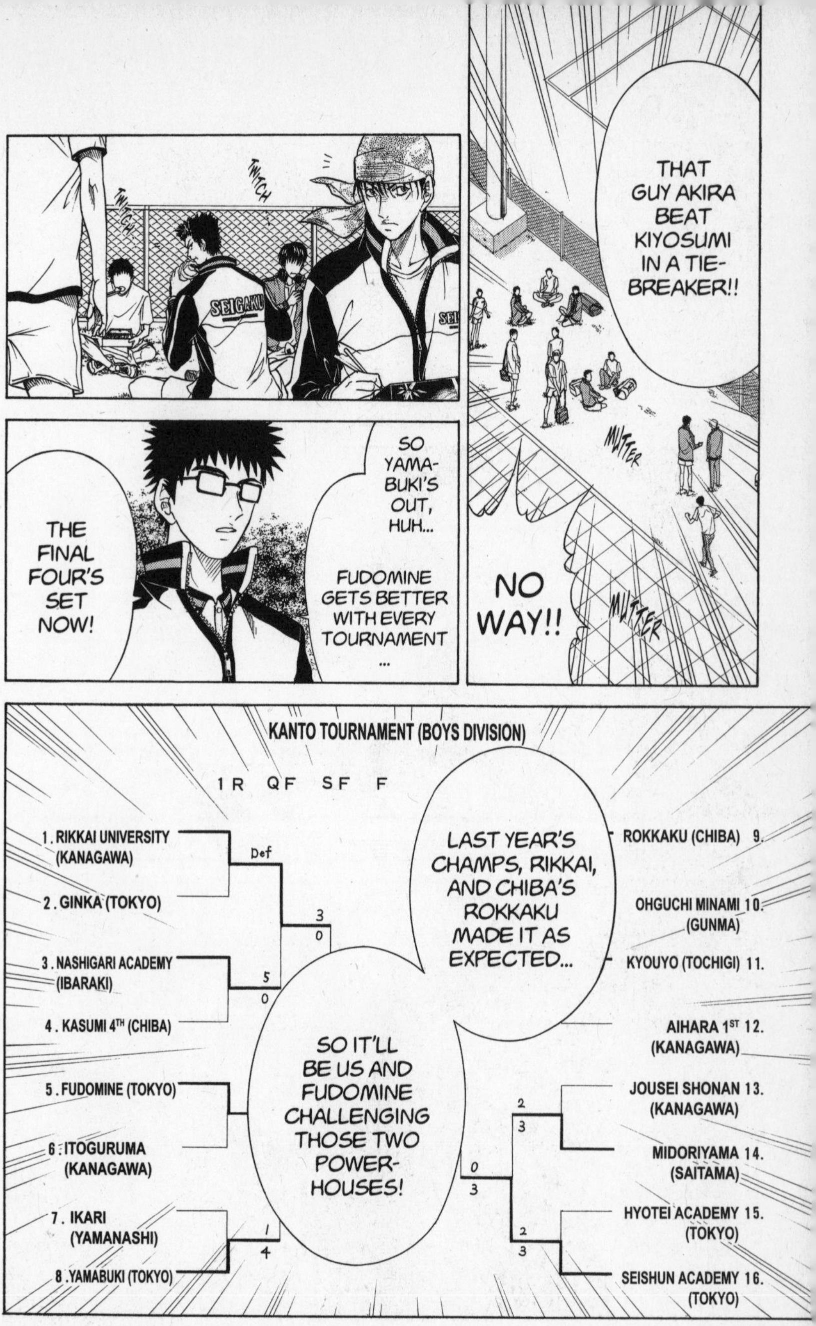
THAT GUY AKIRA BEAT KIYOSUMI IN A TIE-BREAKER!!
MUTTER
NO WAY!!
MUTTER
TWITCH
TWITCH
SO YAMA-BUKI'S OUT, HUH...
FUDOMINE GETS BETTER WITH EVERY TOURNAMENT ...
THE FINAL FOUR'S SET NOW!
KANTO TOURNAMENT (BOYS DIVISION)
1R QF SF F
1. RIKKAI UNIVERSITY (KANAGAWA)
2. GINKA (TOKYO)
3. NASHIGARI ACADEMY (IBARAKI)
4. KASUMI 4TH (CHIBA)
5. FUDOMINE (TOKYO)
6. ITOGURUMA (KANAGAWA)
7. IKARI (YAMANASHI)
8. YAMABUKI (TOKYO)
Def
3
0
5
0
1
4
ROKKAKU (CHIBA) 9.
OHGUCHI MINAMI 10. (GUNMA)
KYOUYO (TOCHIGI) 11.
AIHARA 1ST 12. (KANAGAWA)
JOUSEI SHONAN 13. (KANAGAWA)
MIDORIYAMA 14. (SAITAMA)
HYOTEI ACADEMY 15. (TOKYO)
SEISHUN ACADEMY 16. (TOKYO)
2
3
0
3
2
3
LAST YEAR'S CHAMPS, RIKKAI, AND CHIBA'S ROKKAKU MADE IT AS EXPECTED...
SO IT'LL BE US AND FUDOMINE CHALLENGING THOSE TWO POWER-HOUSES!

READ THIS WAY

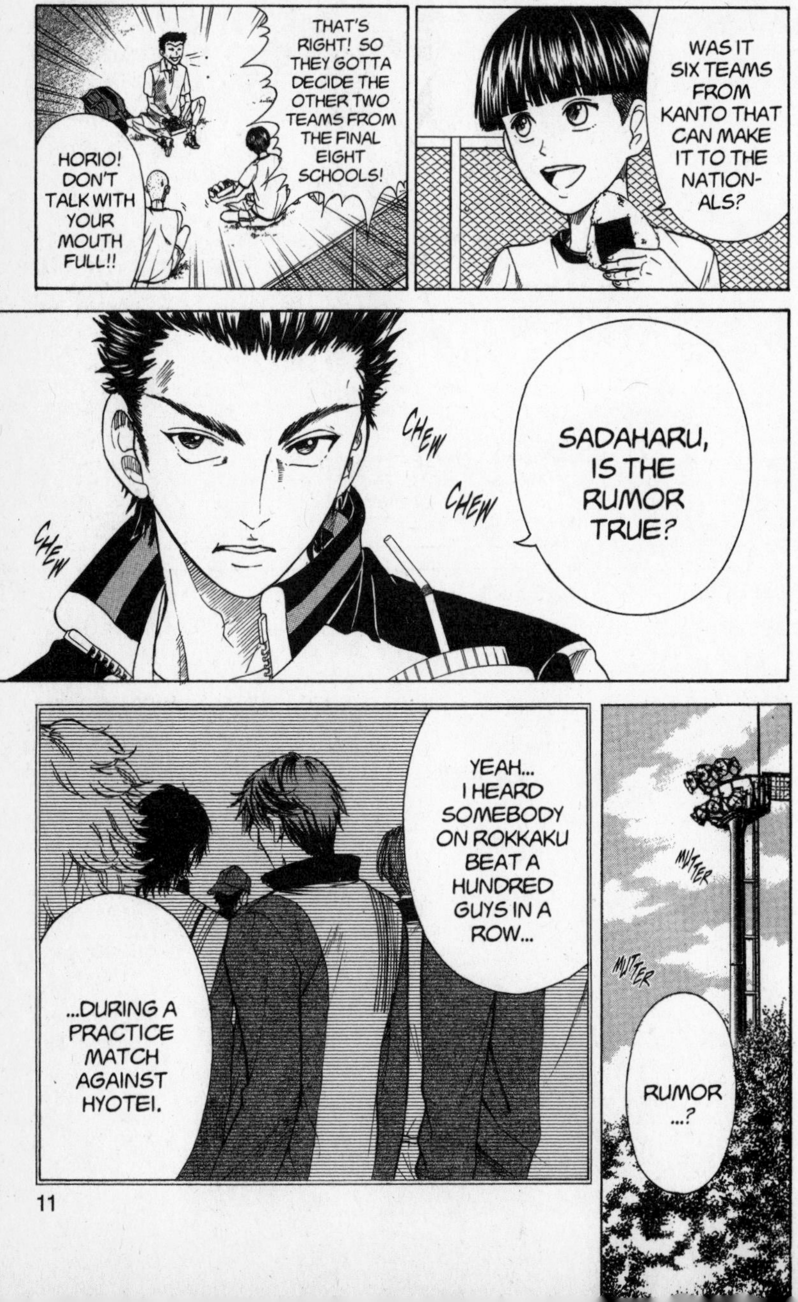

WAS IT SIX TEAMS FROM KANTO THAT CAN MAKE IT TO THE NATION-ALS?
THAT'S RIGHT! SO THEY GOTTA DECIDE THE OTHER TWO TEAMS FROM THE FINAL EIGHT SCHOOLS!
HORIO! DON'T TALK WITH YOUR MOUTH FULL!!
SADAHARU, IS THE RUMOR TRUE?
CHEW
CHEW
CHEW
MUTTER
MUTTER
RUMOR ...?
YEAH... I HEARD SOMEBODY ON ROKKAKU BEAT A HUNDRED GUYS IN A ROW...
...DURING A PRACTICE MATCH AGAINST HYOTEI.

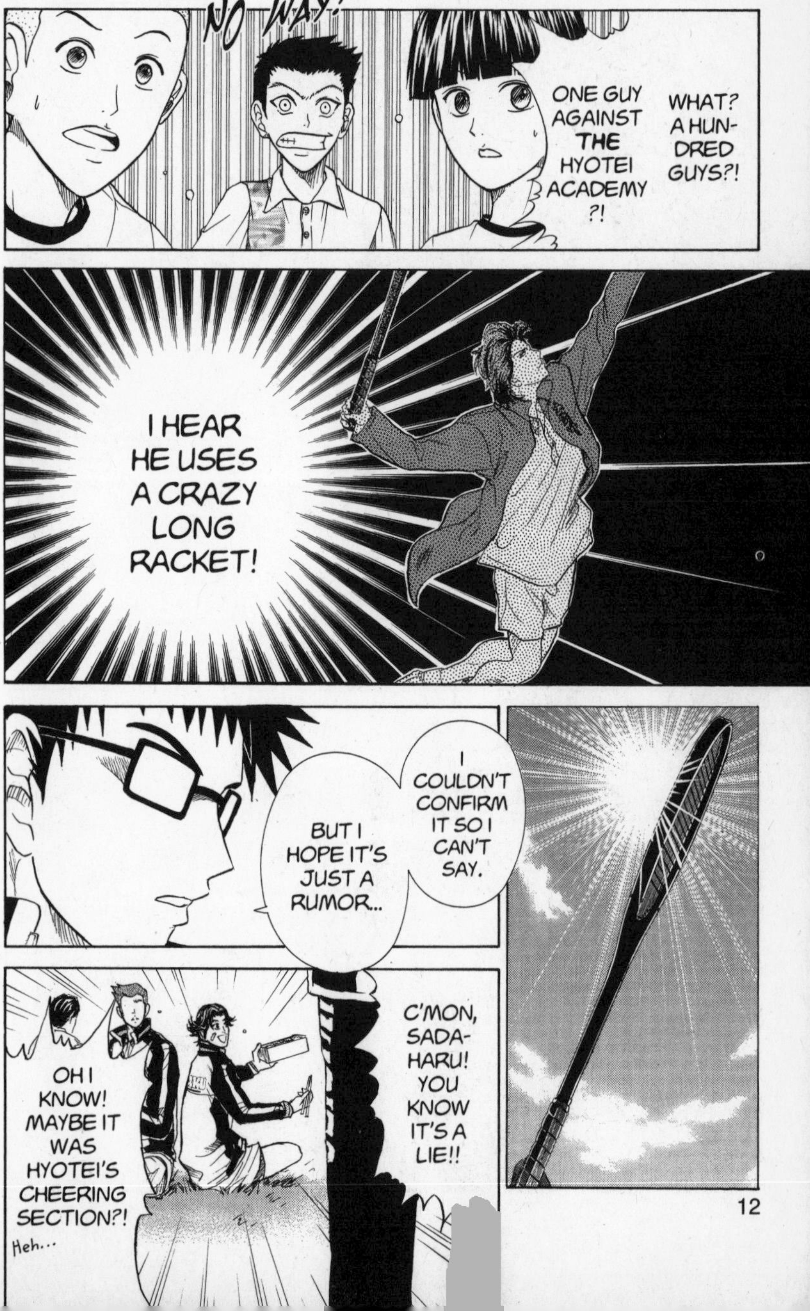
WHAT? A HUN-DRED GUYS?!
ONE GUY AGAINST THE HYOTEI ACADEMY ?!
NO WAY!
I HEAR HE USES A CRAZY LONG RACKET!
I COULDN'T CONFIRM IT SO I CAN'T SAY.
BUT I HOPE IT'S JUST A RUMOR...
C'MON, SADA-HARU! YOU KNOW IT'S A LIE!!
OH I KNOW! MAYBE IT WAS HYOTEI'S CHEERING SECTION?!
Heh...

READ THIS WAY

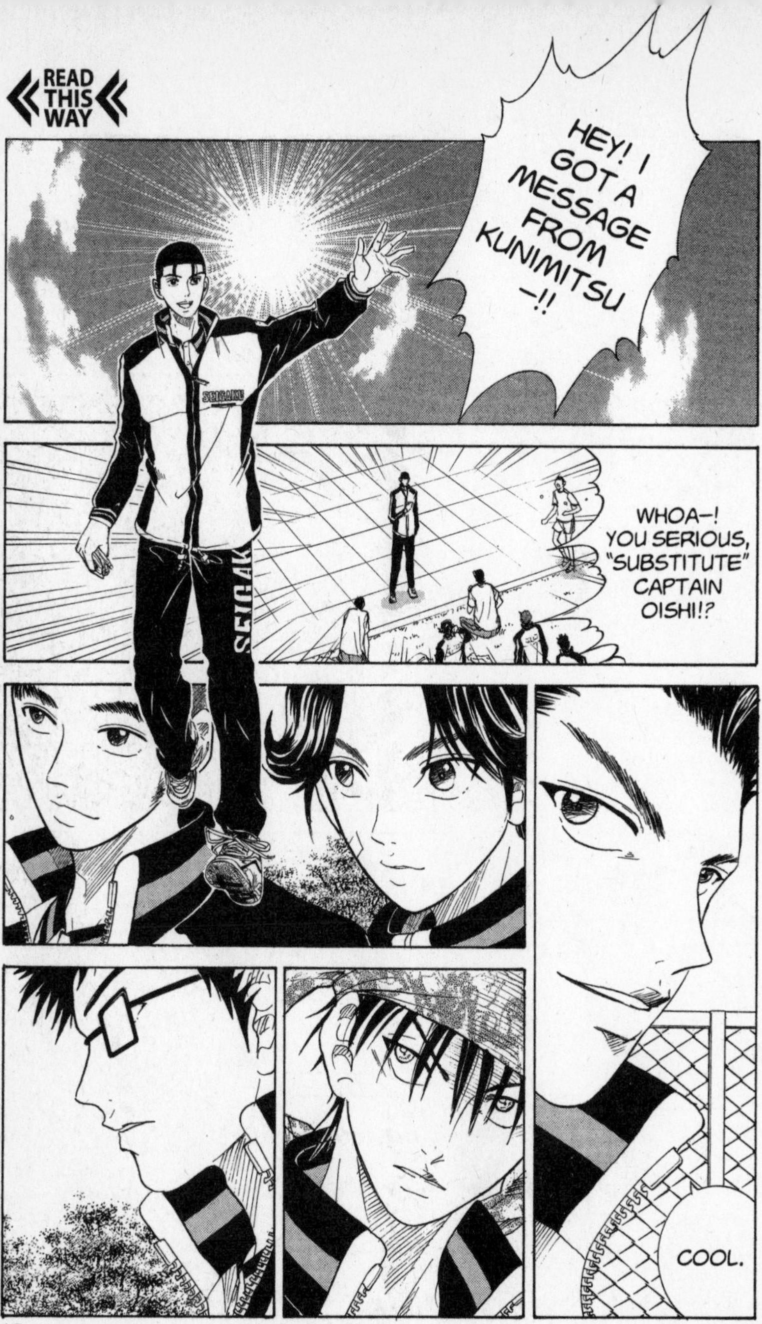

HEY! I GOT A MESSAGE FROM KUNIMITSU–!!
WHOA–! YOU SERIOUS, "SUBSTITUTE" CAPTAIN OISHI!?
COOL.

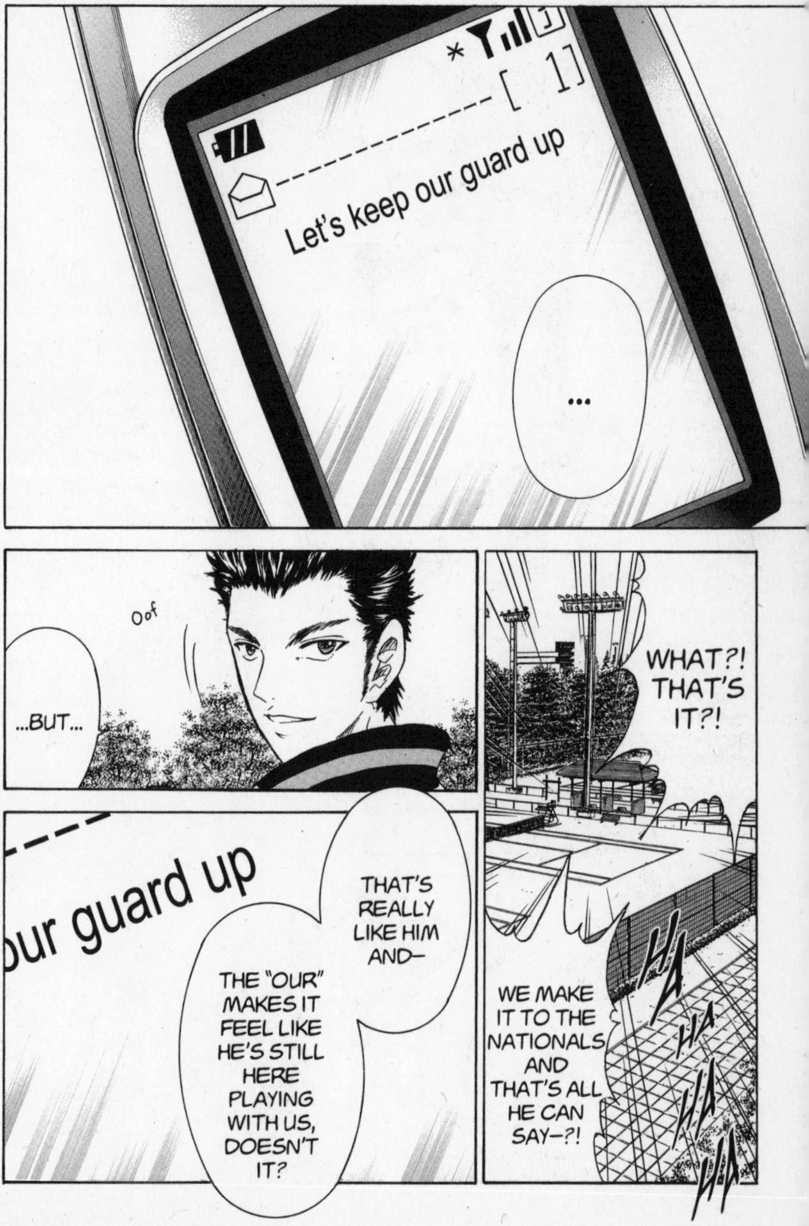
Let's keep our guard up
...
WHAT?! THAT'S IT?!
WE MAKE IT TO THE NATIONALS AND THAT'S ALL HE CAN SAY—?!
HA HA HA HA HA
Oof
...BUT...
our guard up
THAT'S REALLY LIKE HIM AND—
THE "OUR" MAKES IT FEEL LIKE HE'S STILL HERE PLAYING WITH US, DOESN'T IT?

READ THIS WAY

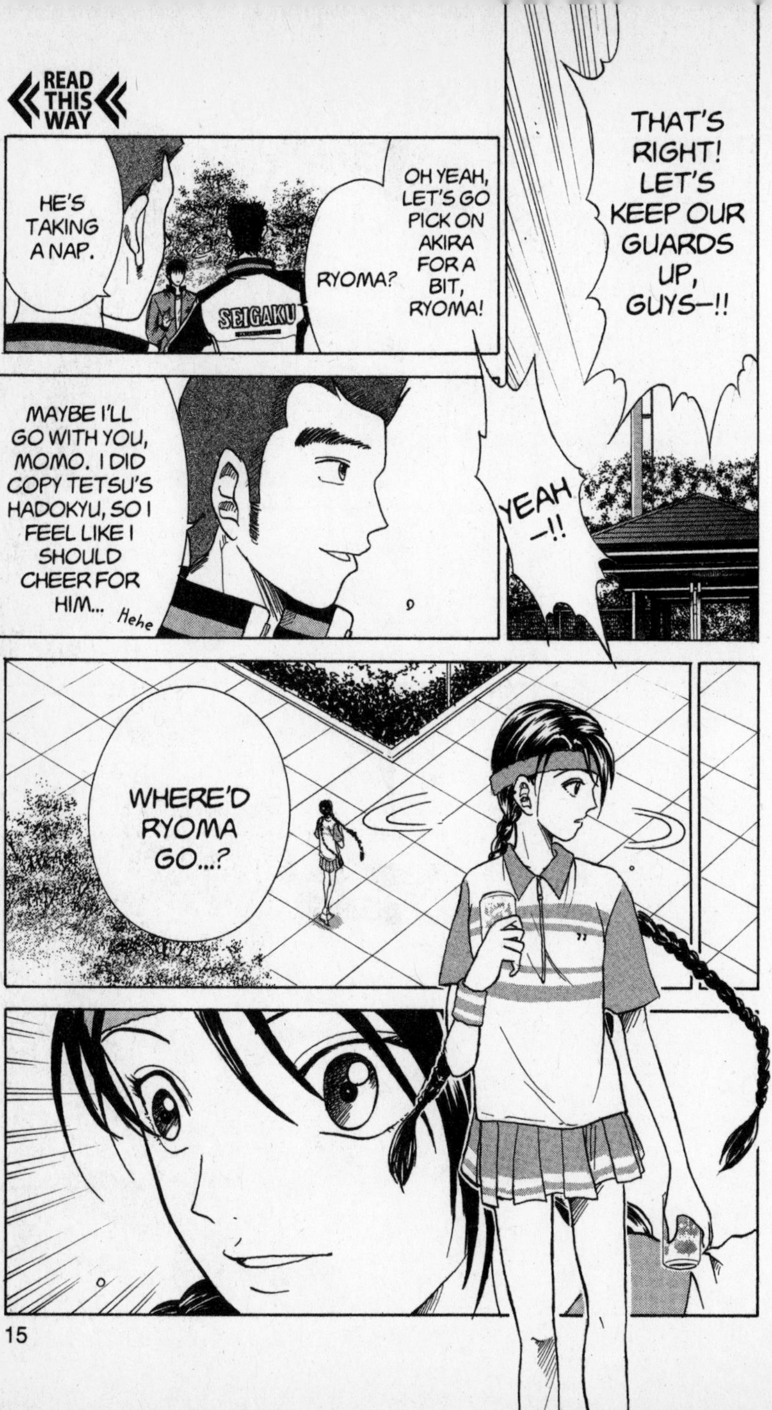
THAT'S RIGHT! LET'S KEEP OUR GUARDS UP, GUYS—!!
YEAH—!!
OH YEAH, LET'S GO PICK ON AKIRA FOR A BIT, RYOMA!
RYOMA?
SEIGAKU
HE'S TAKING A NAP.
MAYBE I'LL GO WITH YOU, MOMO. I DID COPY TETSU'S HADOKYU, SO I FEEL LIKE I SHOULD CHEER FOR HIM...
Hehe
WHERE'D RYOMA GO...?

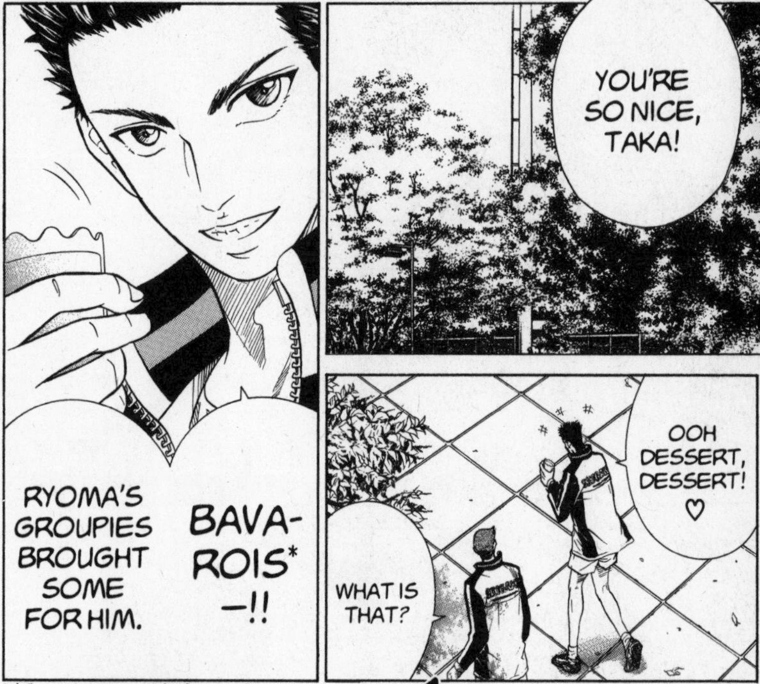
YOU'RE SO NICE, TAKA!
OOH DESSERT, DESSERT! ♡
WHAT IS THAT?
BAVAROIS* —!!
RYOMA'S GROUPIES BROUGHT SOME FOR HIM.

*A French dessert named for Bavarian Cream.

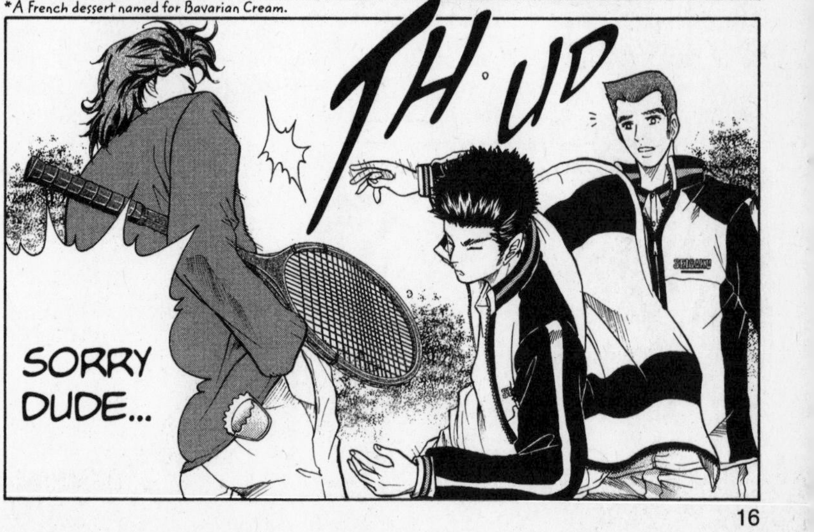
THUD
SORRY DUDE...

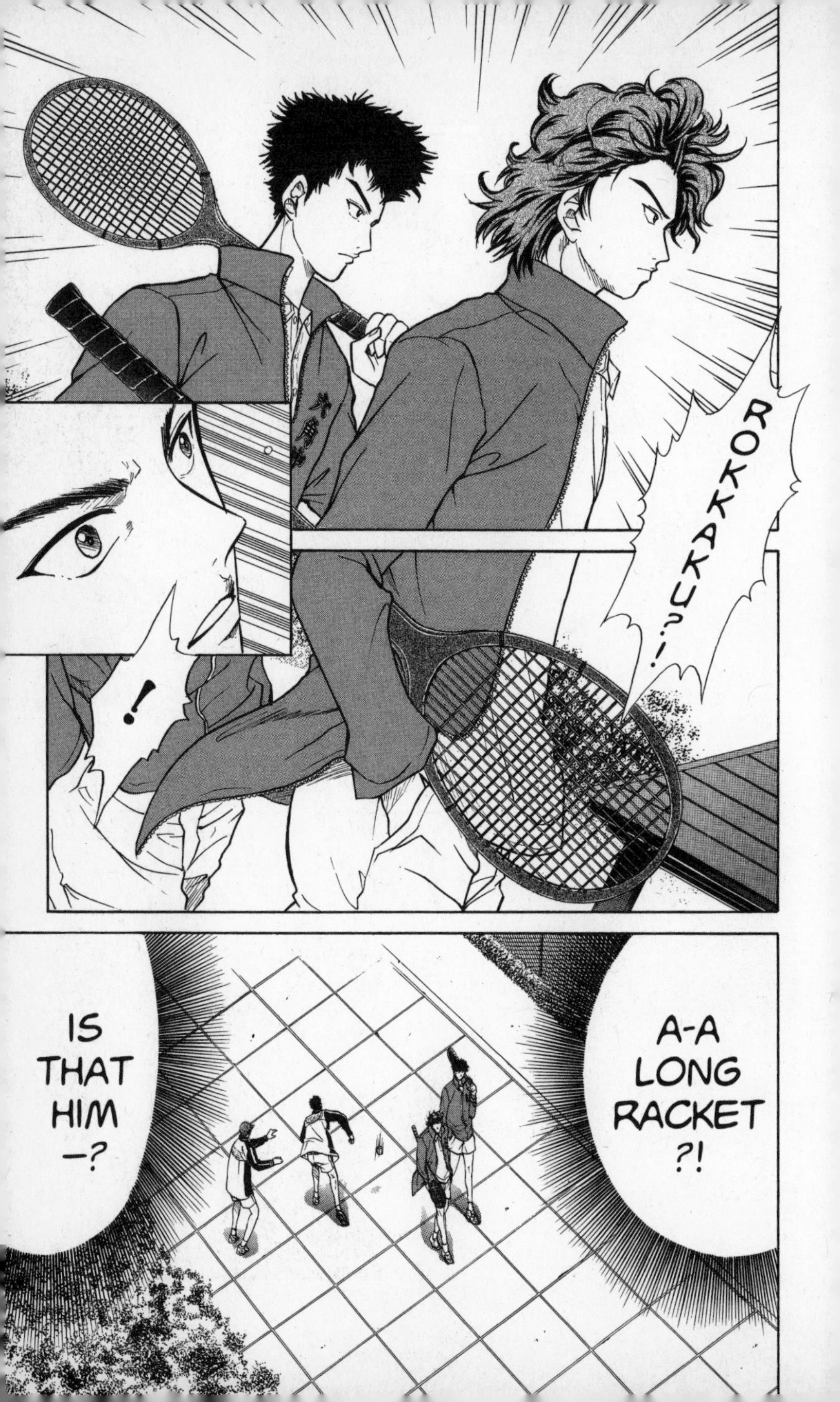
ROKKAKU?!
!
A-A LONG RACKET?!
IS THAT HIM—?

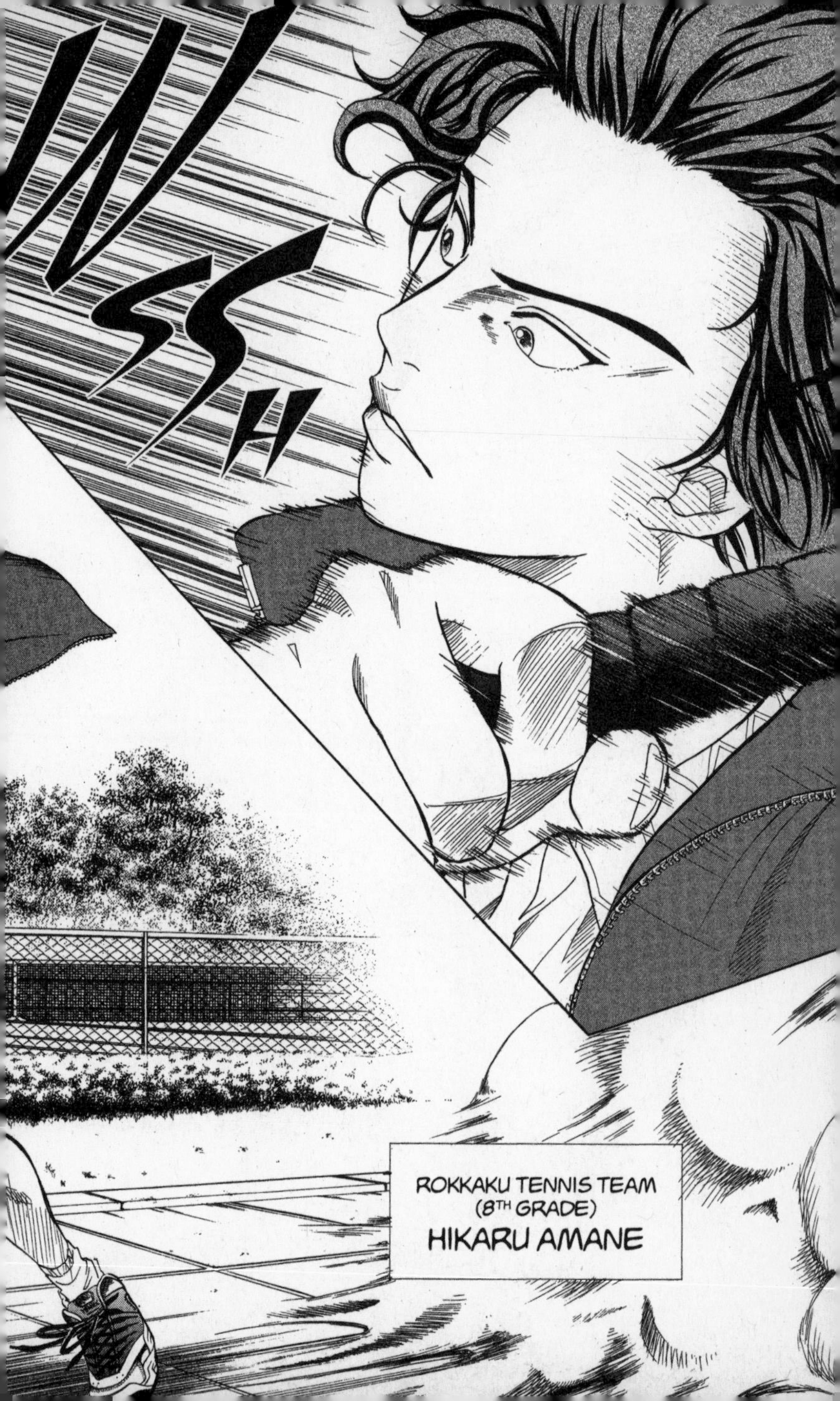
WHSSH
ROKKAKU TENNIS TEAM
(8TH GRADE)
HIKARU AMANE

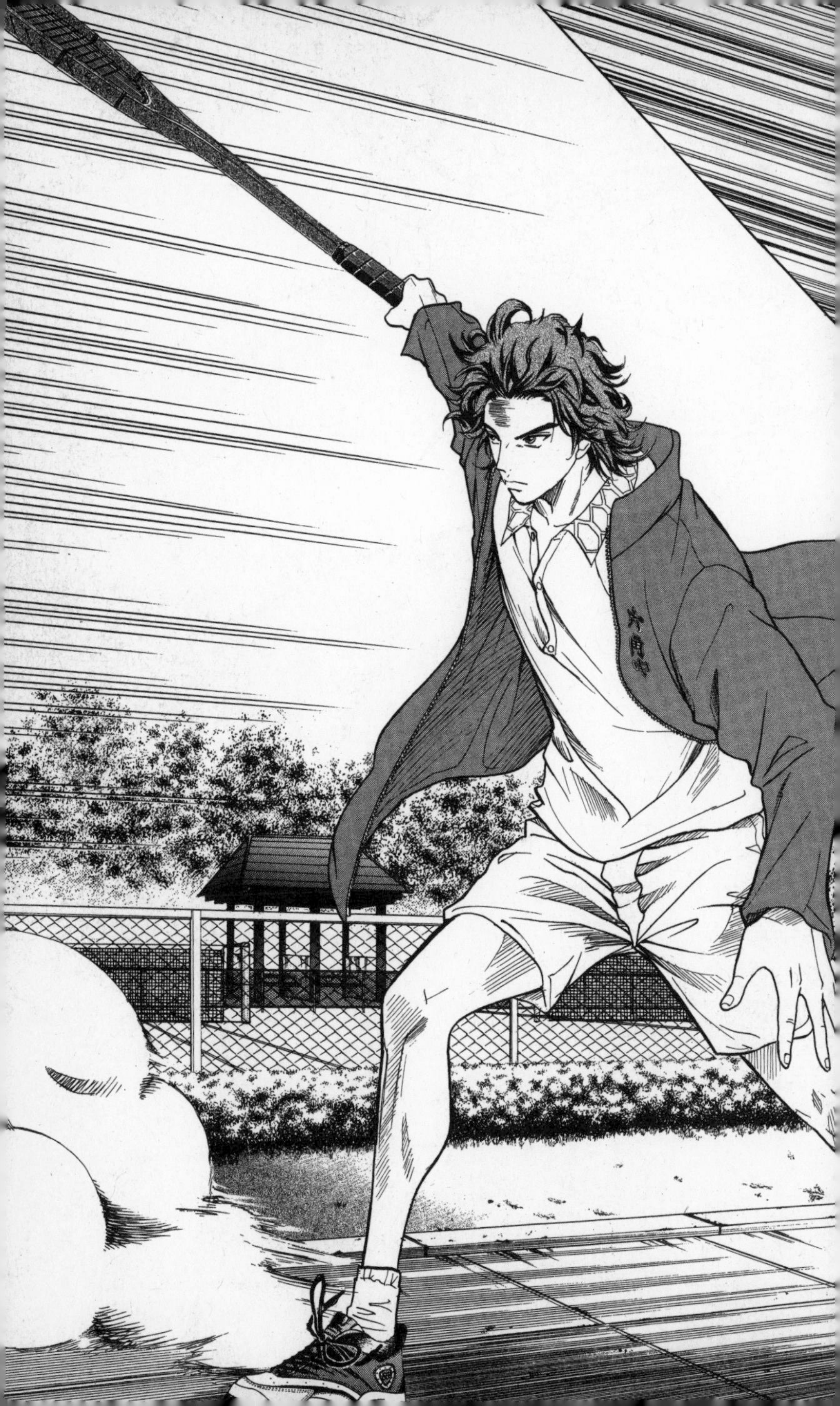

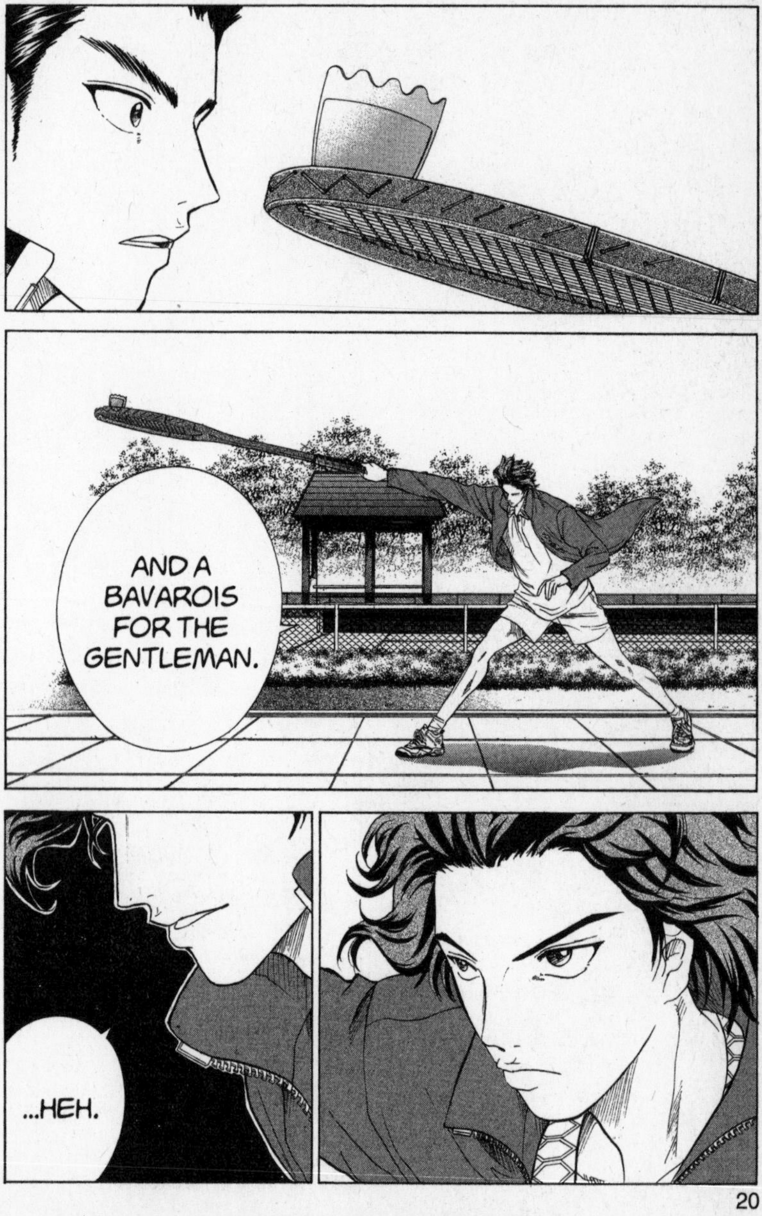
AND A BAVAROIS FOR THE GENTLEMAN.
...HEH.

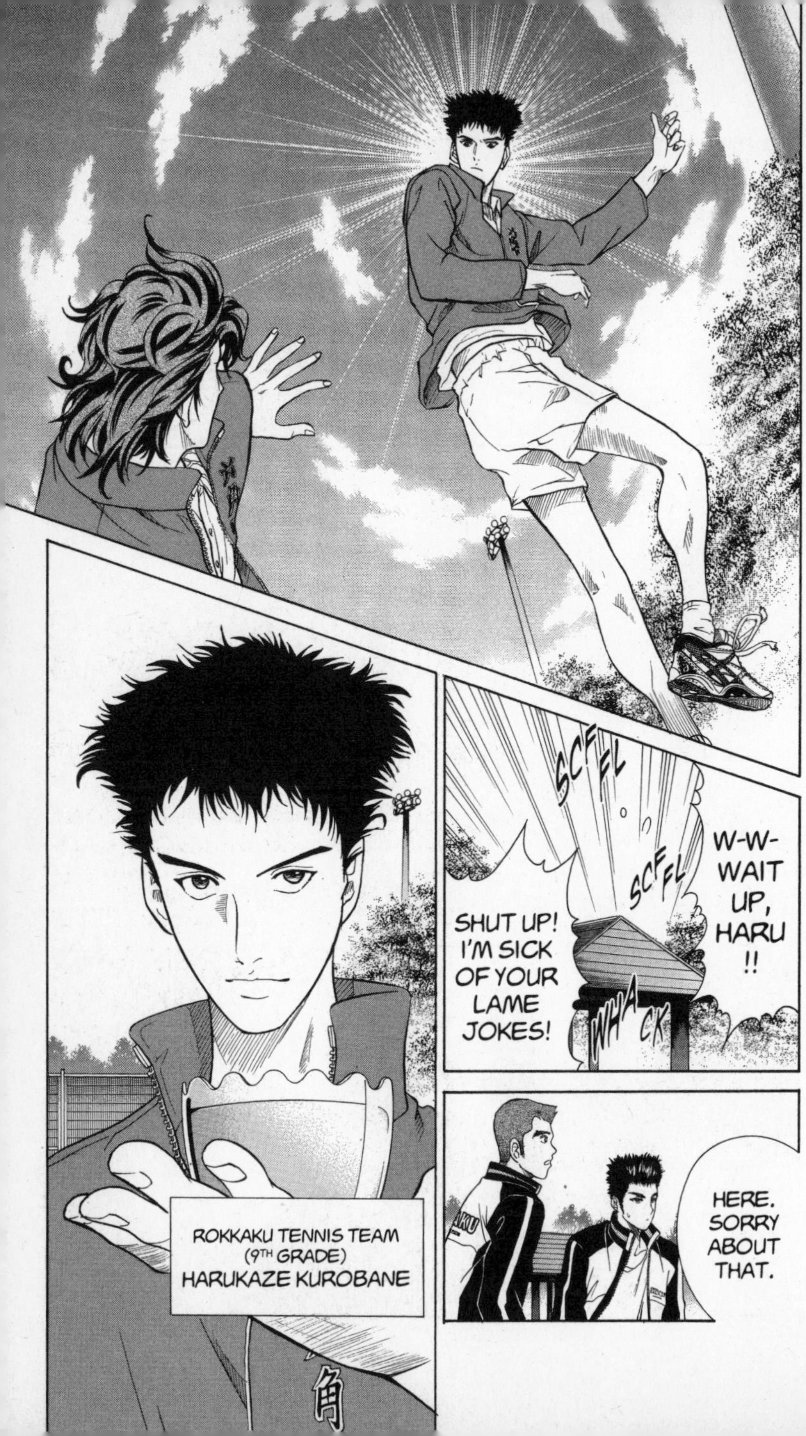
SCFFL
W-W-WAIT UP, HARU!!
SCFFL
SHUT UP! I'M SICK OF YOUR LAME JOKES!
WHACK
HERE. SORRY ABOUT THAT.
ROKKAKU TENNIS TEAM (9TH GRADE) HARUKAZE KUROBANE

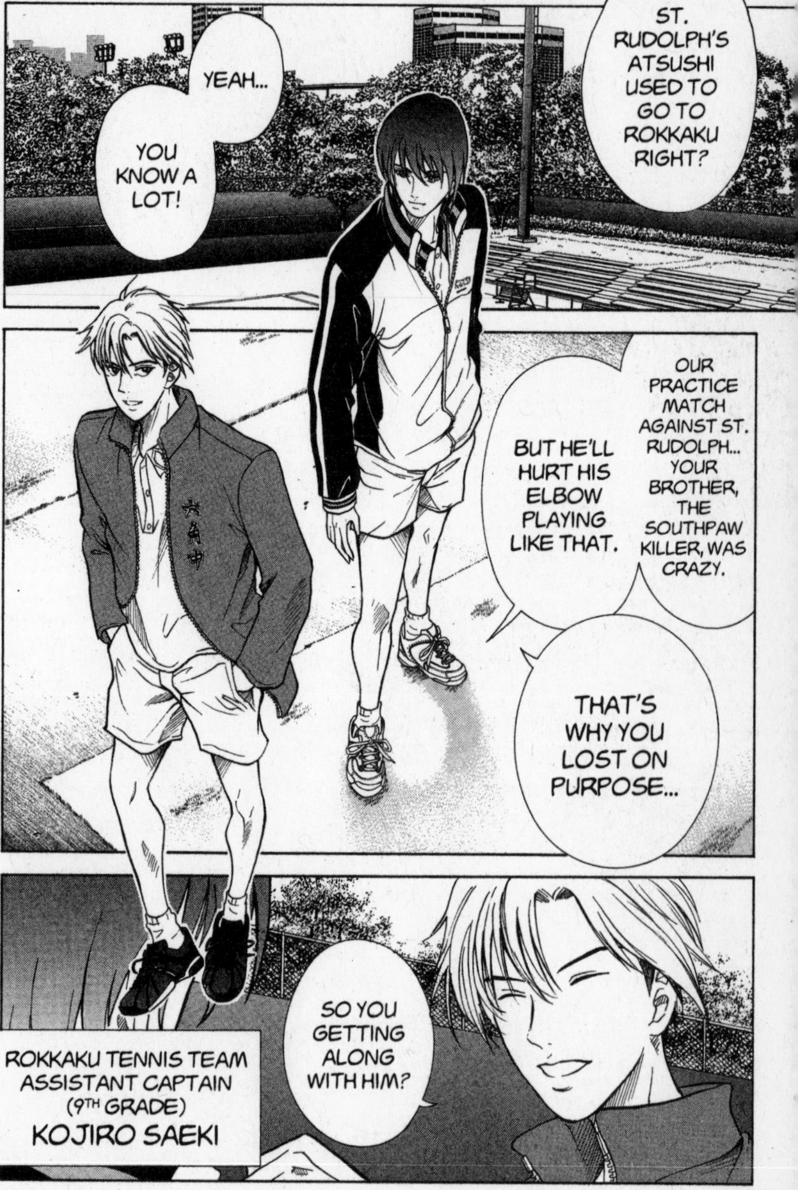
ST. RUDOLPH'S ATSUSHI USED TO GO TO ROKKAKU RIGHT?
YEAH...
YOU KNOW A LOT!
OUR PRACTICE MATCH AGAINST ST. RUDOLPH... YOUR BROTHER, THE SOUTHPAW KILLER, WAS CRAZY.
BUT HE'LL HURT HIS ELBOW PLAYING LIKE THAT.
THAT'S WHY YOU LOST ON PURPOSE...
SO YOU GETTING ALONG WITH HIM?
ROKKAKU TENNIS TEAM ASSISTANT CAPTAIN (9TH GRADE) KOJIRO SAEKI

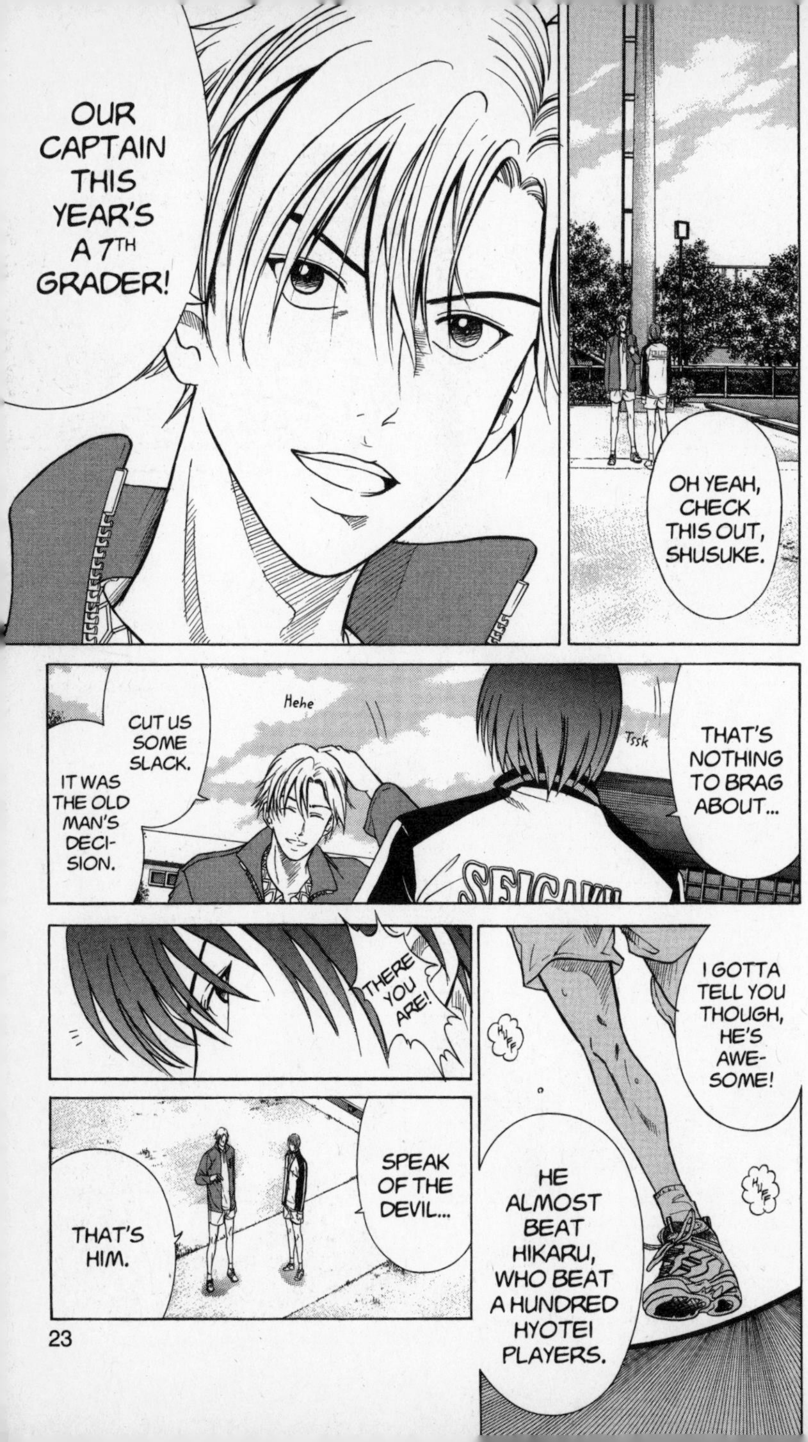
OH YEAH, CHECK THIS OUT, SHUSUKE.
OUR CAPTAIN THIS YEAR'S A 7TH GRADER!
THAT'S NOTHING TO BRAG ABOUT...
Tssk
Hehe
CUT US SOME SLACK.
IT WAS THE OLD MAN'S DECISION.
I GOTTA TELL YOU THOUGH, HE'S AWESOME!
HUFF
HE ALMOST BEAT HIKARU, WHO BEAT A HUNDRED HYOTEI PLAYERS.
HUFF
THERE YOU ARE!
SPEAK OF THE DEVIL...
THAT'S HIM.

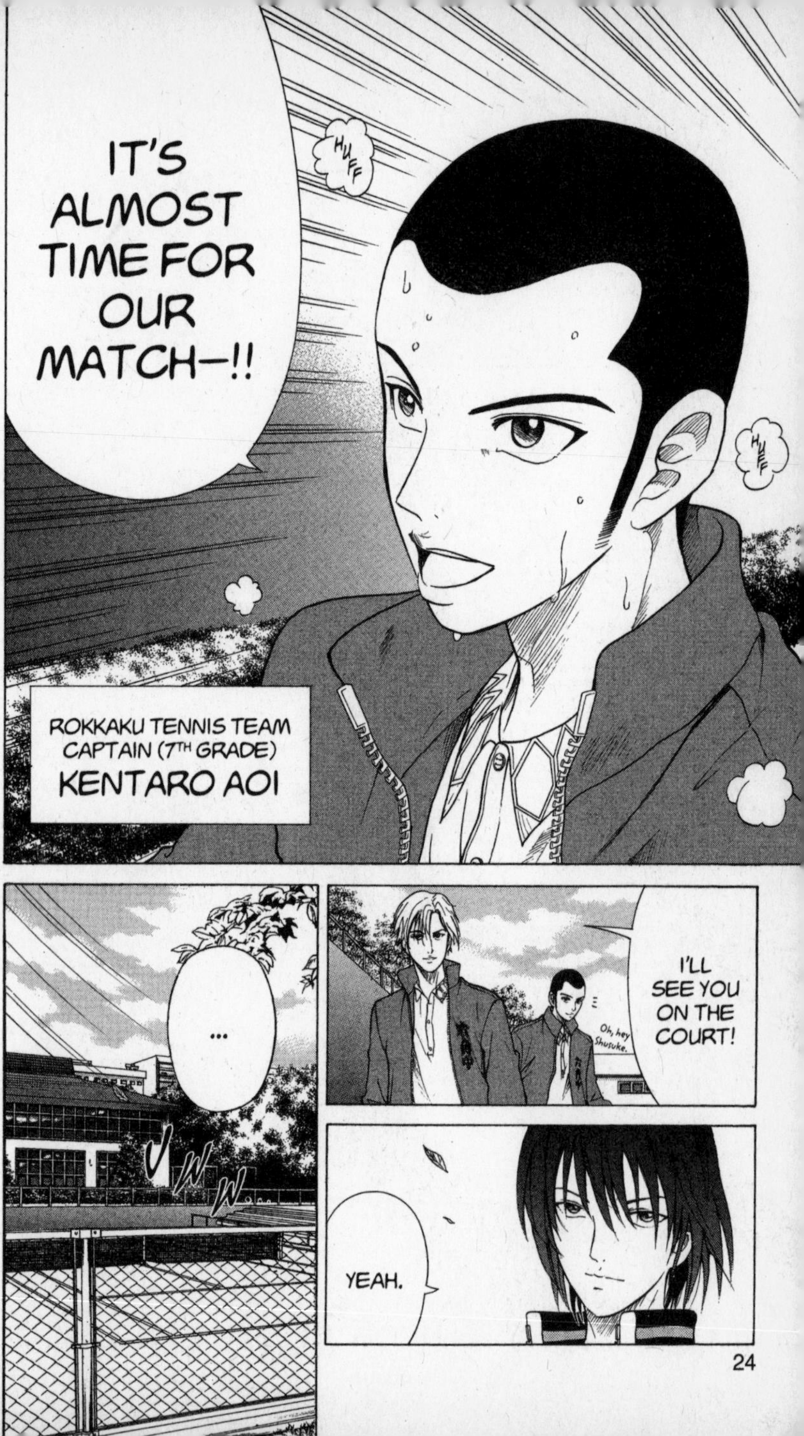
IT'S ALMOST TIME FOR OUR MATCH—!!
HUFF
HUFF
ROKKAKU TENNIS TEAM CAPTAIN (7TH GRADE)
KENTARO AOI
I'LL SEE YOU ON THE COURT!
Oh, hey Shusuke.
YEAH.
...

READ THIS WAY

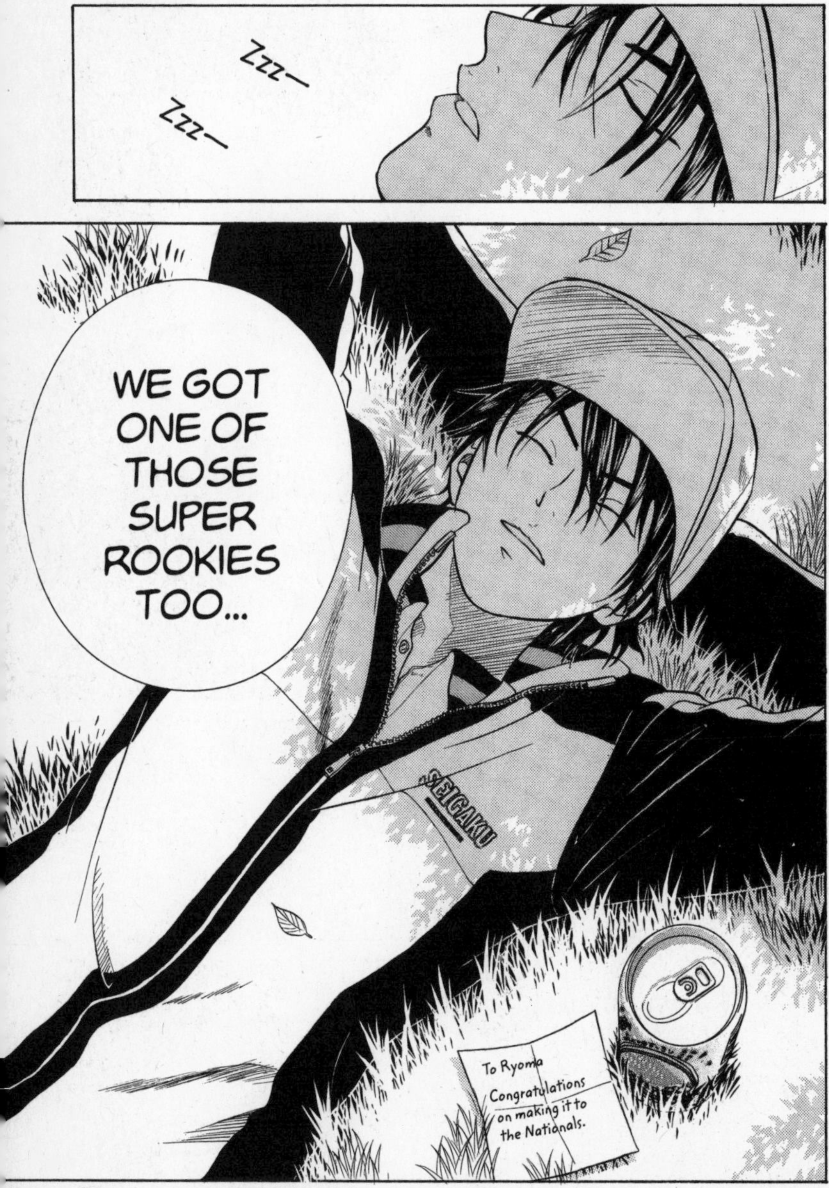
Zzz—
Zzz—
WE GOT ONE OF THOSE SUPER ROOKIES TOO...
SEIGAKU
To Ryoma
Congratulations on making it to the Nationals.

テニスの王子様

THE PRINCE OF TENNIS™

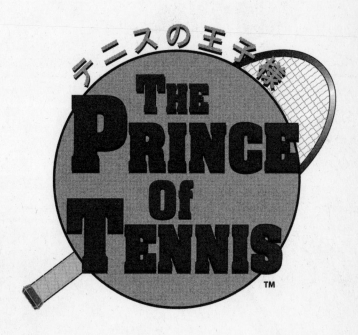

# GENIUS 169: SEISHUN vs. ROKKAKU

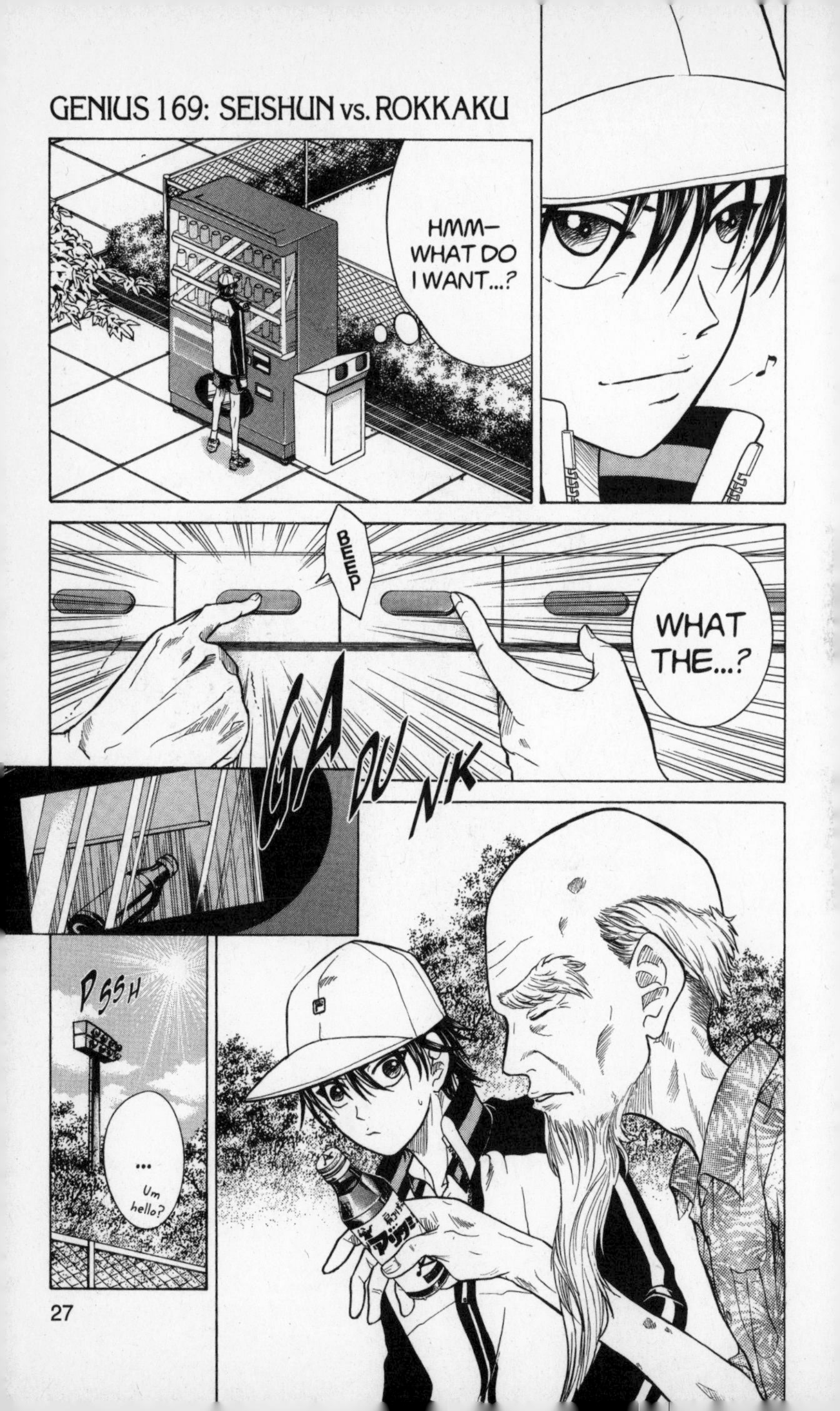
HMM—
WHAT DO
I WANT...?
BEEP
WHAT
THE...?
GADUNK
PSSH
...
Um
hello?

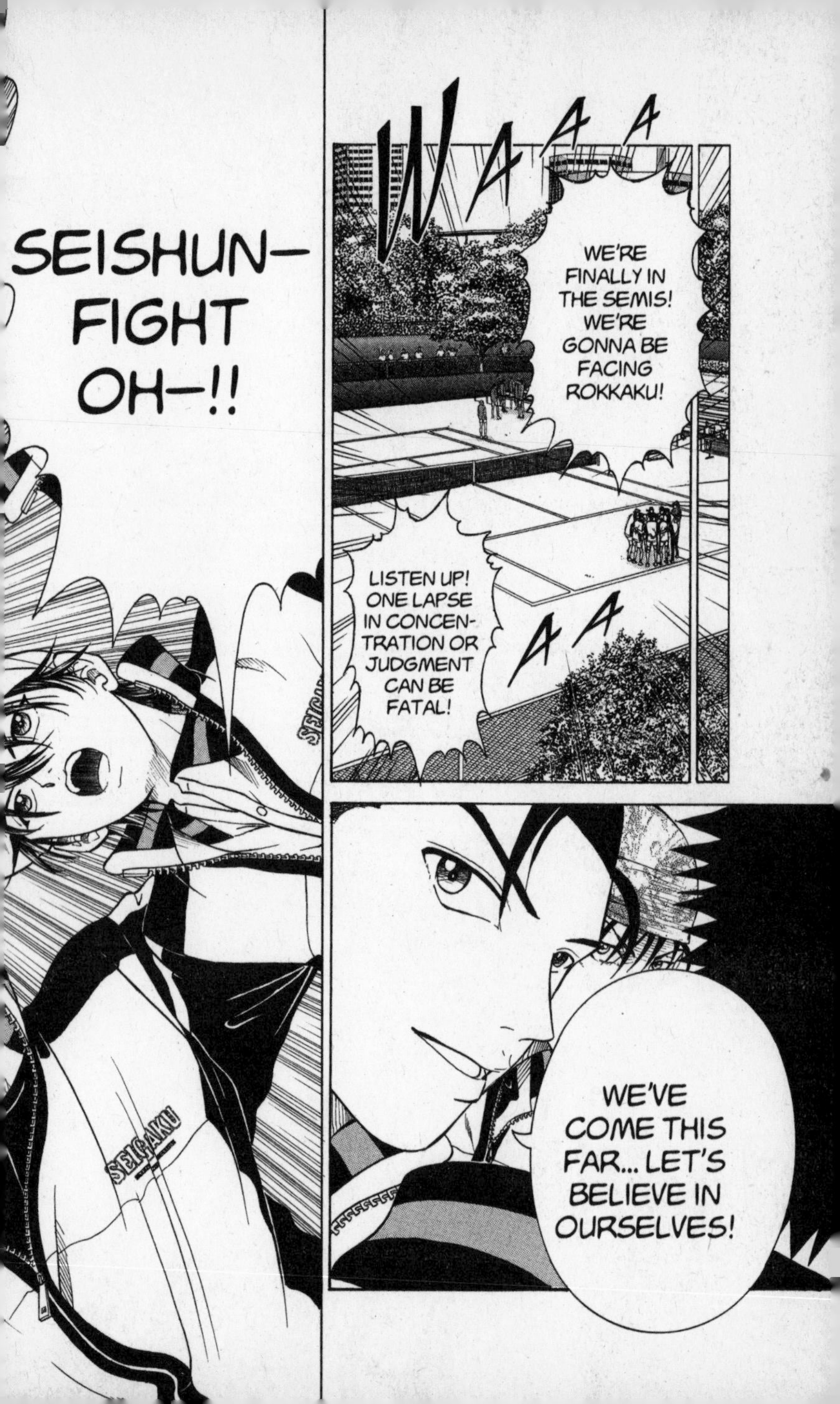
WAAA
WE'RE FINALLY IN THE SEMIS! WE'RE GONNA BE FACING ROKKAKU!
LISTEN UP! ONE LAPSE IN CONCENTRATION OR JUDGMENT CAN BE FATAL!
AA
WE'VE COME THIS FAR... LET'S BELIEVE IN OURSELVES!
SEISHUN-FIGHT OH-!!
SEIGAKU

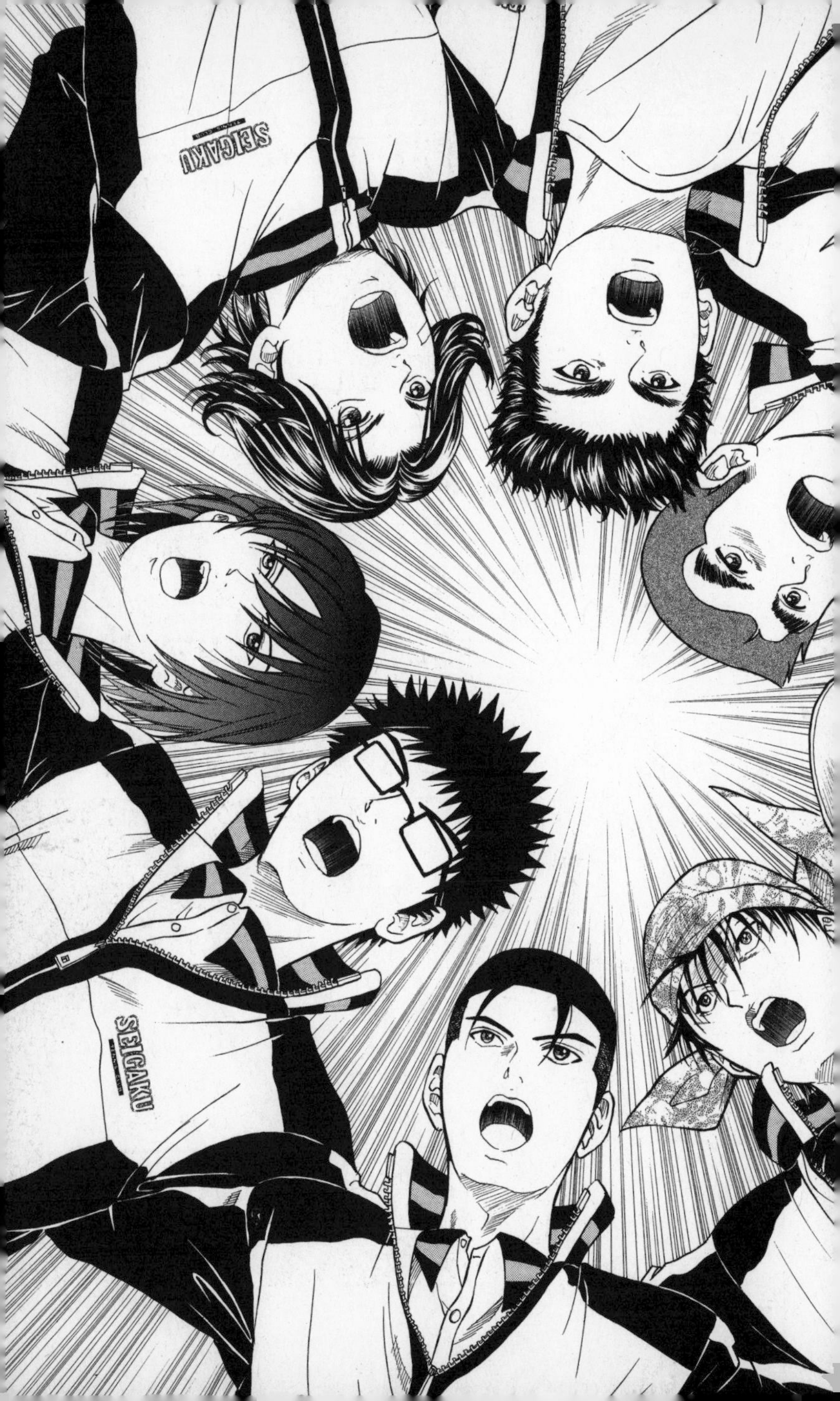
SEIGAKU
SEIGAKU

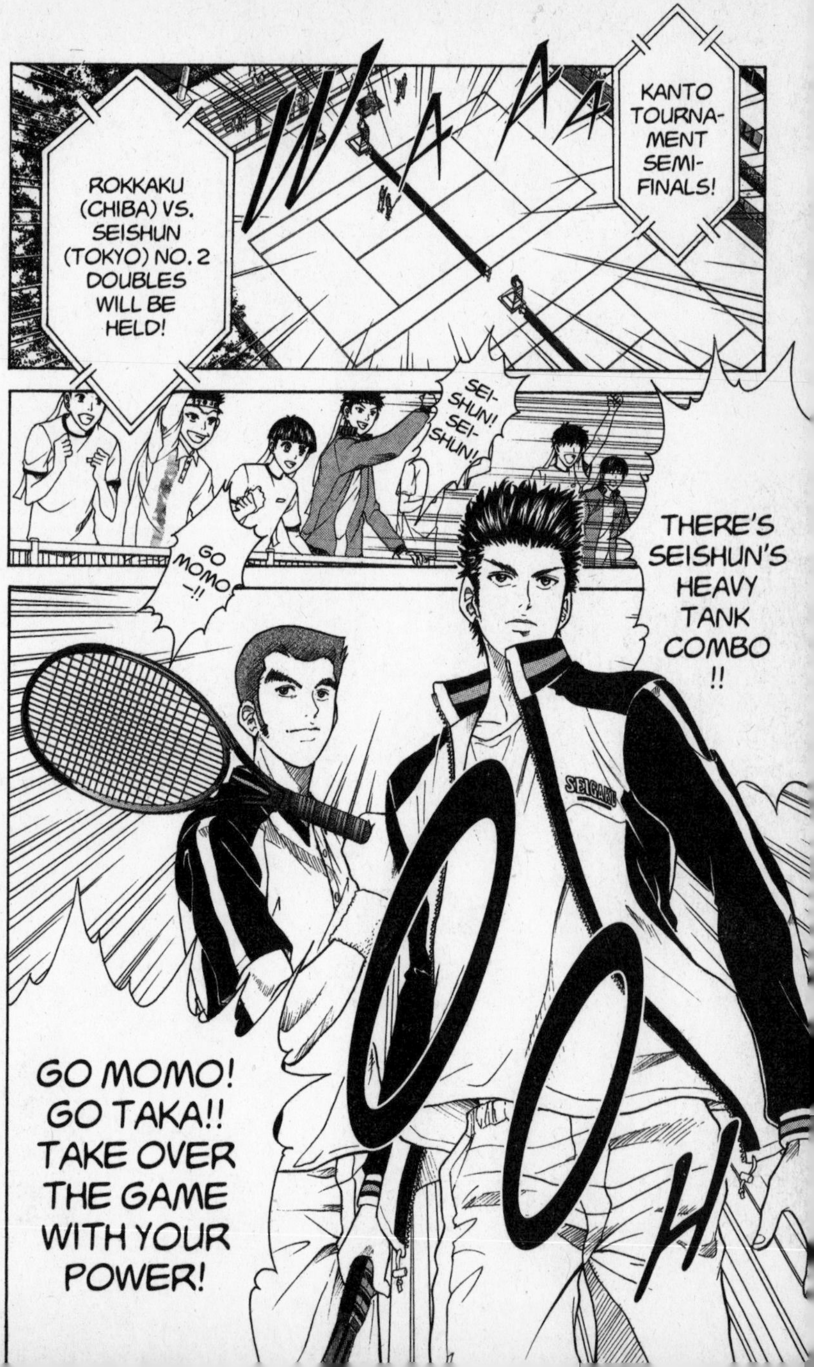
KANTO TOURNAMENT SEMI-FINALS!
ROKKAKU (CHIBA) VS. SEISHUN (TOKYO) NO. 2 DOUBLES WILL BE HELD!
WAAA
SEISHUN! SEISHUN!
GO MOMO—!!
THERE'S SEISHUN'S HEAVY TANK COMBO!!
GO MOMO! GO TAKA!! TAKE OVER THE GAME WITH YOUR POWER!
SEIGAKU
OOOH

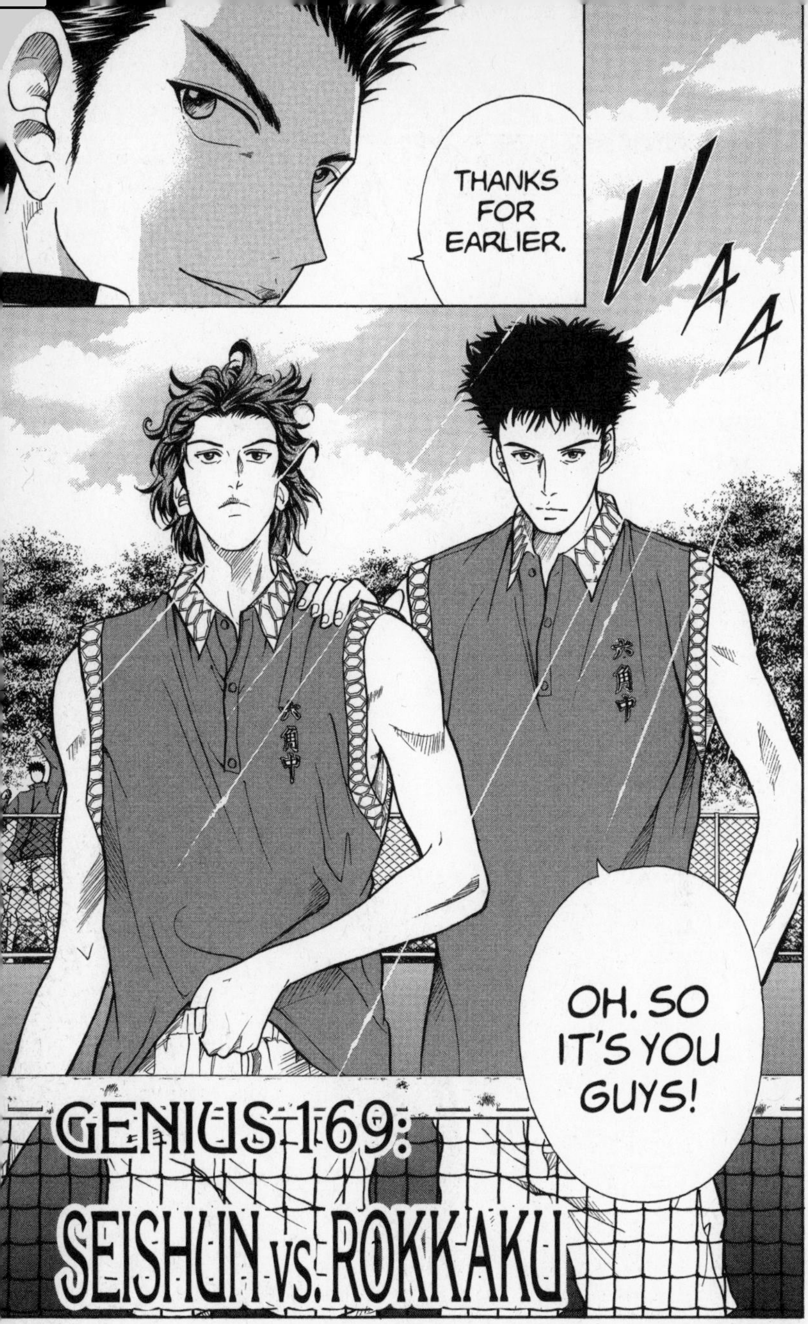
THANKS FOR EARLIER.
WAA
OH. SO IT'S YOU GUYS!
GENIUS 169:
SEISHUN vs. ROKKAKU

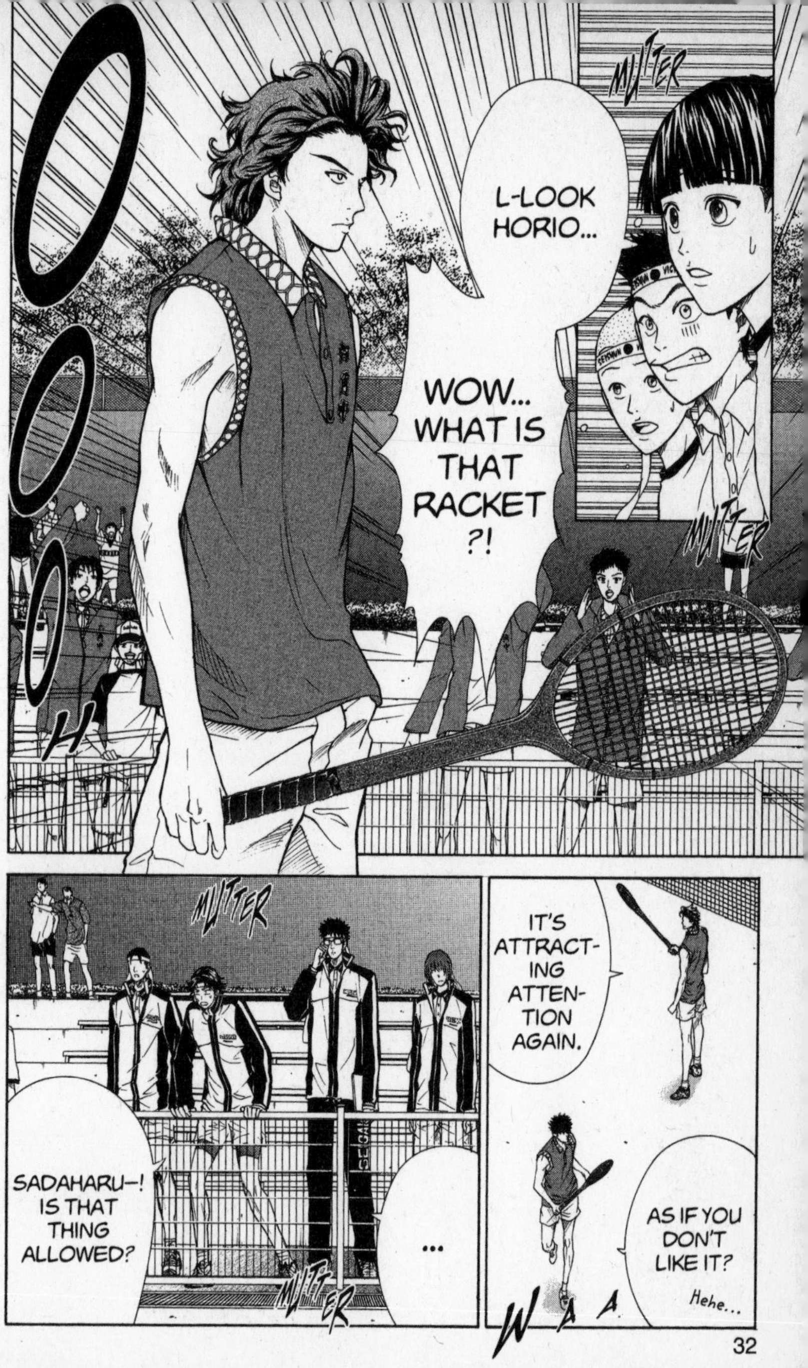
MUTTER
L-LOOK HORIO...
WOW... WHAT IS THAT RACKET?!
MUTTER
OOOOH
IT'S ATTRACT-ING ATTEN-TION AGAIN.
AS IF YOU DON'T LIKE IT?
Hehe...
WAA
MUTTER
...
SADAHARU-! IS THAT THING ALLOWED?
MUTTER

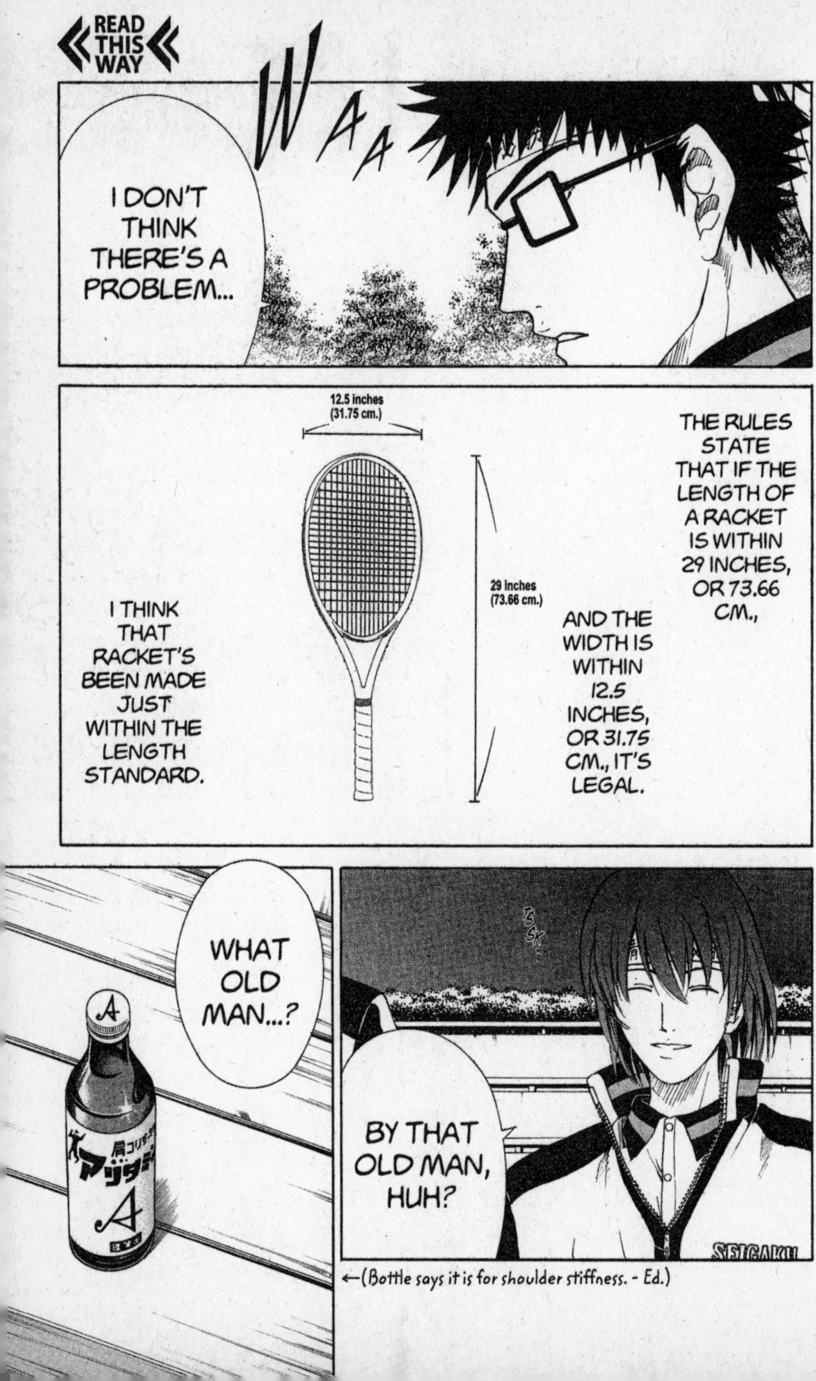
READ THIS WAY
WAA
I DON'T THINK THERE'S A PROBLEM...
THE RULES STATE THAT IF THE LENGTH OF A RACKET IS WITHIN 29 INCHES, OR 73.66 CM.,
AND THE WIDTH IS WITHIN 12.5 INCHES, OR 31.75 CM., IT'S LEGAL.
12.5 inches (31.75 cm.)
29 inches (73.66 cm.)
I THINK THAT RACKET'S BEEN MADE JUST WITHIN THE LENGTH STANDARD.
TSK
BY THAT OLD MAN, HUH?
SEIGAKU
WHAT OLD MAN...?
←(Bottle says it is for shoulder stiffness. - Ed.)

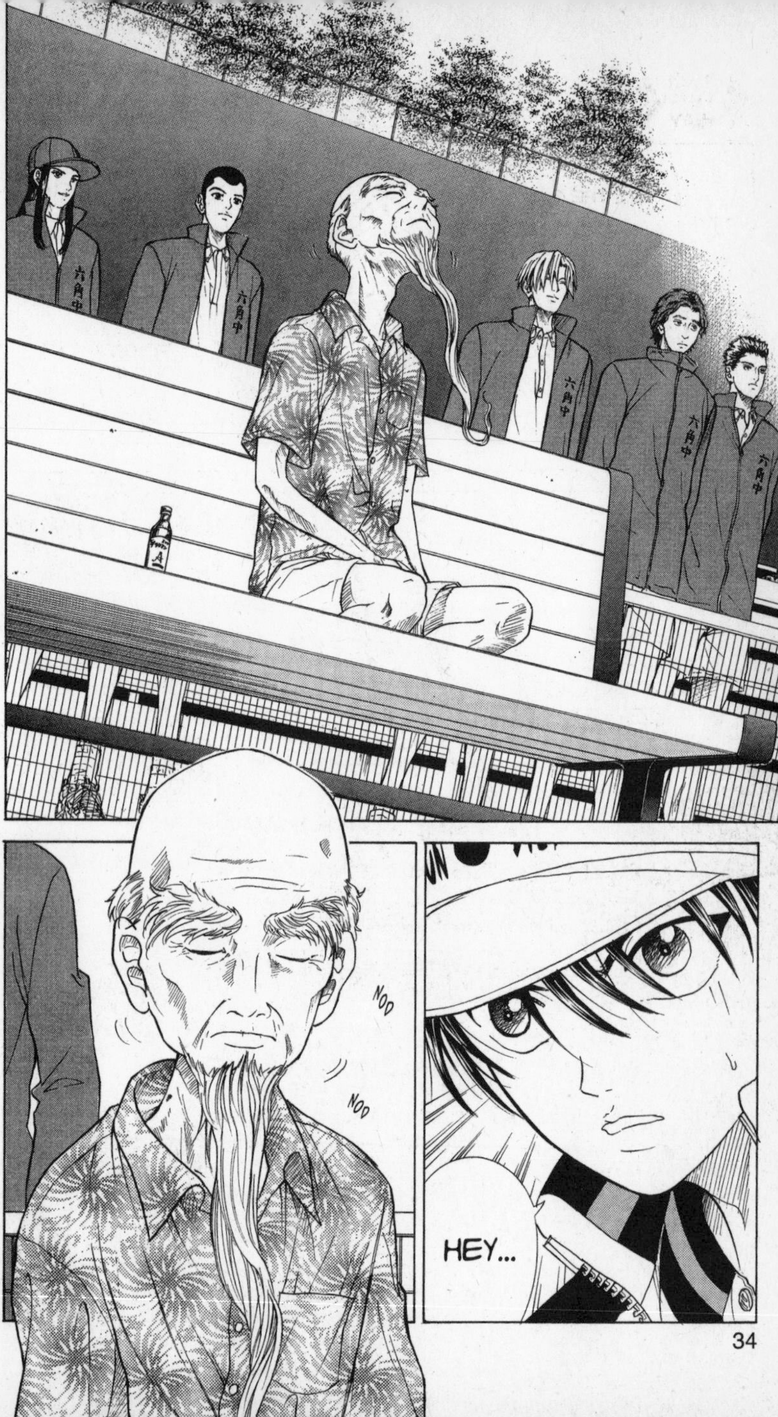
六角中
HEY...
NOD
NOD

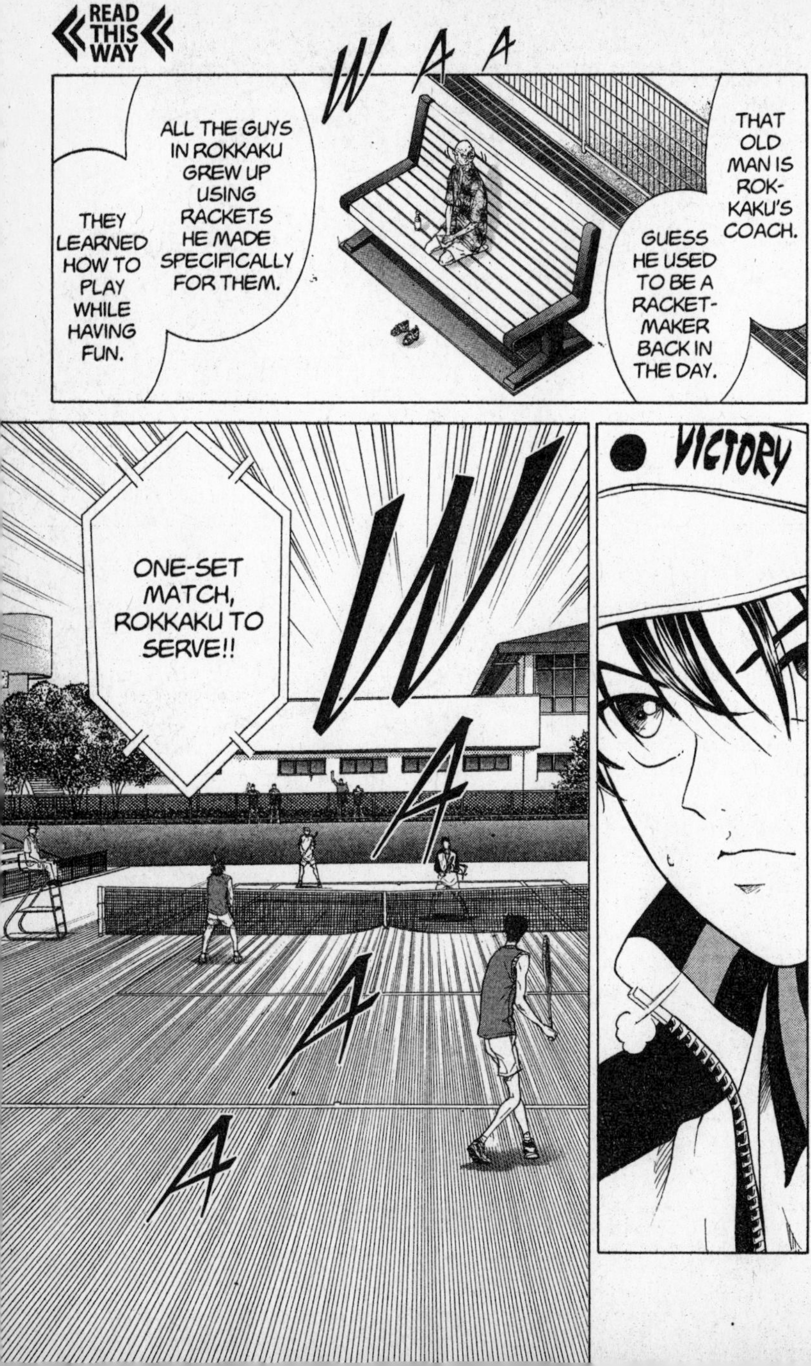
READ THIS WAY
THAT OLD MAN IS ROK-KAKU'S COACH.
GUESS HE USED TO BE A RACKET-MAKER BACK IN THE DAY.
WAA
ALL THE GUYS IN ROKKAKU GREW UP USING RACKETS HE MADE SPECIFICALLY FOR THEM.
THEY LEARNED HOW TO PLAY WHILE HAVING FUN.
VICTORY
ONE-SET MATCH, ROKKAKU TO SERVE!!
WAAAA

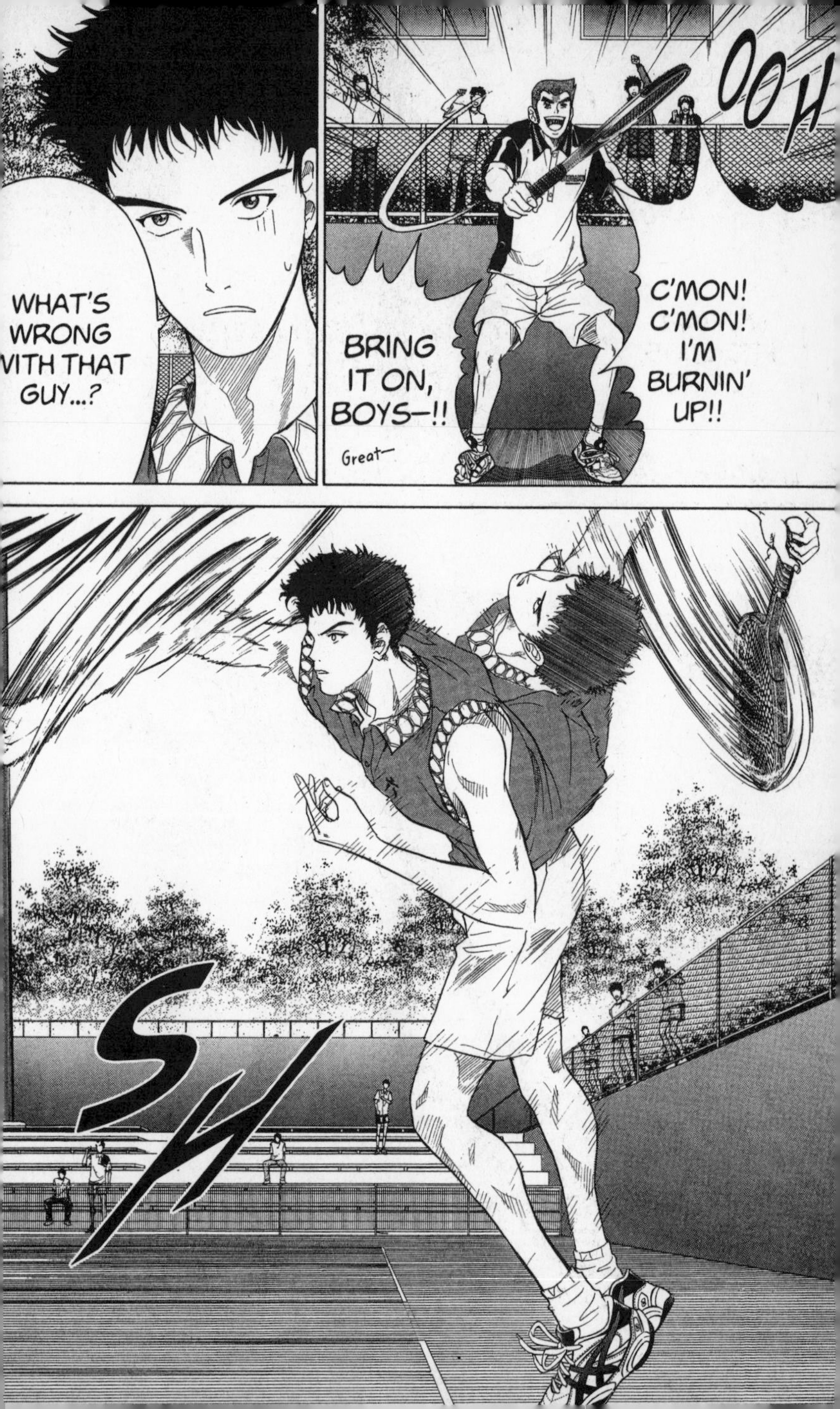

OOH
C'MON! C'MON! I'M BURNIN' UP!!
BRING IT ON, BOYS--!!
Great—
WHAT'S WRONG WITH THAT GUY...?
SH

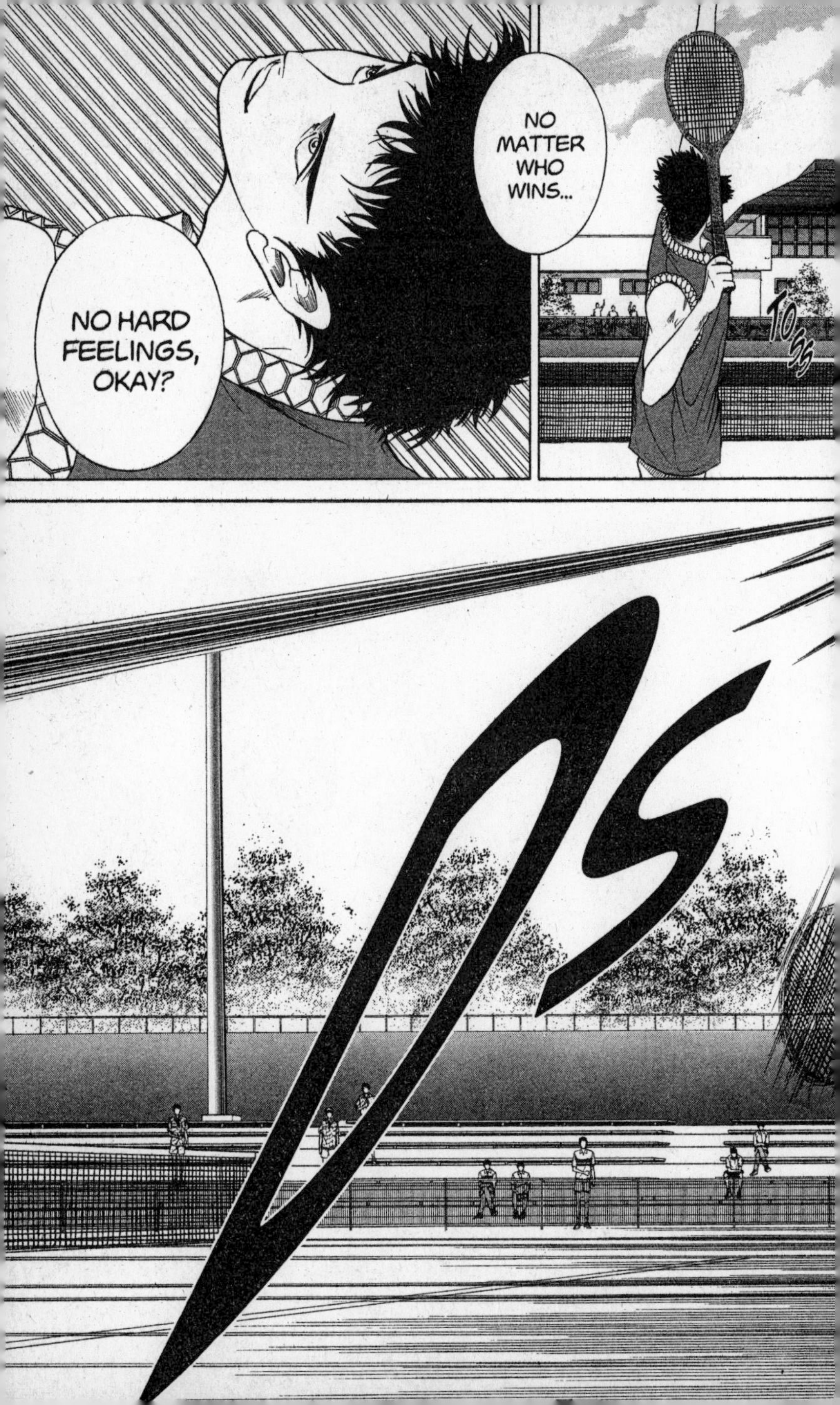
TOSS
NO MATTER WHO WINS...
NO HARD FEELINGS, OKAY?

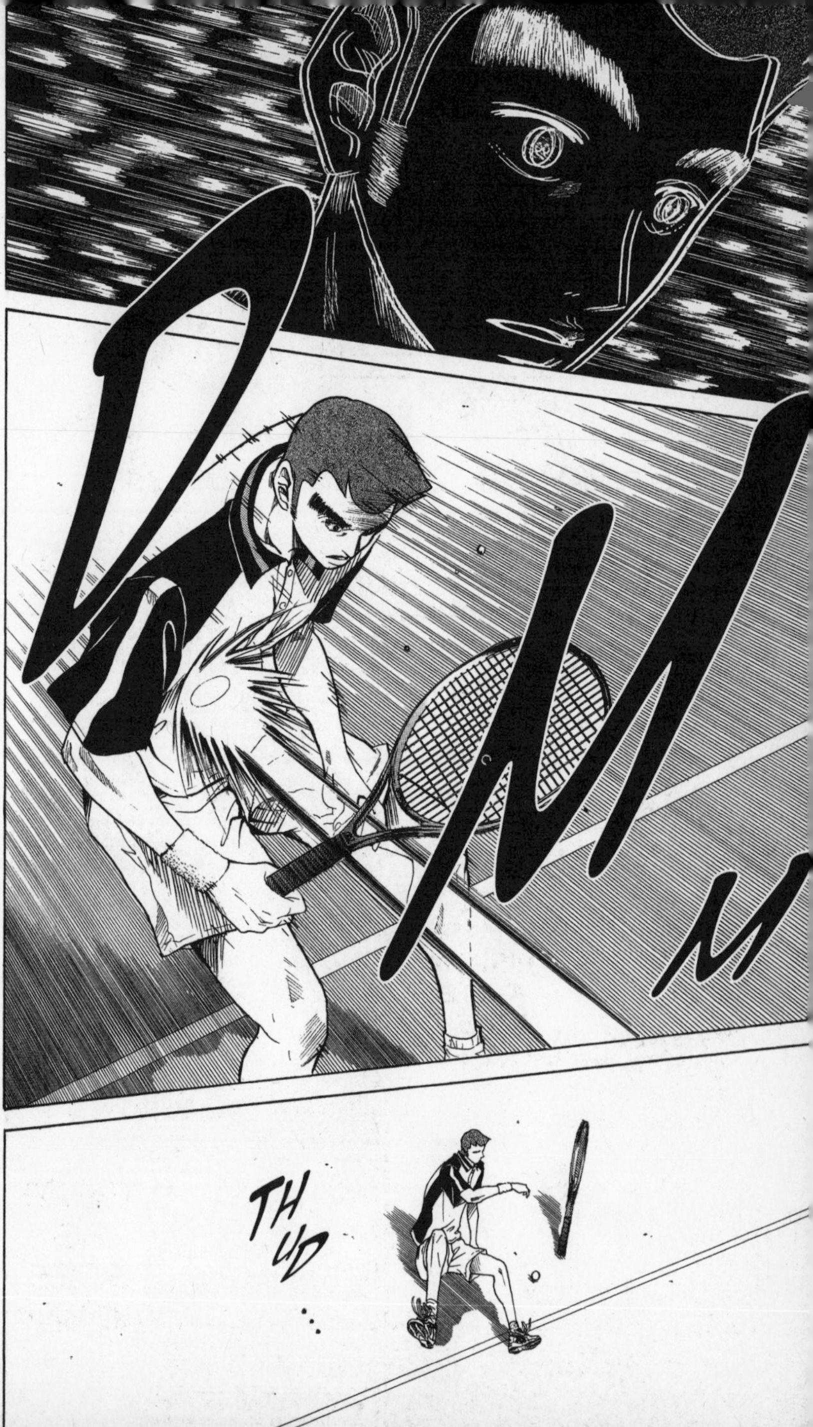
THUD

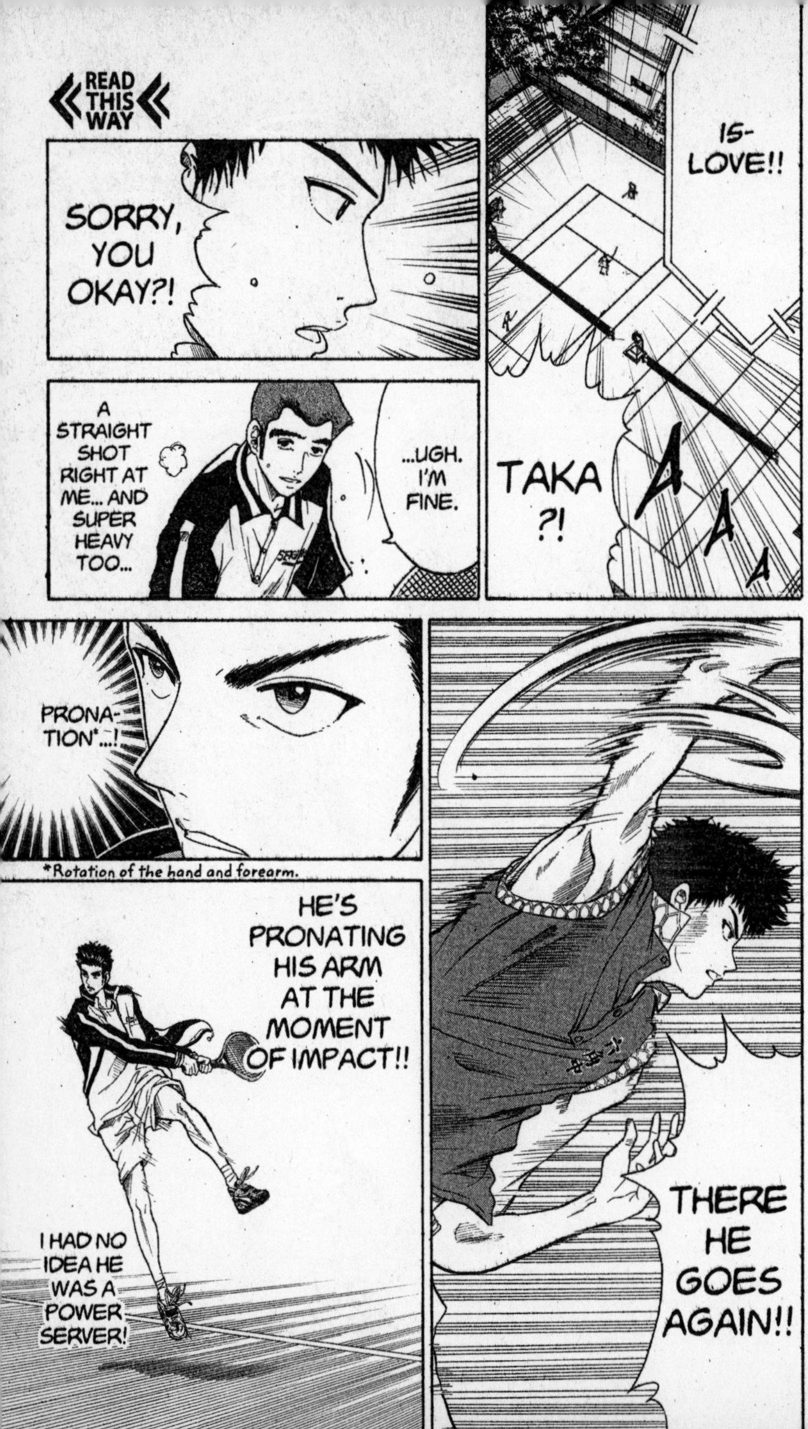
READ THIS WAY
15- LOVE!!
TAKA ?!
SORRY, YOU OKAY?!
...UGH. I'M FINE.
A STRAIGHT SHOT RIGHT AT ME... AND SUPER HEAVY TOO...
THERE HE GOES AGAIN!!
PRONATION*...!
HE'S PRONATING HIS ARM AT THE MOMENT OF IMPACT!!
I HAD NO IDEA HE WAS A POWER SERVER!

*Rotation of the hand and forearm.

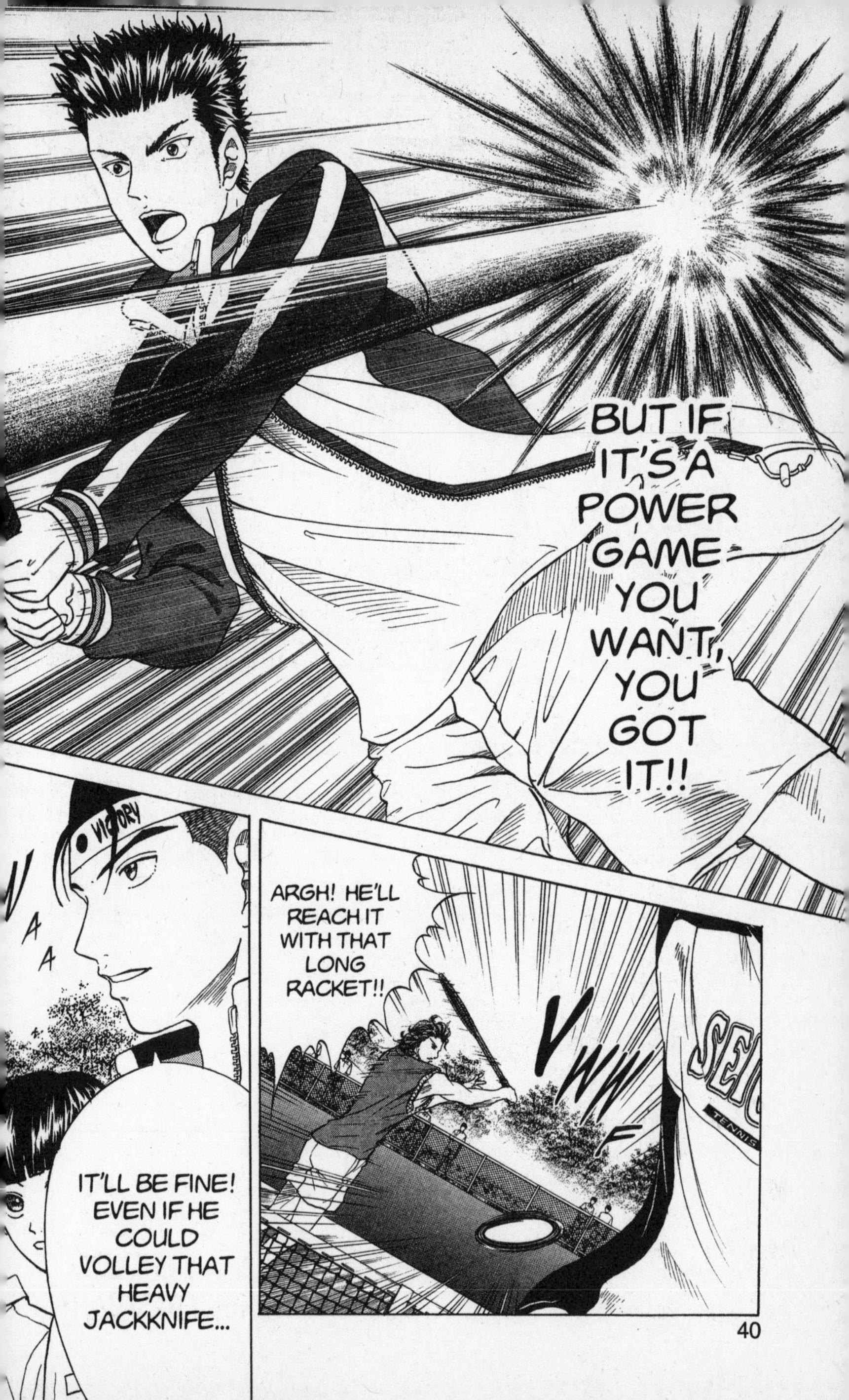
BUT IF IT'S A POWER GAME YOU WANT, YOU GOT IT!!
ARGH! HE'LL REACH IT WITH THAT LONG RACKET!!
VWWF
VICTORY
IT'LL BE FINE! EVEN IF HE COULD VOLLEY THAT HEAVY JACKKNIFE...

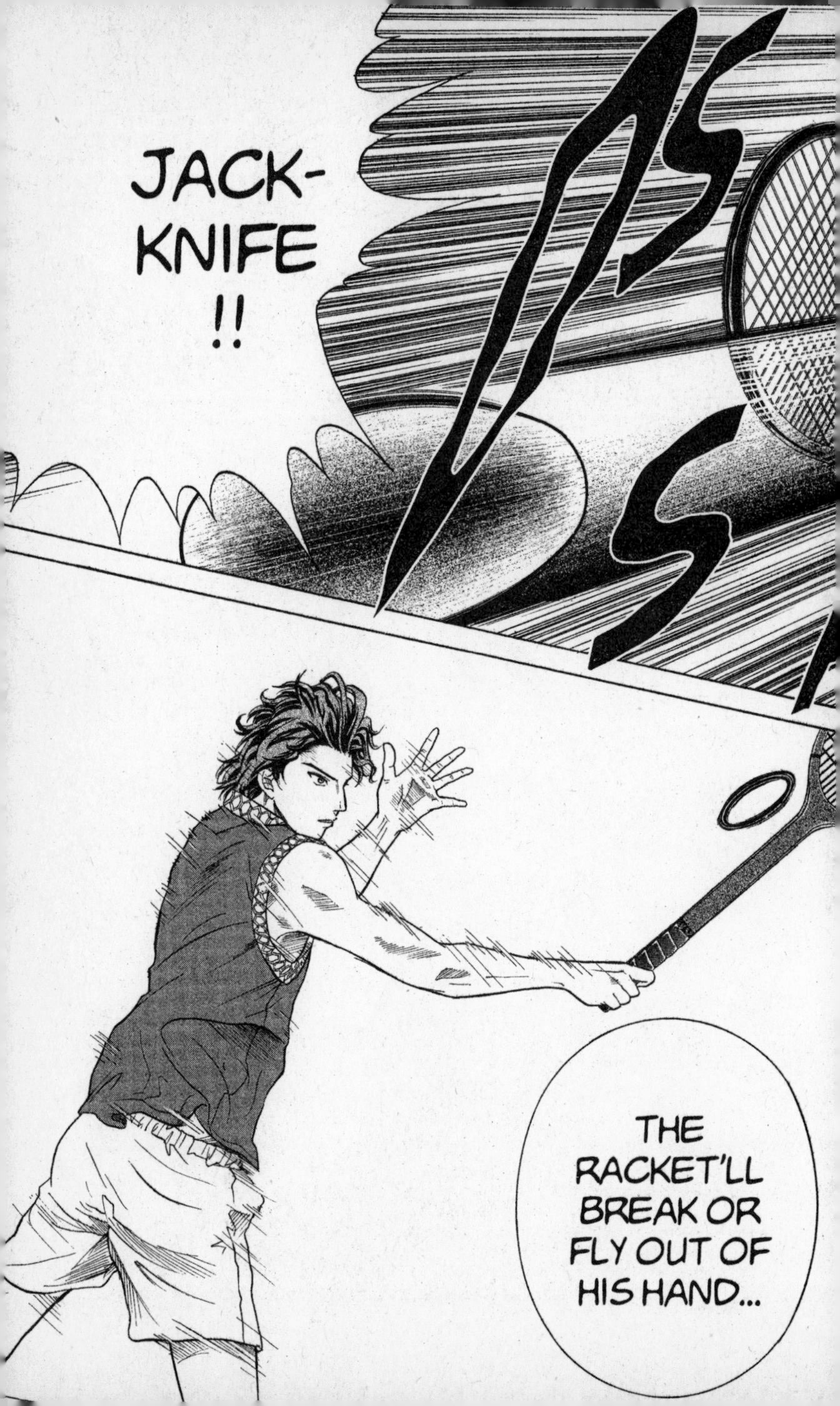
JACK-KNIFE!!
THE RACKET'LL BREAK OR FLY OUT OF HIS HAND...

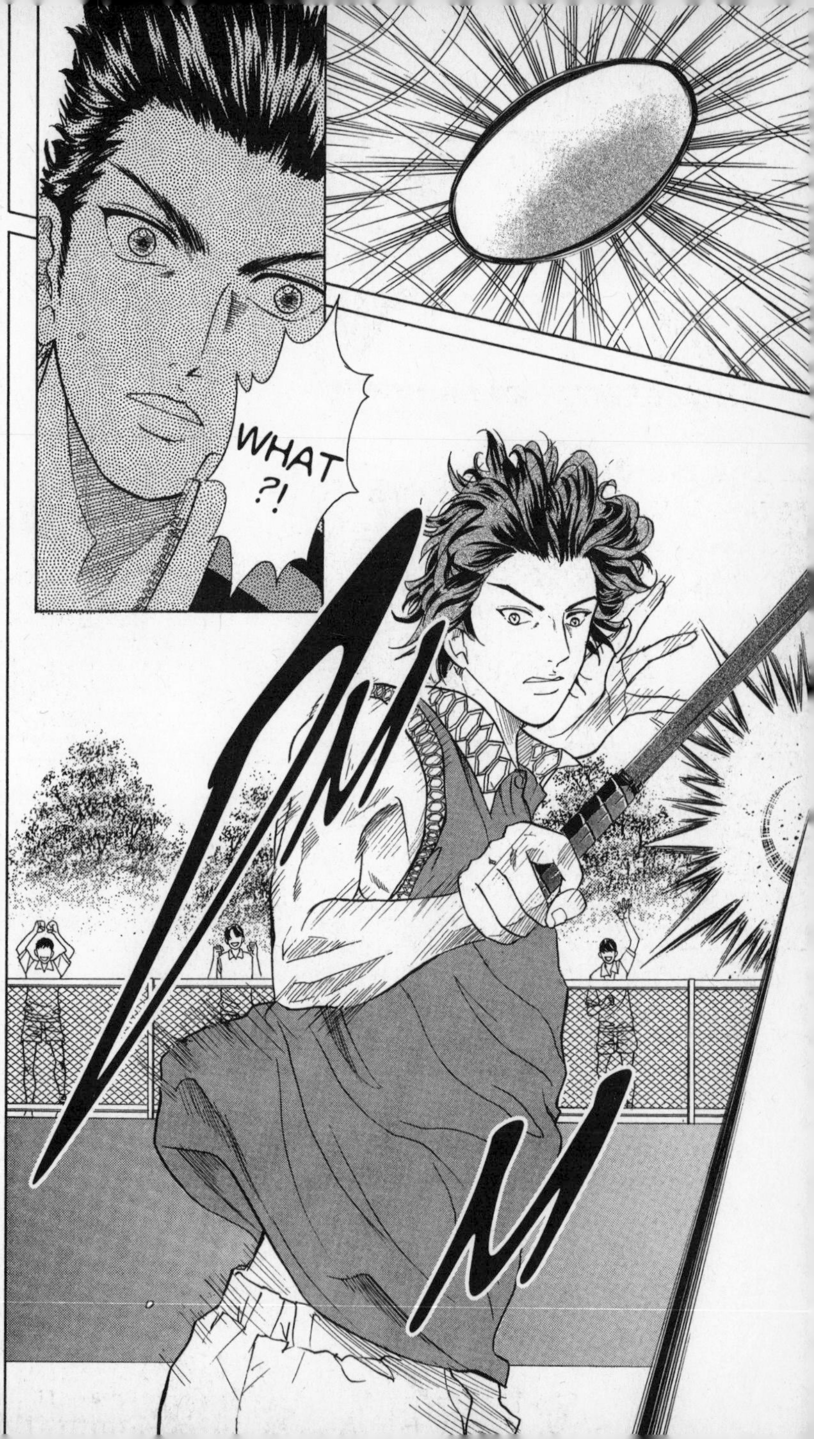
WHAT ?!

READ THIS WAY

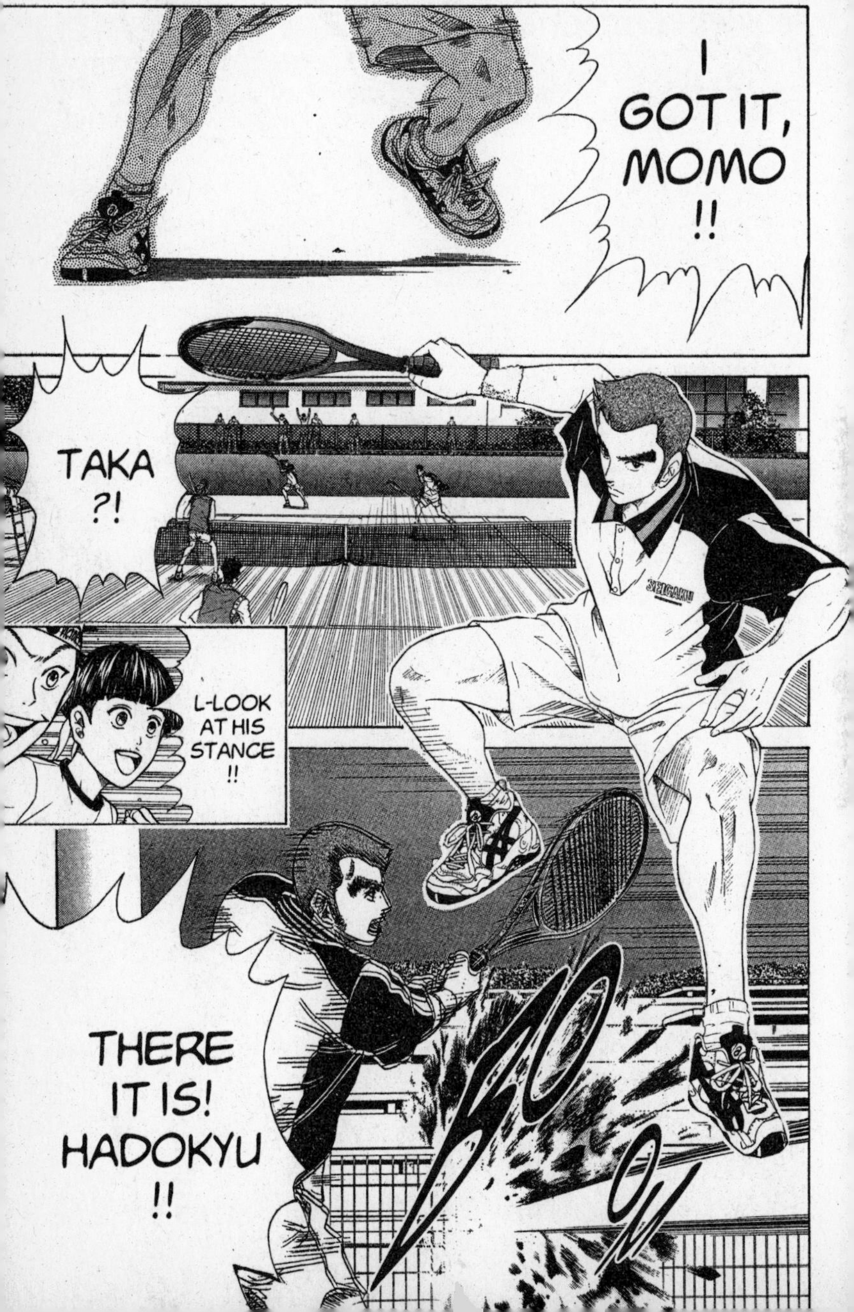
I GOT IT, MOMO !!
TAKA ?!
L-LOOK AT HIS STANCE !!
THERE IT IS! HADOKYU !!

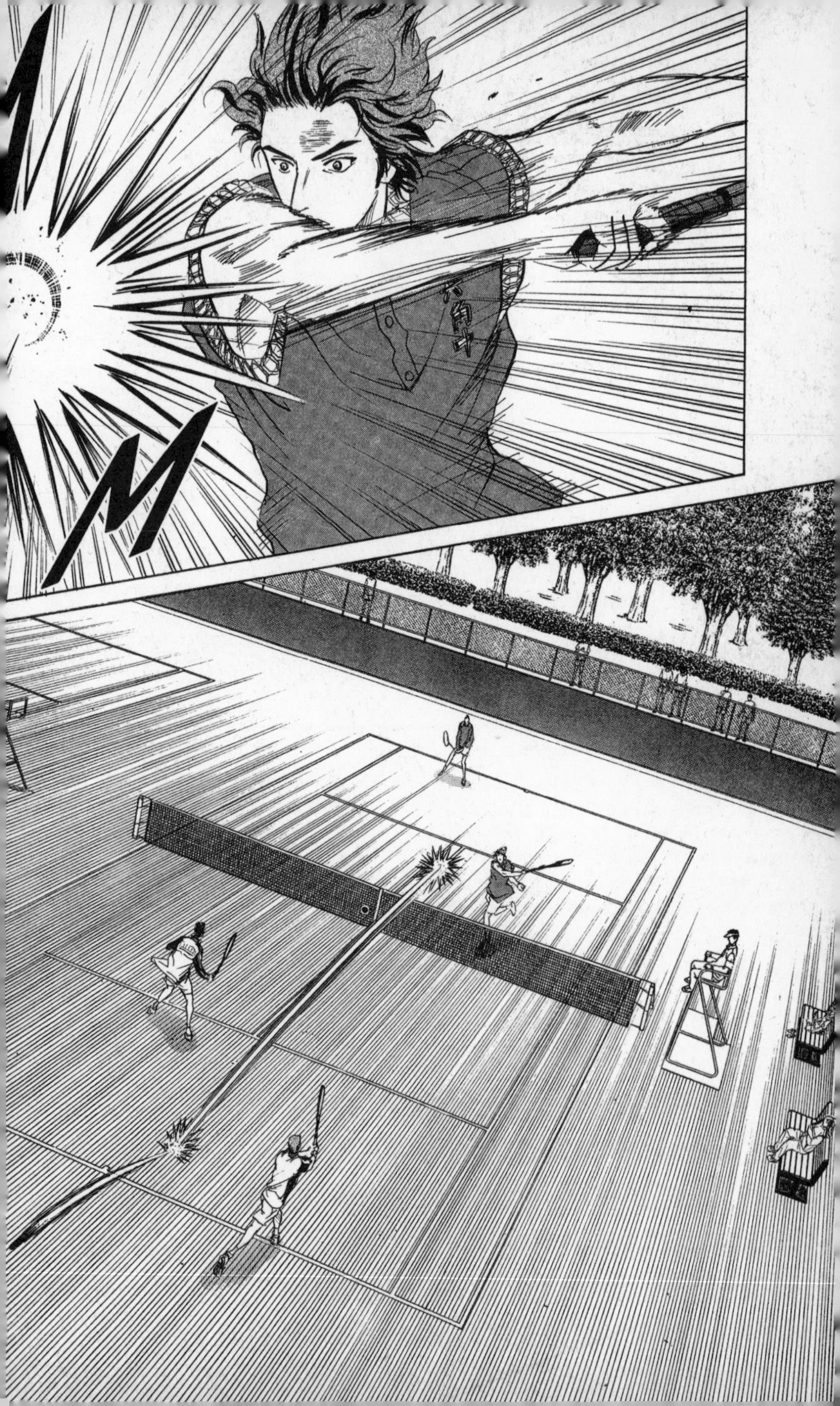

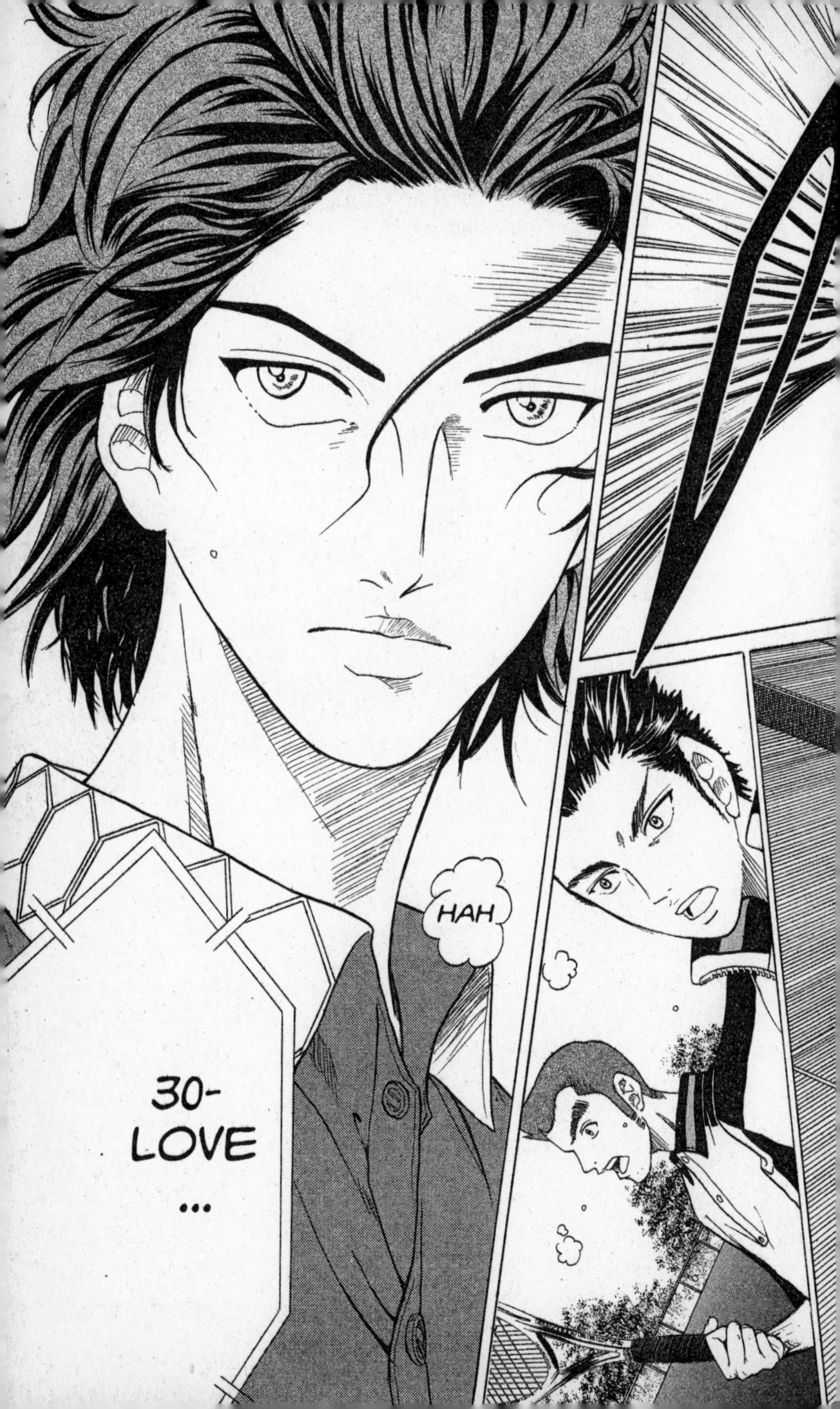
HAH
30-LOVE ...

Typical
Jock

## Harukaze Kurobane / Right-Handed

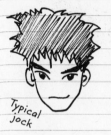

Rokkaku Junior High School 9th Grade, Class A
Height: 184 cm. / Blood Type: A / Birthday: 9/29
Best move: Aerial Combo
Favorite food: Grilled corn
Hobby / Recent pastime: Hanging out at the beach

Statue
of
David
Beat 100 Hyotei players—
do not underestimate!

## Hikaru Amane / Right-Handed
(Nickname: David)

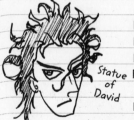

Rokkaku Junior High School 8th Grade, Class B
Height: 180 cm. / Blood Type: A / Birthday: 11/22
Best move: Joke Attack
Favorite food: Strawberry Chocolate Super Deluxe Parfait
Hobby / Recent pastime: Hanging out at the beach

(Selected from Sadaharu Inui Secret Data Note No. 132)

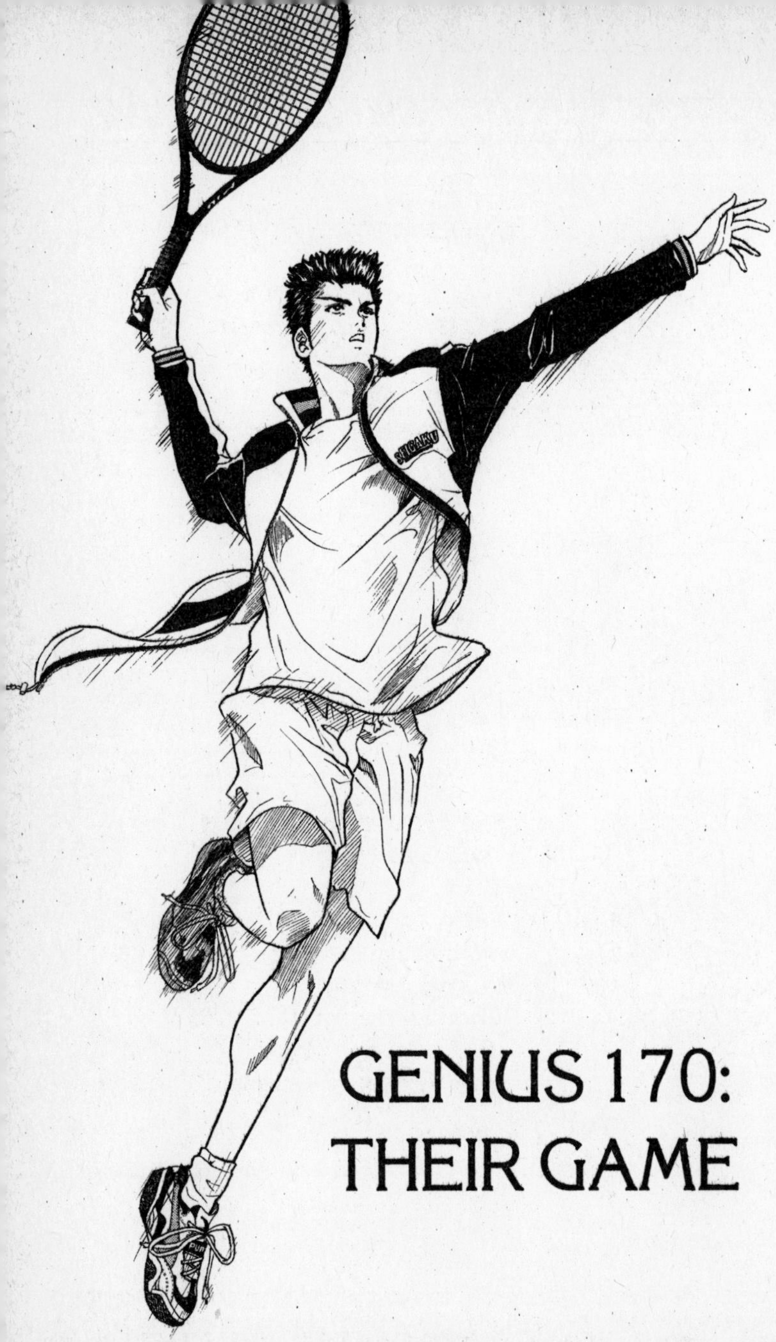

# GENIUS 170: THEIR GAME

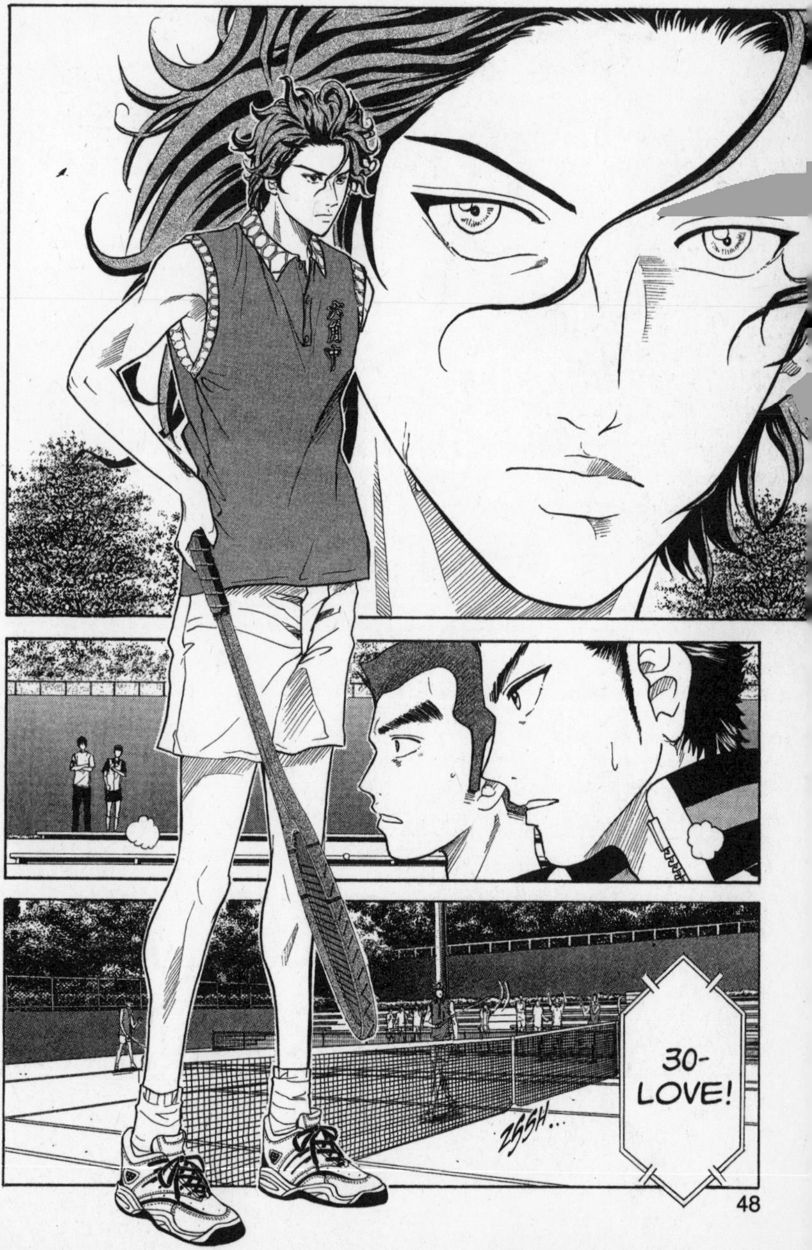
30-
LOVE!
ZSSH...

READ THIS WAY

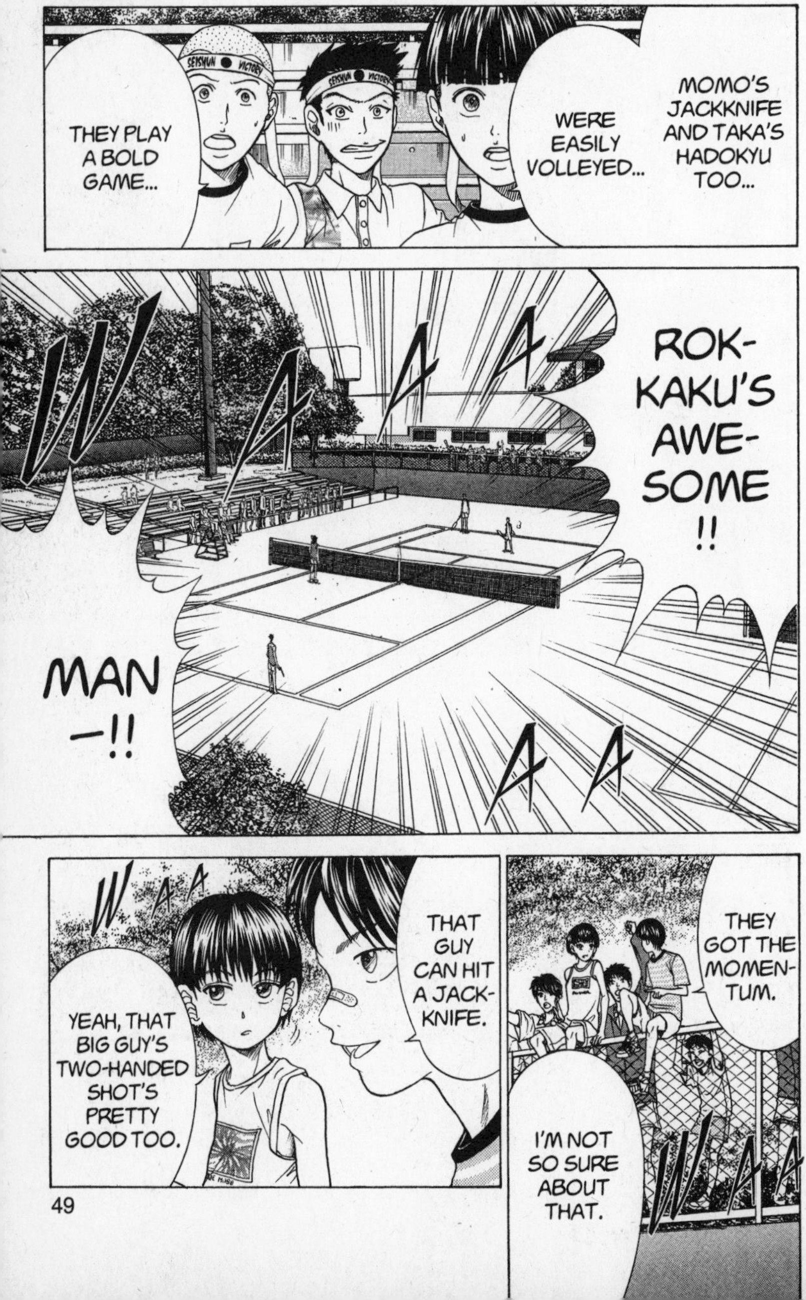

MOMO'S JACKKNIFE AND TAKA'S HADOKYU TOO...
WERE EASILY VOLLEYED...
THEY PLAY A BOLD GAME...
WAAAAA
ROKKAKU'S AWESOME!!
MAN—!!
THEY GOT THE MOMENTUM.
I'M NOT SO SURE ABOUT THAT.
WAA
WAA
THAT GUY CAN HIT A JACKKNIFE.
YEAH, THAT BIG GUY'S TWO-HANDED SHOT'S PRETTY GOOD TOO.

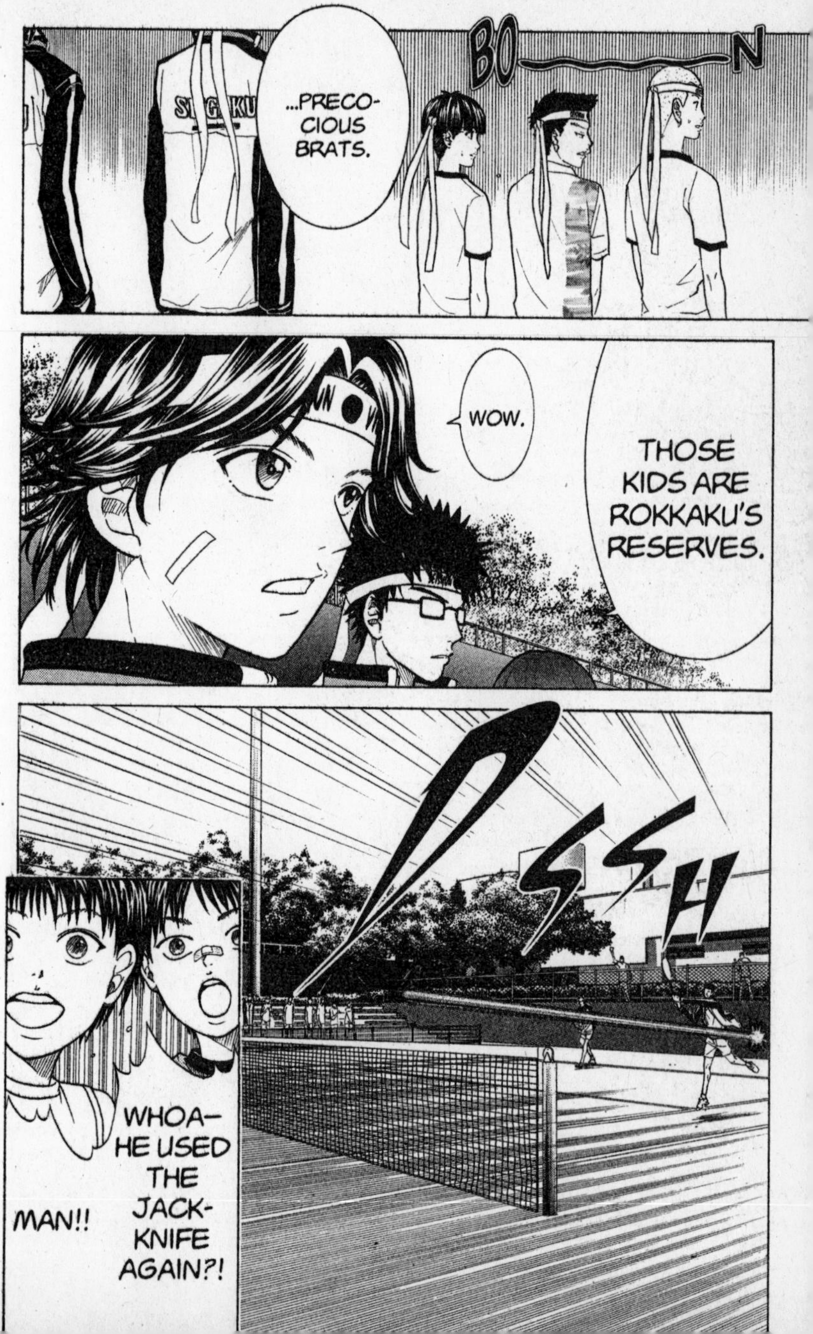
BO———N
...PRECO-CIOUS BRATS.
THOSE KIDS ARE ROKKAKU'S RESERVES.
WOW.
VSSH
WHOA- HE USED THE JACK-KNIFE AGAIN?!
MAN!!

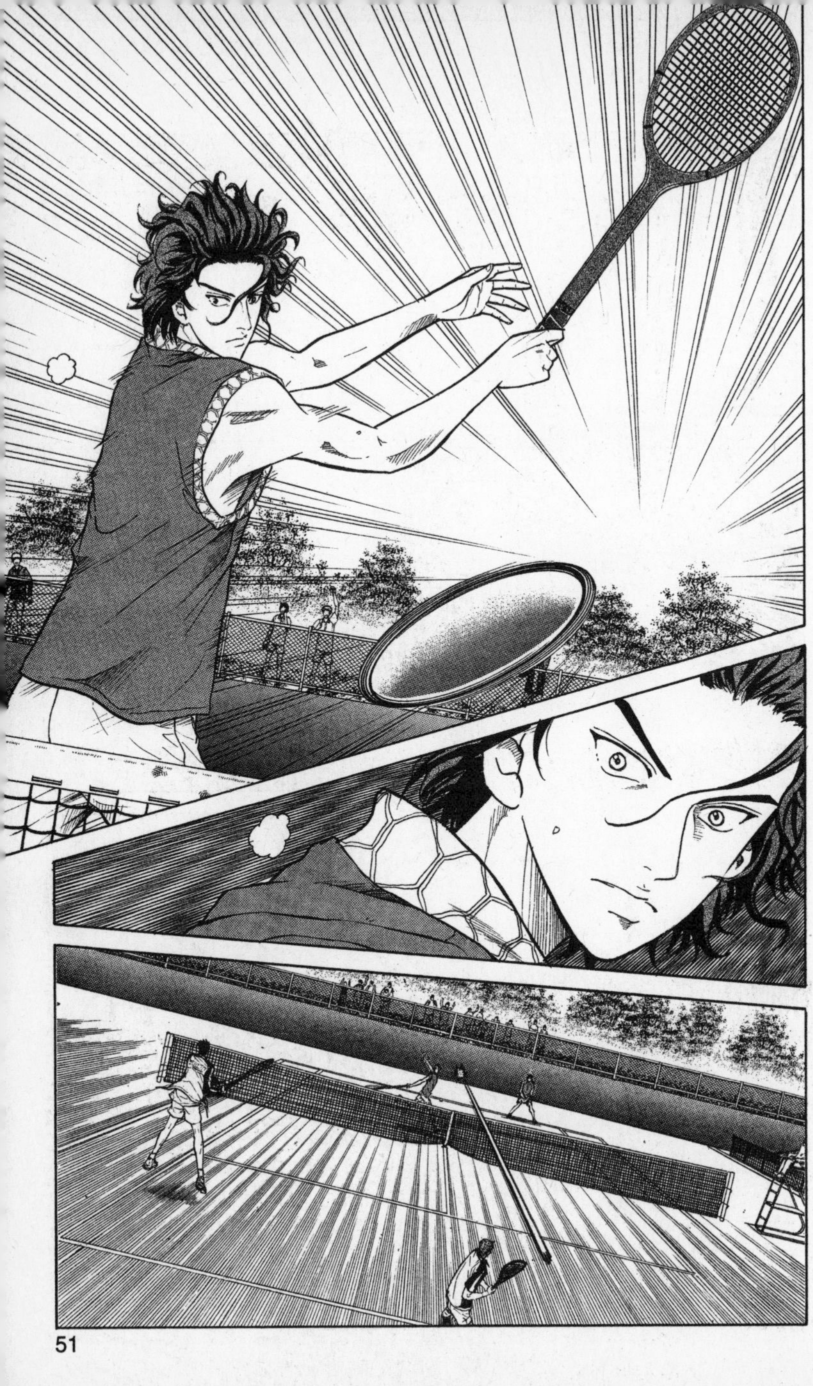

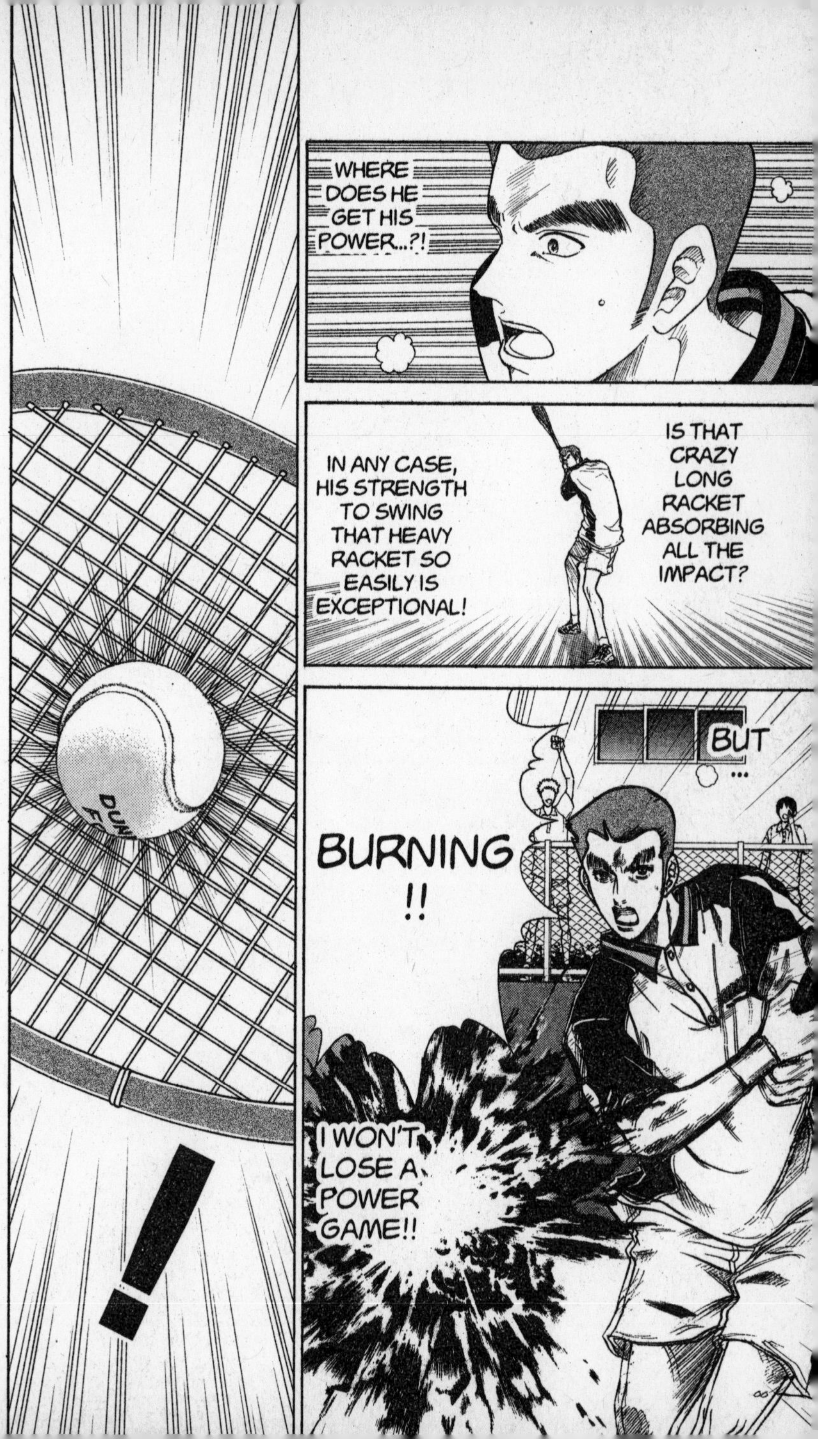
WHERE DOES HE GET HIS POWER...?!
IS THAT CRAZY LONG RACKET ABSORBING ALL THE IMPACT?
IN ANY CASE, HIS STRENGTH TO SWING THAT HEAVY RACKET SO EASILY IS EXCEPTIONAL!
BUT ...
BURNING !!
I WON'T LOSE A POWER GAME!!
!

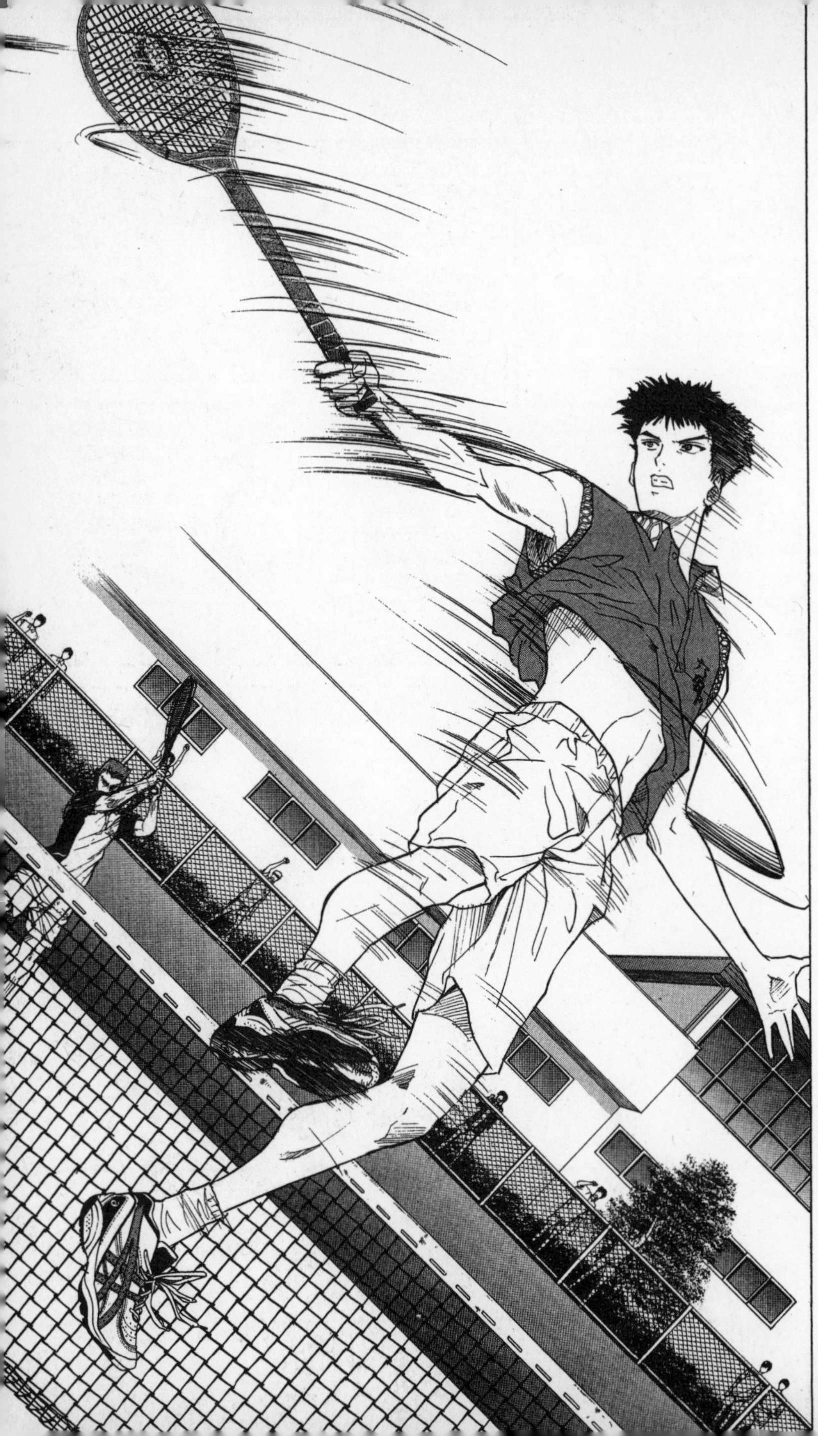

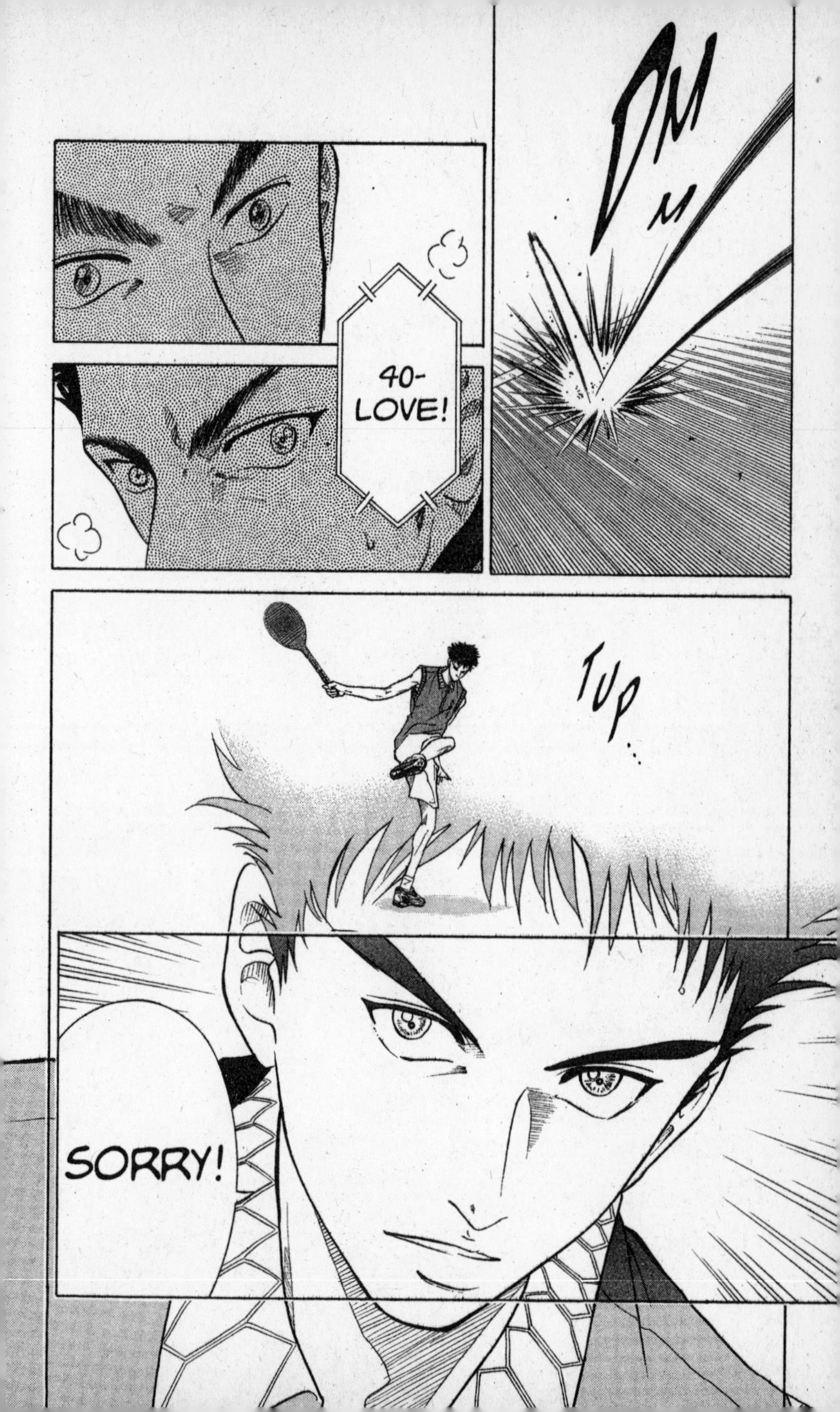
DMM
40-LOVE!
TUP...
SORRY!

READ THIS WAY

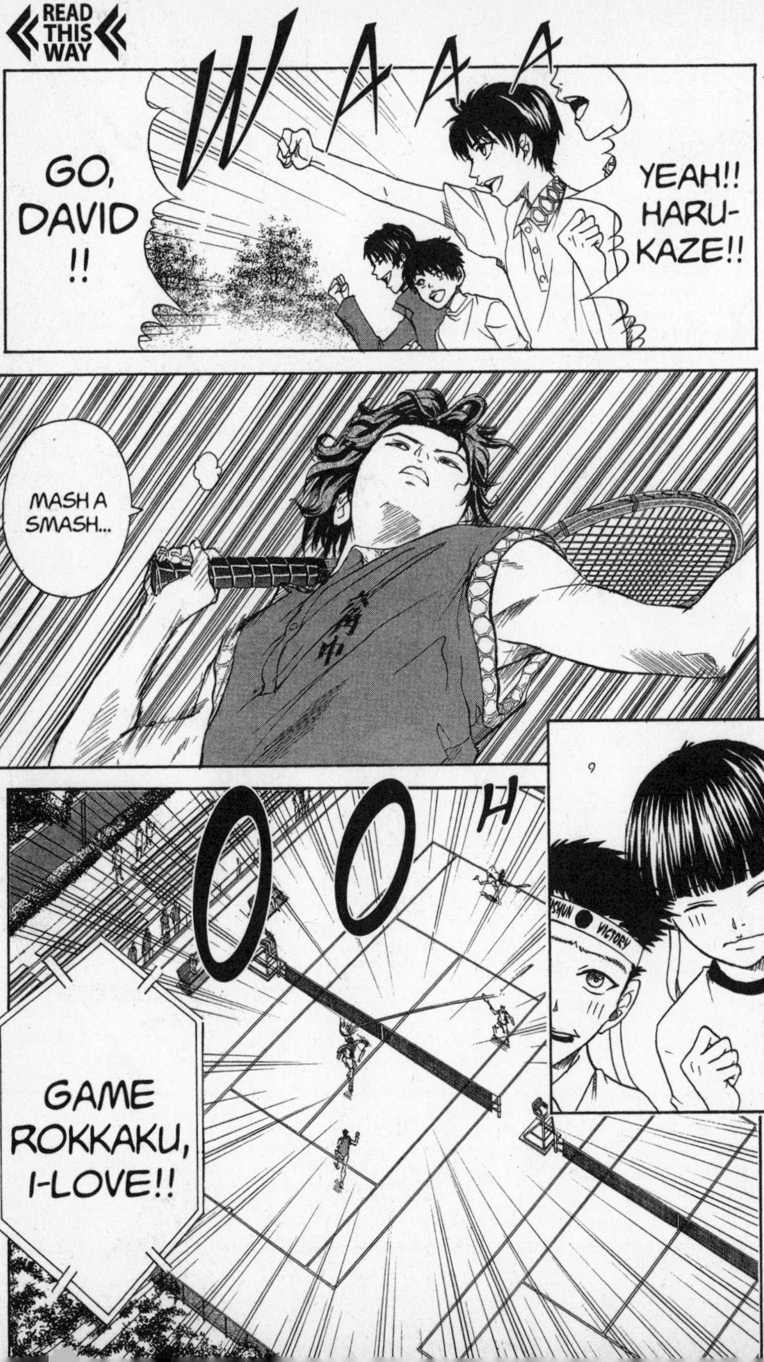

WAAA
YEAH!! HARU-KAZE!!
GO, DAVID!!
MASH A SMASH...
OOH
GAME ROKKAKU, 1-LOVE!!

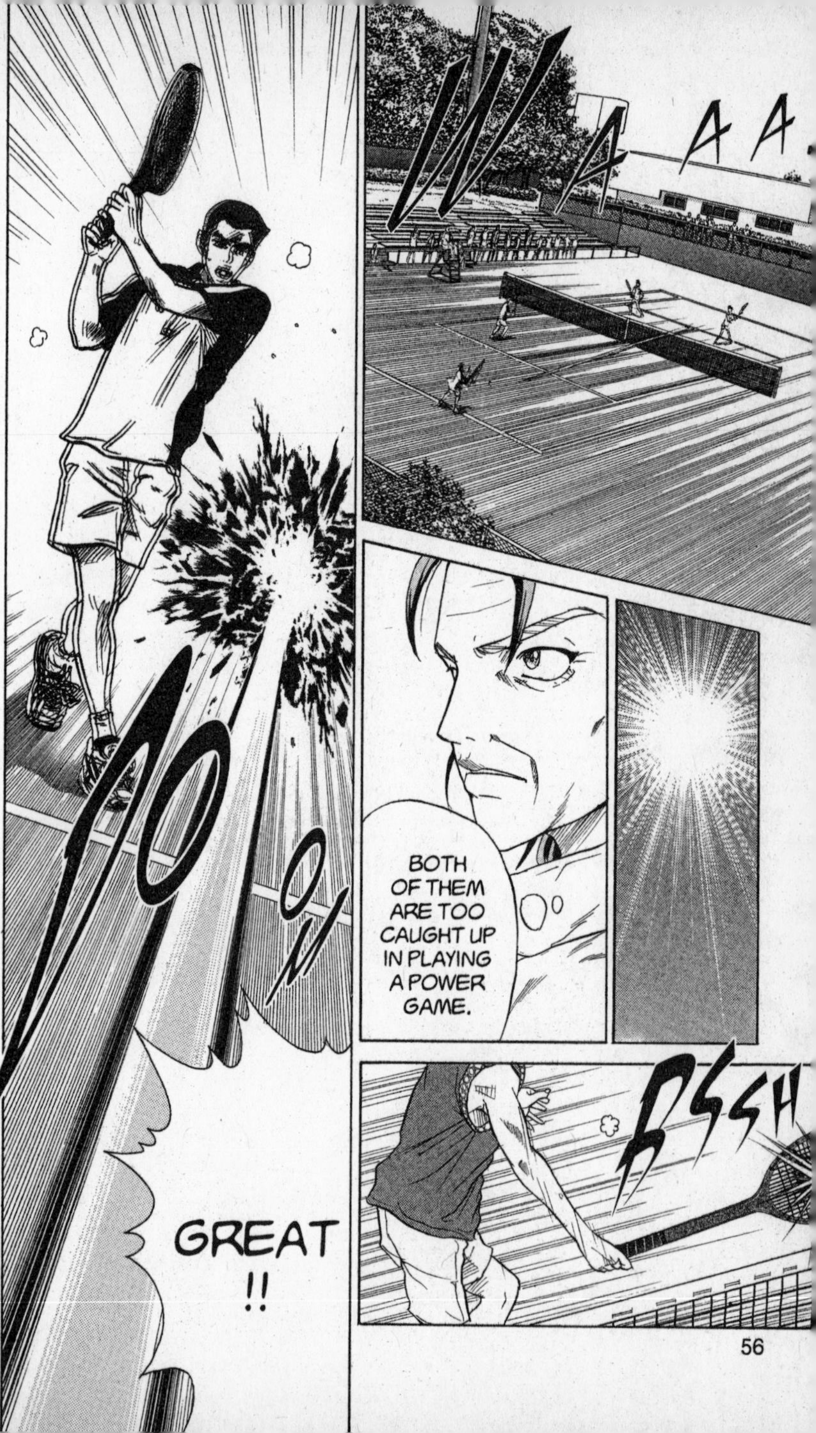
WAAA
BOTH OF THEM ARE TOO CAUGHT UP IN PLAYING A POWER GAME.
BSSH
GREAT !!

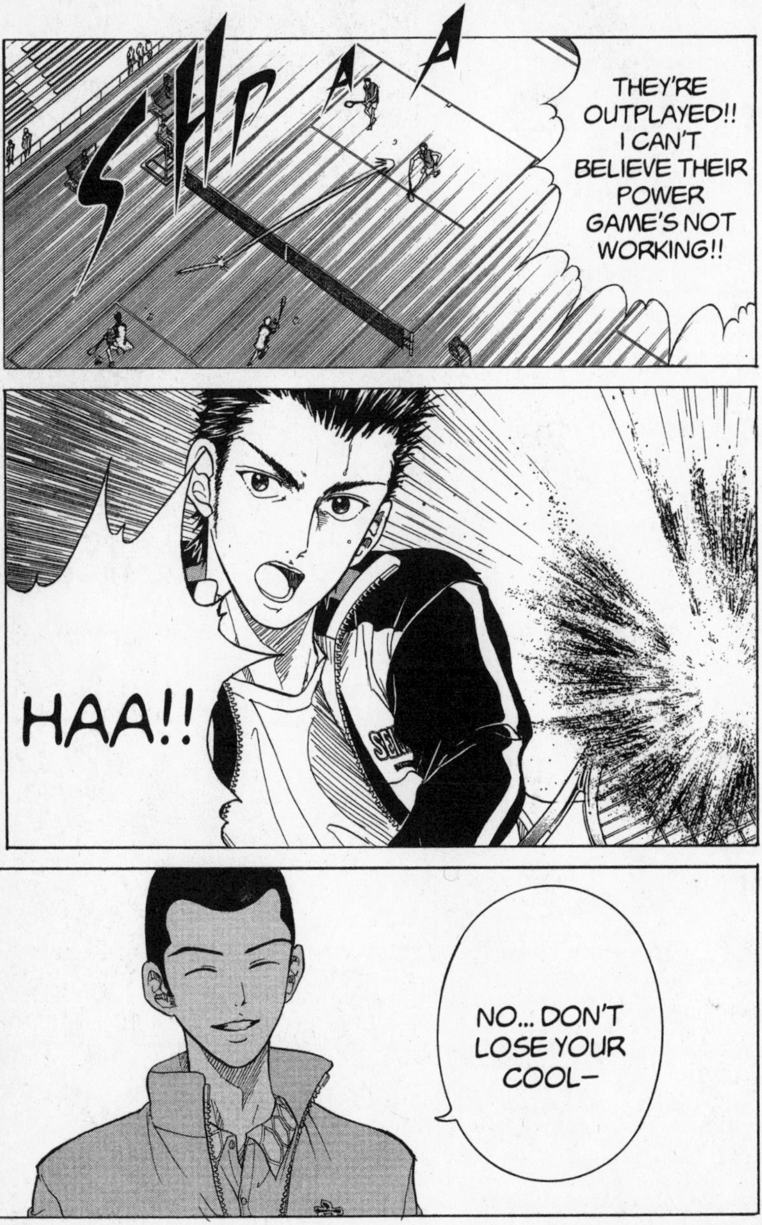
SHPAAA
THEY'RE OUTPLAYED!! I CAN'T BELIEVE THEIR POWER GAME'S NOT WORKING!!
HAA!!
NO... DON'T LOSE YOUR COOL-

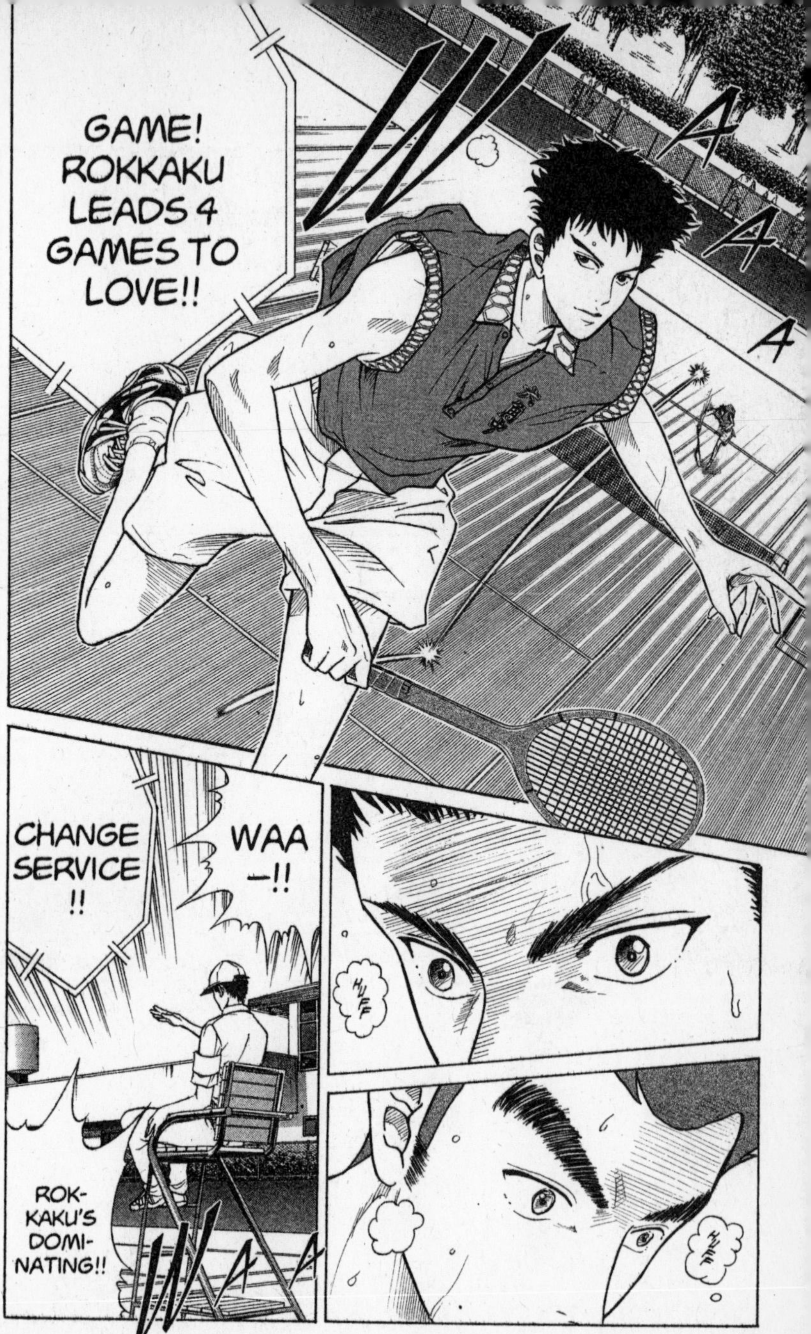
WAAA
GAME! ROKKAKU LEADS 4 GAMES TO LOVE!!
HUFF
HUFF
WAA—!!
CHANGE SERVICE!!
ROK-KAKU'S DOMI-NATING!!
WAA

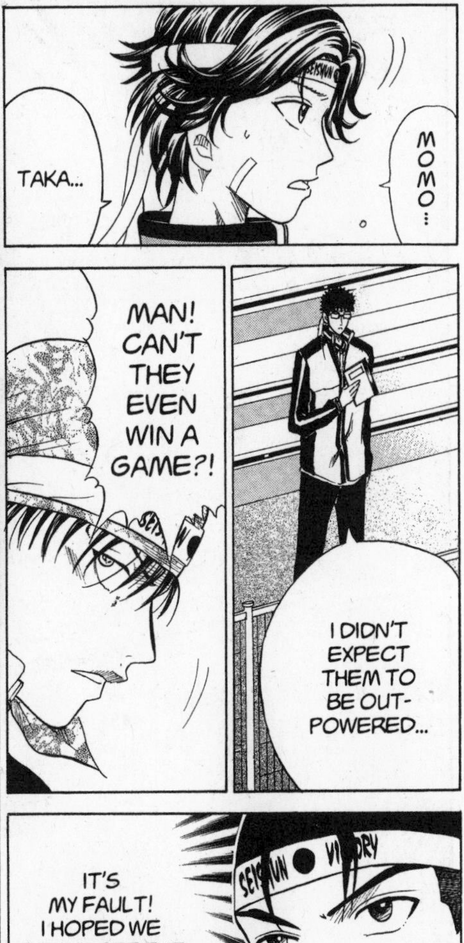
MOMO...
TAKA...
I DIDN'T EXPECT THEM TO BE OUT-POWERED...
MAN! CAN'T THEY EVEN WIN A GAME?!
IT'S MY FAULT! I HOPED WE COULD GET THE MOMENTUM BY SHOWING OFF OUR POWER FROM THE GET-GO BUT...
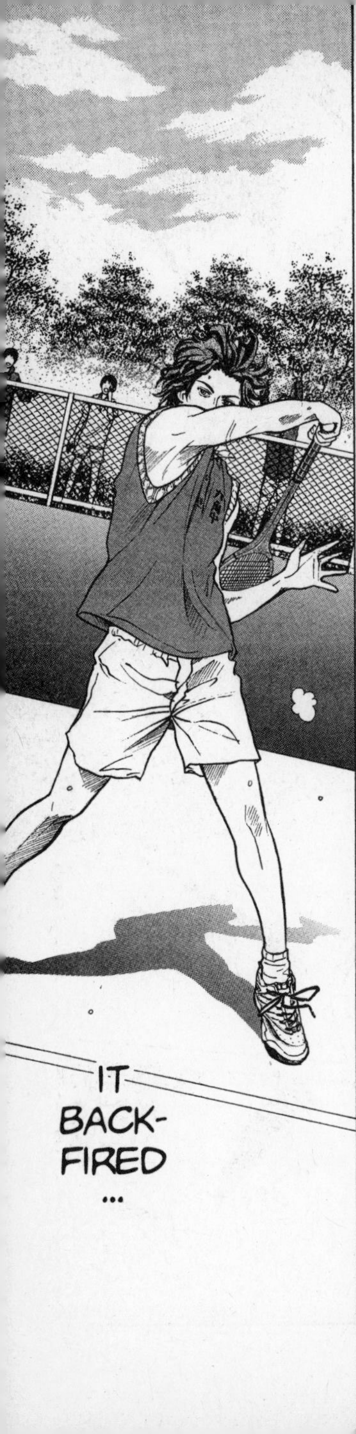
IT BACK-FIRED...

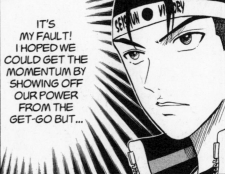

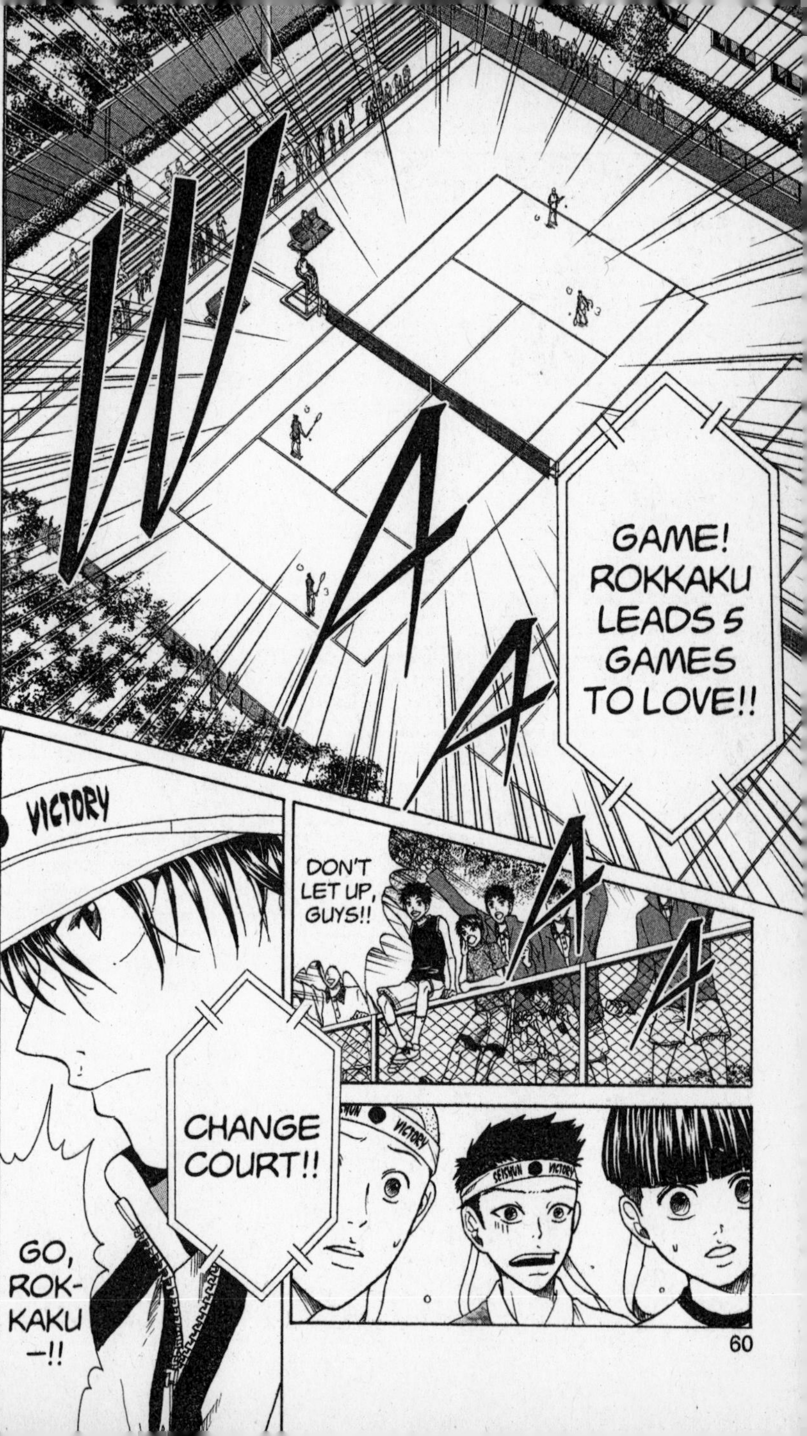
WAAAAA
GAME! ROKKAKU LEADS 5 GAMES TO LOVE!!
DON'T LET UP, GUYS!!
SEISHUN VICTORY
CHANGE COURT!!
VICTORY
GO, ROK-KAKU—!!

YOU'RE ON FIRE TODAY, DAVID!

PANTS ON FIRE!

ONE MORE GAME! FIRE, FIRE...

...HEHE.

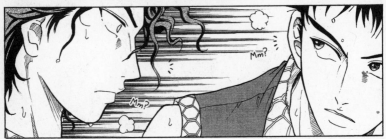

Mm?

Mm?

...

61

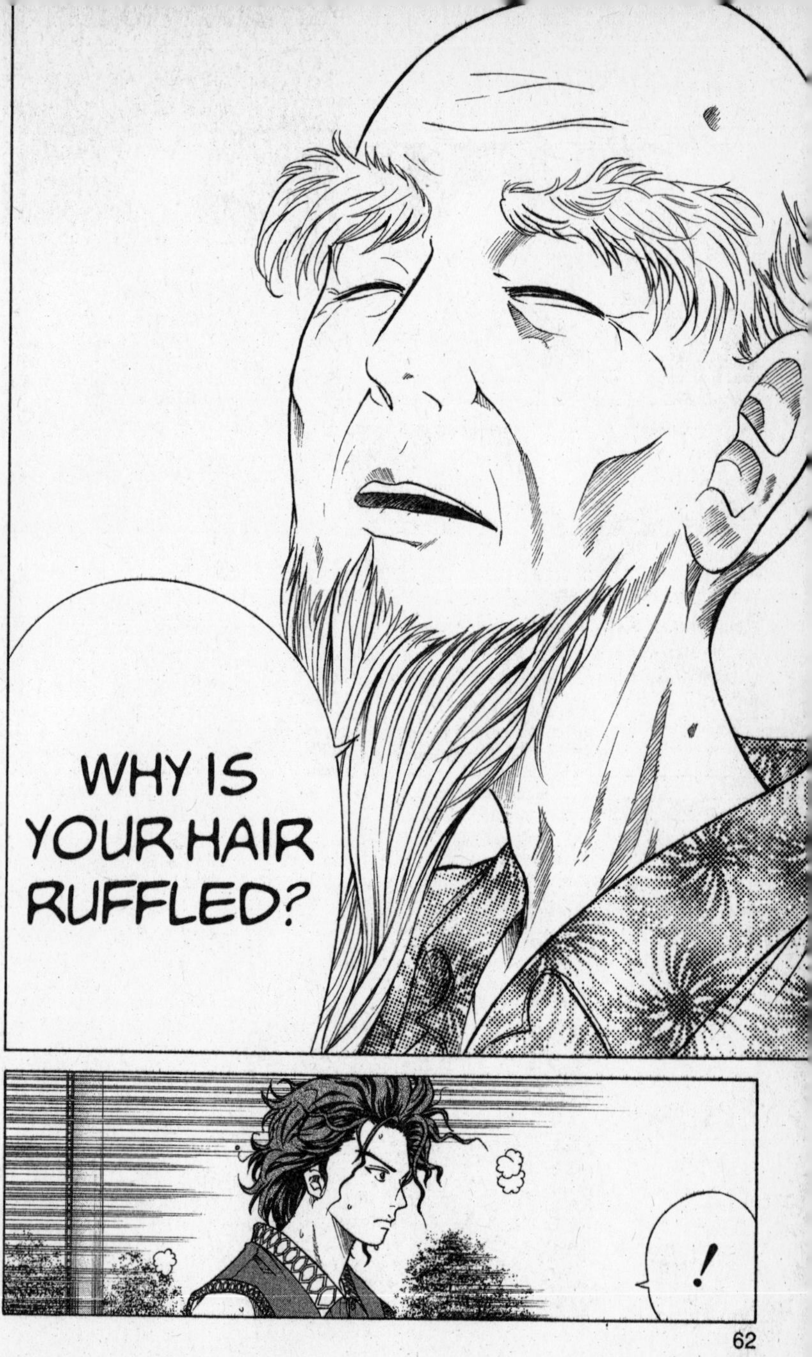
WHY IS YOUR HAIR RUFFLED?
!

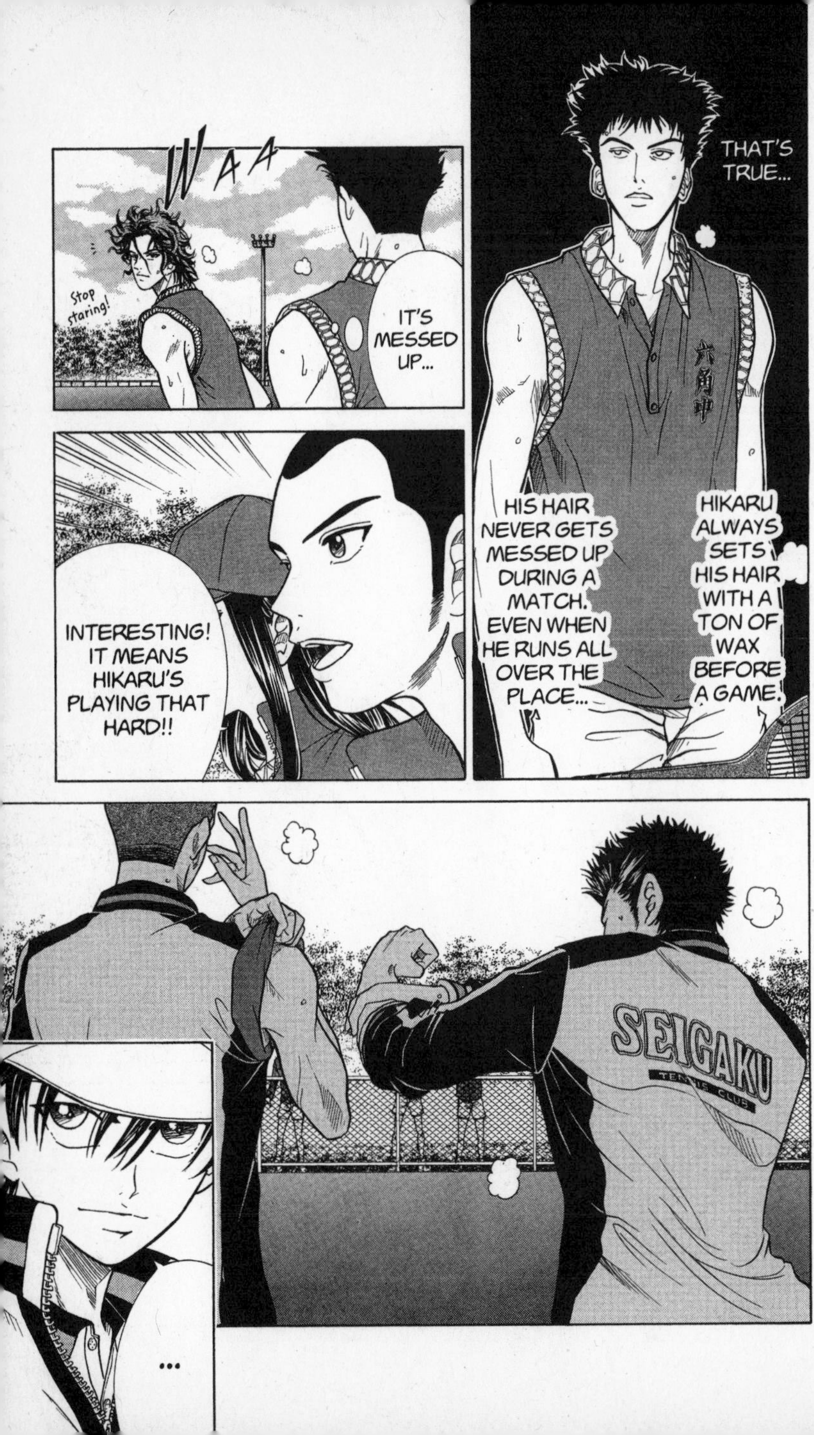
THAT'S TRUE...
HIKARU ALWAYS SETS HIS HAIR WITH A TON OF WAX BEFORE A GAME.
HIS HAIR NEVER GETS MESSED UP DURING A MATCH. EVEN WHEN HE RUNS ALL OVER THE PLACE...
WAA
IT'S MESSED UP...
Stop staring!
INTERESTING! IT MEANS HIKARU'S PLAYING THAT HARD!!
SEIGAKU
TENNIS CLUB
...

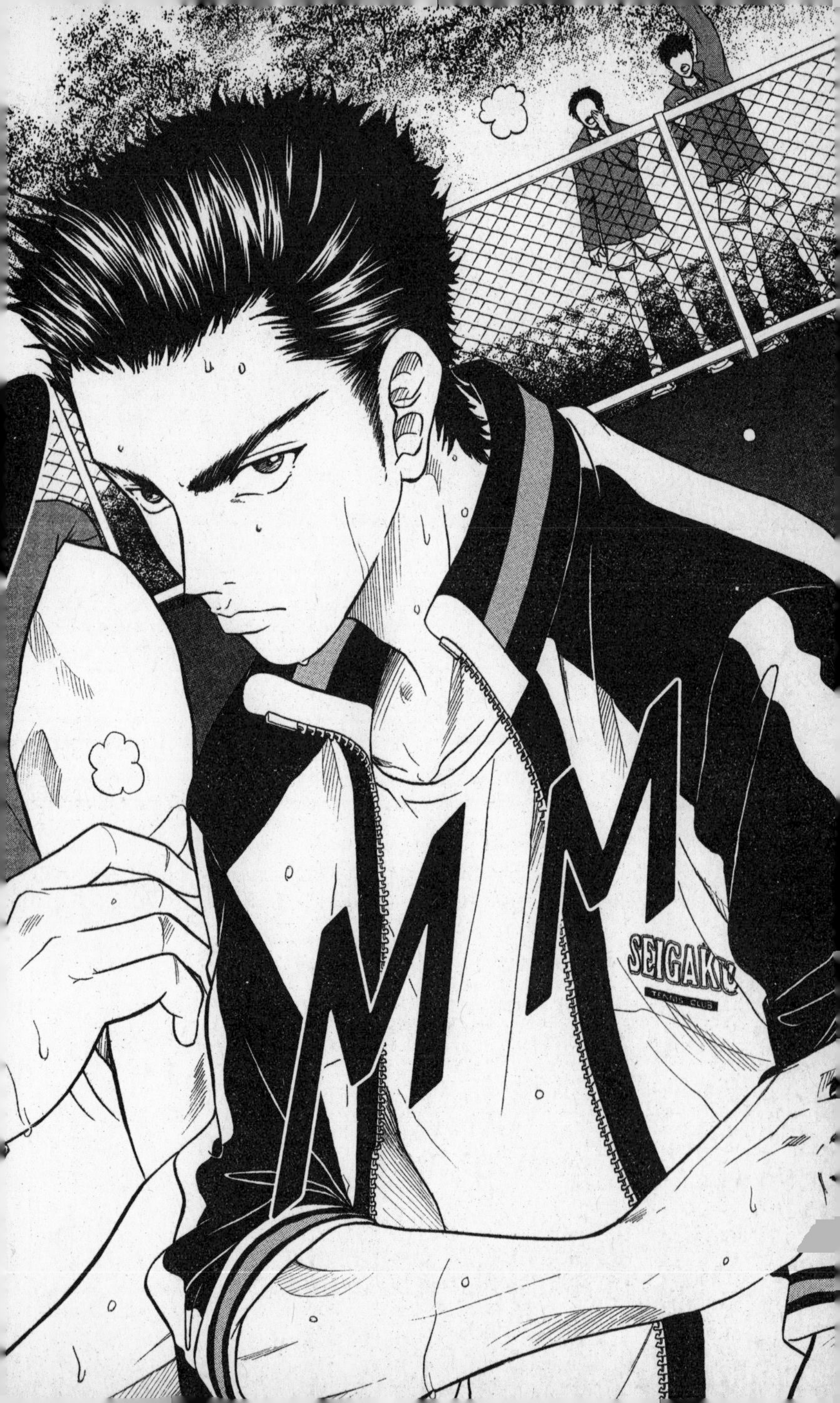
SEIGAKU

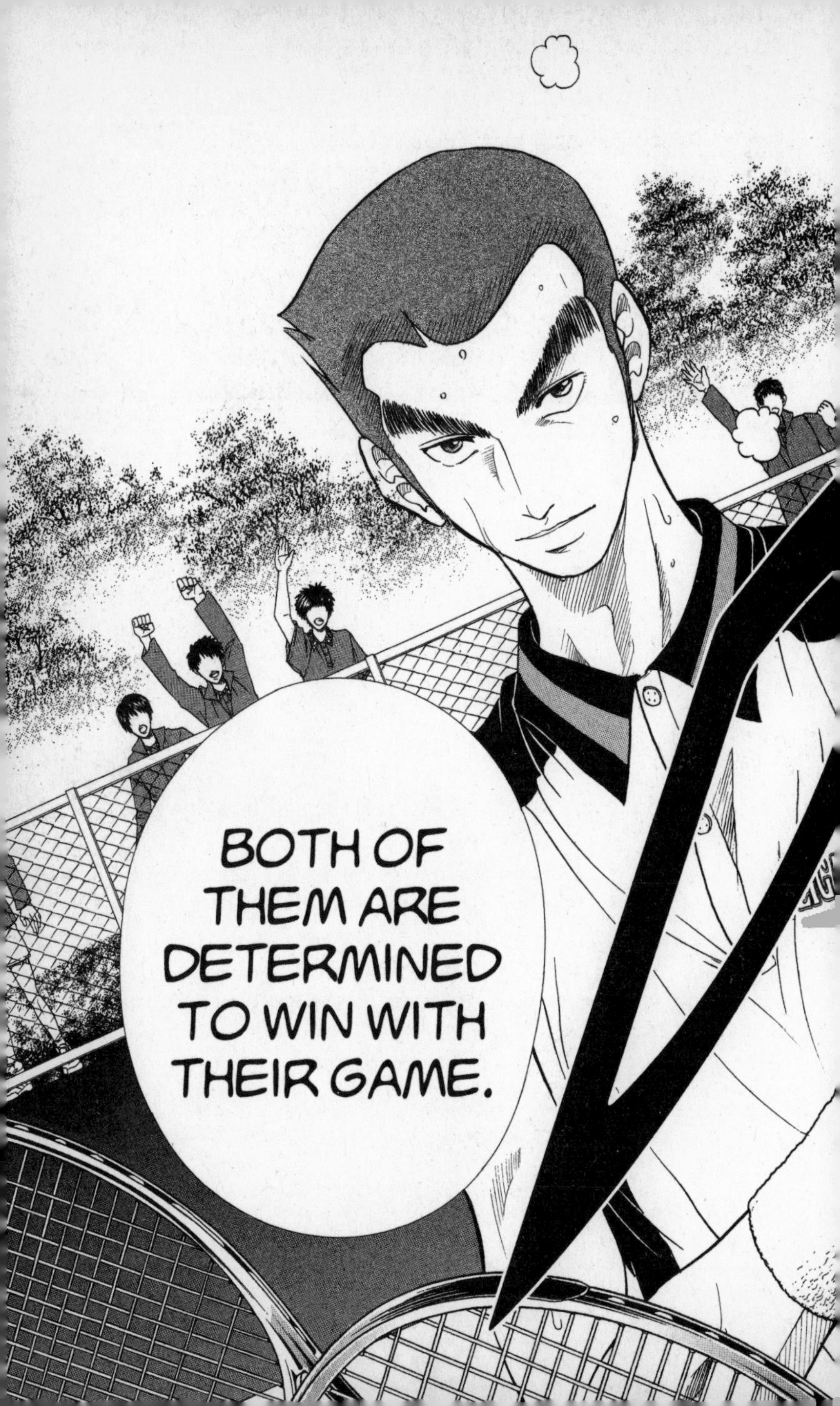
BOTH OF THEM ARE DETERMINED TO WIN WITH THEIR GAME.

Date . . No. 133

## Kojiro Saeki / Left-Handed

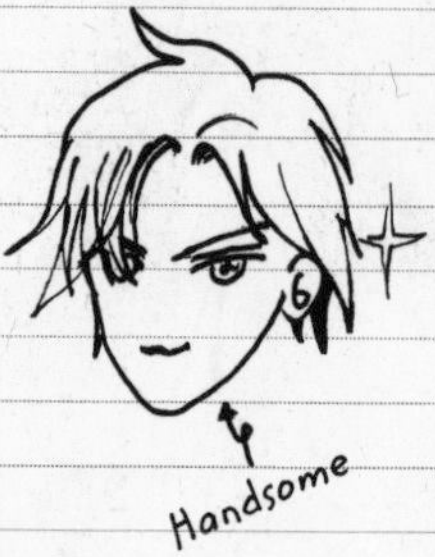
Handsome

Rokkaku Junior High School 9th Grade, Class C
Height: 174 cm. / Blood Type: O / Birthday: 10/18
Best move: Marking/Dynamic Vision
Favorite food: Okara (tofu lees)
Grilled uni (half-cooked)
Hobby / Recent pastime: Hanging out at the beach

## Marehiko Itsuki / Right-Handed

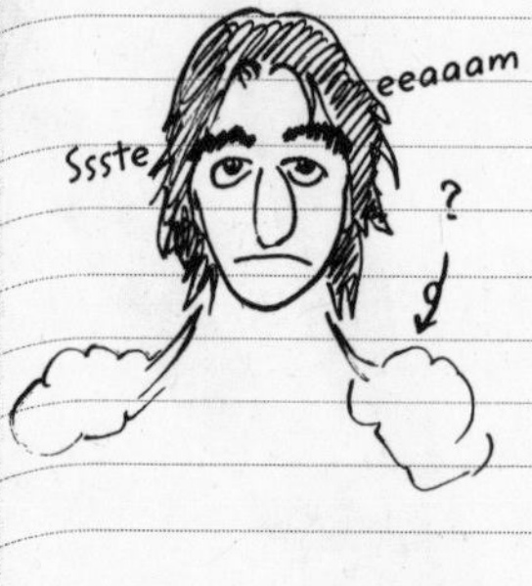
Ssste
eeaaam
?

Rokkaku Junior High School 9th Grade, Class B
Height: 174 cm. / Blood Type: AB / Birthday: 8/31
Best move: Blowing Away Dust with Nose
Favorite food: Vegetable curry
Hobby / Recent pastime: Hanging out at the beach

(Selected from Sadaharu Inui Secret Data Note No. 133)

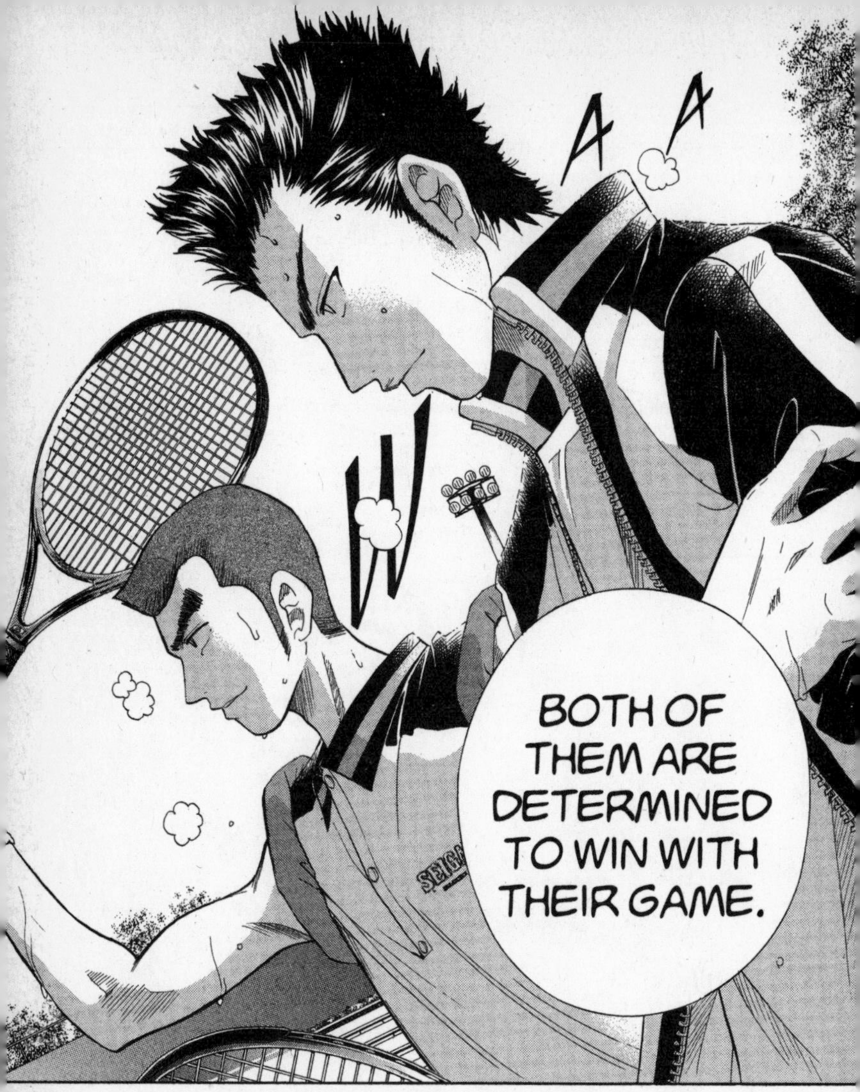
BOTH OF THEM ARE DETERMINED TO WIN WITH THEIR GAME.

# GENIUS 171: HEAD-ON BATTLE!

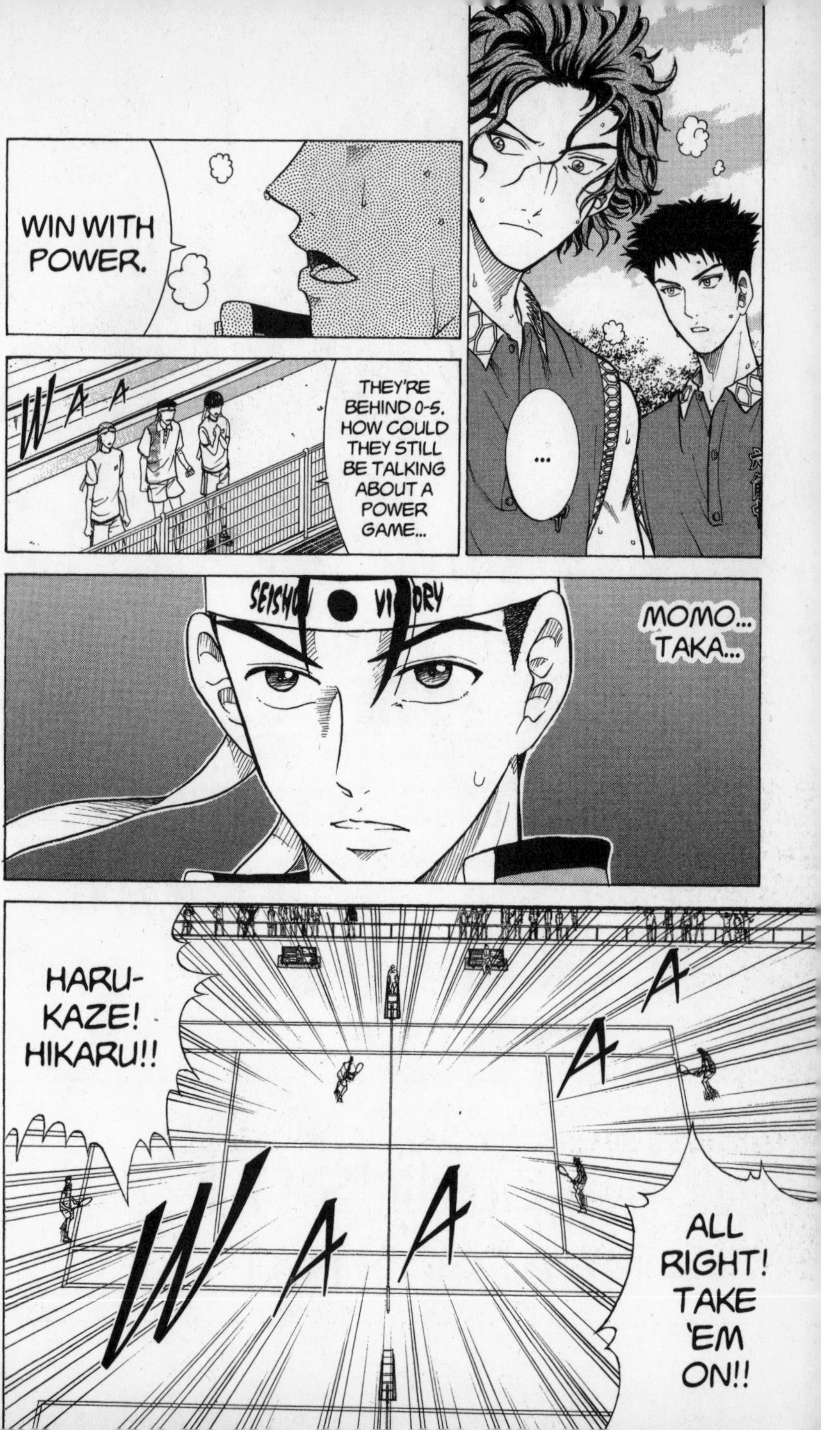
...
WIN WITH POWER.
THEY'RE BEHIND 0-5. HOW COULD THEY STILL BE TALKING ABOUT A POWER GAME...
WAA
MOMO... TAKA...
AA
ALL RIGHT! TAKE 'EM ON!!
HARU-KAZE! HIKARU!!
WAA

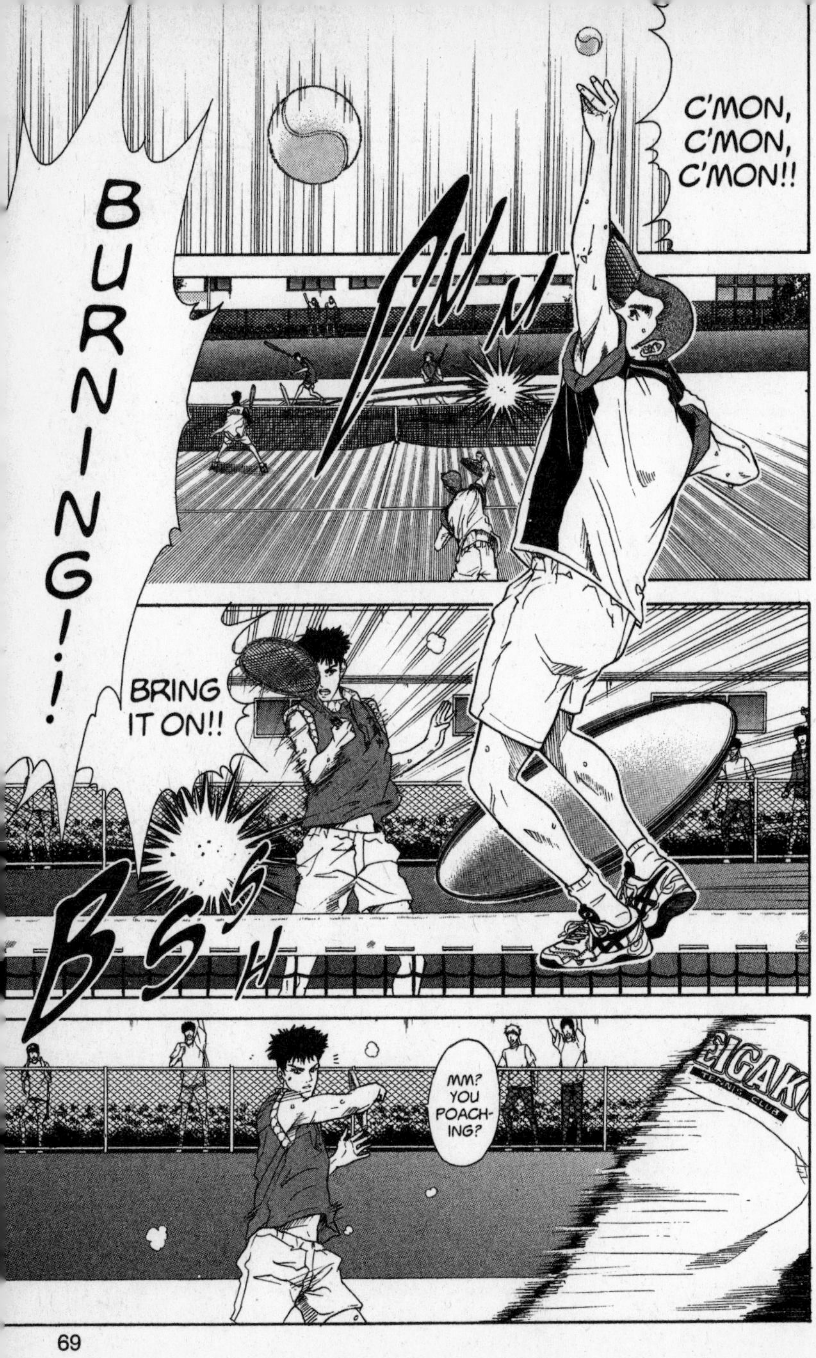
C'MON, C'MON, C'MON!!
BURNING!!
BRING IT ON!!
BSSSH
MM? YOU POACH-ING?

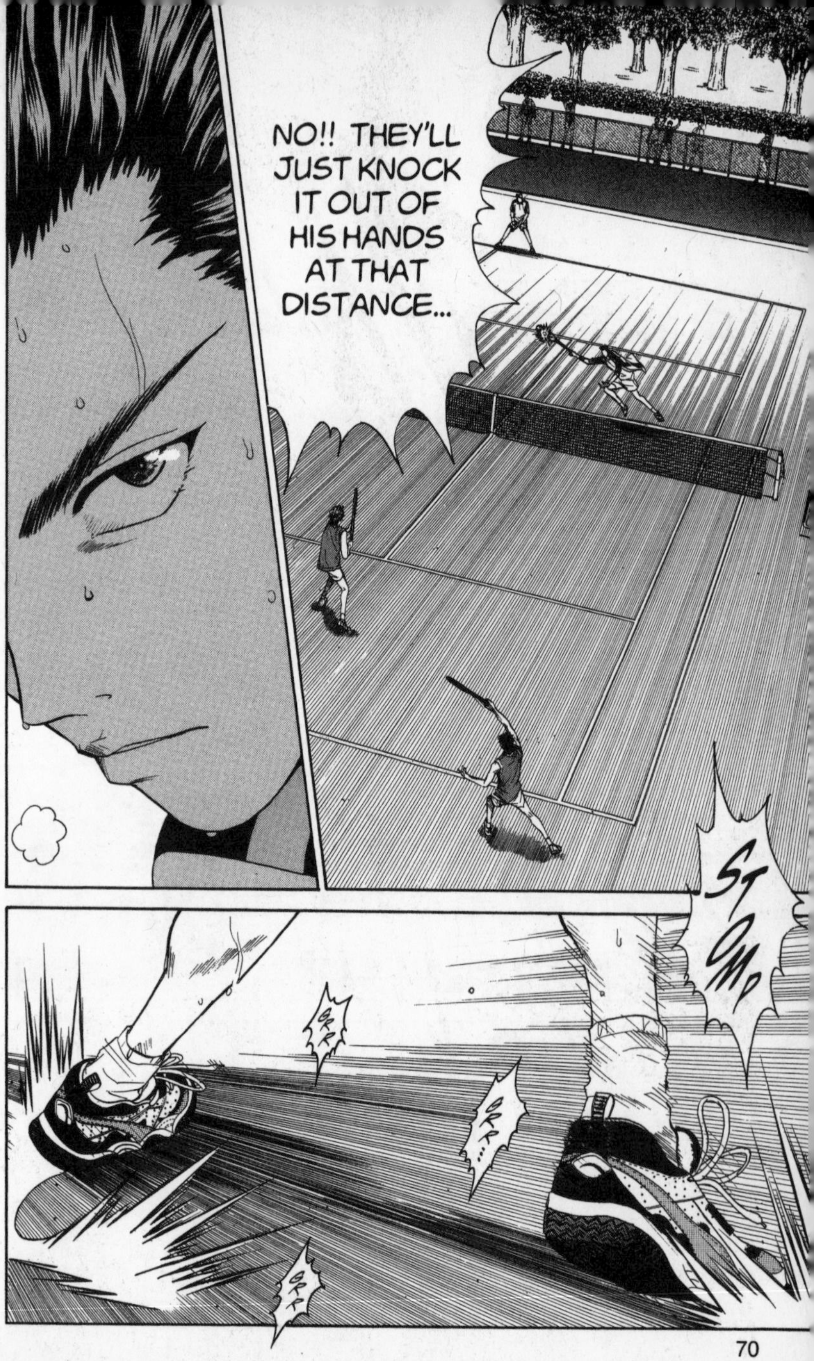
NO!! THEY'LL JUST KNOCK IT OUT OF HIS HANDS AT THAT DISTANCE...
STOMP
GRR...
GRR
GRR

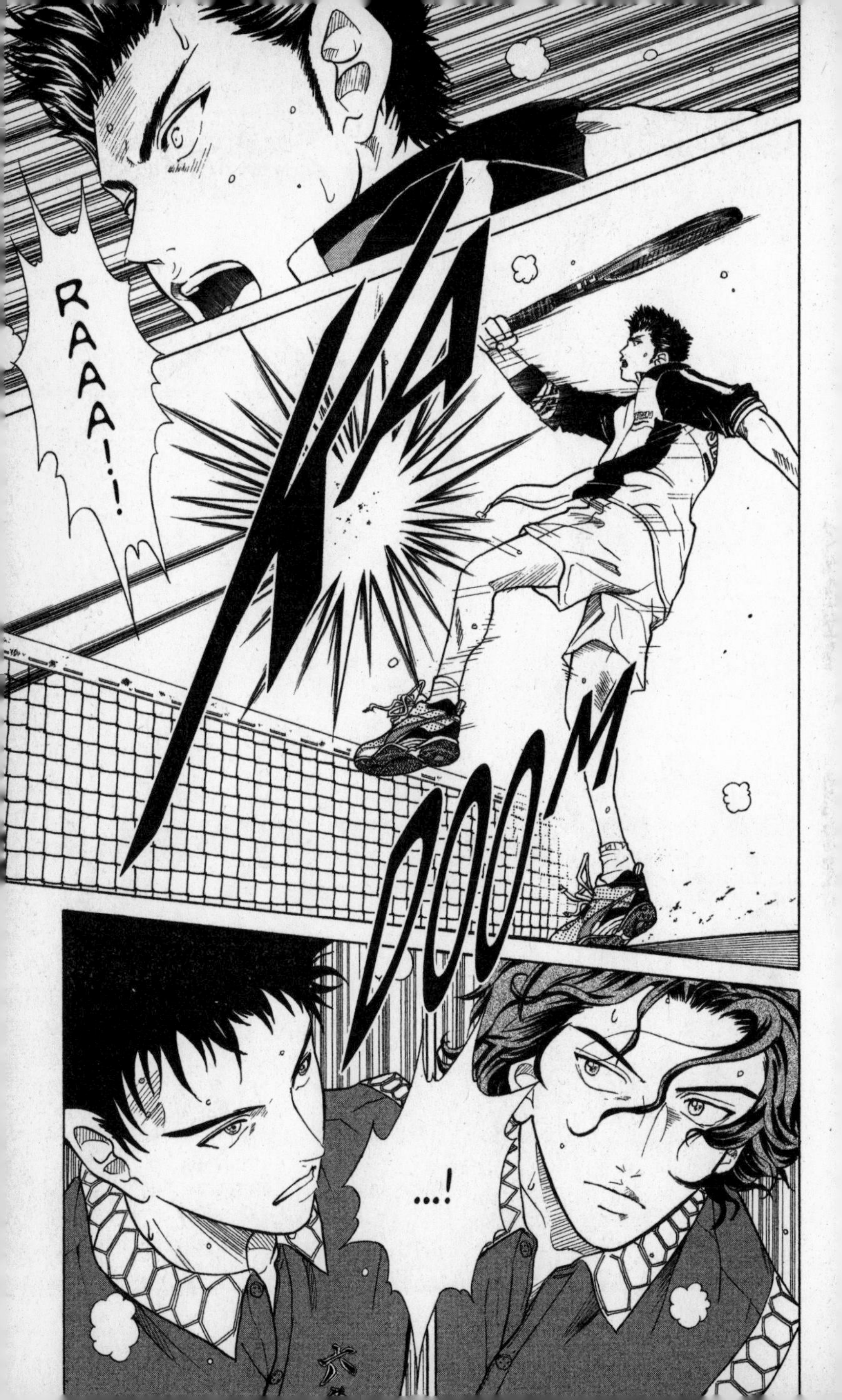
RAAA!!
KA
DOOOM
...!

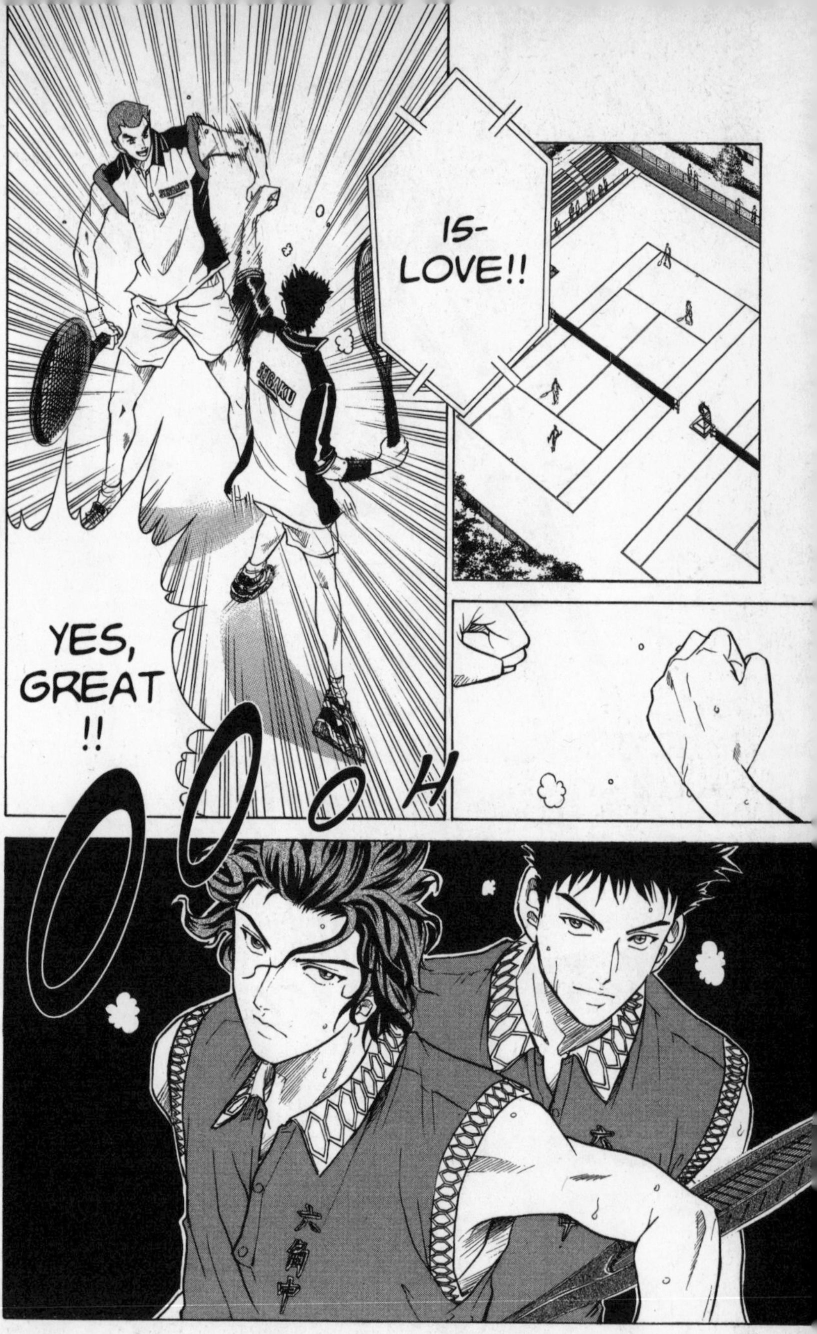
15-
LOVE!!
YES, GREAT !!
OOOH

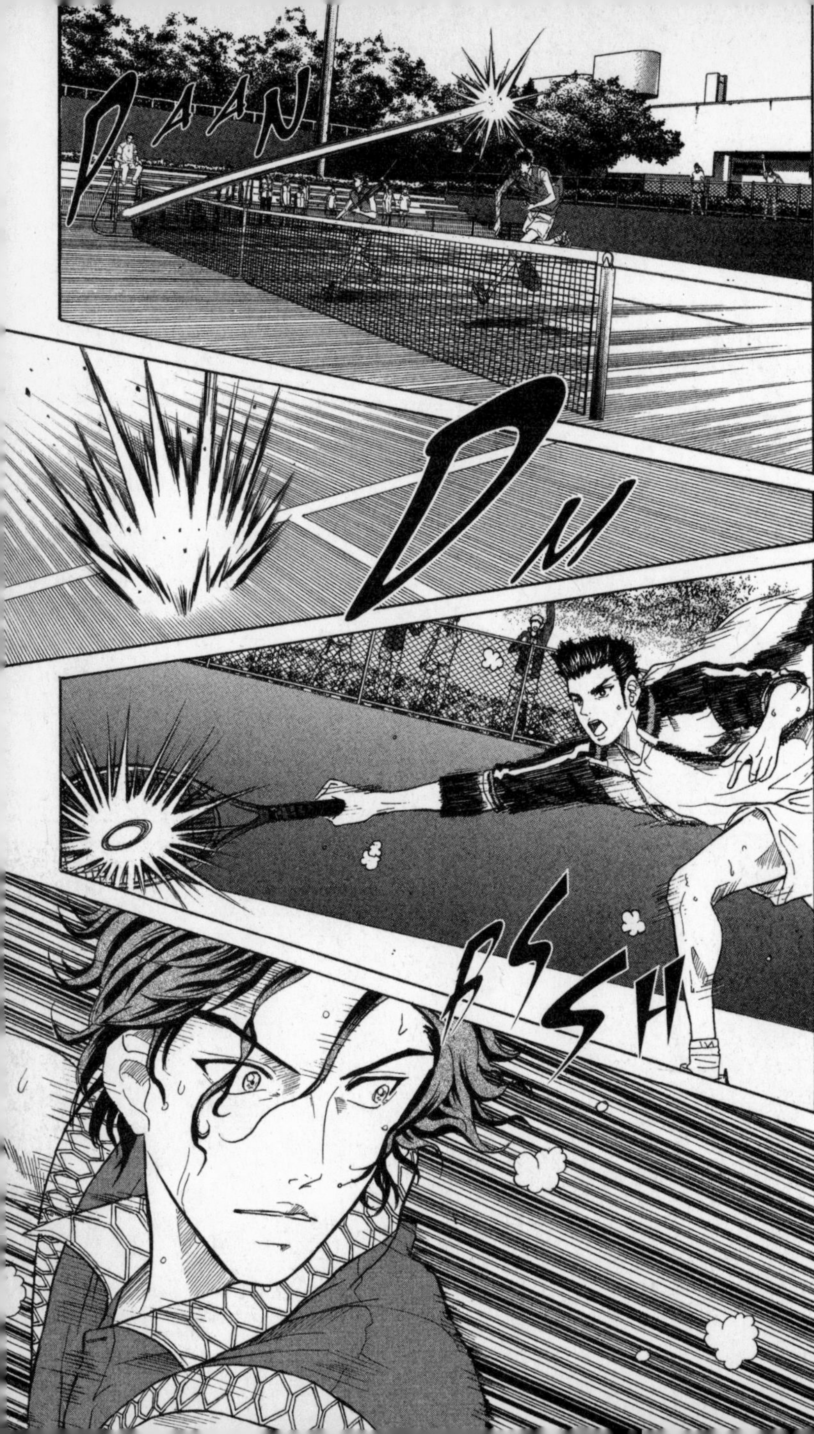

DAAN
DM
FSSH

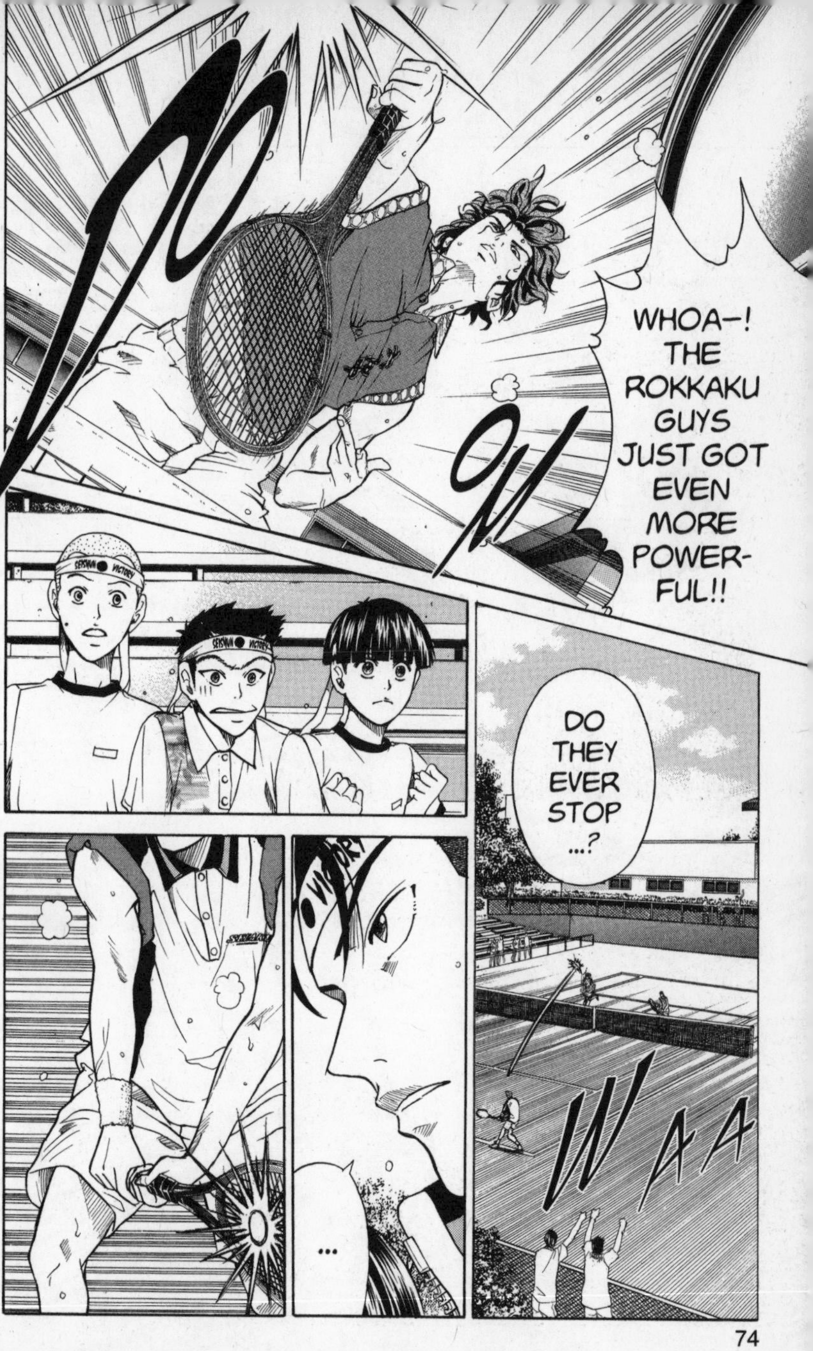

WHOA-! THE ROKKAKU GUYS JUST GOT EVEN MORE POWER-FUL!!
DO THEY EVER STOP ...?
WAA
...

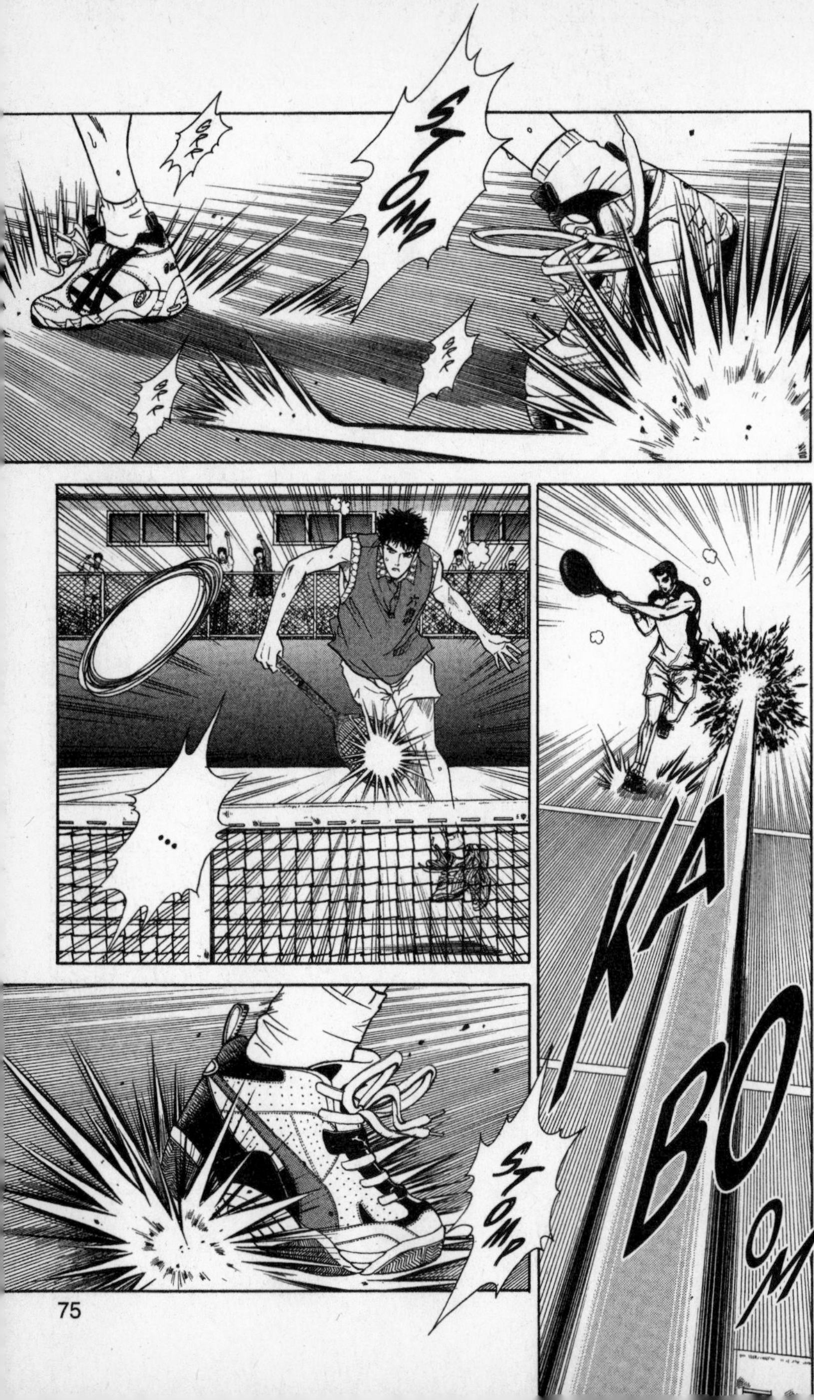
STOMP
GRR
GRR
GRR
KABOOM
...
STOMP

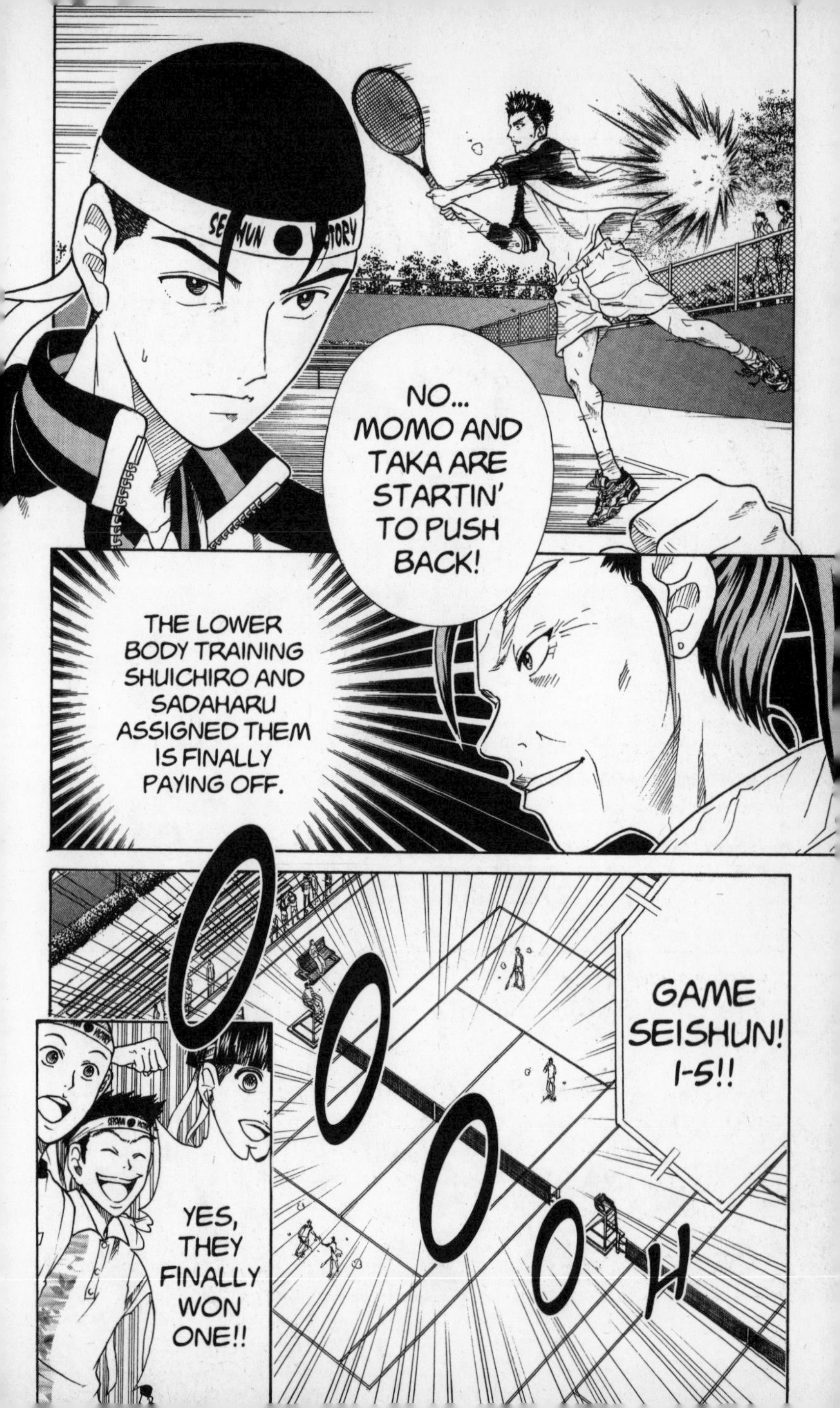
NO... MOMO AND TAKA ARE STARTIN' TO PUSH BACK!
THE LOWER BODY TRAINING SHUICHIRO AND SADAHARU ASSIGNED THEM IS FINALLY PAYING OFF.
GAME SEISHUN! 1-5!!
OOOOOH
YES, THEY FINALLY WON ONE!!

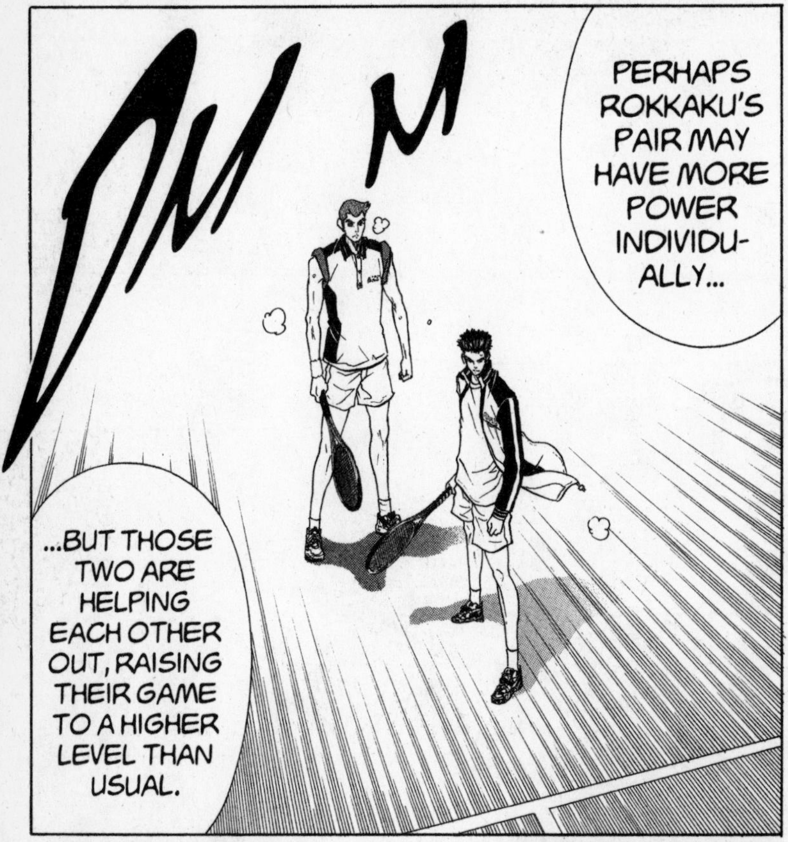
PERHAPS ROKKAKU'S PAIR MAY HAVE MORE POWER INDIVIDU-ALLY...
...BUT THOSE TWO ARE HELPING EACH OTHER OUT, RAISING THEIR GAME TO A HIGHER LEVEL THAN USUAL.
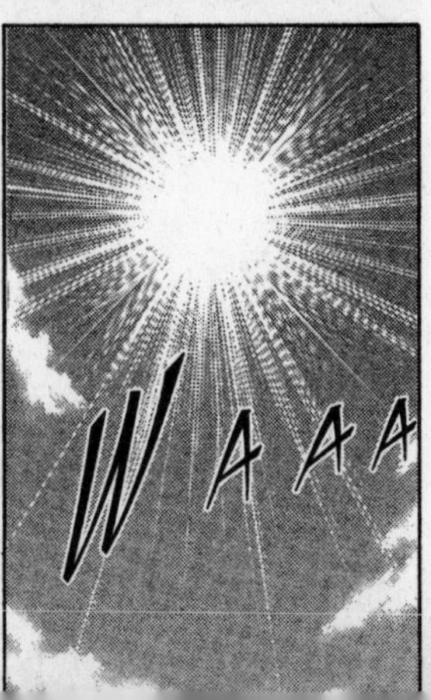
WAAA
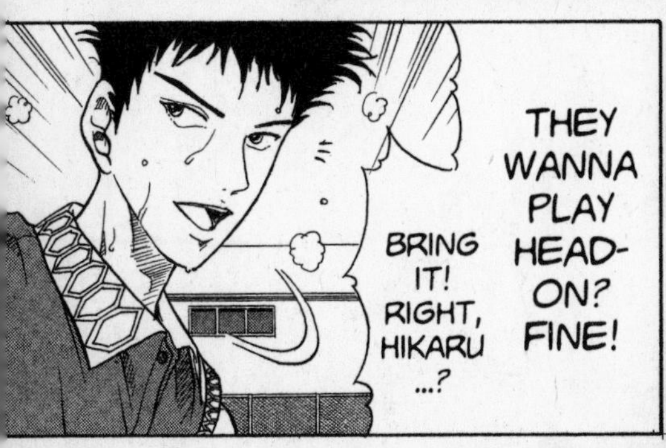
THEY WANNA PLAY HEAD-ON? FINE!
BRING IT! RIGHT, HIKARU ...?

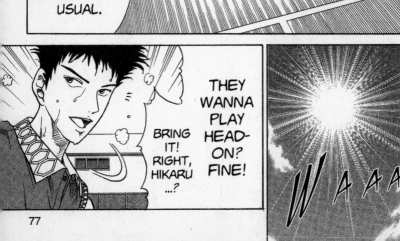

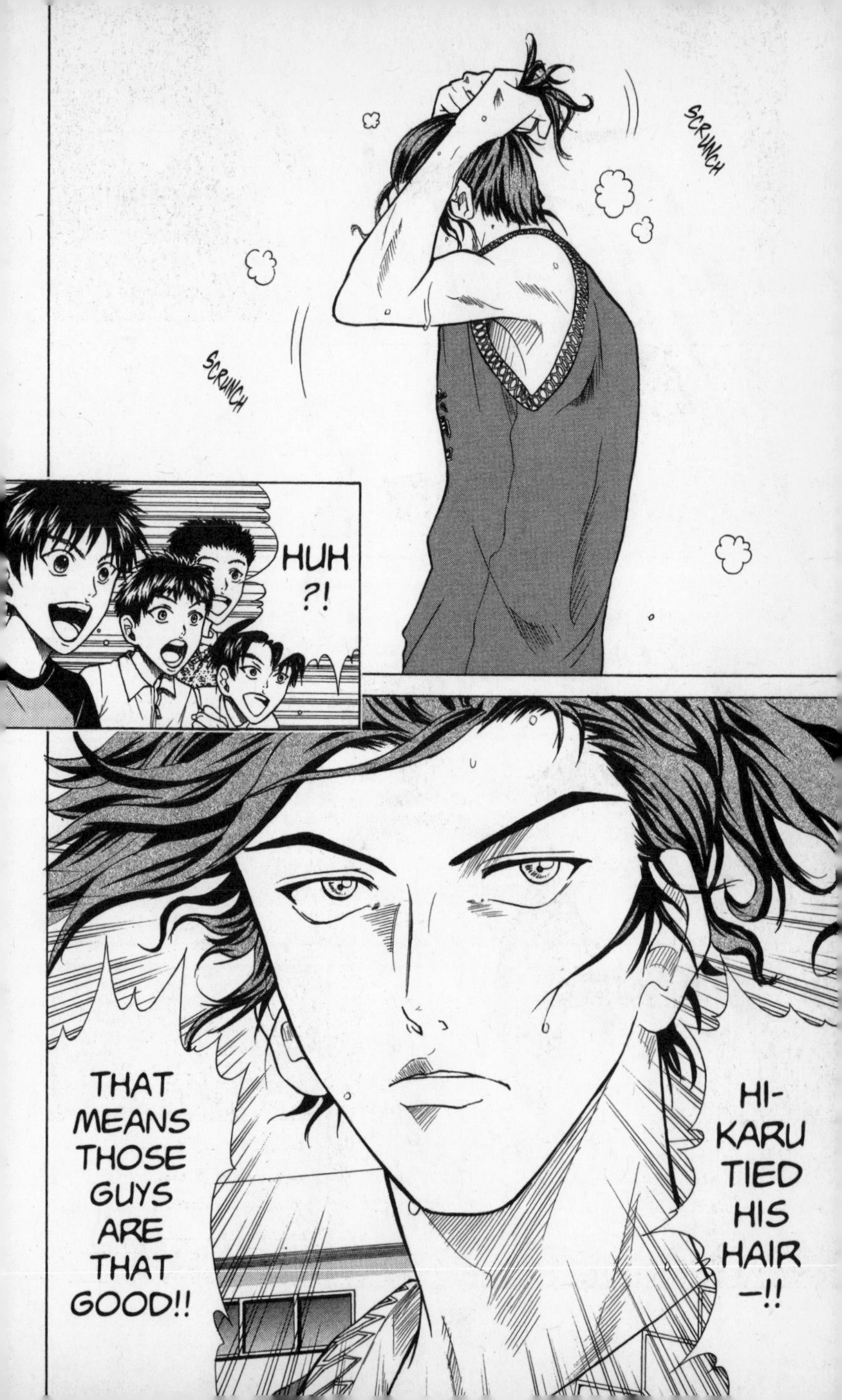
SCRUNCH
SCRUNCH
HUH ?!
HI-KARU TIED HIS HAIR—!!
THAT MEANS THOSE GUYS ARE THAT GOOD!!

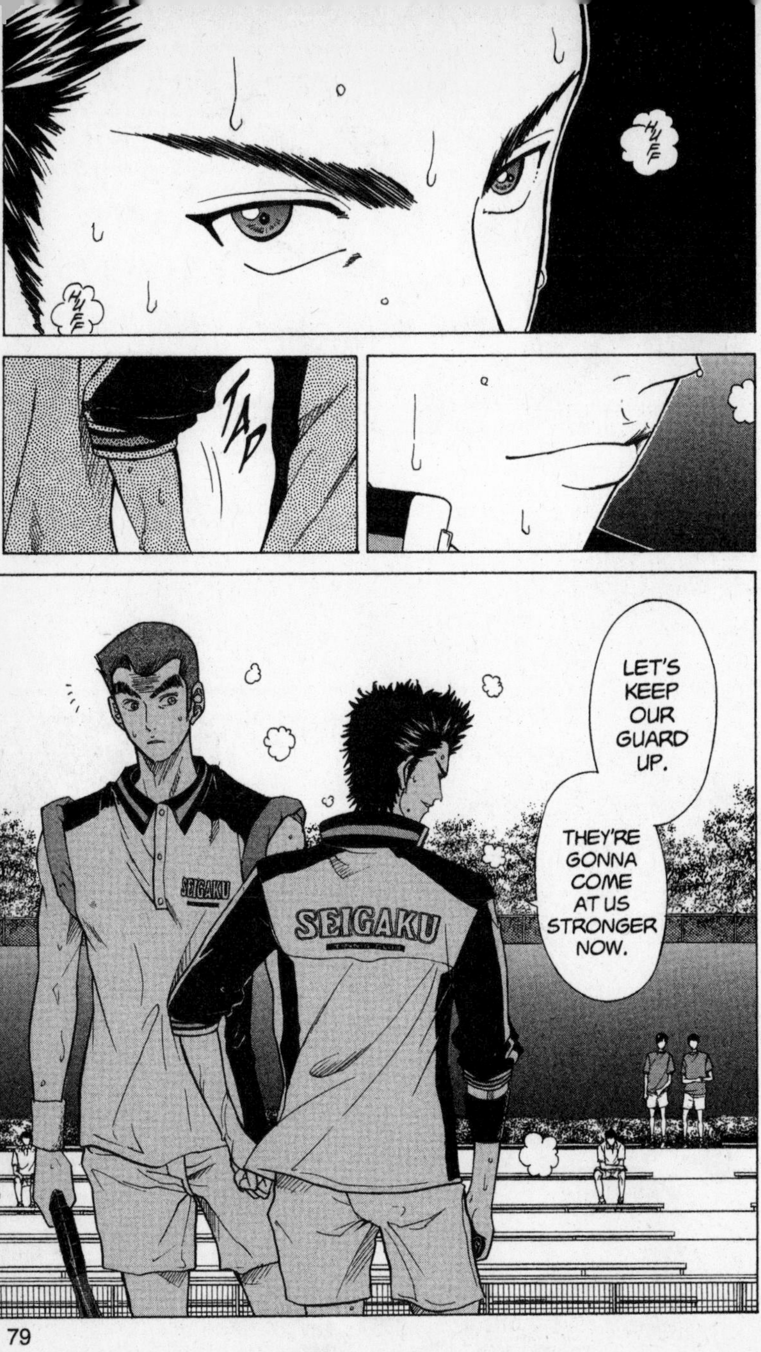
HUFF
HUFF
TAP
LET'S KEEP OUR GUARD UP.
THEY'RE GONNA COME AT US STRONGER NOW.

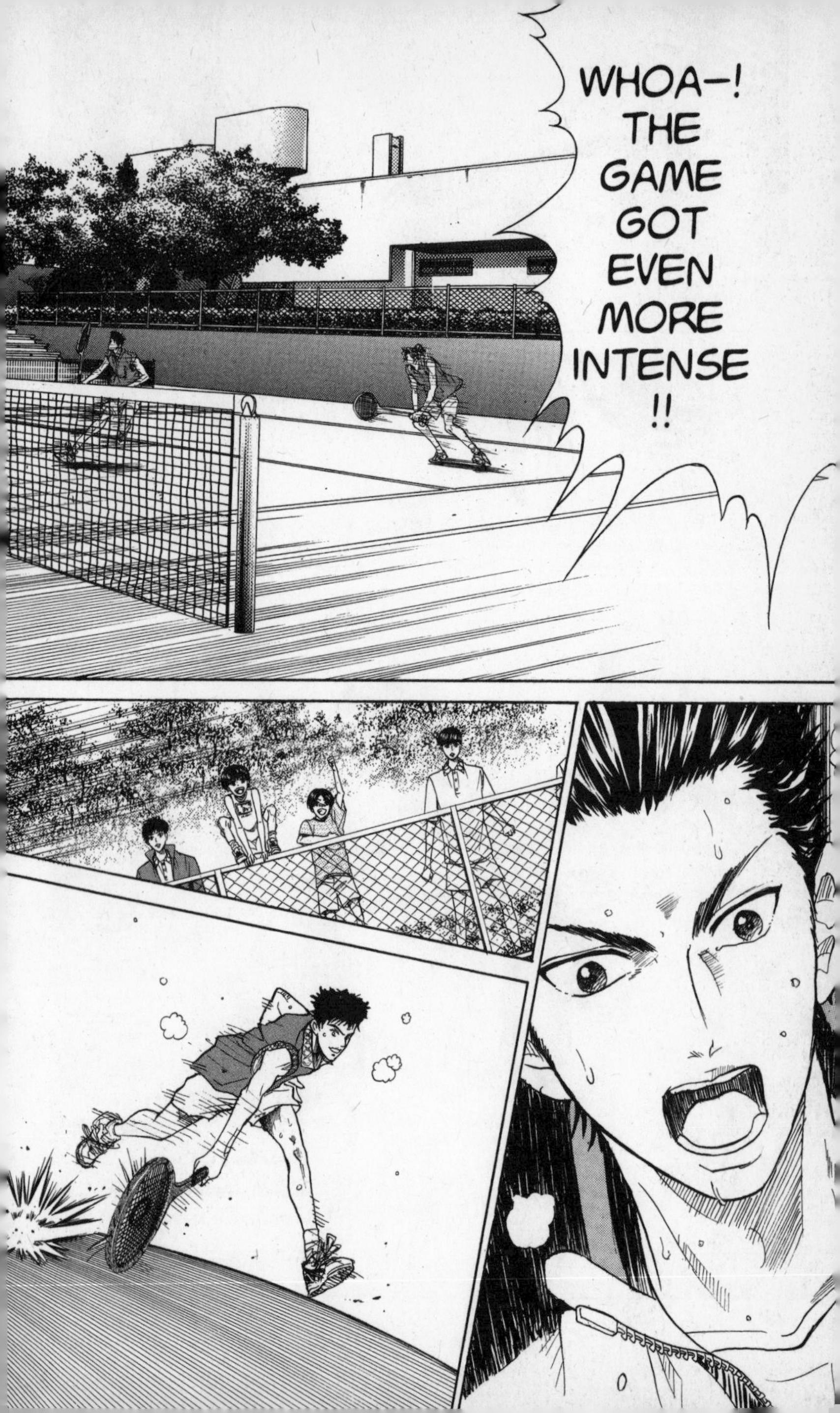
WHOA-! THE GAME GOT EVEN MORE INTENSE !!

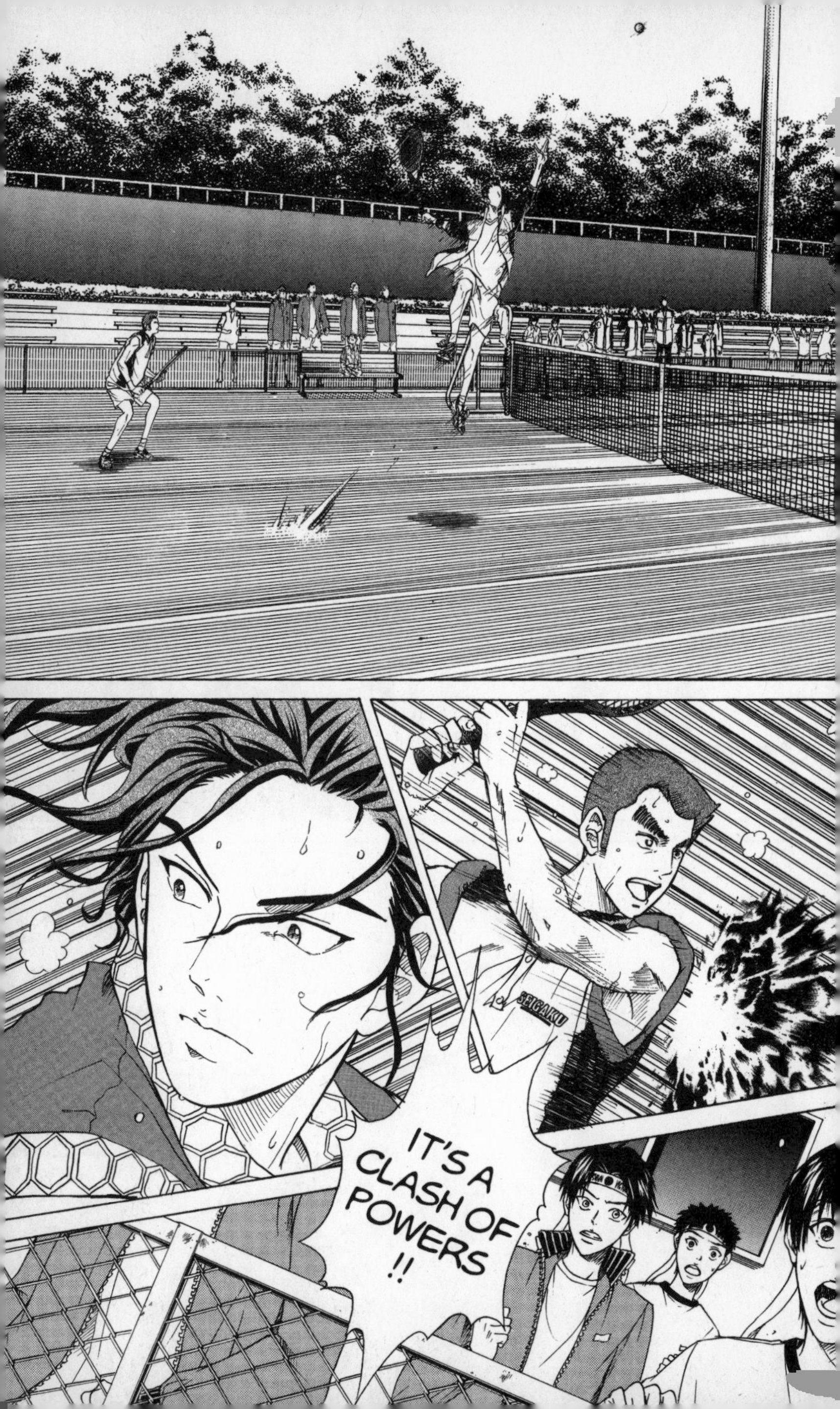
SEIGAKU
IT'S A CLASH OF POWERS !!

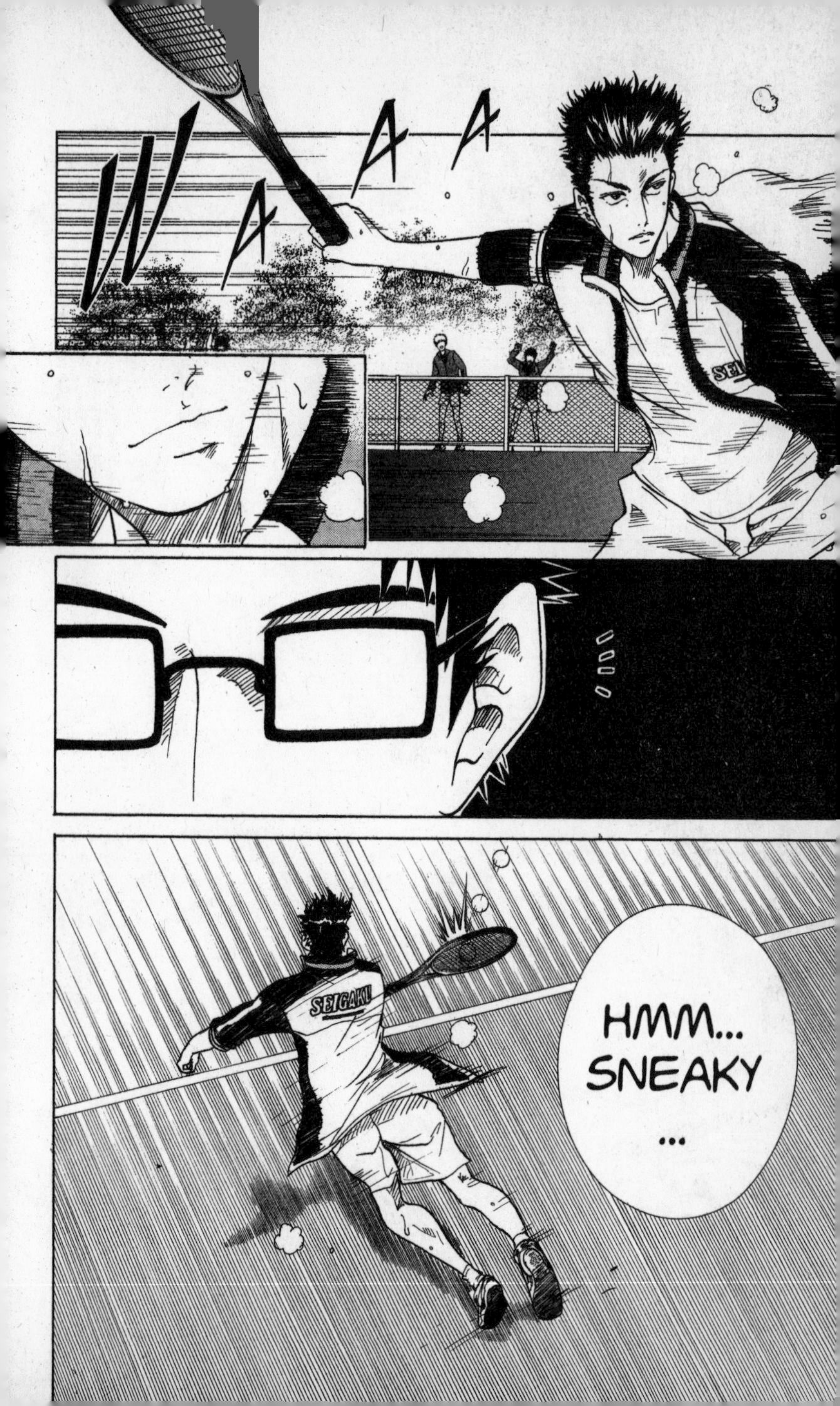
WAAAA
HMM... SNEAKY ...

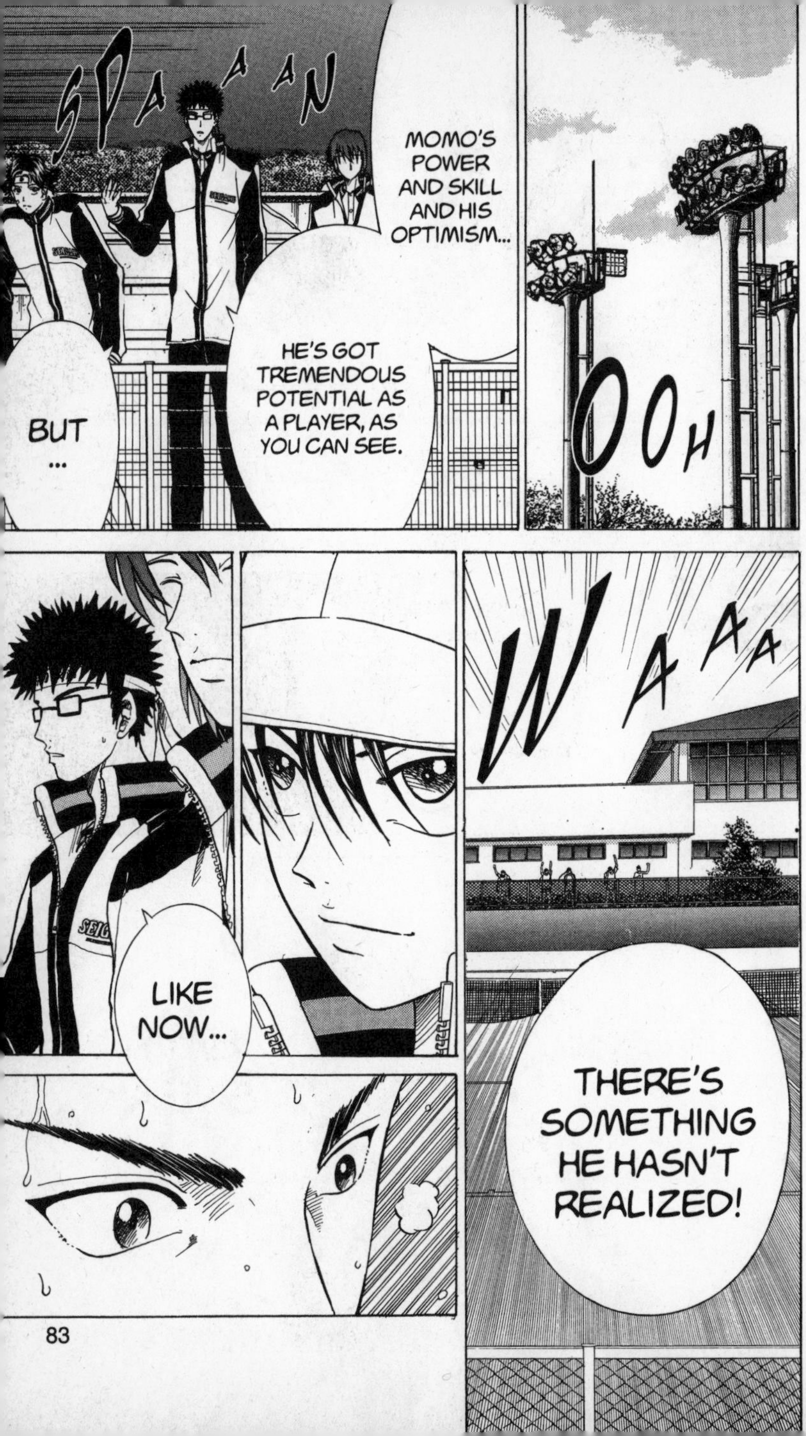
OOH
SPAAAN
MOMO'S POWER AND SKILL AND HIS OPTIMISM...
HE'S GOT TREMENDOUS POTENTIAL AS A PLAYER, AS YOU CAN SEE.
BUT ...
WAAA
THERE'S SOMETHING HE HASN'T REALIZED!
LIKE NOW...

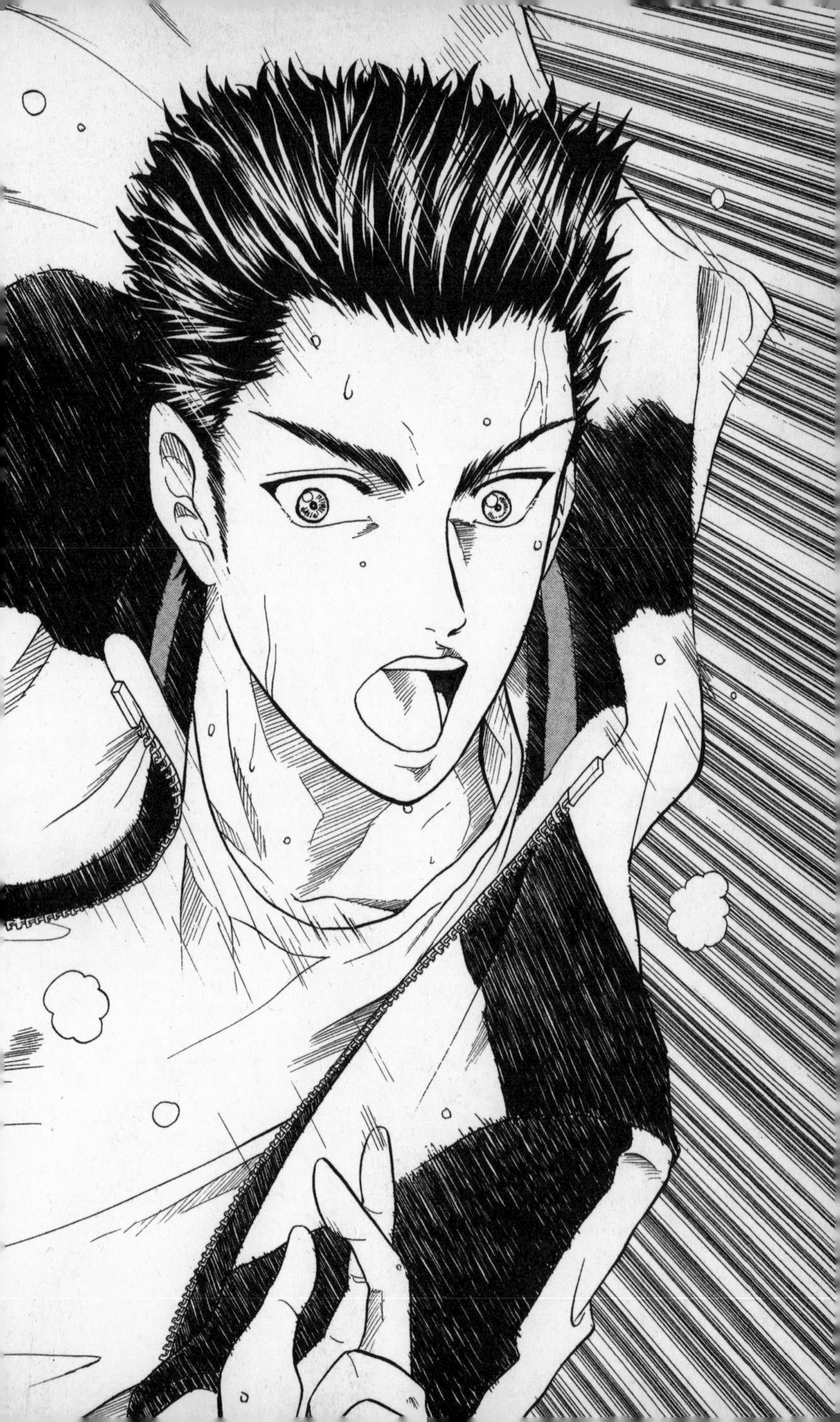

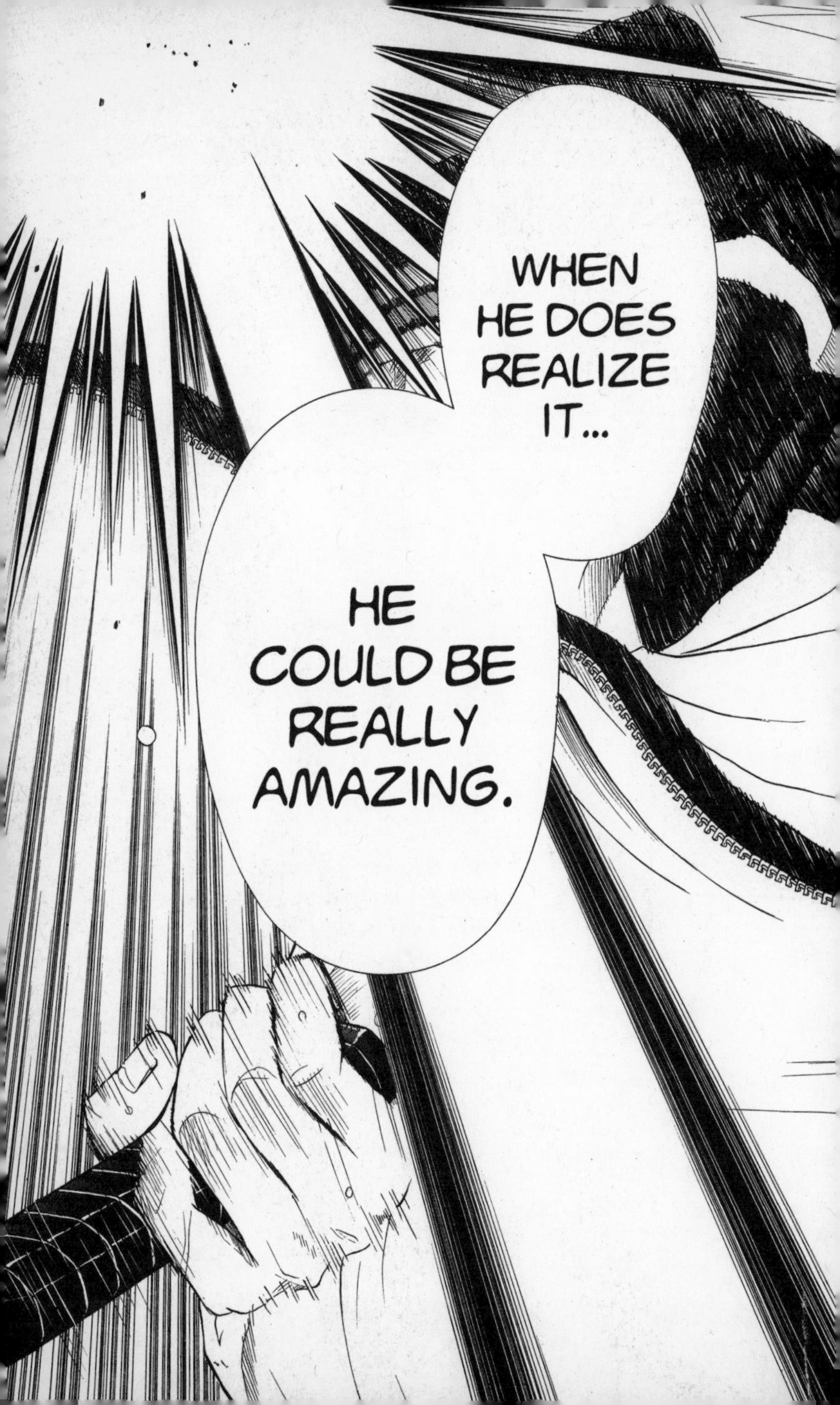
WHEN HE DOES REALIZE IT...
HE COULD BE REALLY AMAZING.

Date · · No. 134

## Kentaro Aoi / Right-Handed

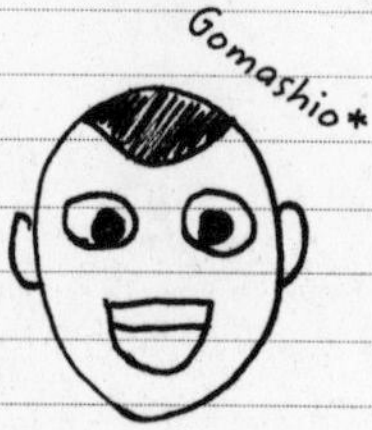
Gomashio*

Rokkaku Junior High School 7th Grade, Class A
Height: 165 cm. / Blood Type: O / Birthday: 12/20
Best move: Net-cord Ball
Favorite food: Korean barbecue
Hobby / Recent pastime: Hanging out at the beach

## Satoshi Shudo / Right-Handed

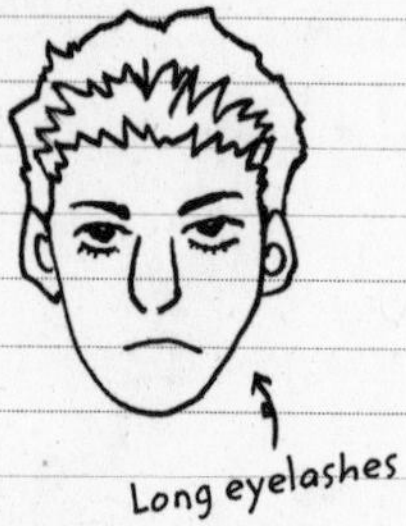
Long eyelashes

Rokkaku Junior High School 9th Grade, Class A
Height: 176 cm. / Blood Type: B / Birthday: 4/15
Best move: Short Cross
Favorite food: Mefun (salted fish innards)
Seaweed
Hobby / Recent pastime: Hanging out at the beach
Doing laundry

*Black-and-white sesame salt — Ed.

(Selected from Sadaharu Inui Secret Data Note No. 134)

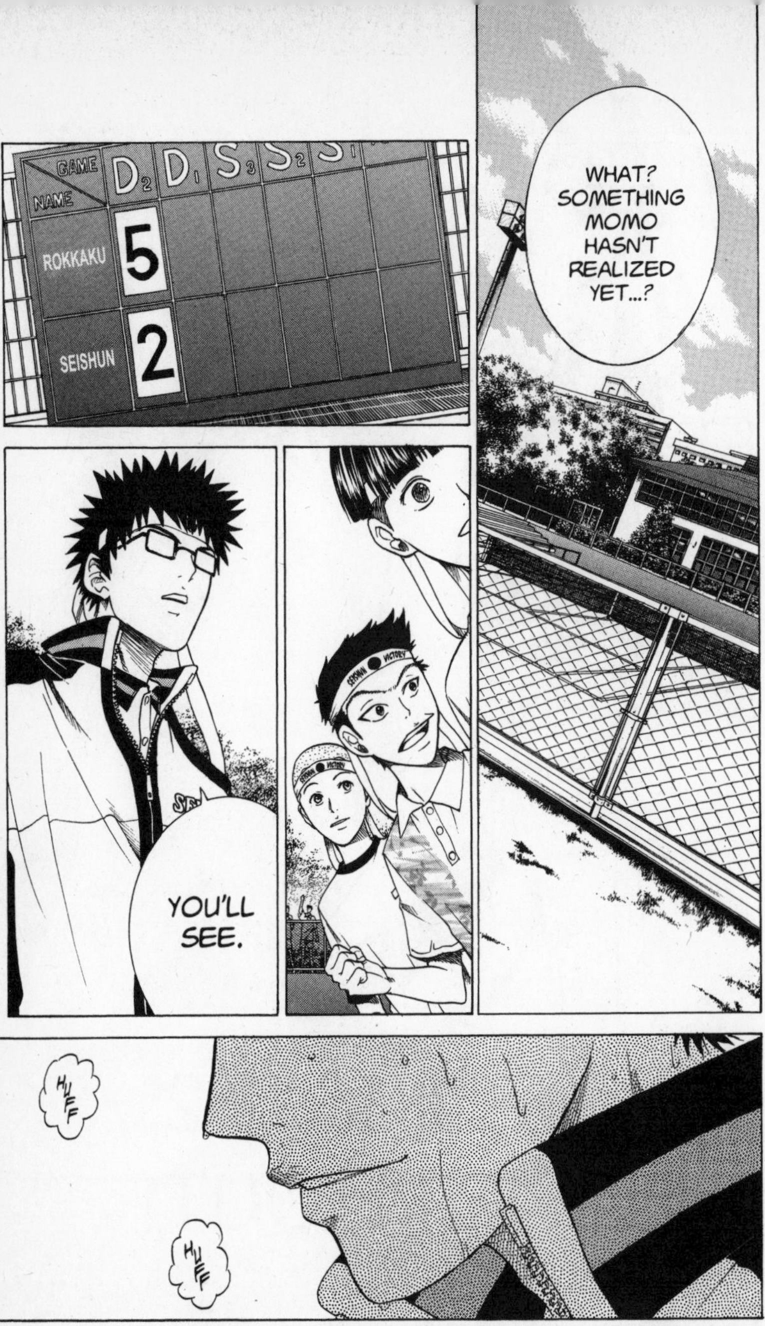
WHAT? SOMETHING MOMO HASN'T REALIZED YET...?
GAME
NAME
D2 D1 S3 S2 S1
ROKKAKU 5
SEISHUN 2
YOU'LL SEE.
HUFF
HUFF



# GENIUS 172: WATCH OUT!

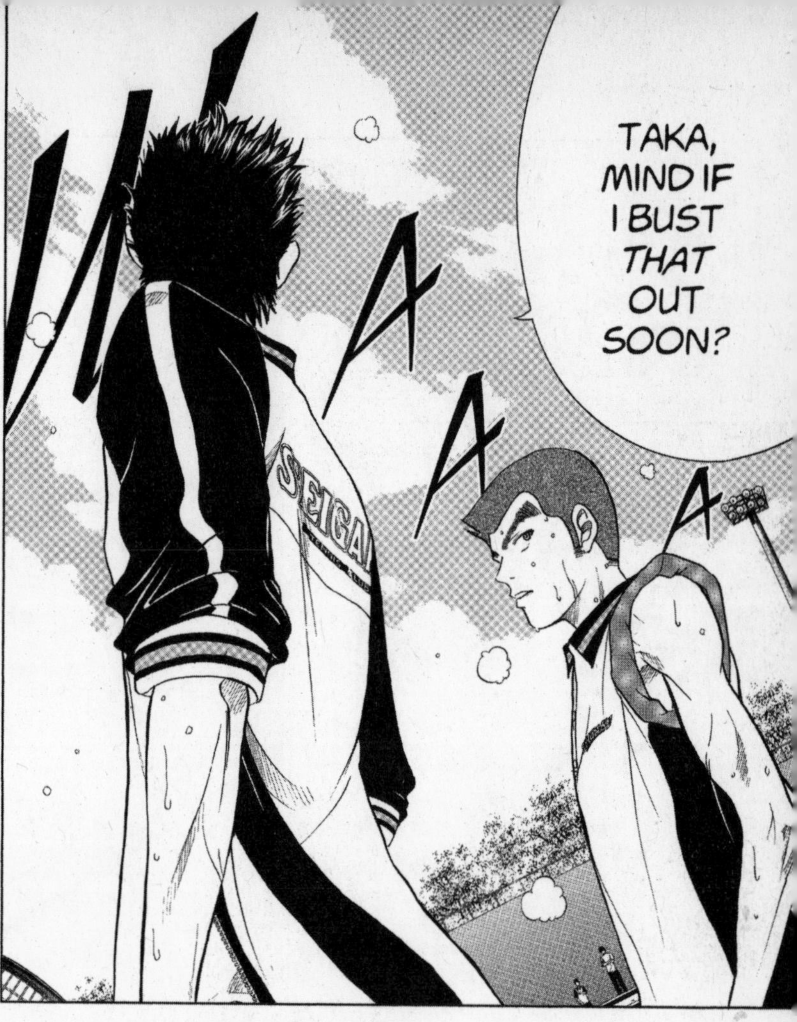
TAKA, MIND IF I BUST THAT OUT SOON?

# GENIUS 172: WATCH OUT!

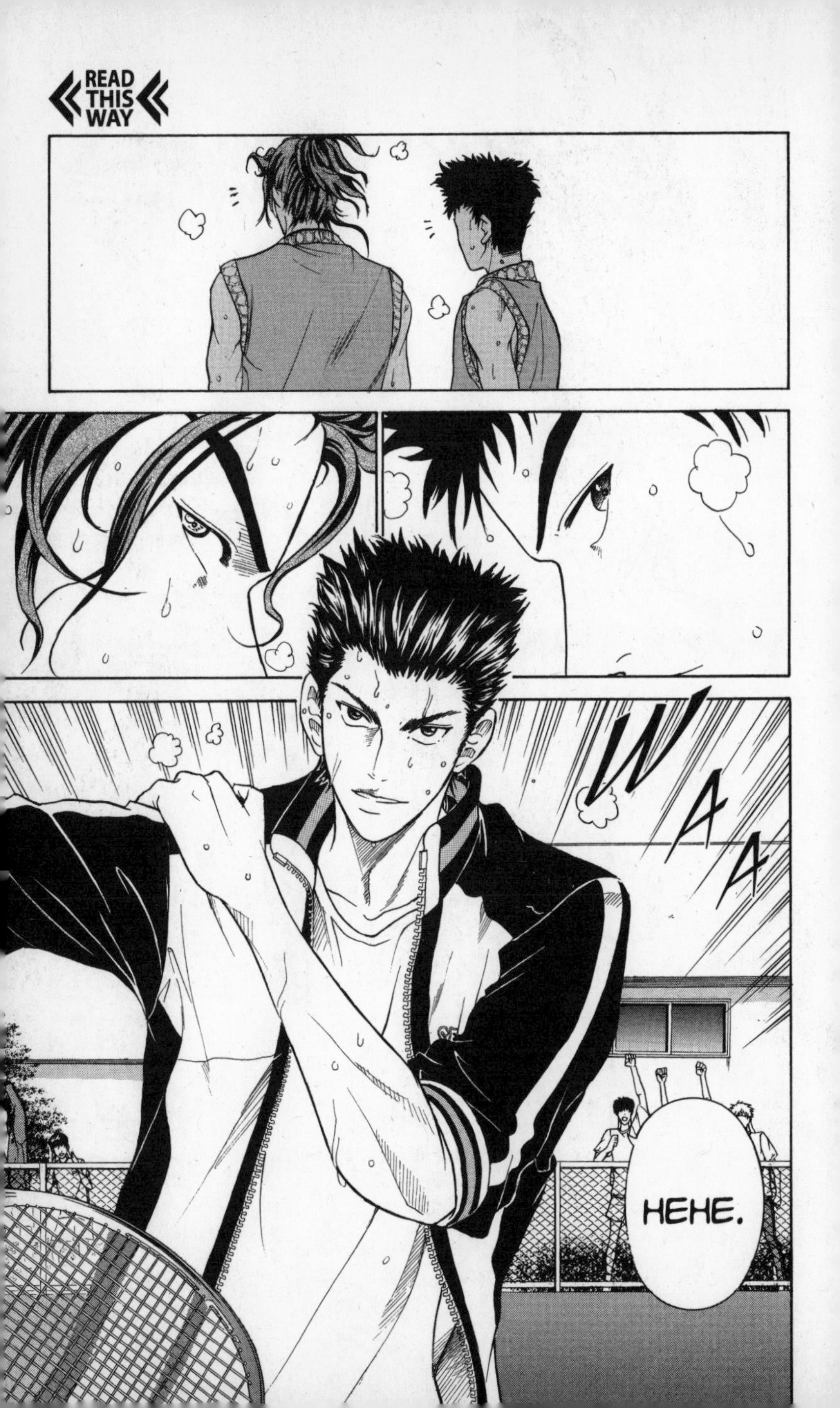
READ THIS WAY
WAA
HEHE.

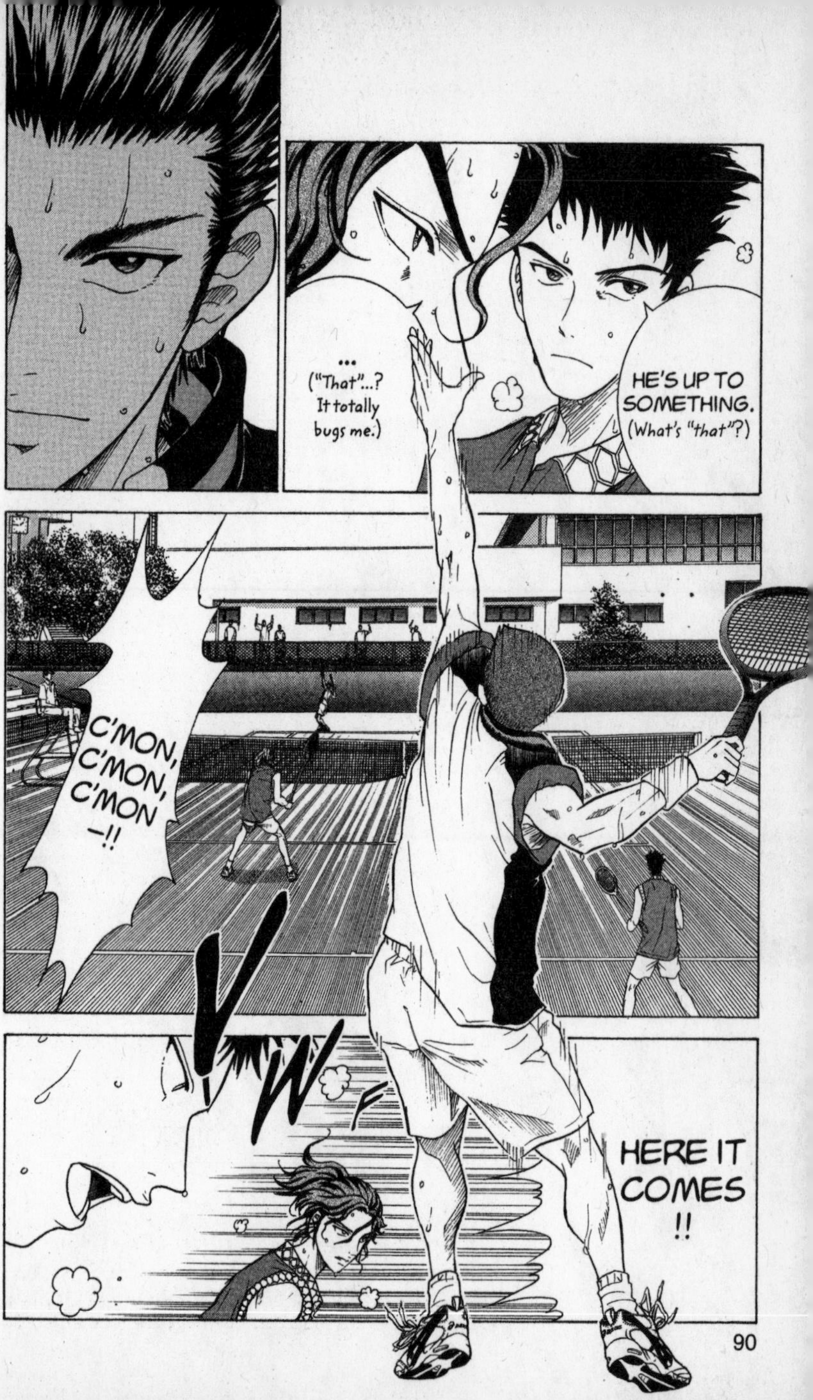
HE'S UP TO SOMETHING. (What's "that"?)
... ("That"...? It totally bugs me.)
C'MON, C'MON, C'MON—!!
VWF
HERE IT COMES!!

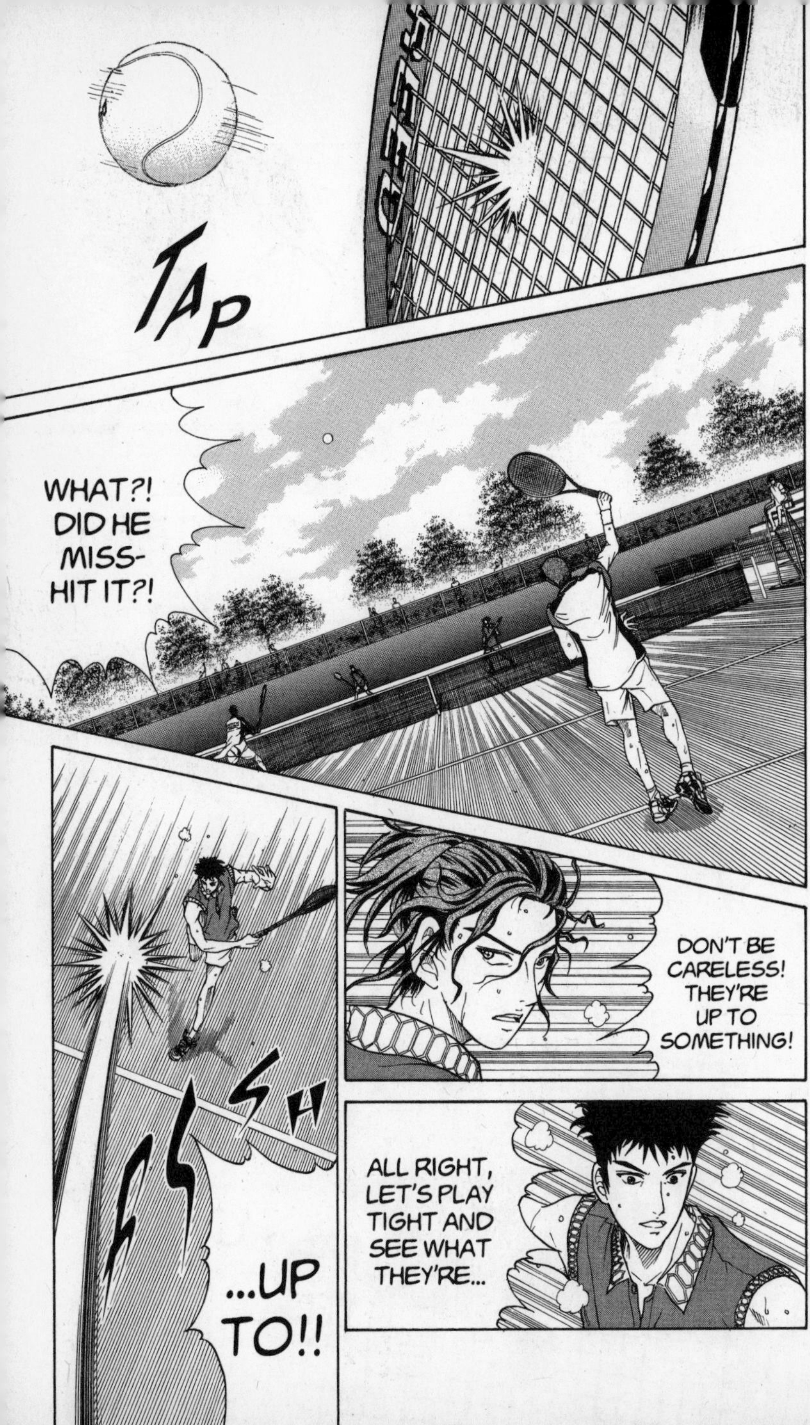
TAP
WHAT?! DID HE MISS-HIT IT?!
DON'T BE CARELESS! THEY'RE UP TO SOMETHING!
ALL RIGHT, LET'S PLAY TIGHT AND SEE WHAT THEY'RE...
FSSH
...UP TO!!

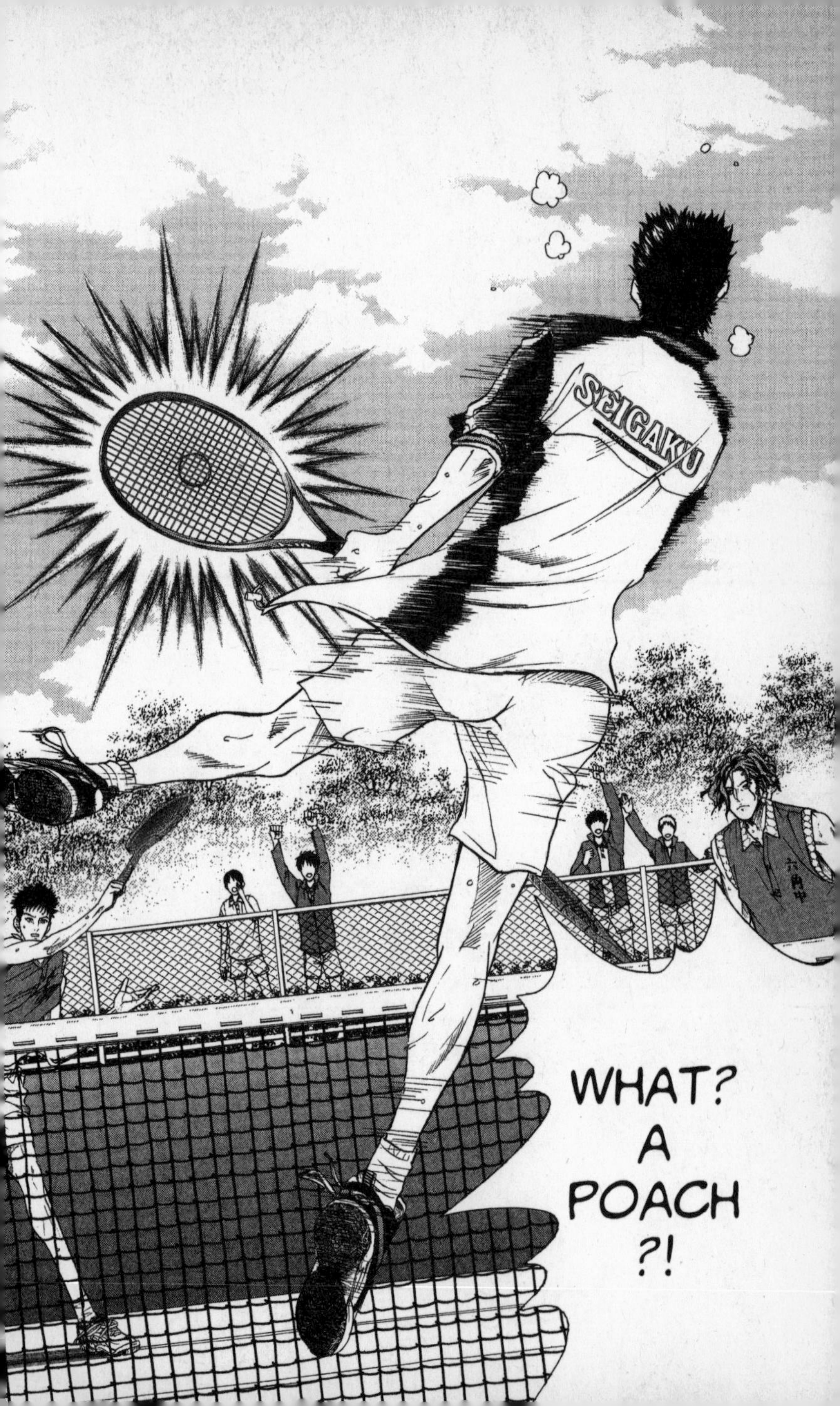
SEIGAKU
WHAT? A POACH ?!

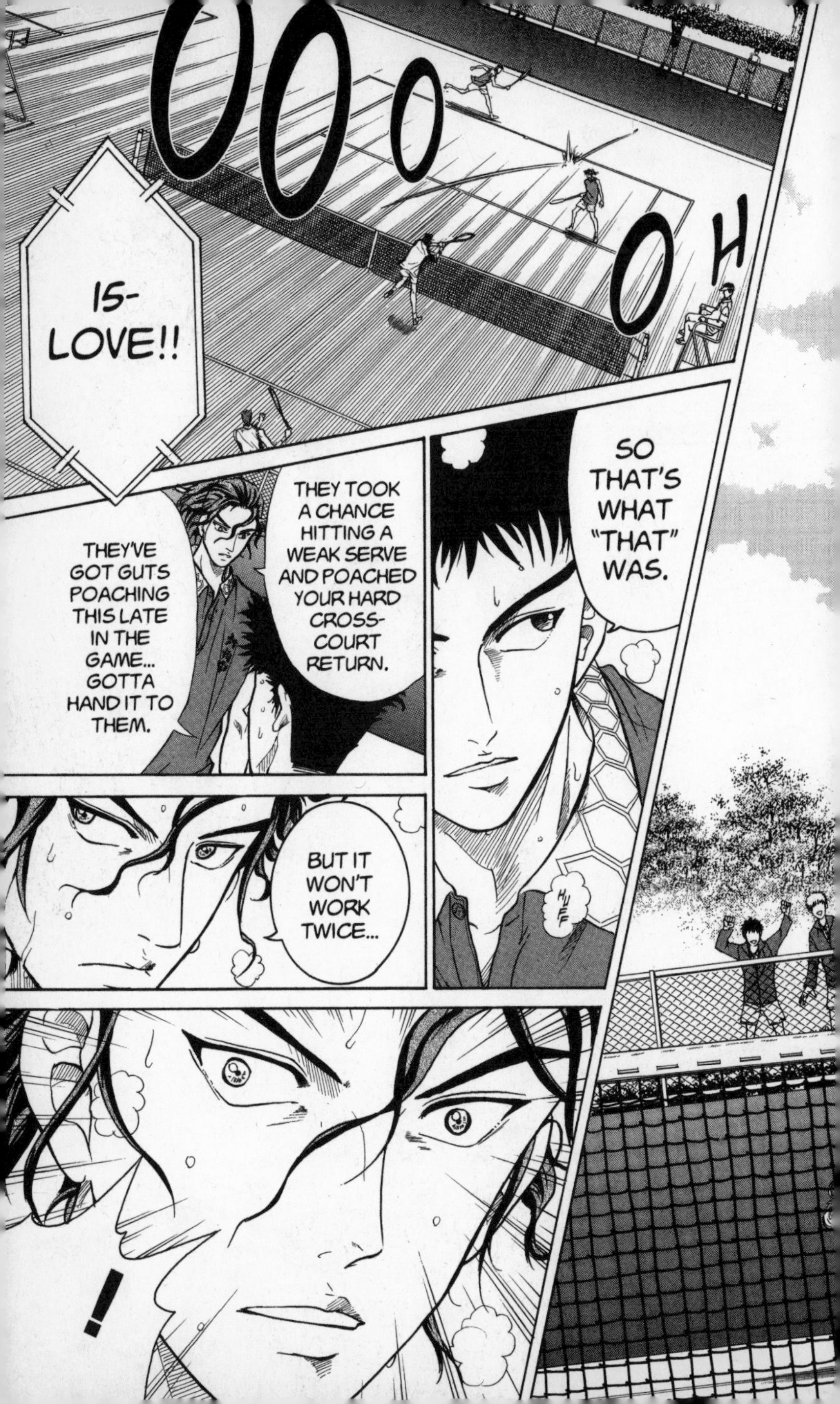
OOOOOOH
15-LOVE!!
SO THAT'S WHAT "THAT" WAS.
HUFF
THEY TOOK A CHANCE HITTING A WEAK SERVE AND POACHED YOUR HARD CROSS-COURT RETURN.
THEY'VE GOT GUTS POACHING THIS LATE IN THE GAME... GOTTA HAND IT TO THEM.
BUT IT WON'T WORK TWICE...
!

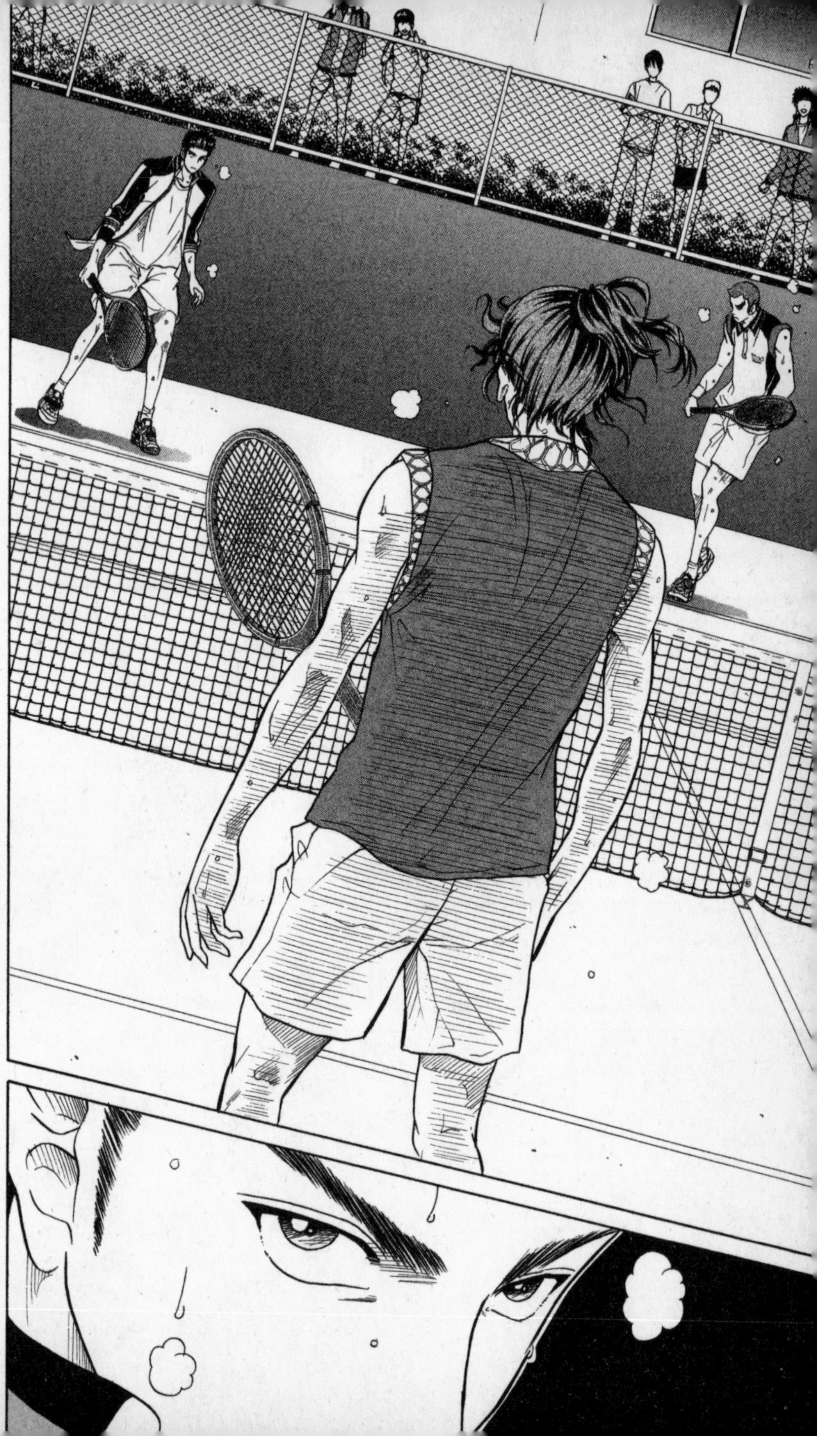

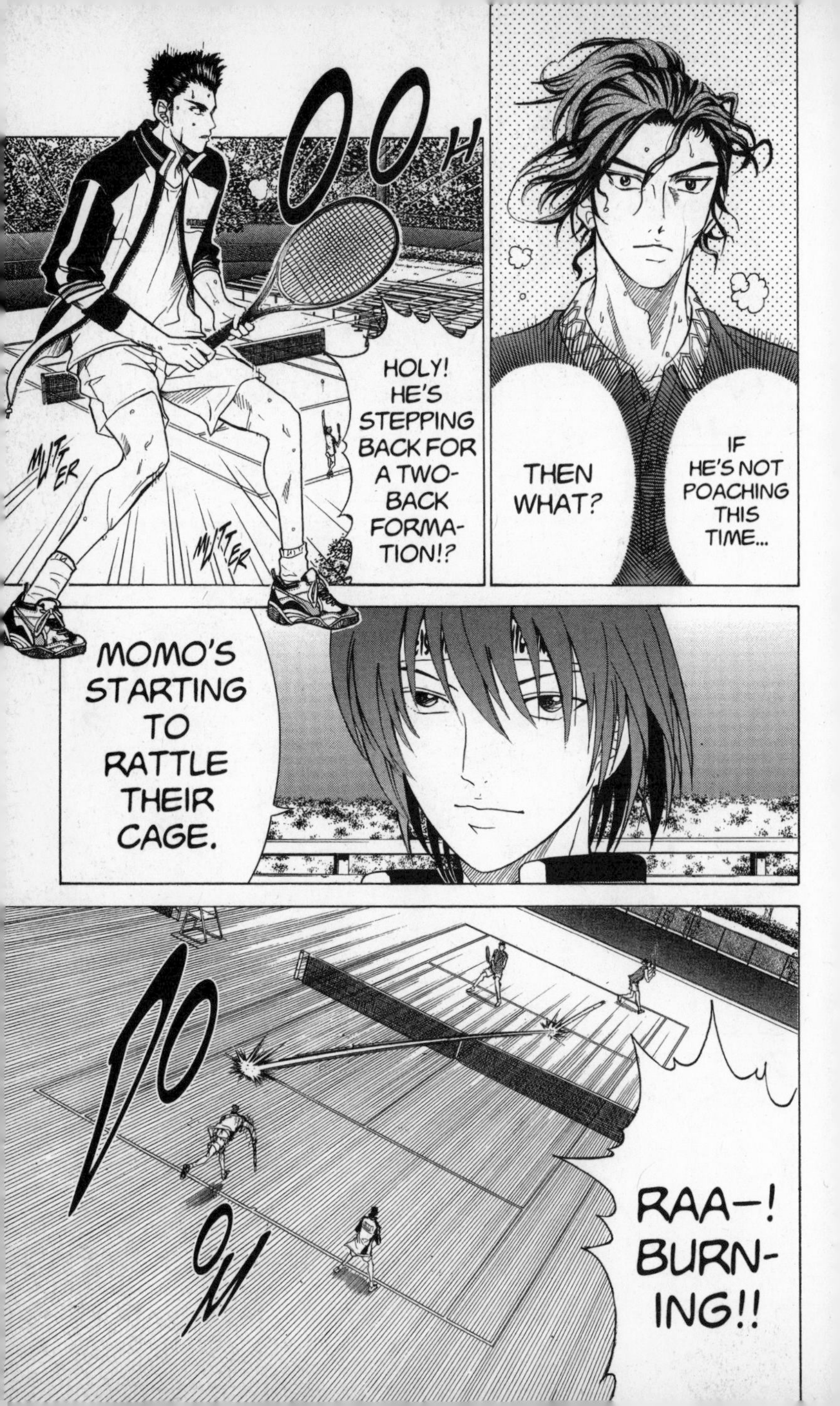
IF HE'S NOT POACHING THIS TIME...
THEN WHAT?
OOOH
HOLY! HE'S STEPPING BACK FOR A TWO-BACK FORMATION!?
MUTTER
MUTTER
MOMO'S STARTING TO RATTLE THEIR CAGE.
RAA—! BURNING!!

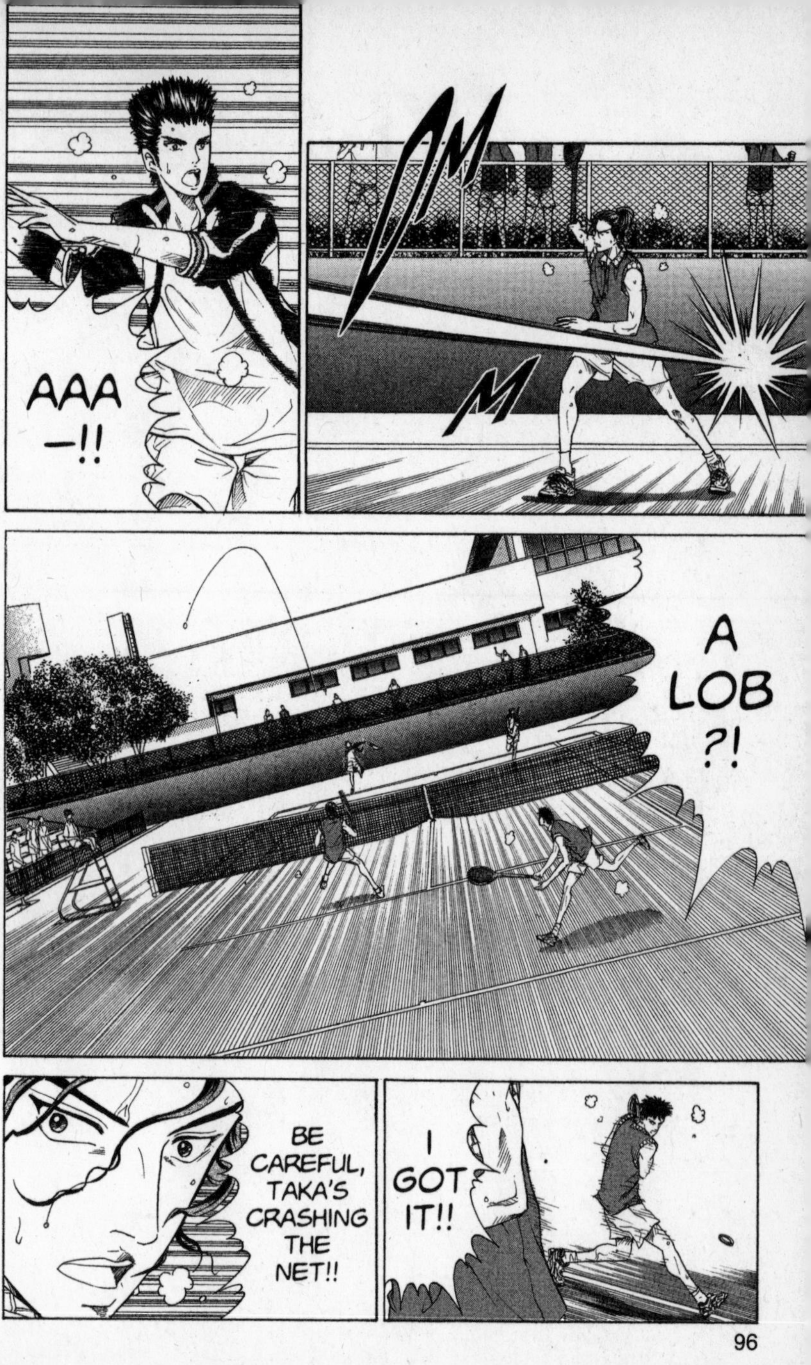

AAA —!!
A LOB ?!
I GOT IT!!
BE CAREFUL, TAKA'S CRASHING THE NET!!

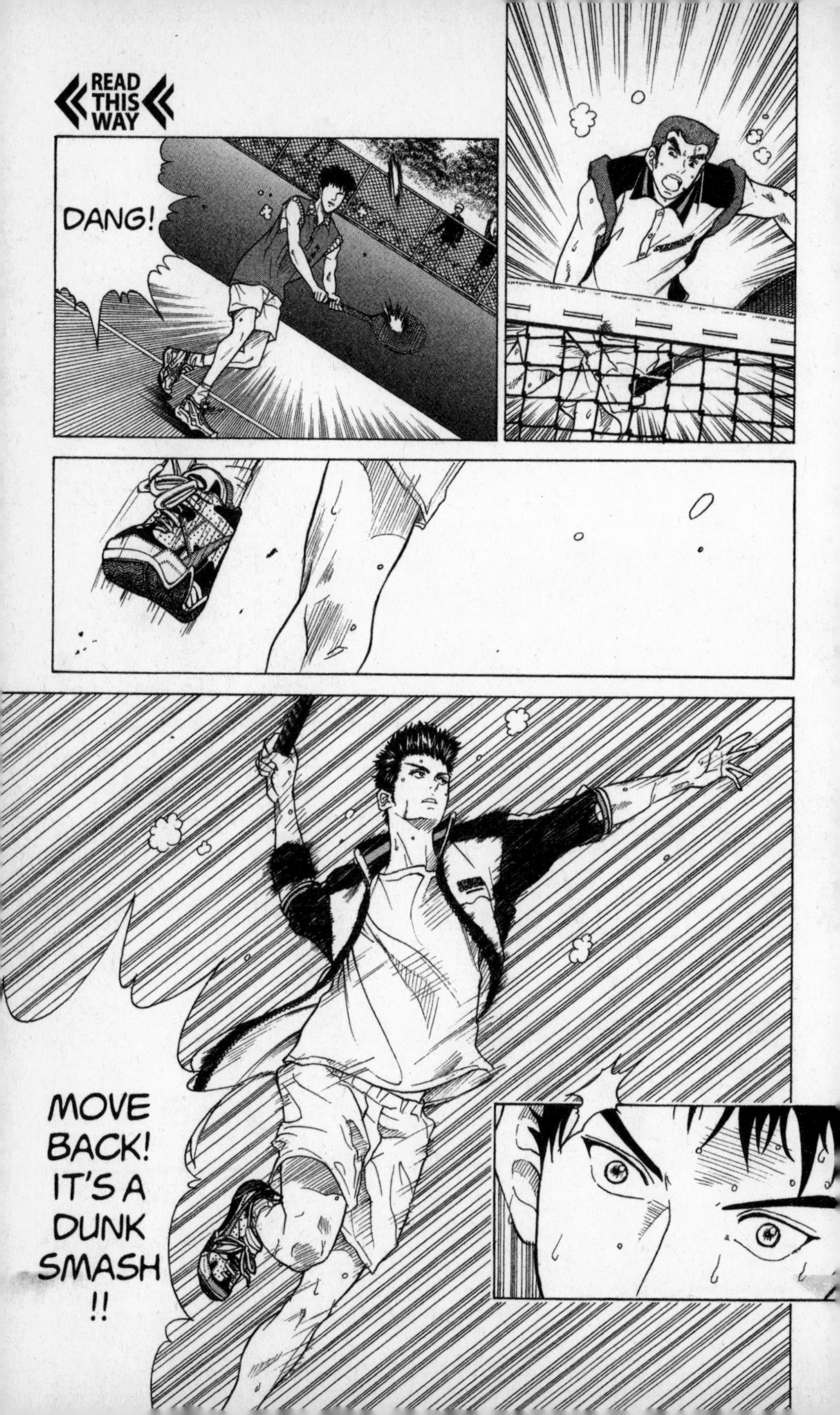
READ THIS WAY
DANG!
MOVE BACK! IT'S A DUNK SMASH!!

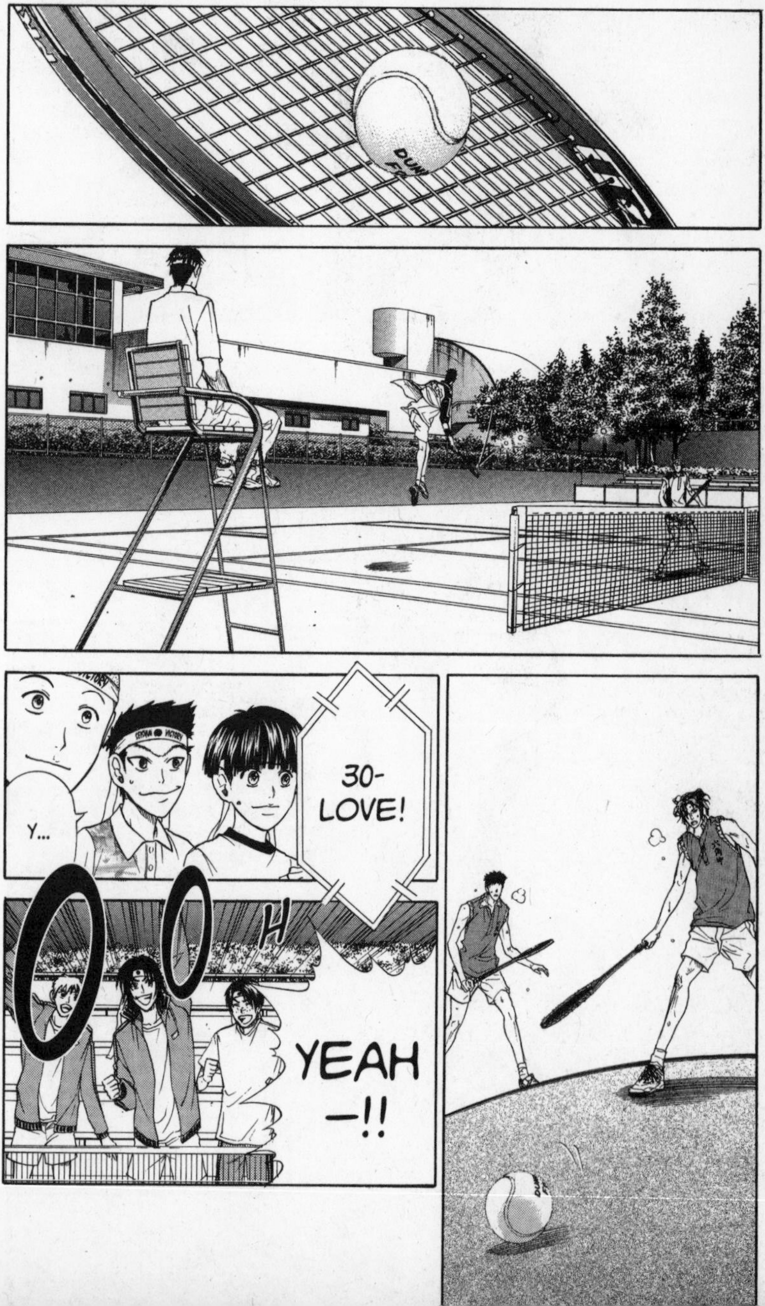
30-
LOVE!
Y...
OOH
YEAH
—!!

READ THIS WAY

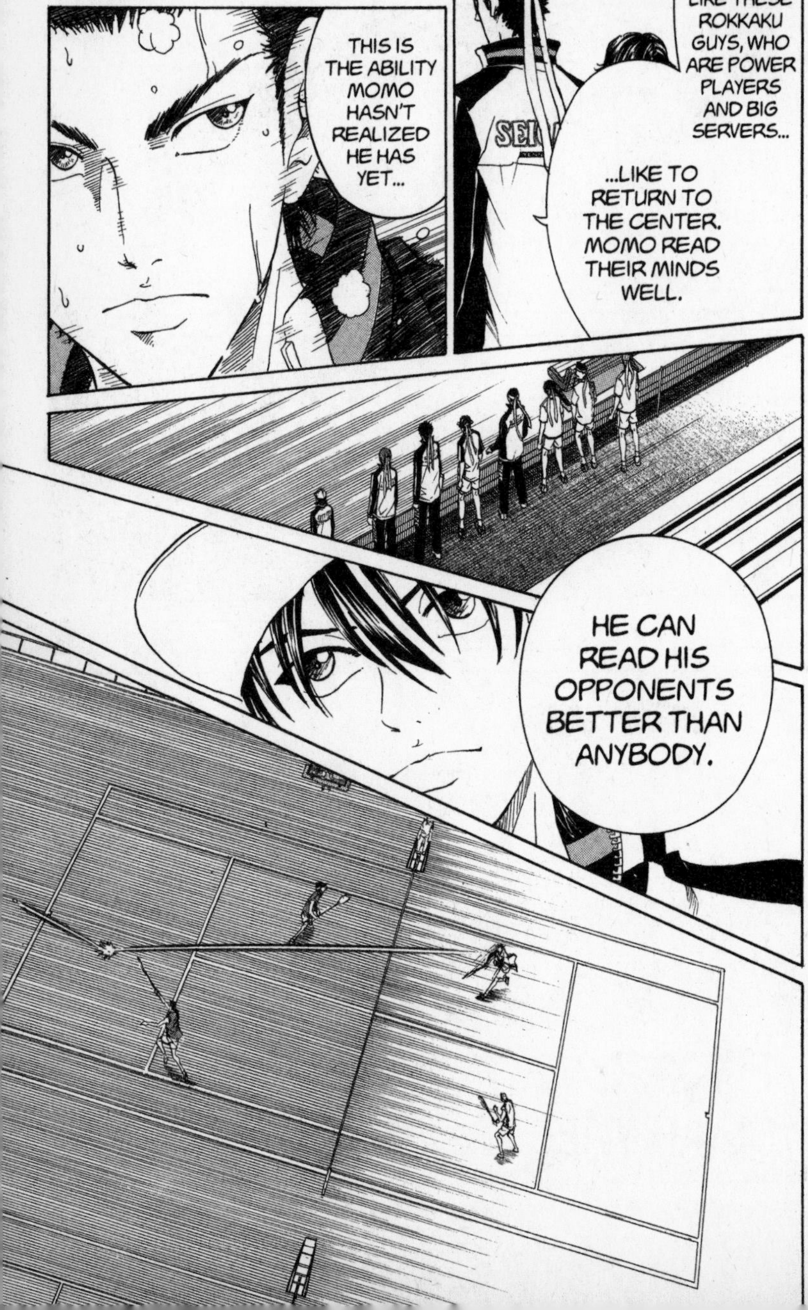
DOUBLES PARTNERS LIKE THESE ROKKAKU GUYS, WHO ARE POWER PLAYERS AND BIG SERVERS...
...LIKE TO RETURN TO THE CENTER. MOMO READ THEIR MINDS WELL.
THIS IS THE ABILITY MOMO HASN'T REALIZED HE HAS YET...
HE CAN READ HIS OPPONENTS BETTER THAN ANYBODY.

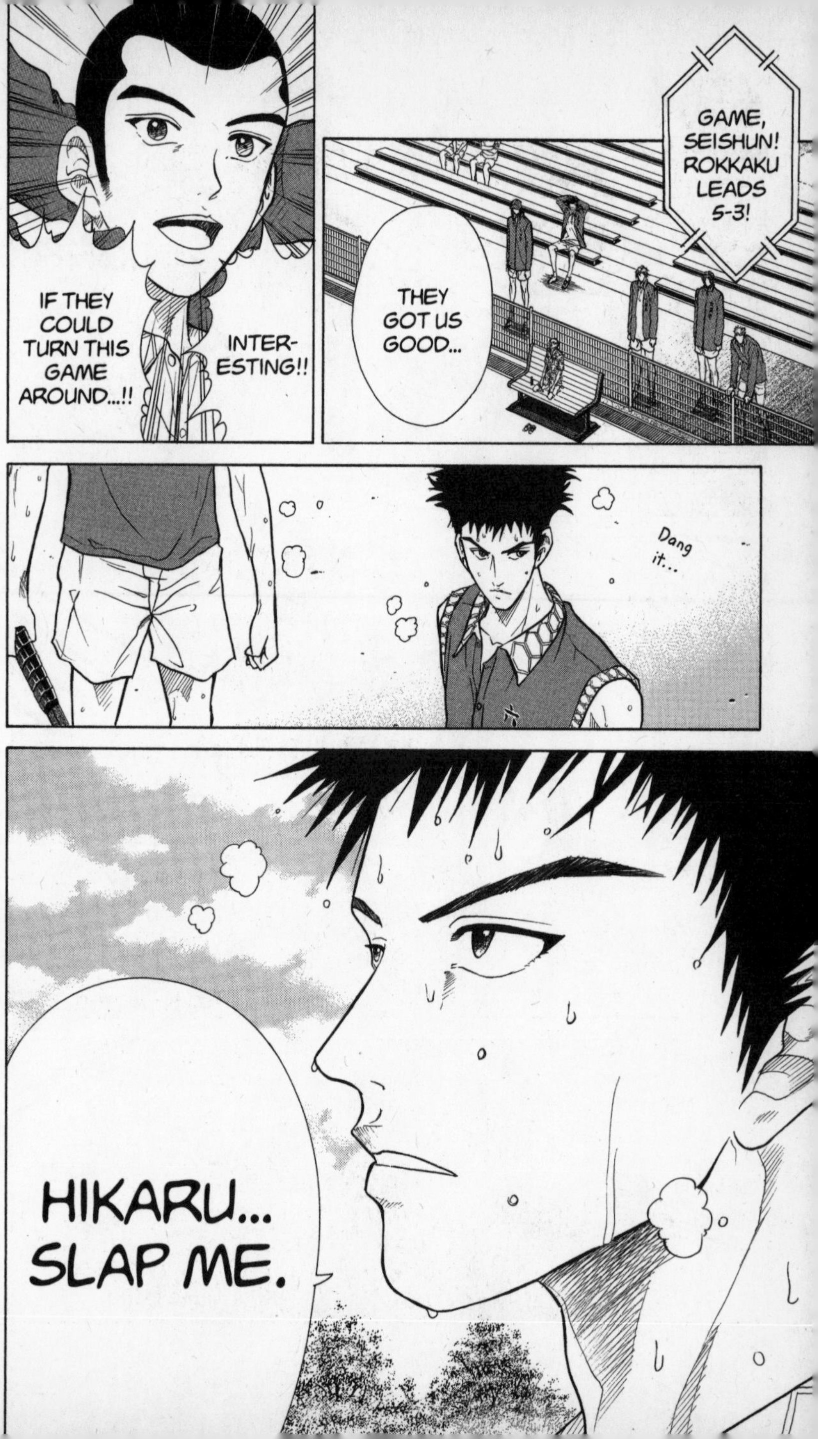
GAME, SEISHUN! ROKKAKU LEADS 5-3!
THEY GOT US GOOD...
INTER-ESTING!!
IF THEY COULD TURN THIS GAME AROUND...!!
Dang it...
HIKARU... SLAP ME.

READ THIS WAY

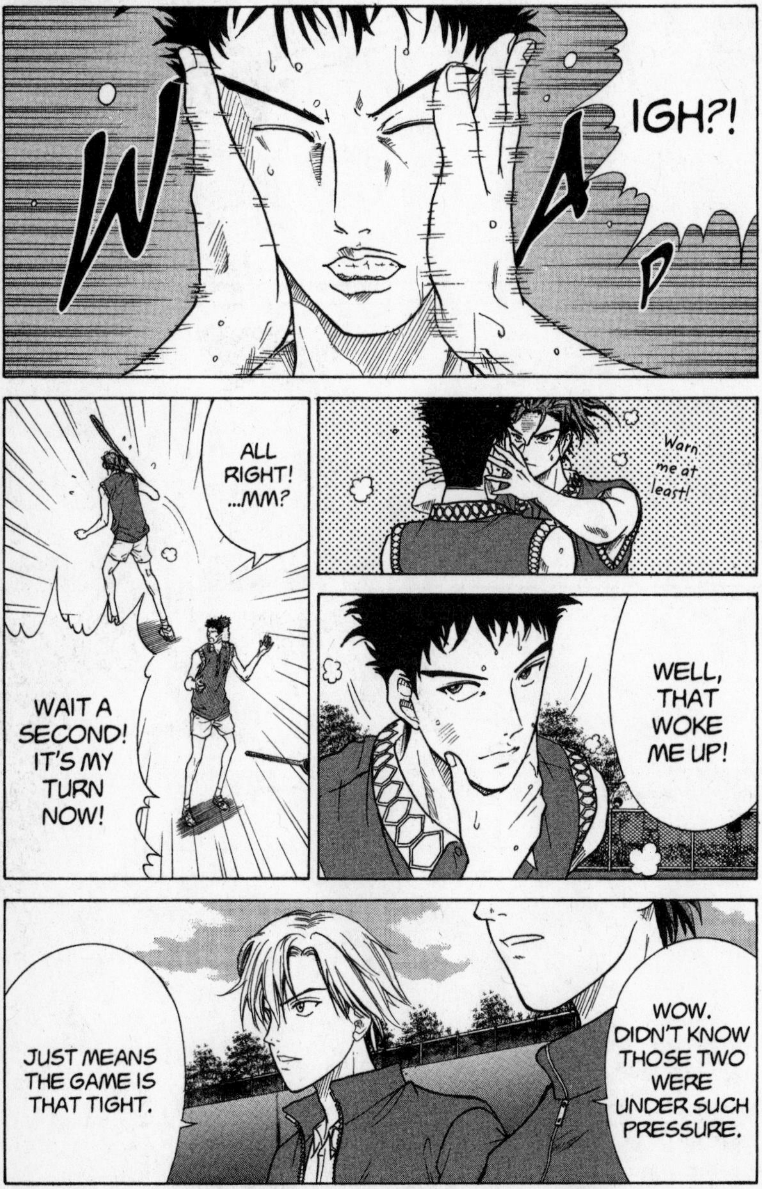
W
A
D
IGH?!
Warn me at least!
WELL, THAT WOKE ME UP!
ALL RIGHT! ...MM?
WAIT A SECOND! IT'S MY TURN NOW!
WOW. DIDN'T KNOW THOSE TWO WERE UNDER SUCH PRESSURE.
JUST MEANS THE GAME IS THAT TIGHT.

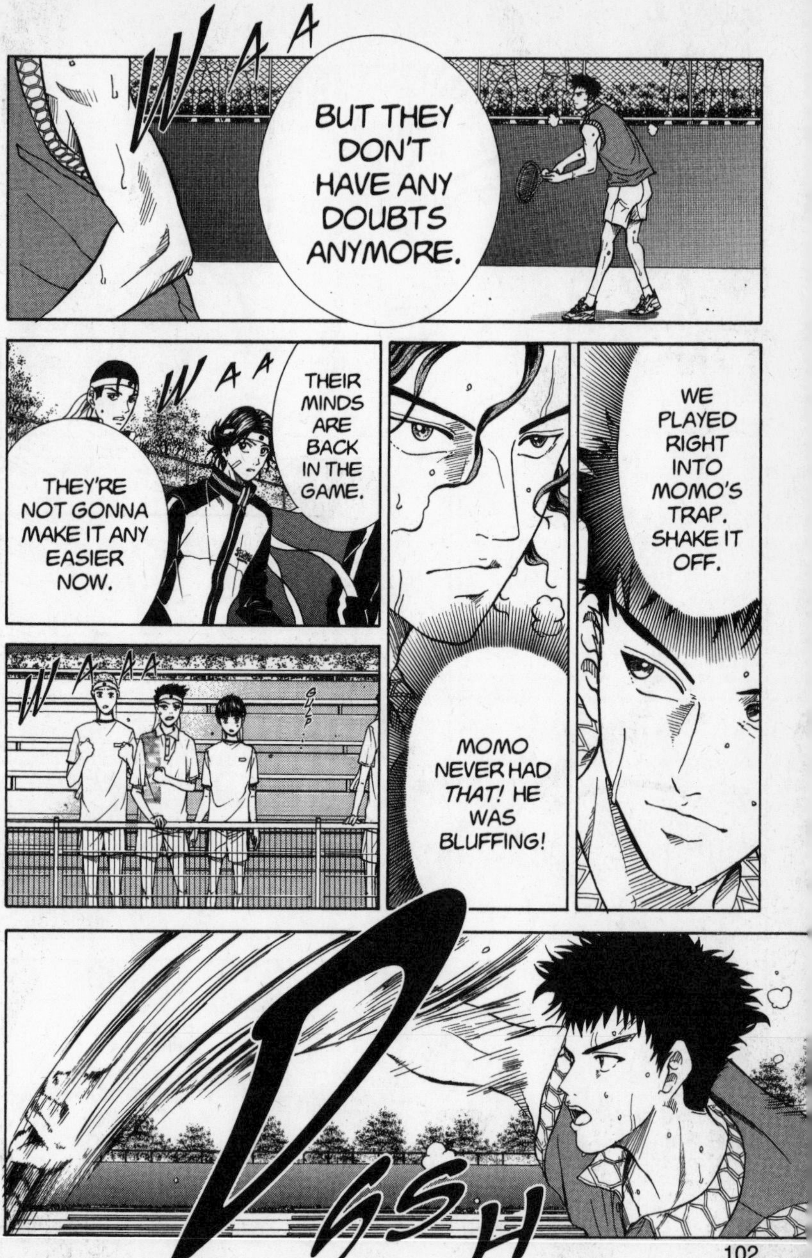
WAAA
BUT THEY DON'T HAVE ANY DOUBTS ANYMORE.
WE PLAYED RIGHT INTO MOMO'S TRAP. SHAKE IT OFF.
MOMO NEVER HAD THAT! HE WAS BLUFFING!
WAA
THEIR MINDS ARE BACK IN THE GAME.
THEY'RE NOT GONNA MAKE IT ANY EASIER NOW.
WAAA
GULP
DSSH

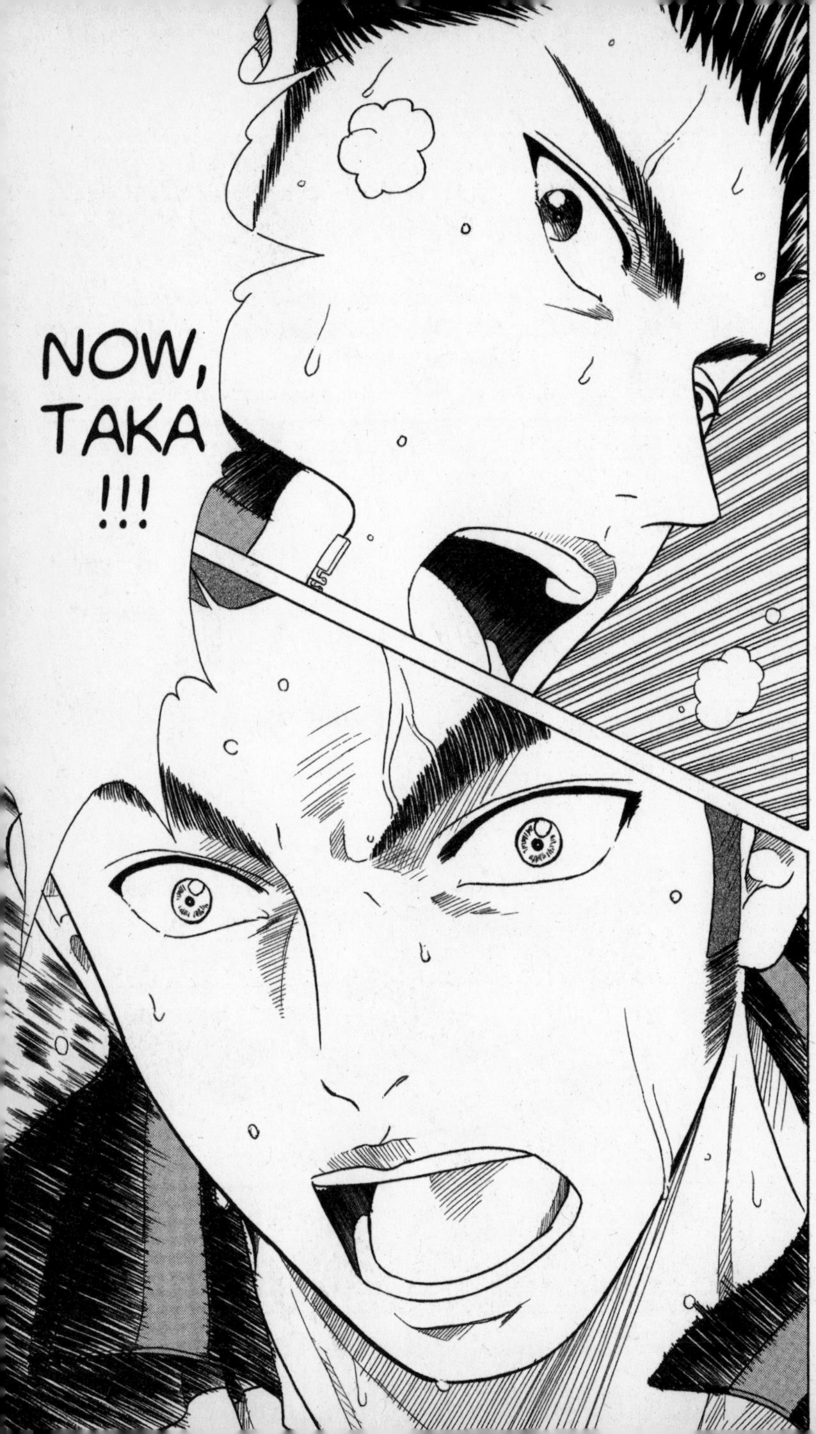
NOW, TAKA !!!

8。

...。

。？ No. 135

## Ryo Kisarazu / Right-Handed

The twin brother of St. Rudolph's Kisarazu

Rokkaku Junior High School 9th Grade, Class B
Height: 163 cm. / Blood Type: O / Birthday: 11/20
Best move: Sky-High Volley
Favorite food: Chicken nuggets
Hobby / Recent pastime: Hanging out at the beach
Movies

## Oji / ??

Oji...

Rokkaku Junior High School Tennis Team Coach
Height: 150 cm. / Blood Type: ? / Born: ?/?
Best move: ?
Favorite food: Asari clams boiled in soy sauce
Aritamin A
Hobby / Recent pastime: Making rackets
Hula Dancing

(Selected from Sadaharu Inui Secret Data Note No. 135)

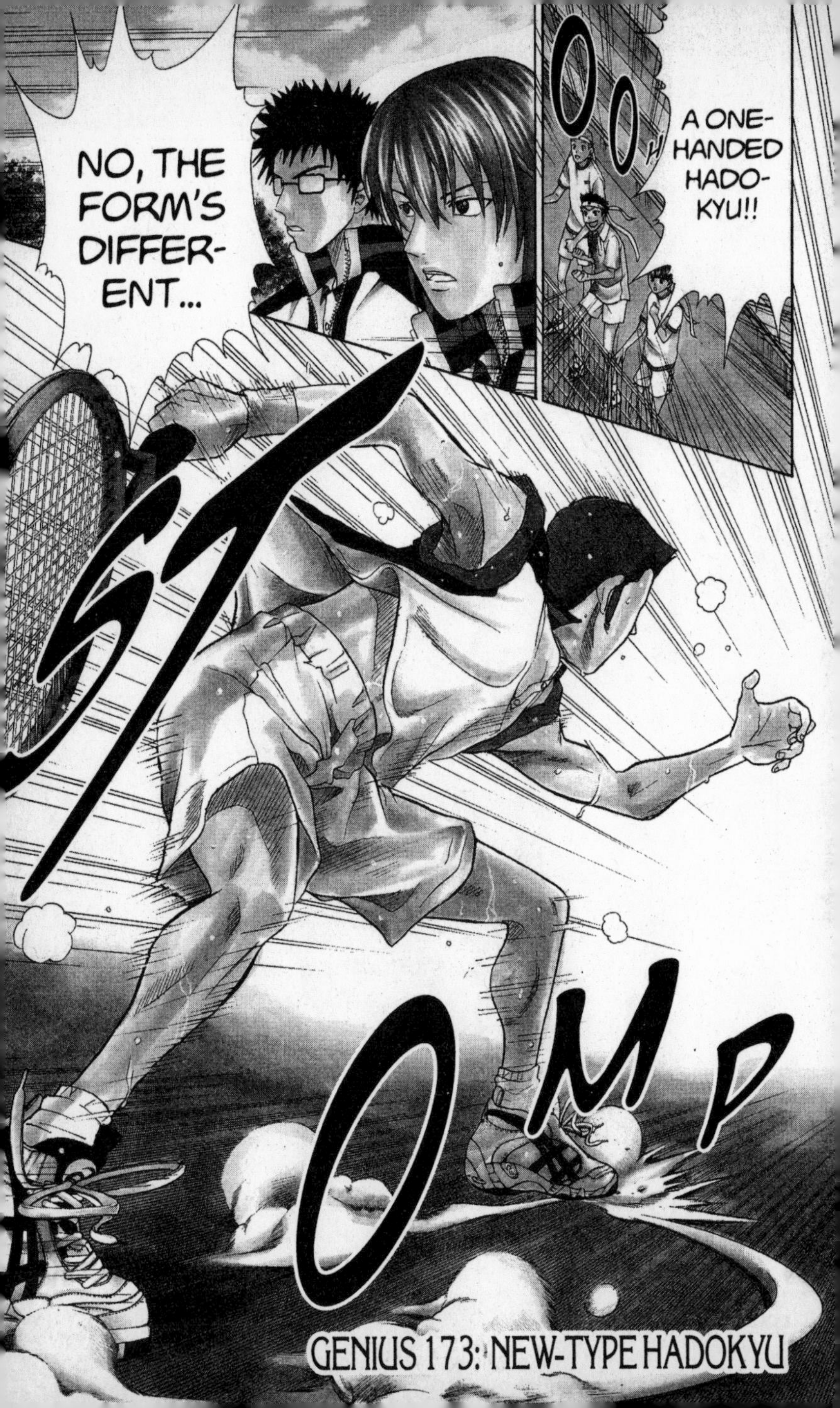
OOH
A ONE-HANDED HADO-KYU!!
NO, THE FORM'S DIFFERENT...
STOMP
GENIUS 173: NEW-TYPE HADOKYU

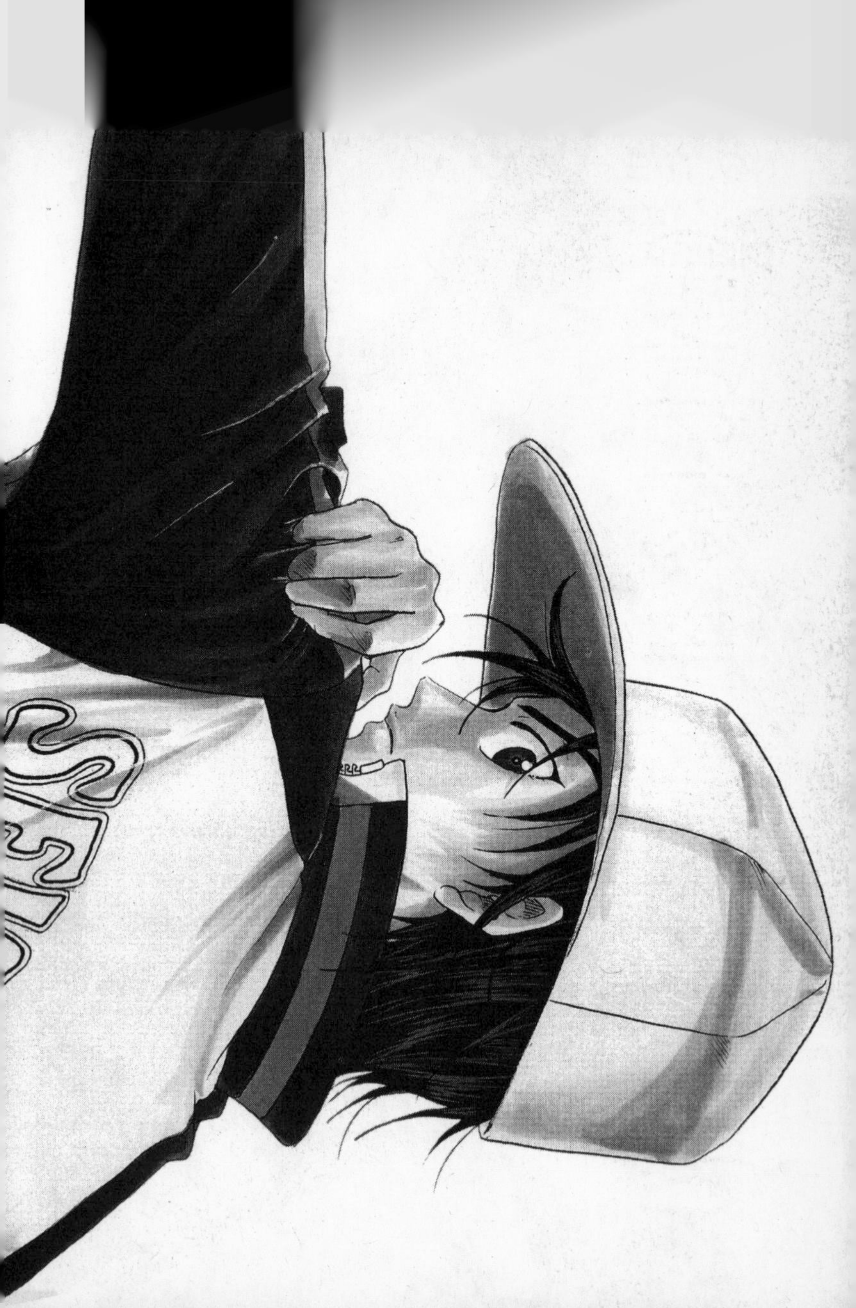

# GENIUS 173: NEW-TYPE HADOKYU

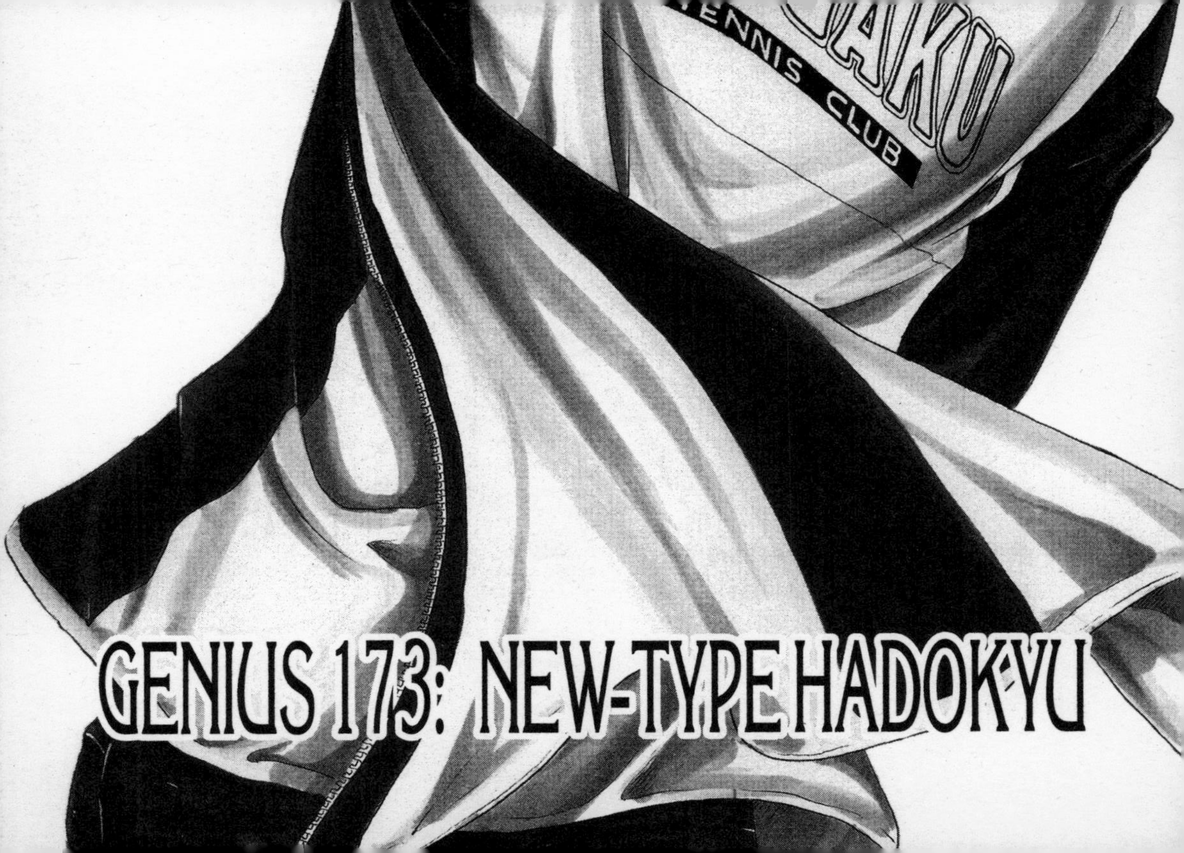

テニスの王子様

THE PRINCE OF TENNIS™

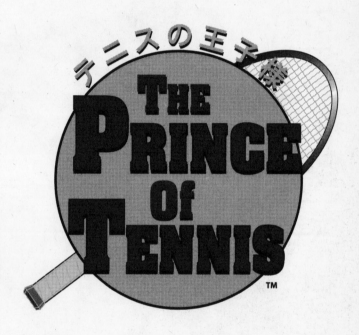

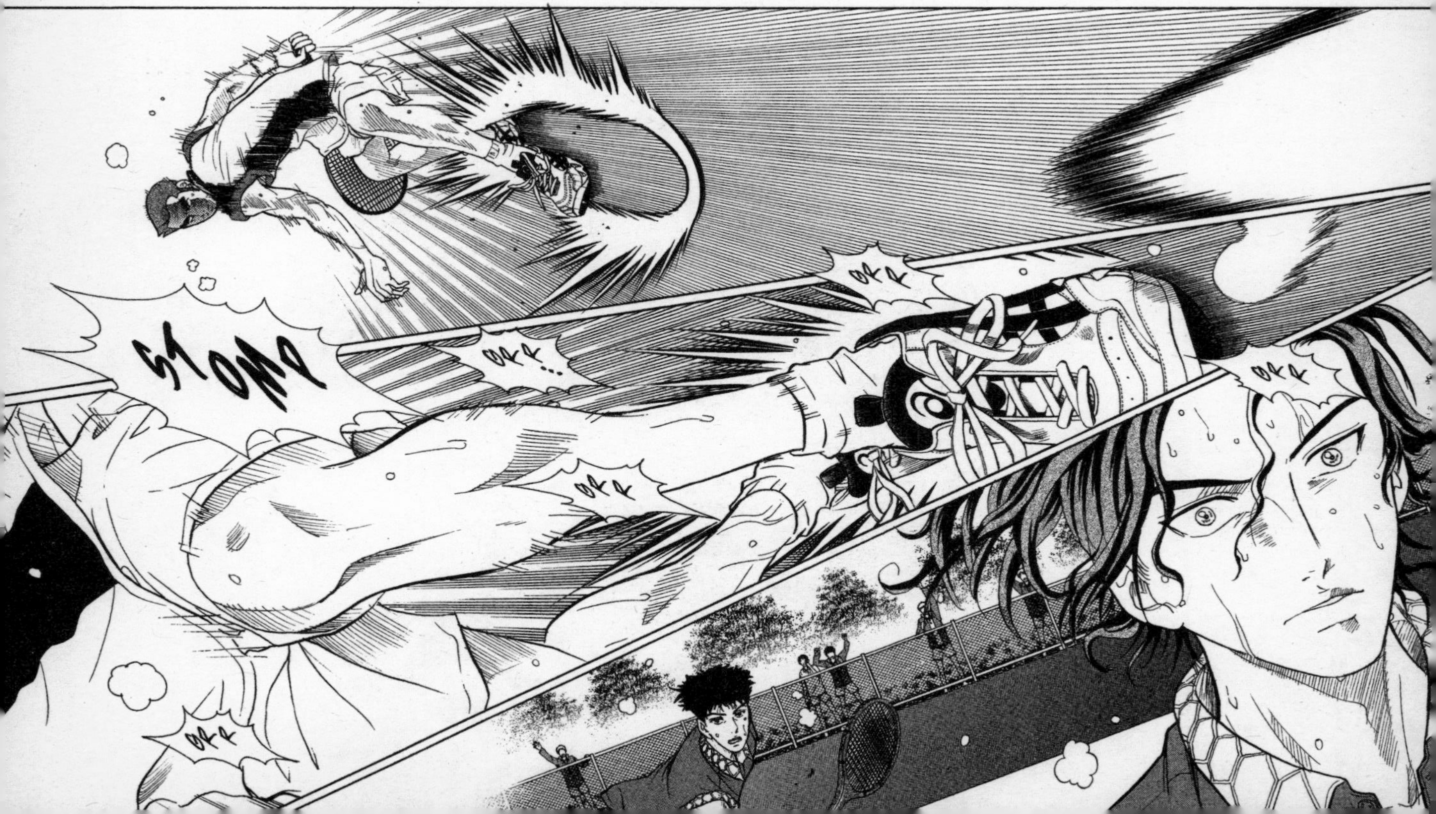
STOMP
GRR
GRR...
GRR
GRR
GRR
GRR

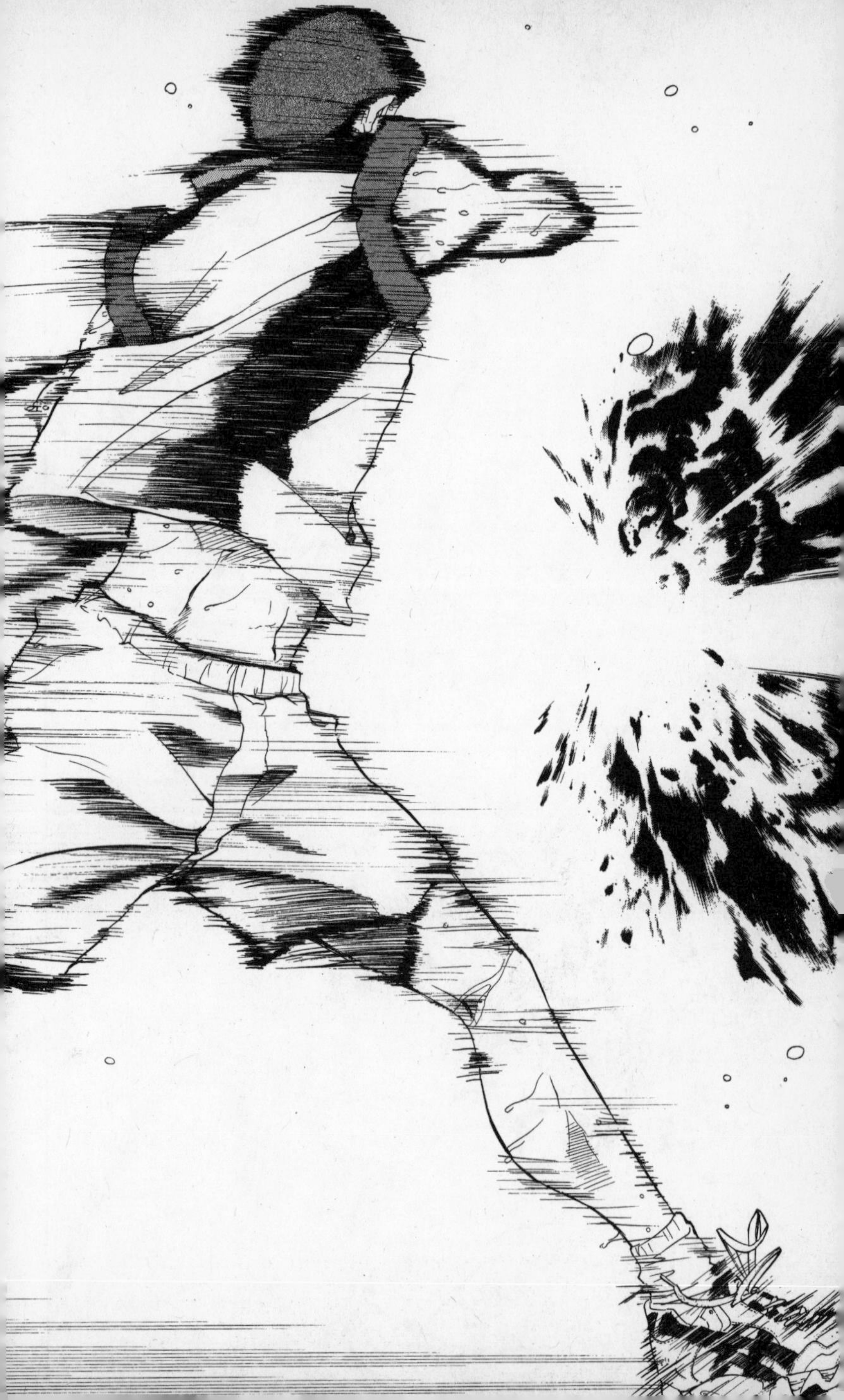

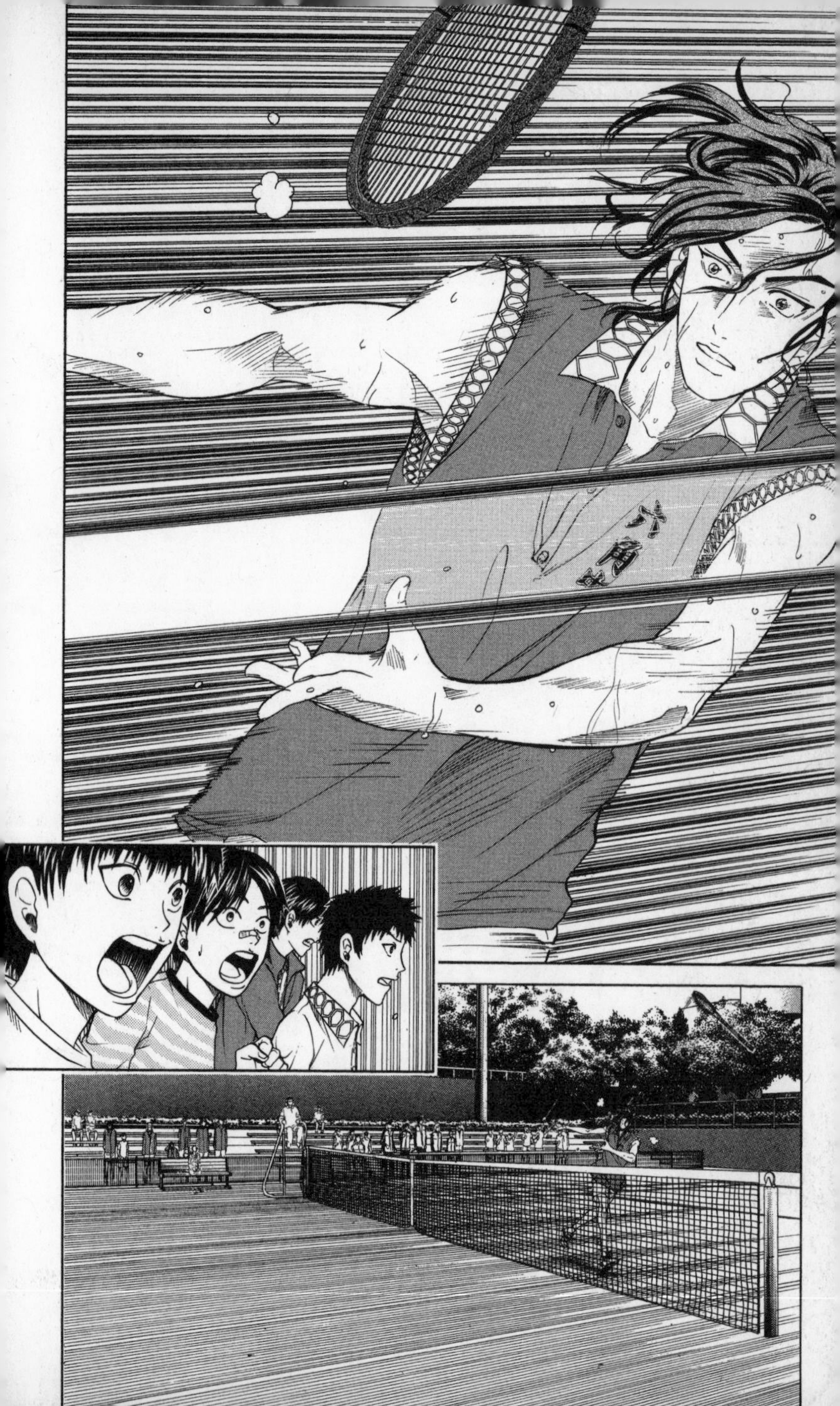
六角中

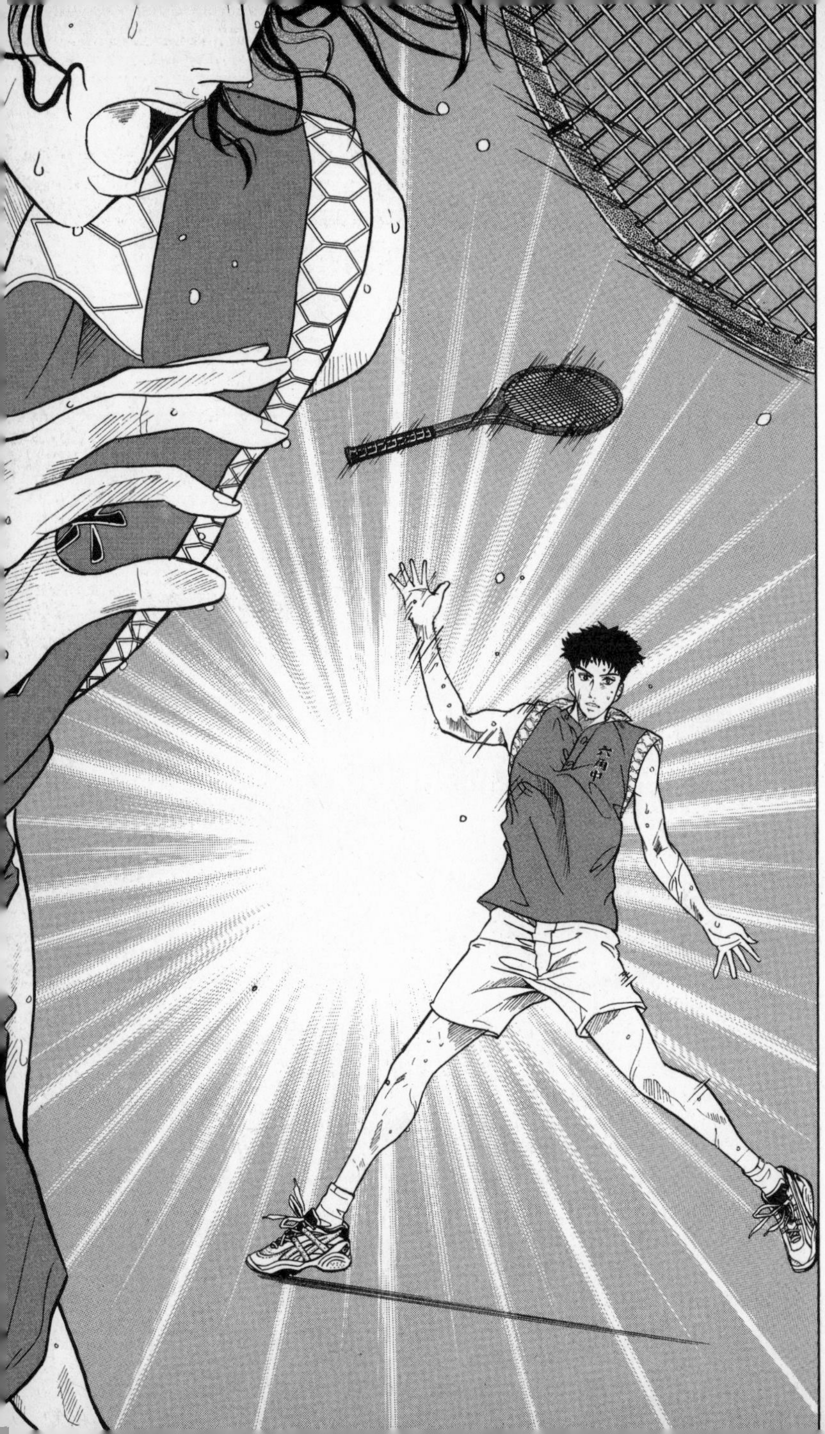
六角中

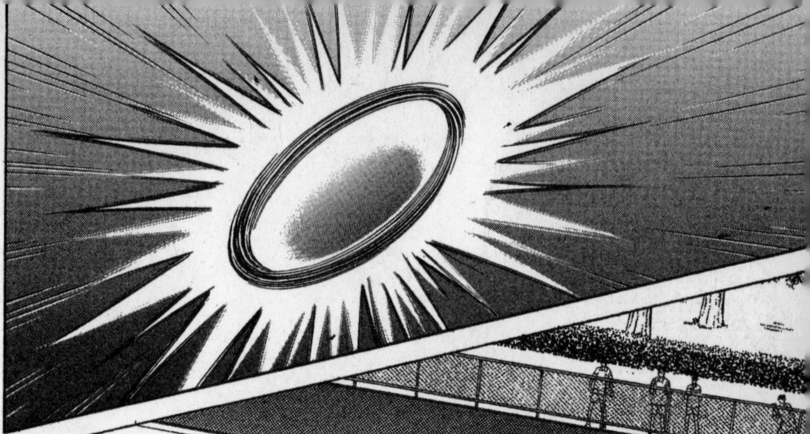
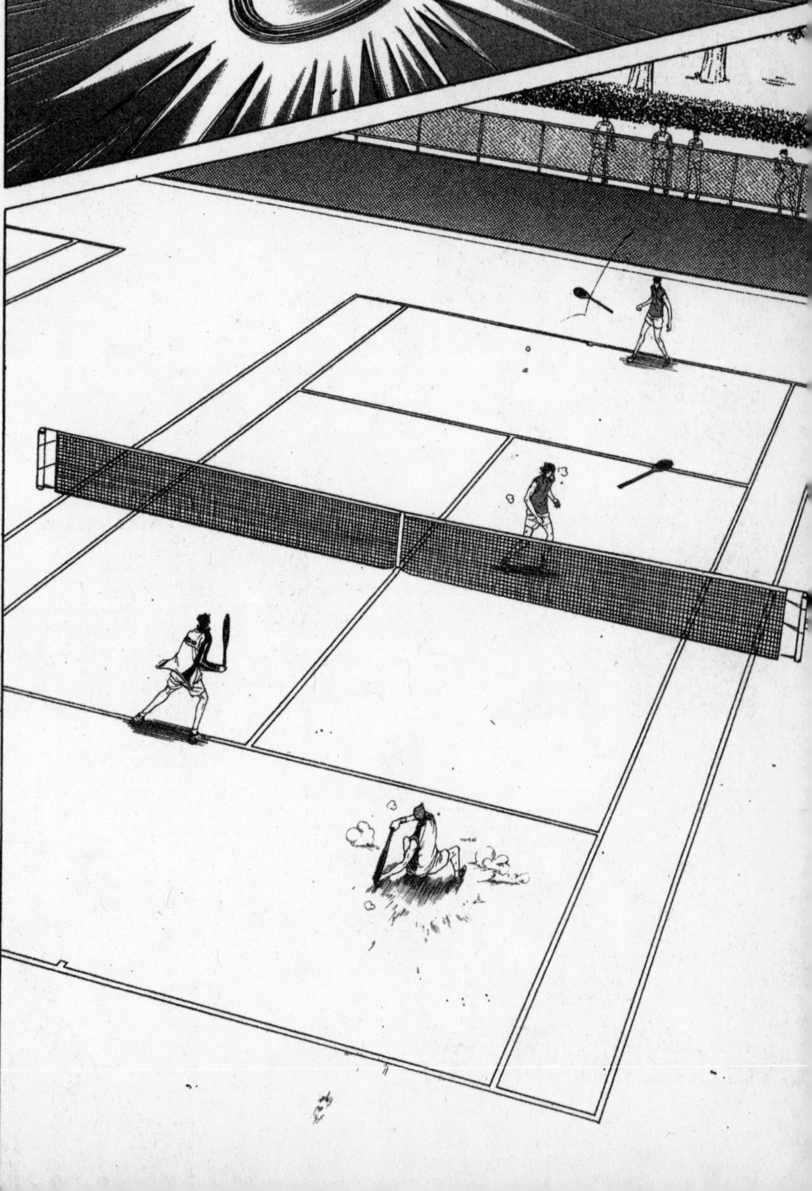

READ THIS WAY

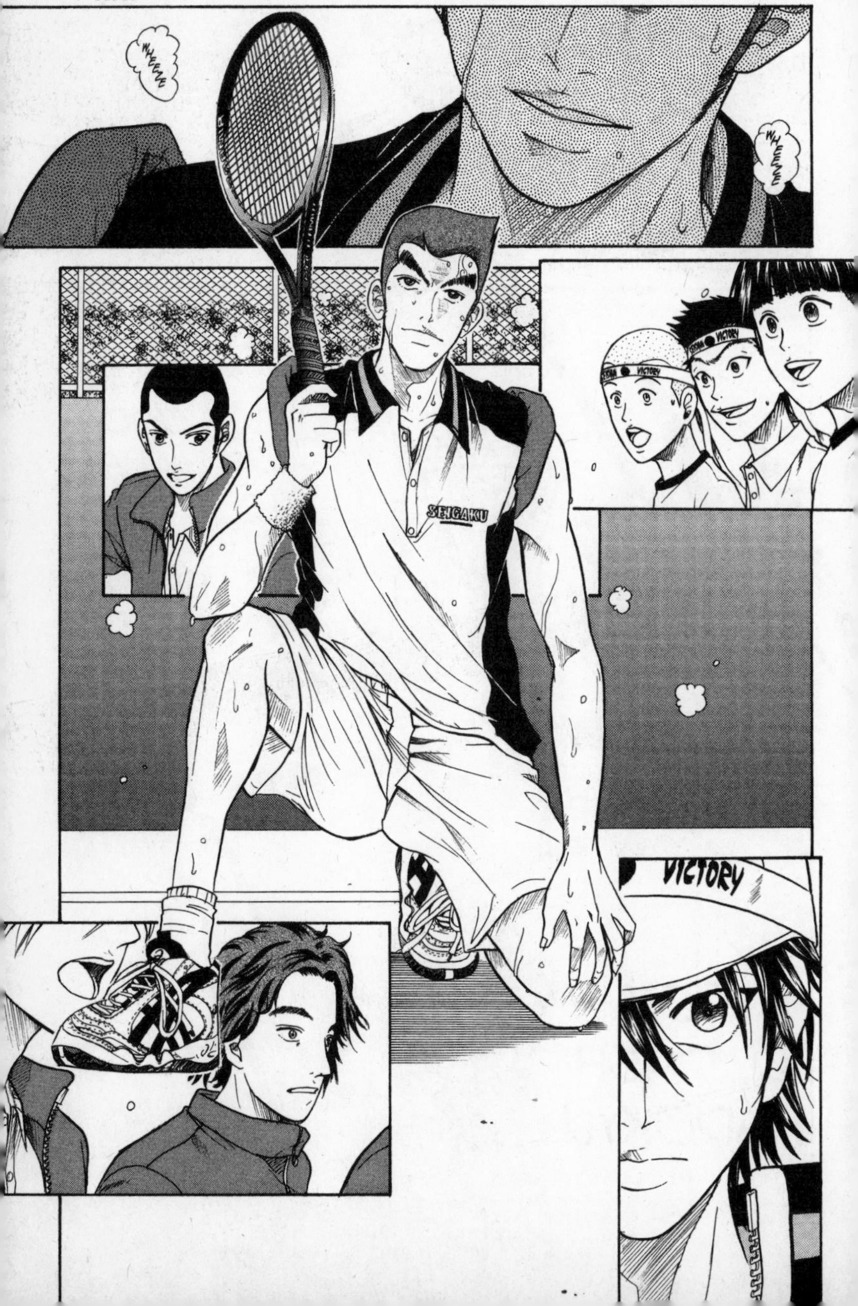
WHEEZE
WHEEZE
SEIGAKU
VICTORY

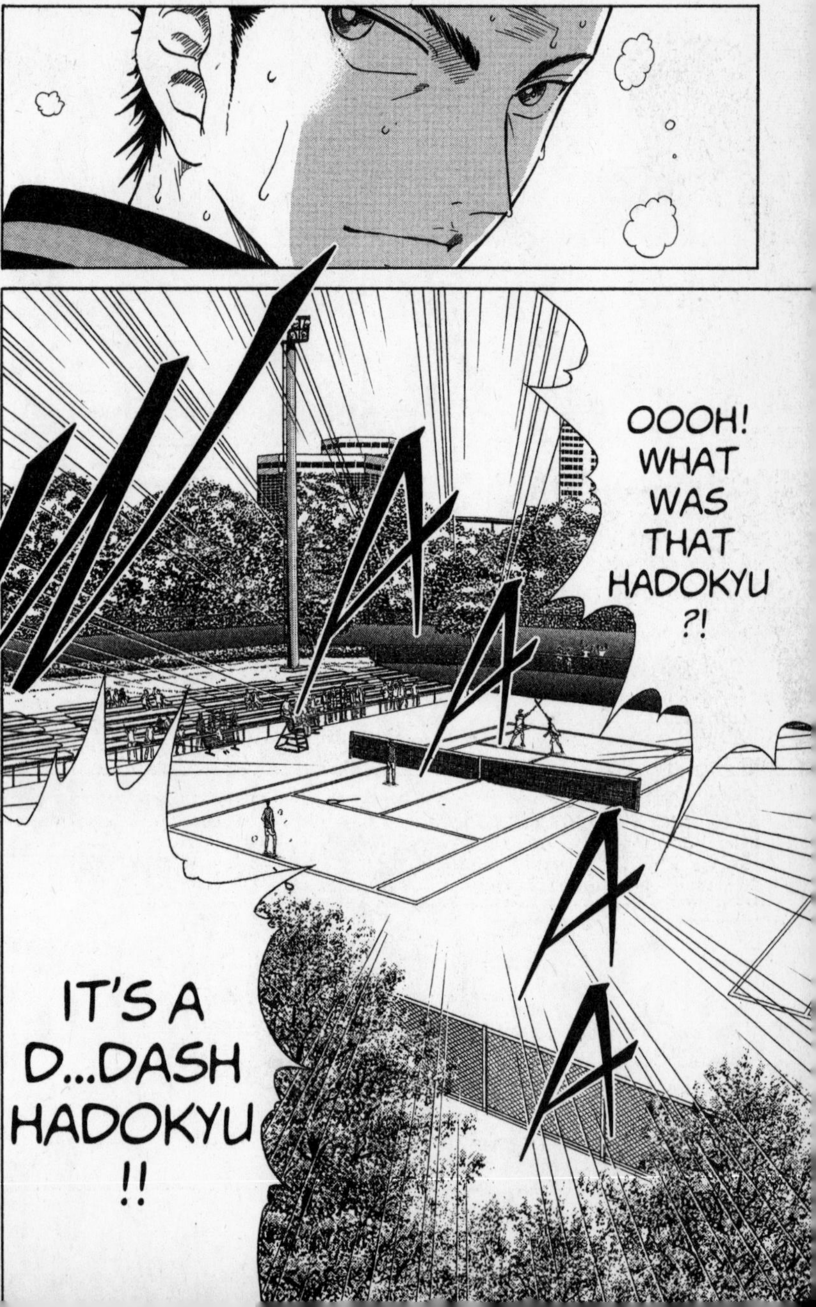
OOOH! WHAT WAS THAT HADOKYU ?!
WAAAA
IT'S A D...DASH HADOKYU !!

READ THIS WAY

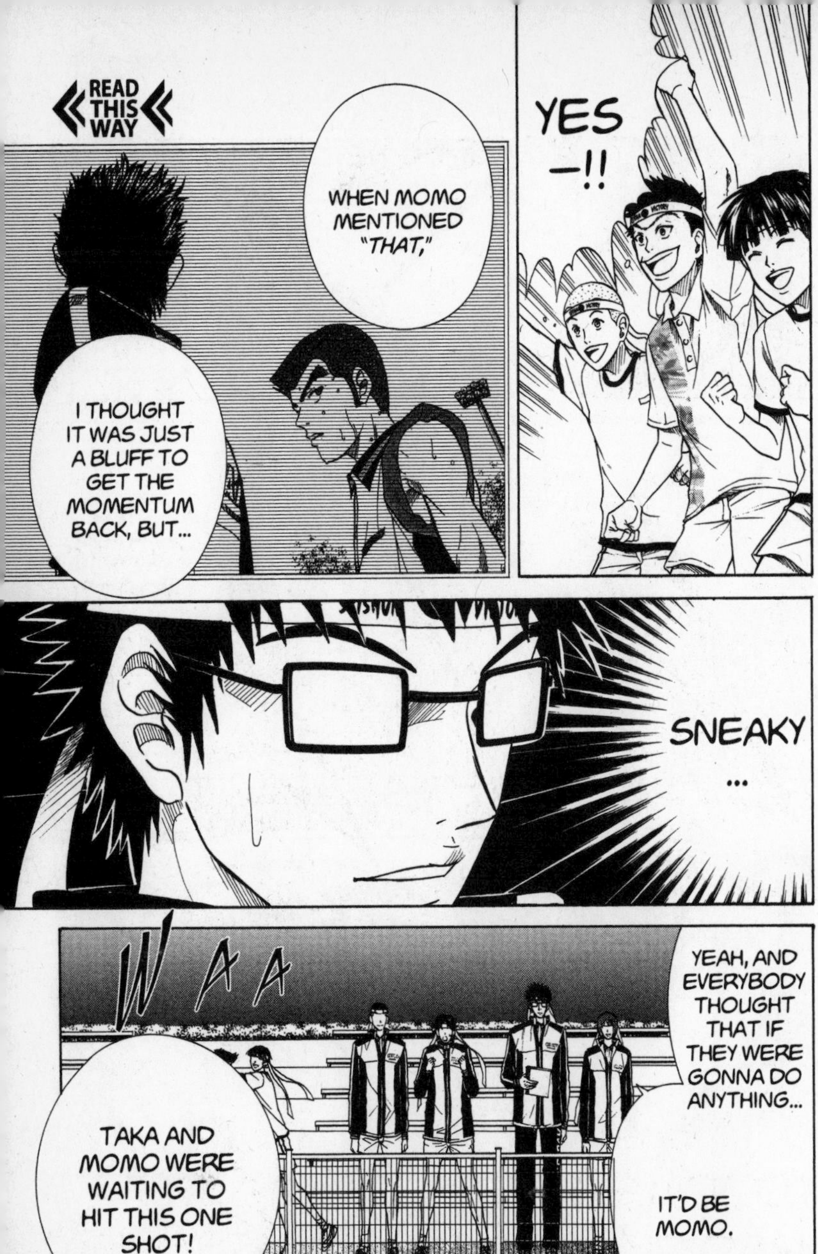

YES —!!
WHEN MOMO MENTIONED "THAT,"
I THOUGHT IT WAS JUST A BLUFF TO GET THE MOMENTUM BACK, BUT...
SNEAKY ...
YEAH, AND EVERYBODY THOUGHT THAT IF THEY WERE GONNA DO ANYTHING...
IT'D BE MOMO.
WAA
TAKA AND MOMO WERE WAITING TO HIT THIS ONE SHOT!

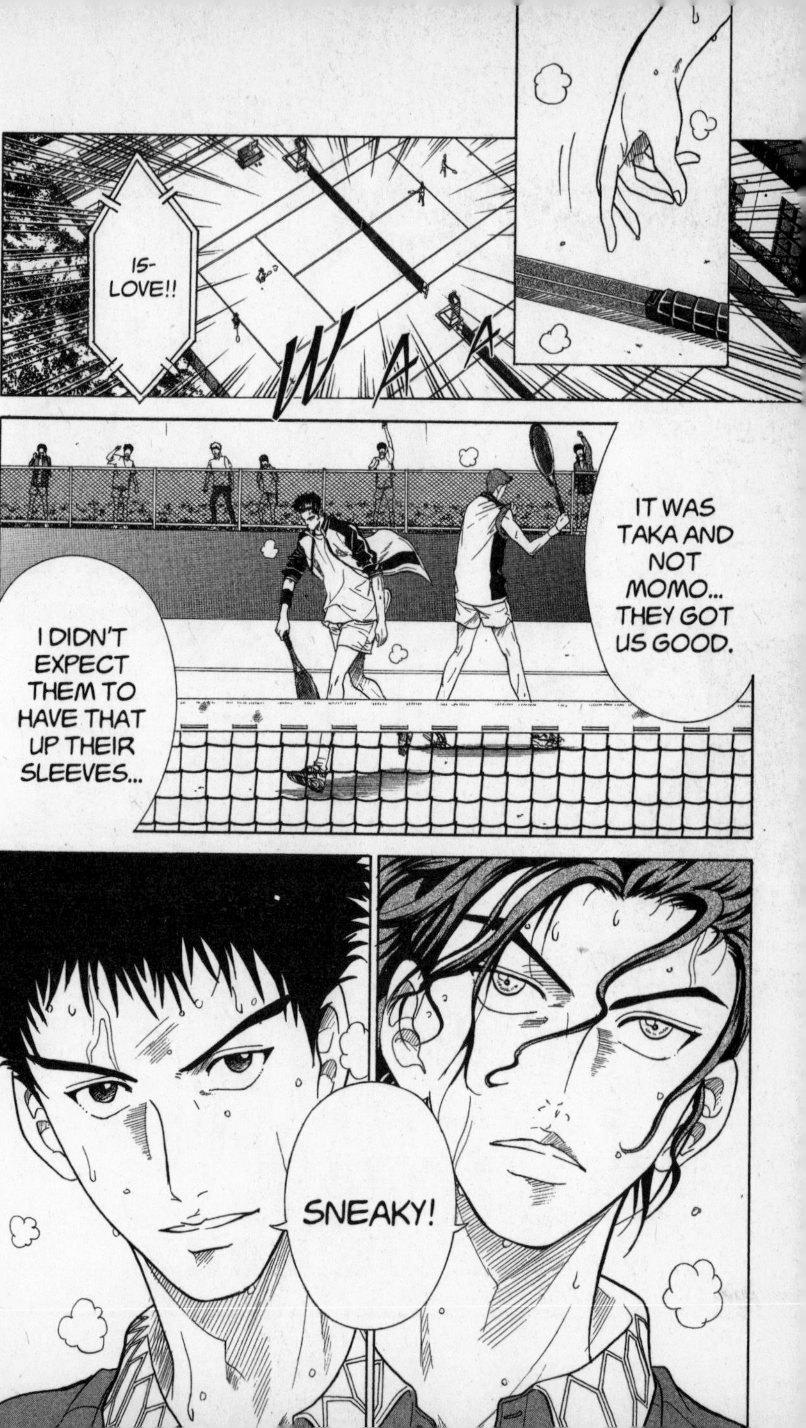
IS-
LOVE!!
WAA
IT WAS TAKA AND NOT MOMO... THEY GOT US GOOD.
I DIDN'T EXPECT THEM TO HAVE THAT UP THEIR SLEEVES...
SNEAKY!

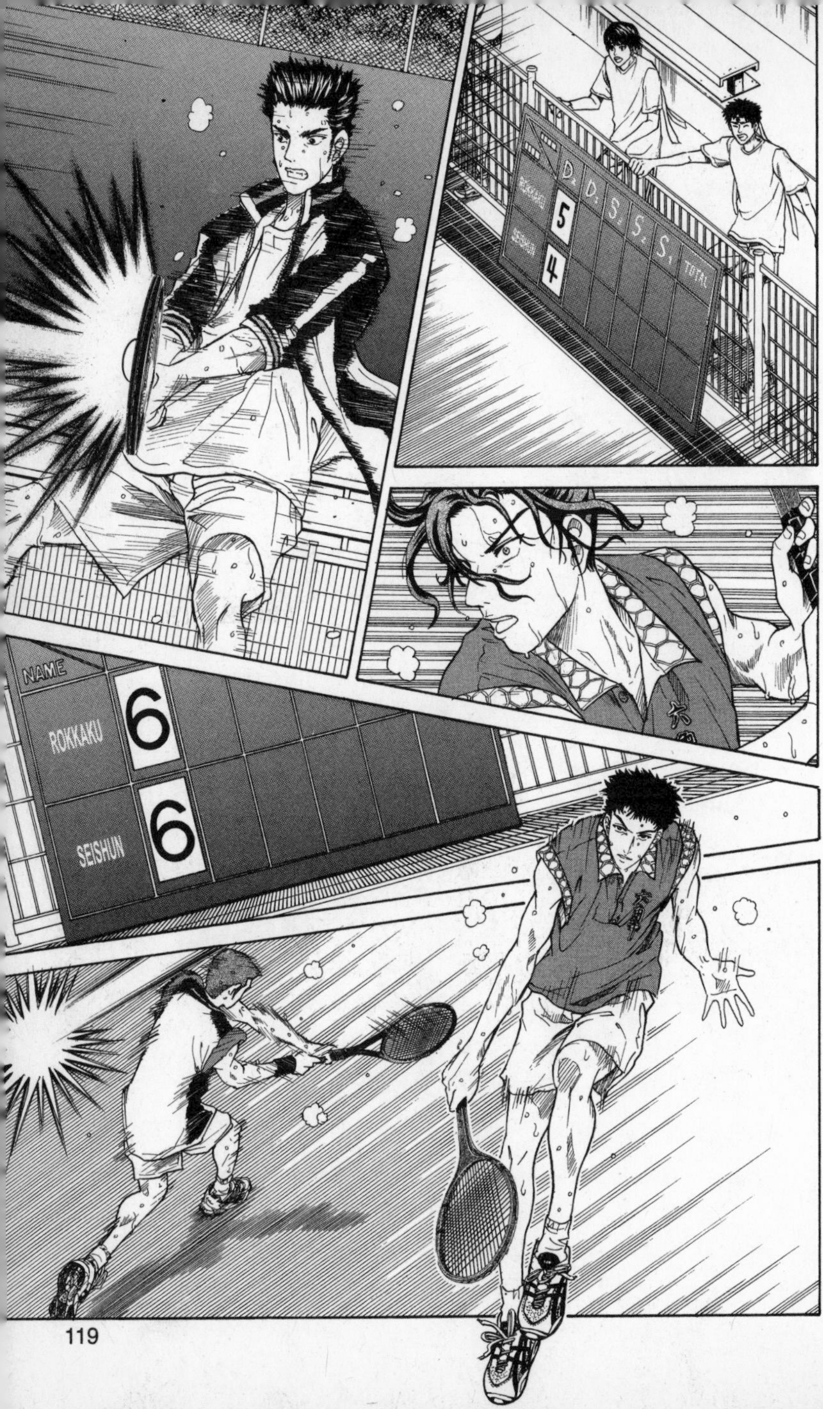
D.
D.
S.
S.
S.
TOTAL
ROKKAKU
5
SEISHUN
4
NAME
ROKKAKU
6
SEISHUN
6

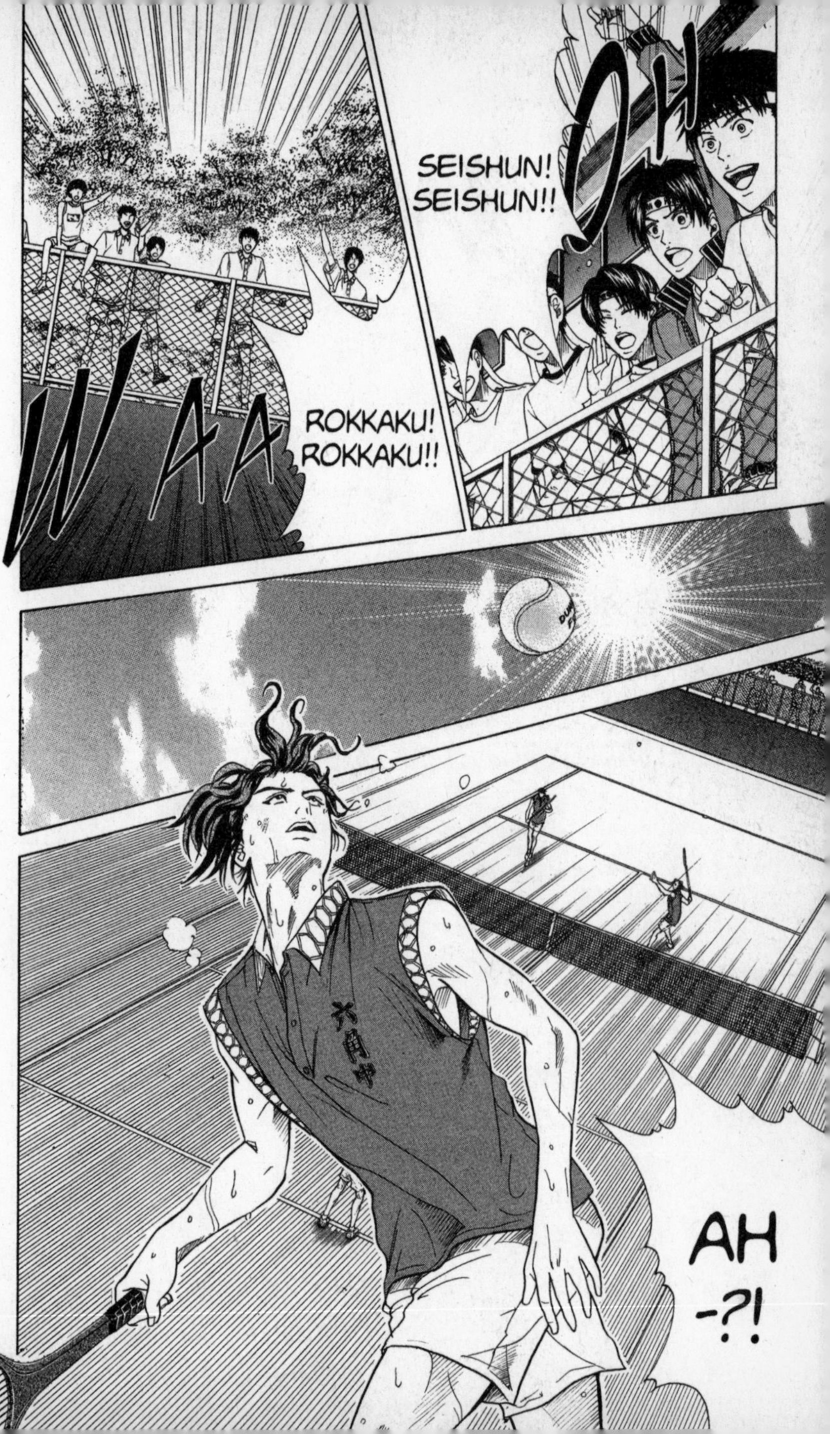
OH
SEISHUN! SEISHUN!!
WAA
ROKKAKU! ROKKAKU!!
AH -?!

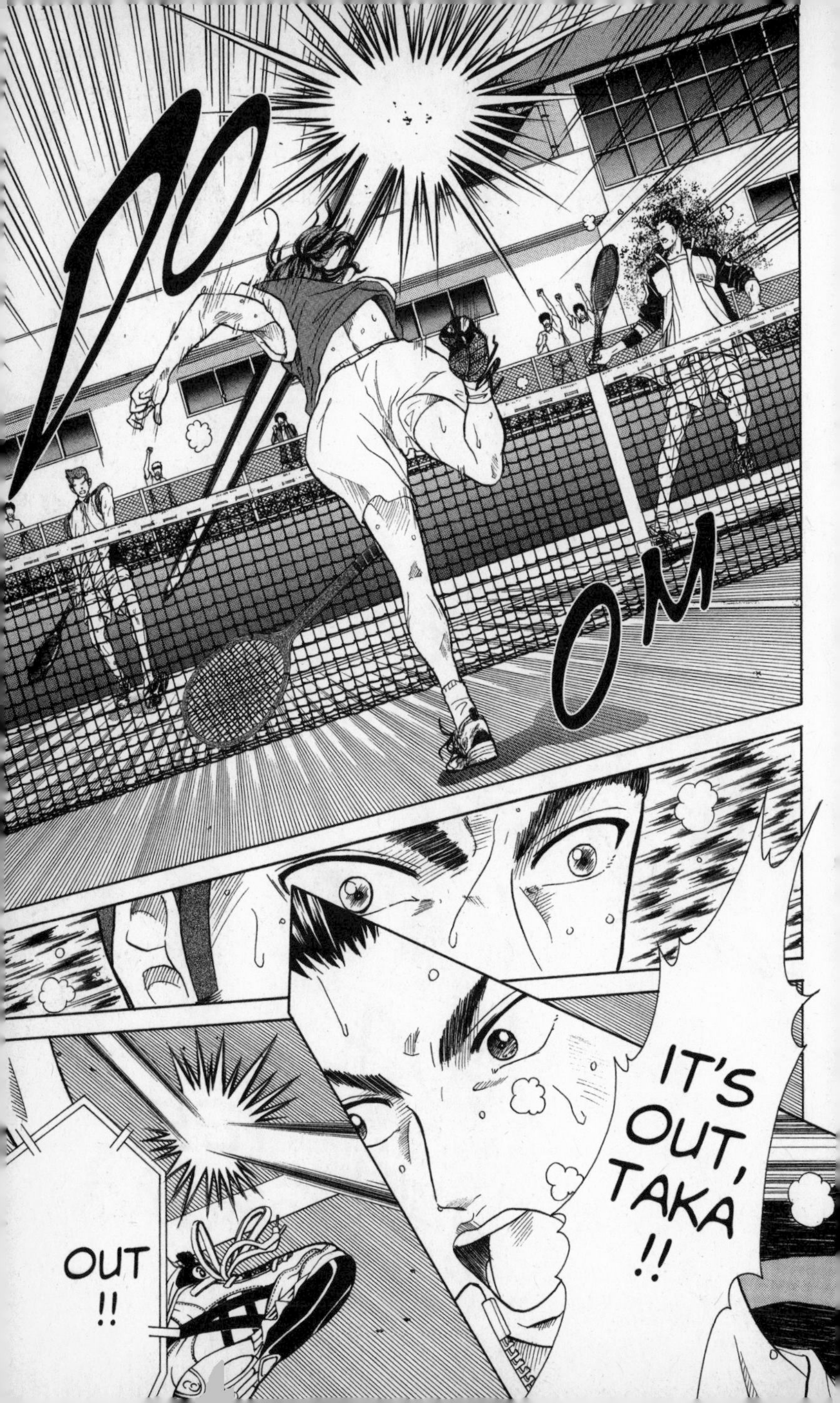
FWOOM
IT'S OUT, TAKA!!
OUT!!

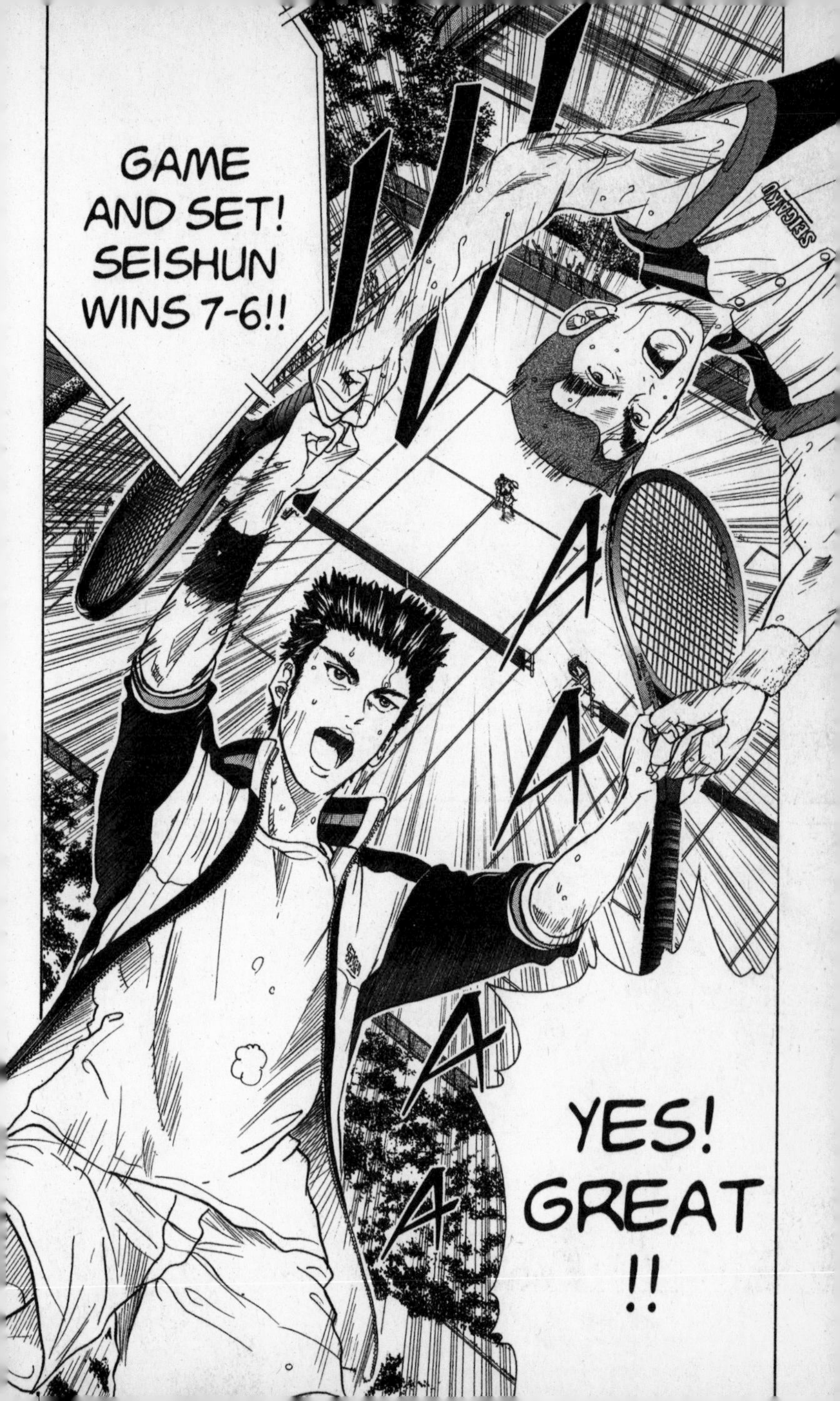
GAME AND SET! SEISHUN WINS 7-6!!
WAAAAA
YES! GREAT !!
SEIGAKU

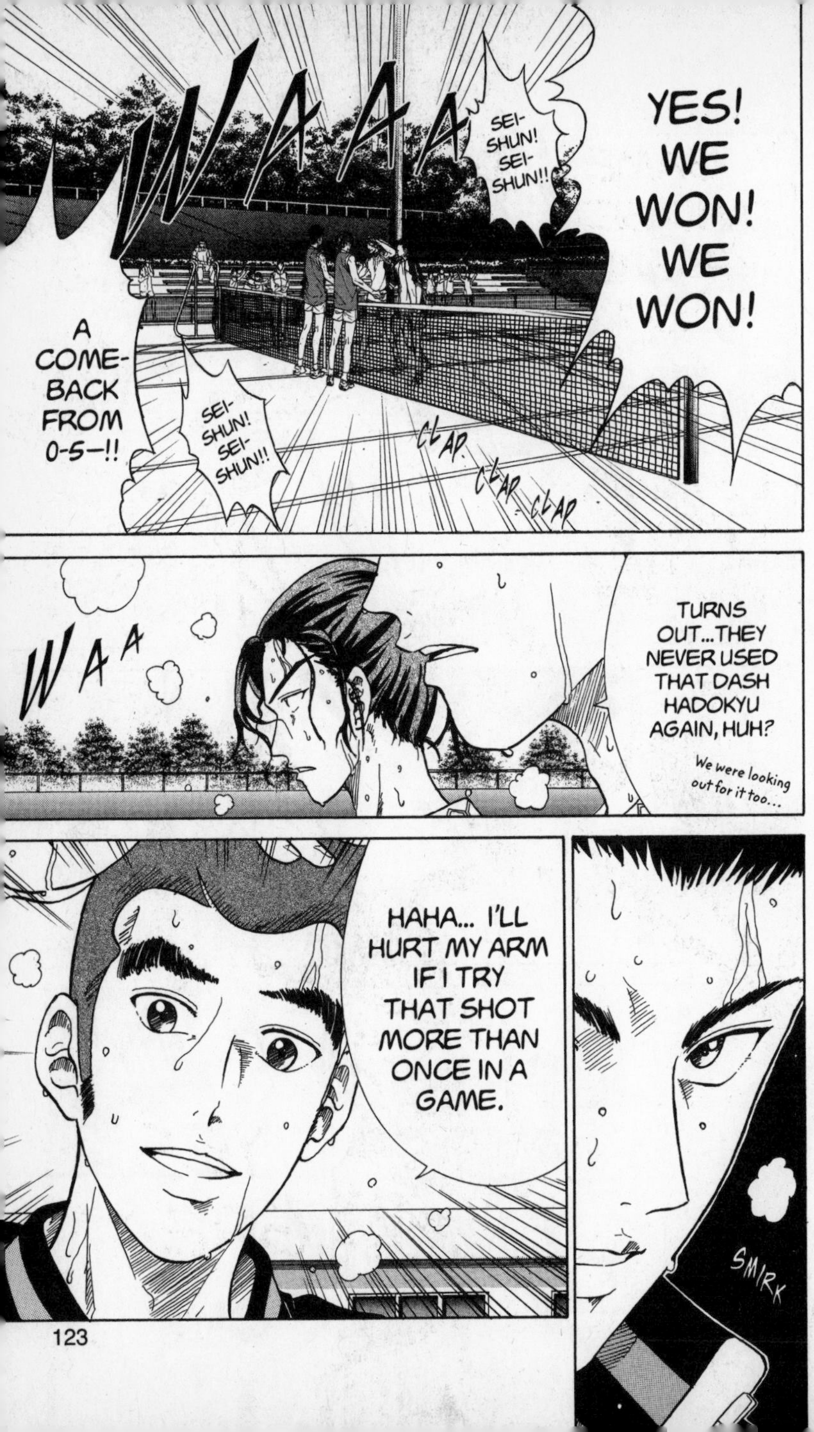
YES! WE WON! WE WON!
SEI-SHUN! SEI-SHUN!!
WAAAA
A COME-BACK FROM 0-5—!!
SEI-SHUN! SEI-SHUN!!
CLAP CLAP CLAP
TURNS OUT...THEY NEVER USED THAT DASH HADOKYU AGAIN, HUH?
We were looking out for it too...
WAA
SMIRK
HAHA... I'LL HURT MY ARM IF I TRY THAT SHOT MORE THAN ONCE IN A GAME.

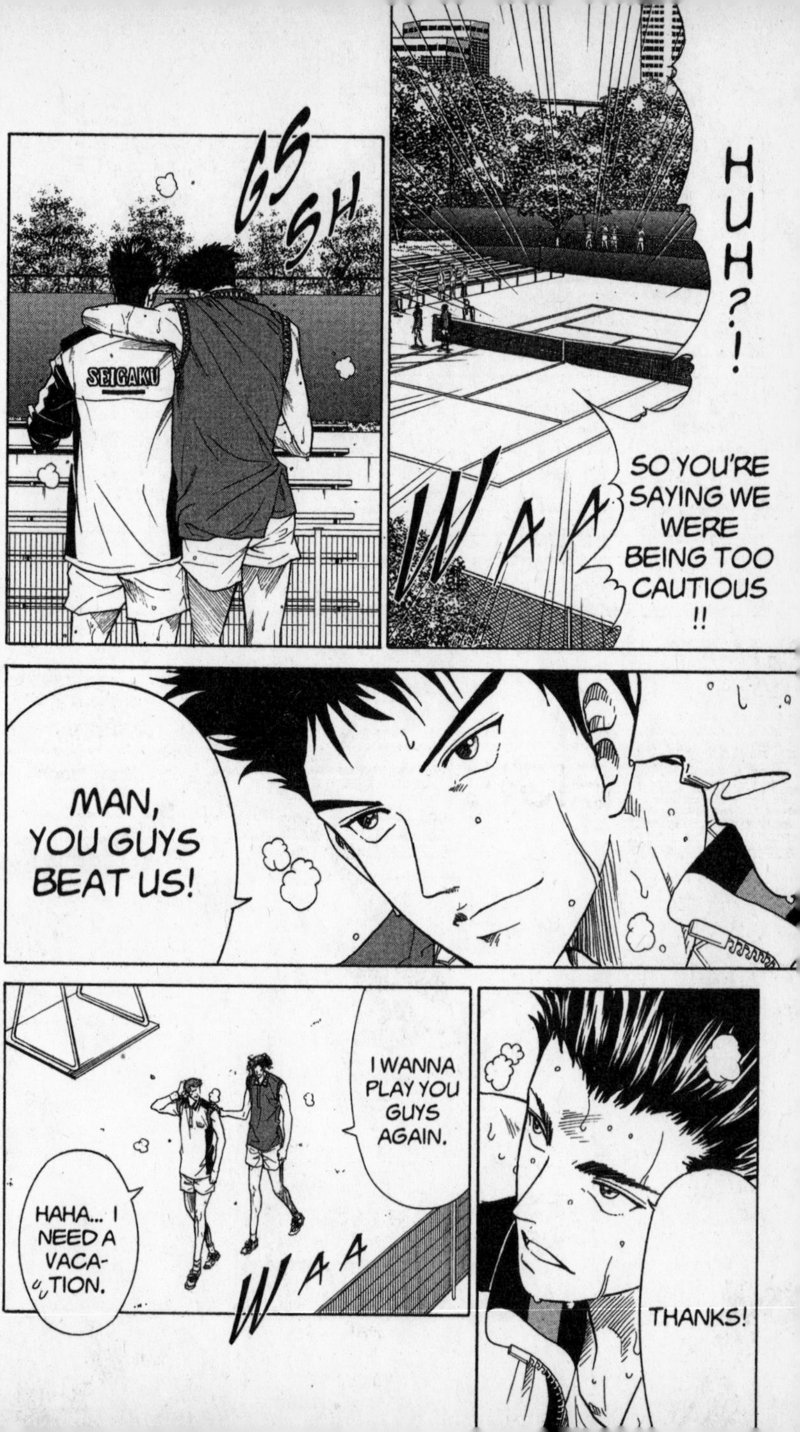
HUH?!
SO YOU'RE SAYING WE WERE BEING TOO CAUTIOUS !!
WAA
GSSH
SEIGAKU
MAN, YOU GUYS BEAT US!
THANKS!
I WANNA PLAY YOU GUYS AGAIN.
HAHA... I NEED A VACA-TION.
WAA

READ THIS WAY

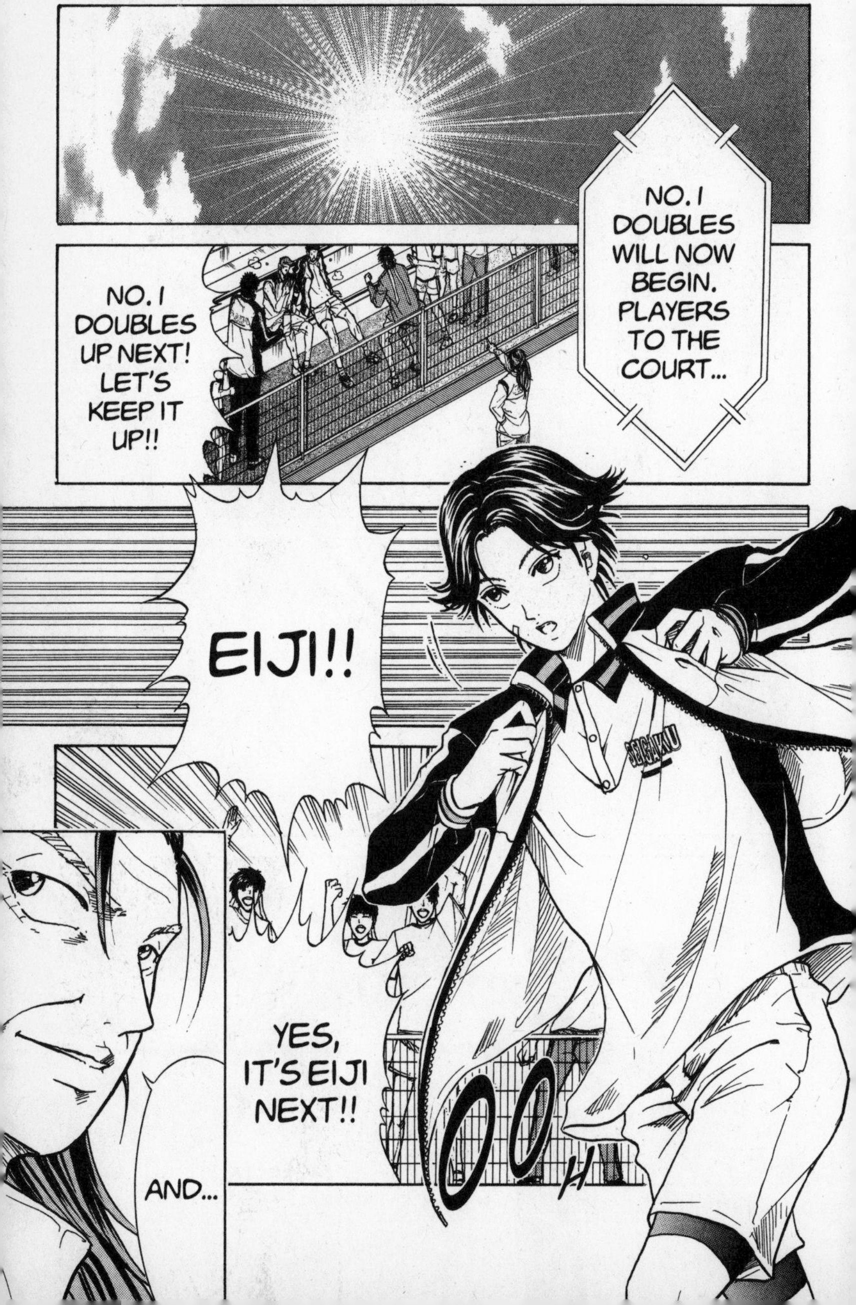
NO. 1 DOUBLES WILL NOW BEGIN. PLAYERS TO THE COURT...
NO. 1 DOUBLES UP NEXT! LET'S KEEP IT UP!!
EIJI!!
YES, IT'S EIJI NEXT!!
OOH
AND...

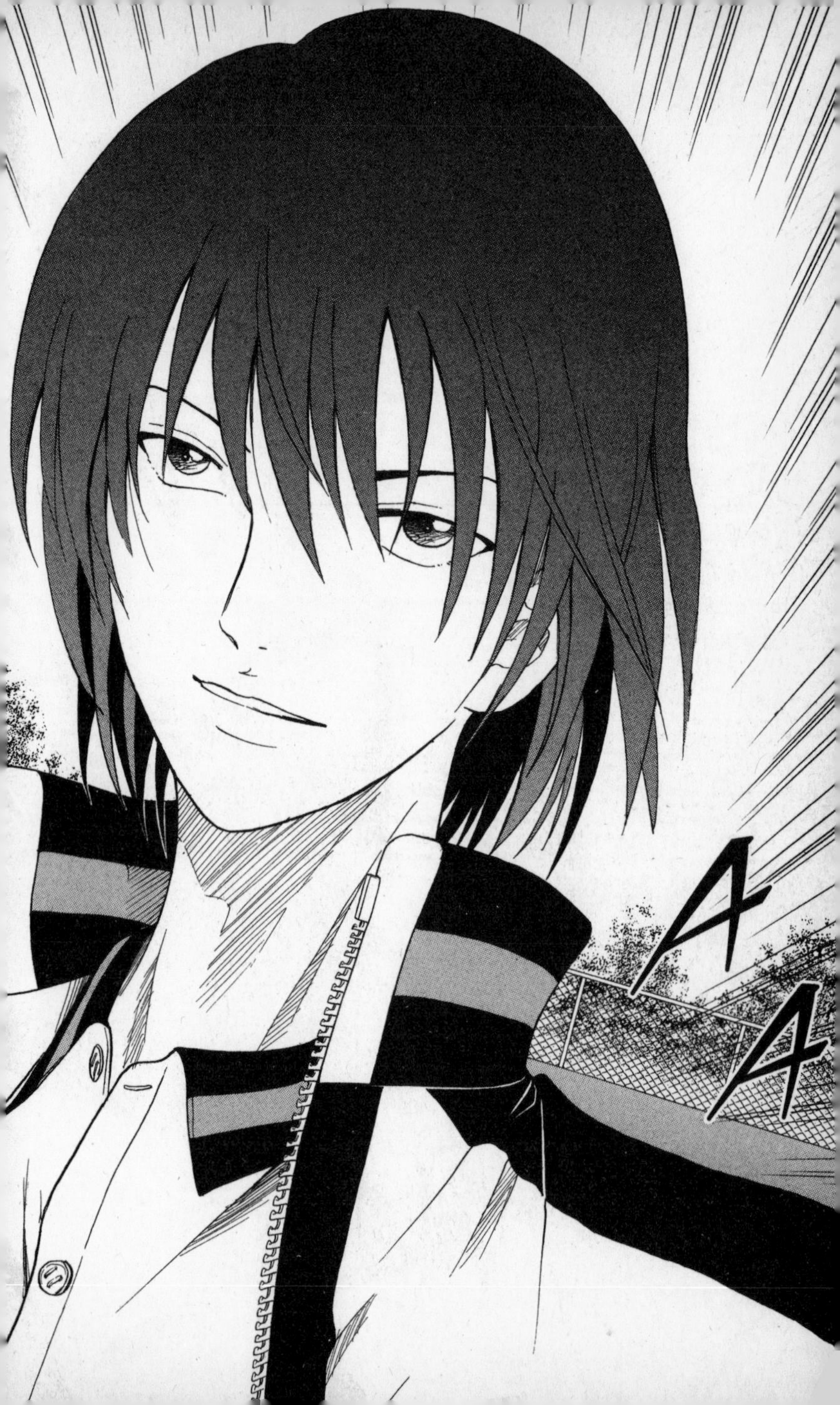
ムム

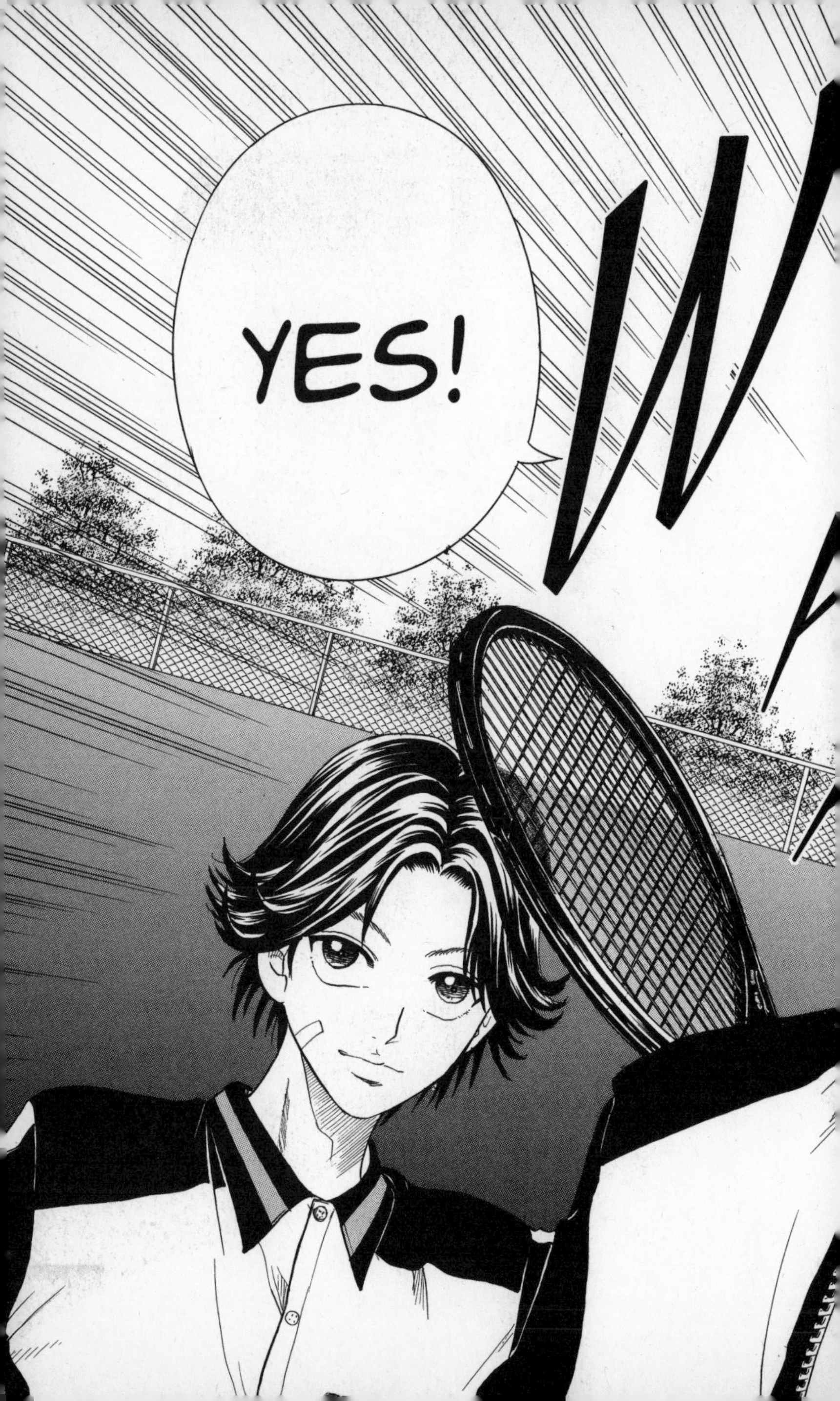
YES!

テニスの王子様

THE PRINCE OF TENNIS™

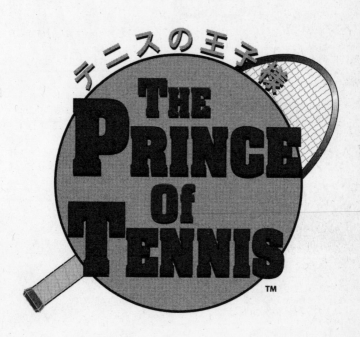

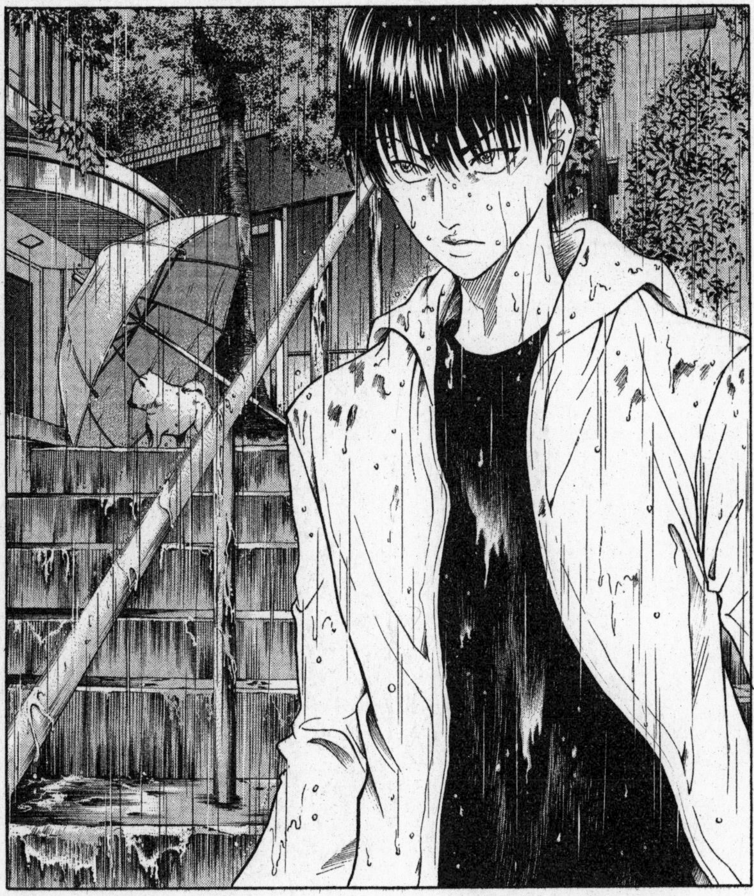

# GENIUS 174: INITIATIVE

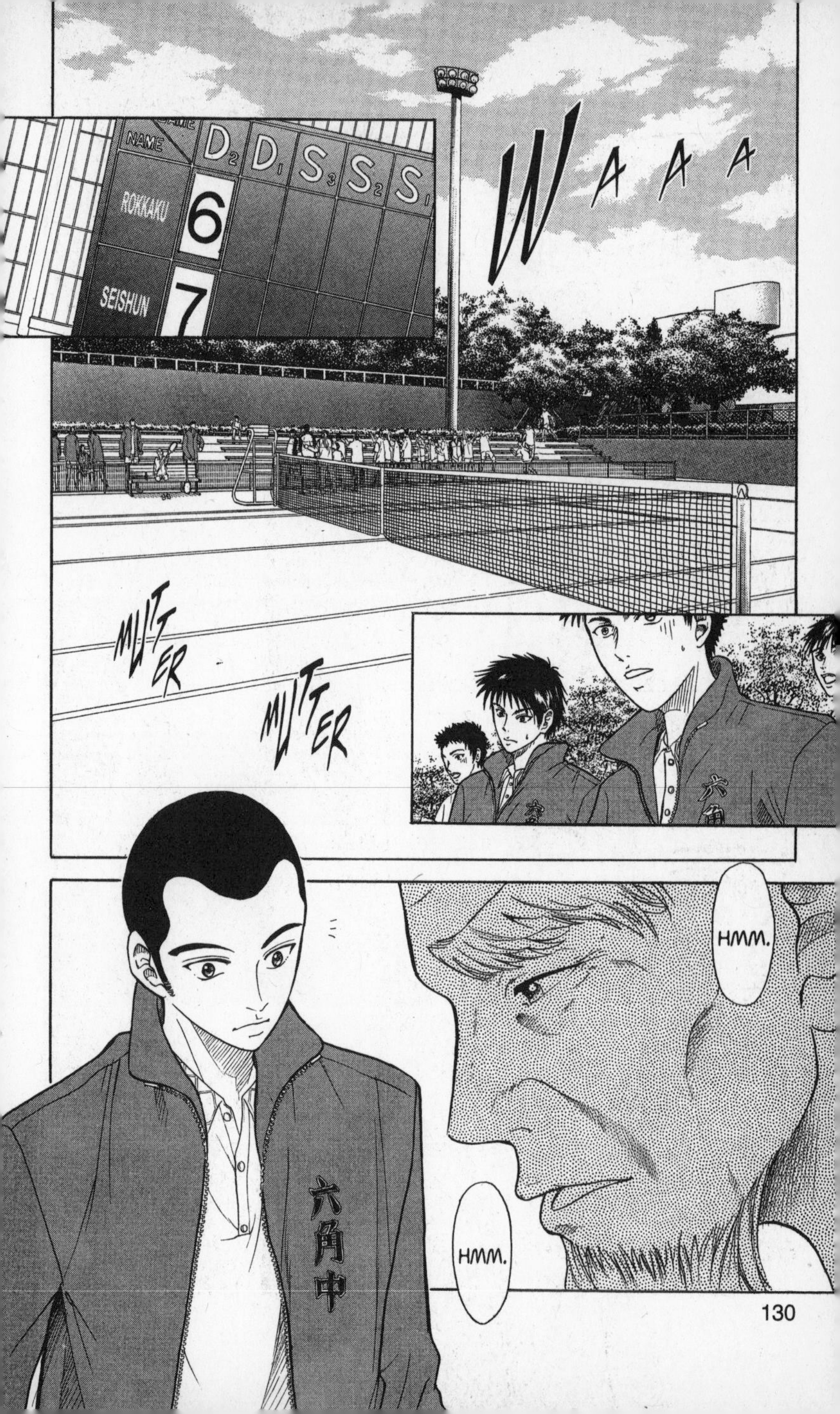
GAME
NAME
D2 D1 S3 S2 S1
ROKKAKU 6
SEISHUN 7
WAAA
MUTTER
MUTTER
HMM.
HMM.

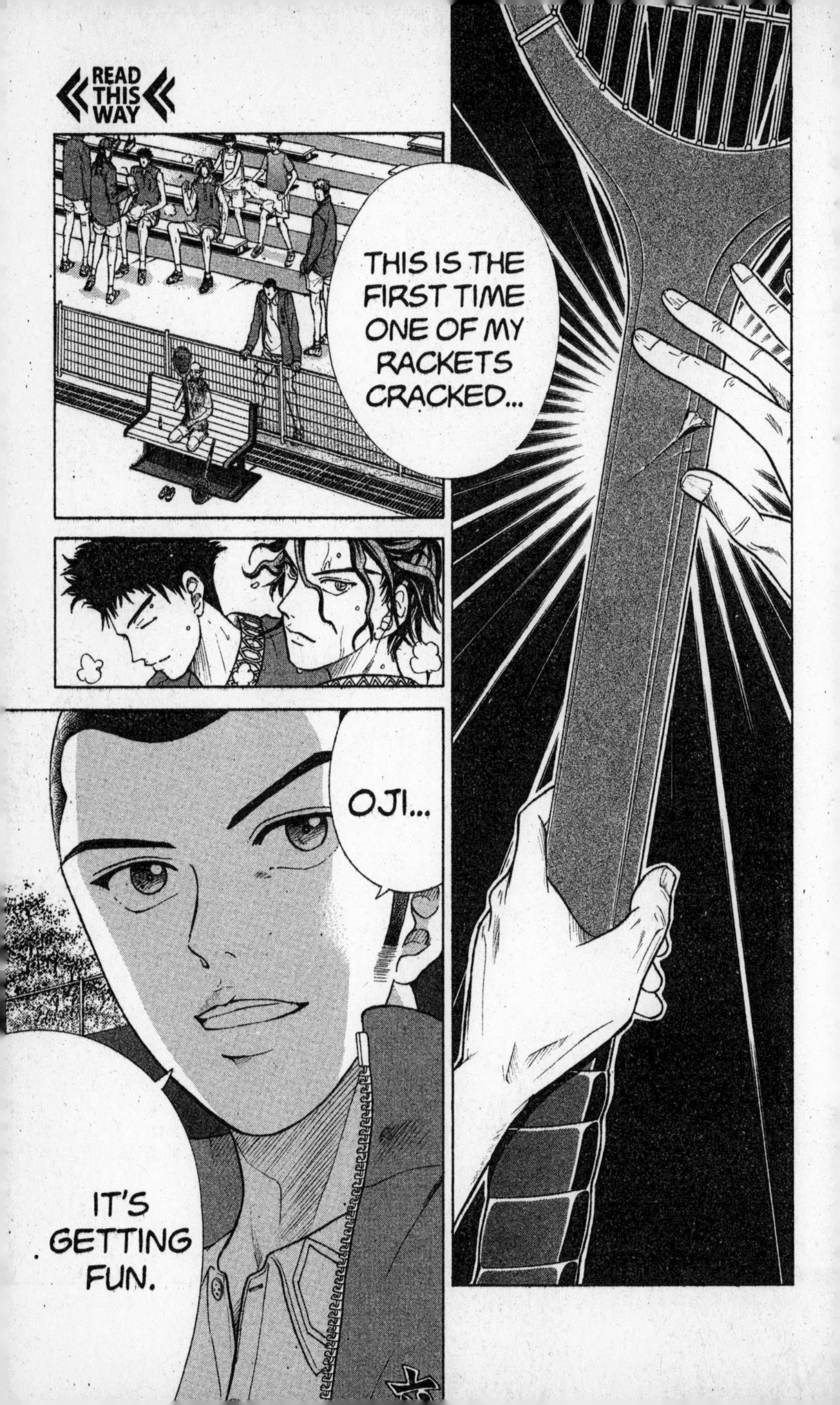
READ THIS WAY
THIS IS THE FIRST TIME ONE OF MY RACKETS CRACKED...
OJI...
IT'S GETTING FUN.

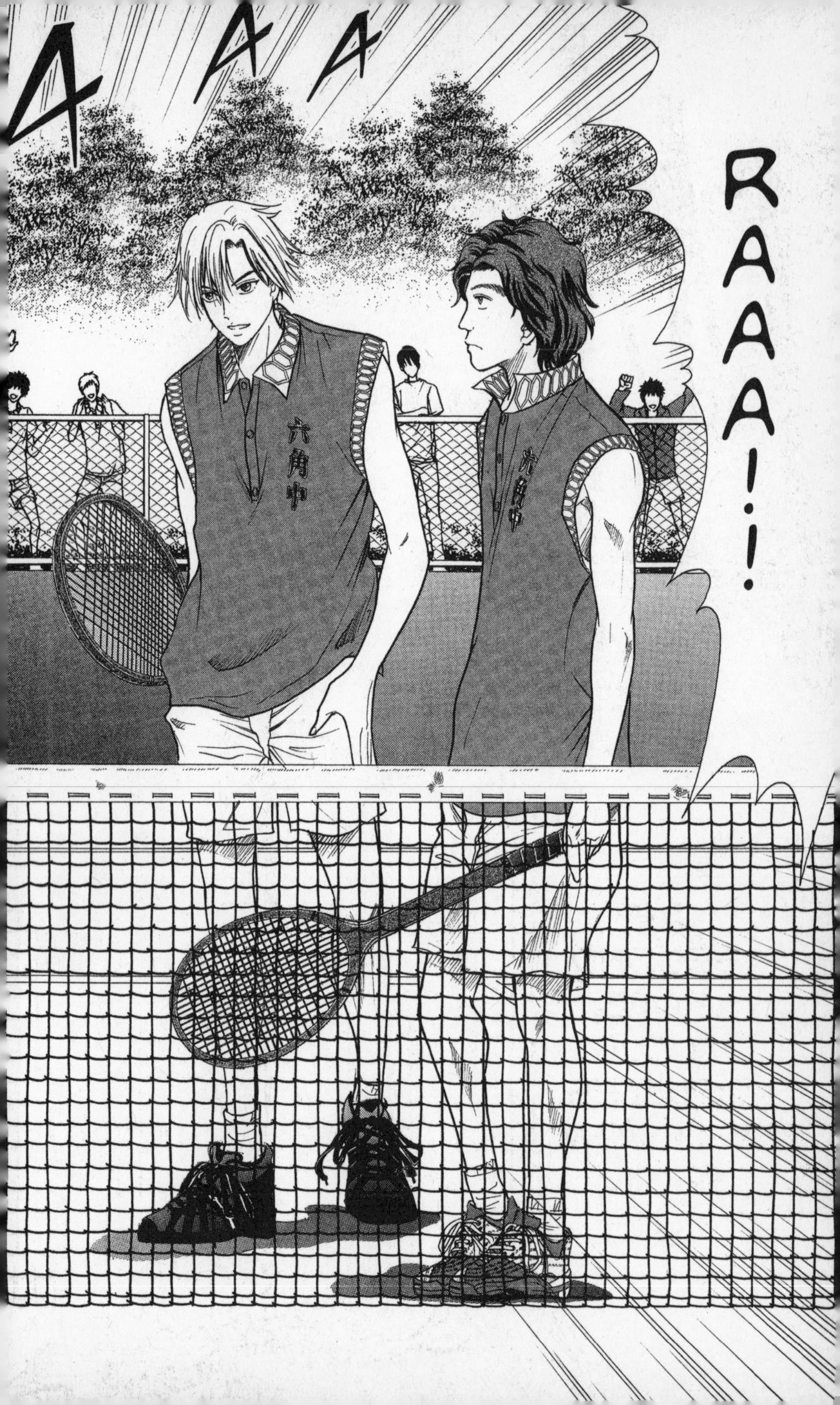
AAA
RAAA!!
六角中

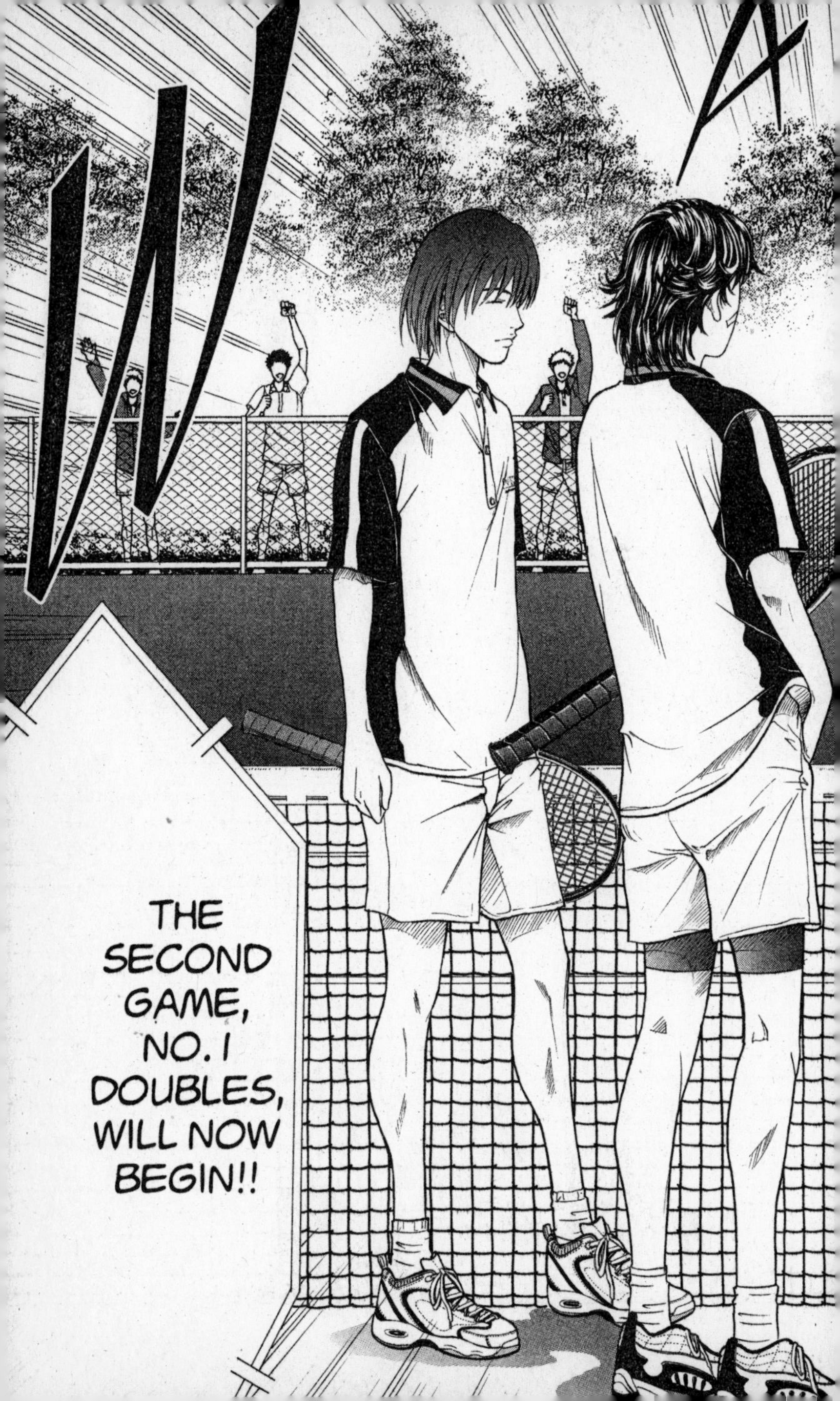
WA
THE SECOND GAME, NO. 1 DOUBLES, WILL NOW BEGIN!!

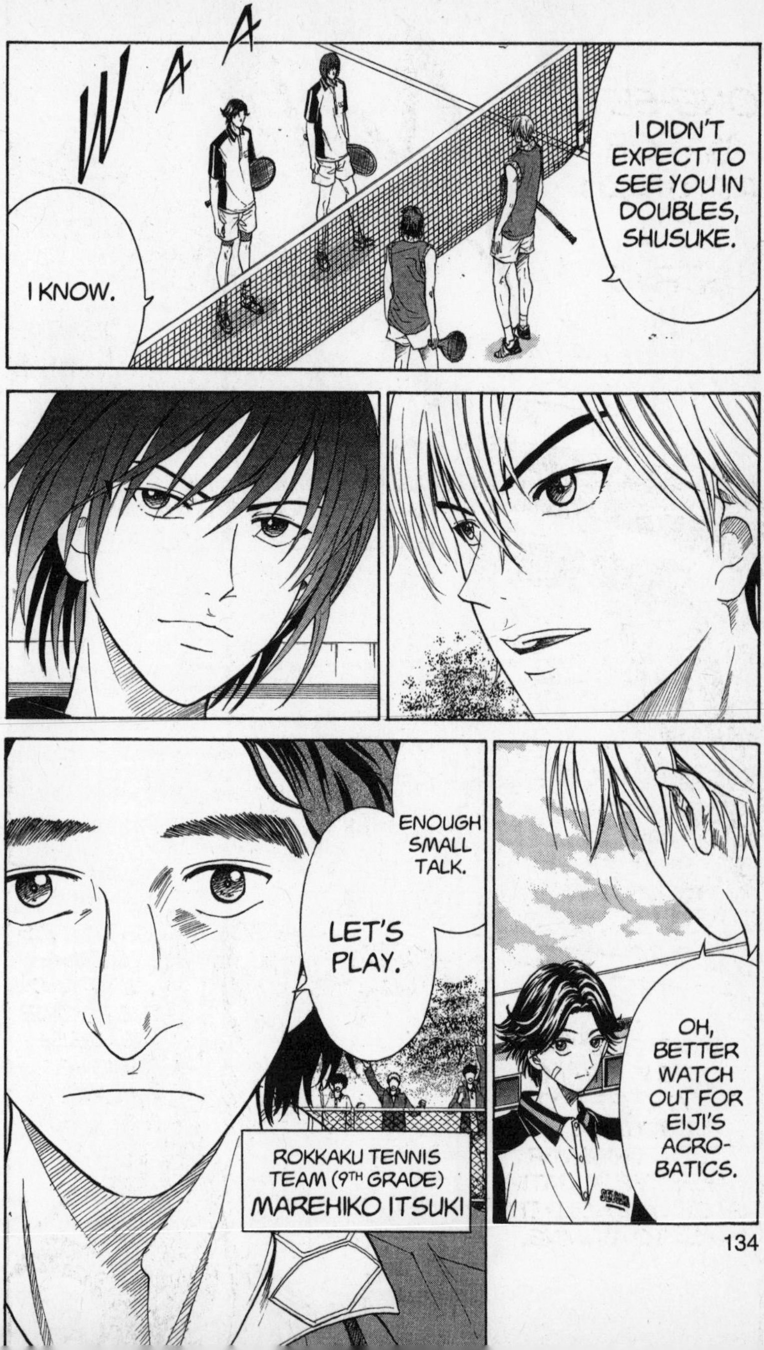
WAA
I DIDN'T EXPECT TO SEE YOU IN DOUBLES, SHUSUKE.
I KNOW.
OH, BETTER WATCH OUT FOR EIJI'S ACRO-BATICS.
ENOUGH SMALL TALK.
LET'S PLAY.
ROKKAKU TENNIS TEAM (9TH GRADE) MAREHIKO ITSUKI

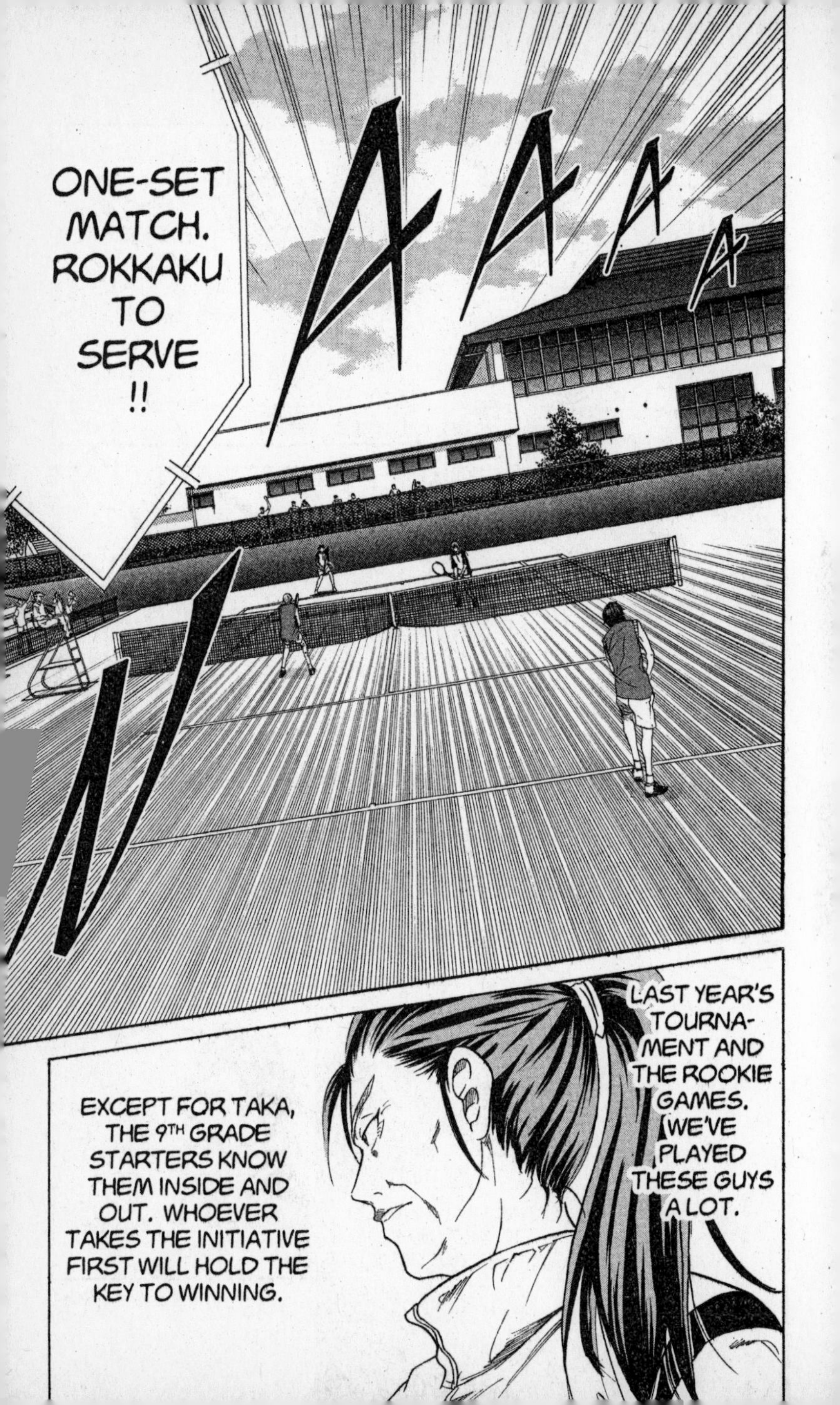
WAAAAA
ONE-SET MATCH. ROKKAKU TO SERVE!!
LAST YEAR'S TOURNAMENT AND THE ROOKIE GAMES. WE'VE PLAYED THESE GUYS A LOT.
EXCEPT FOR TAKA, THE 9TH GRADE STARTERS KNOW THEM INSIDE AND OUT. WHOEVER TAKES THE INITIATIVE FIRST WILL HOLD THE KEY TO WINNING.

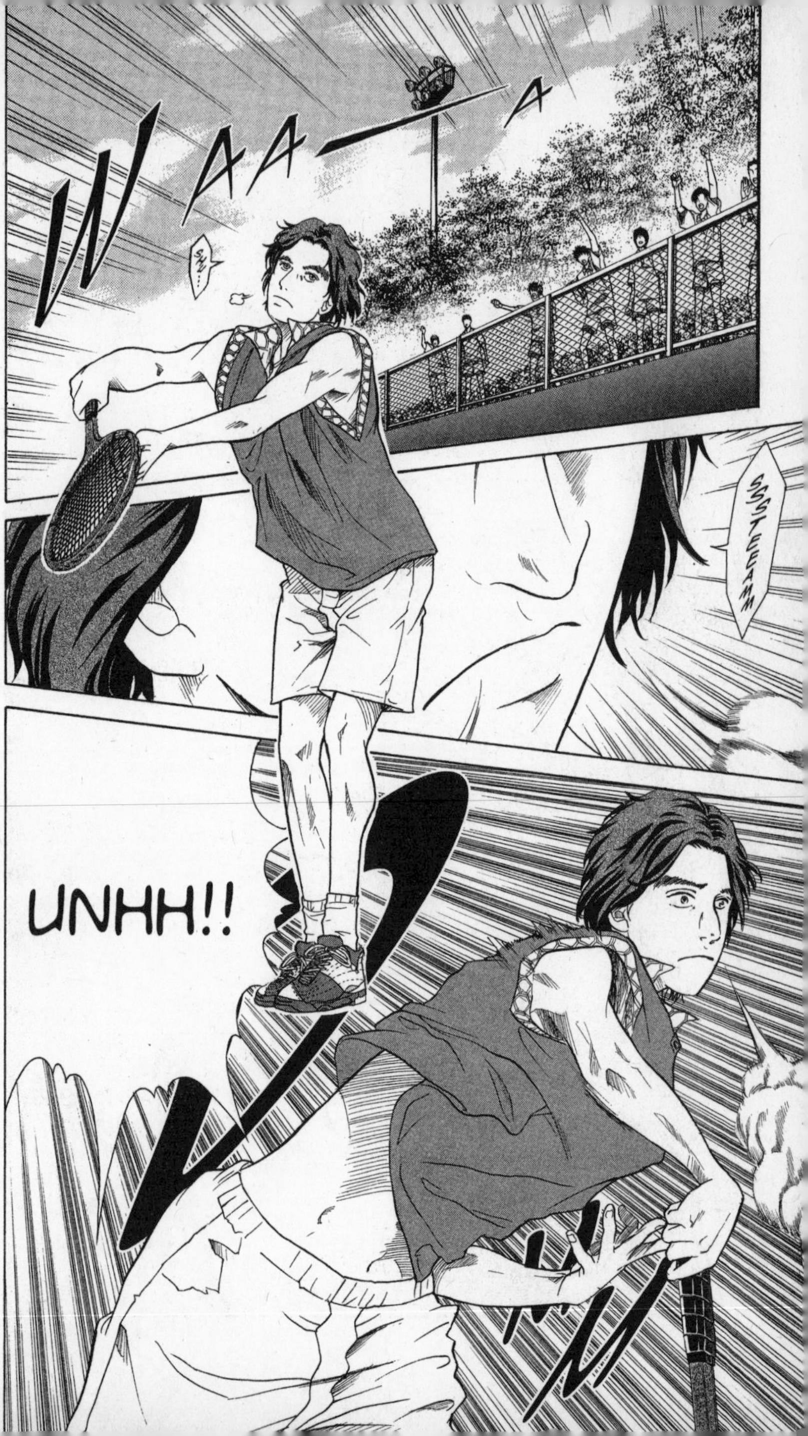

WAA—A
SHU...
SSSTEEAMM
UNHH!!

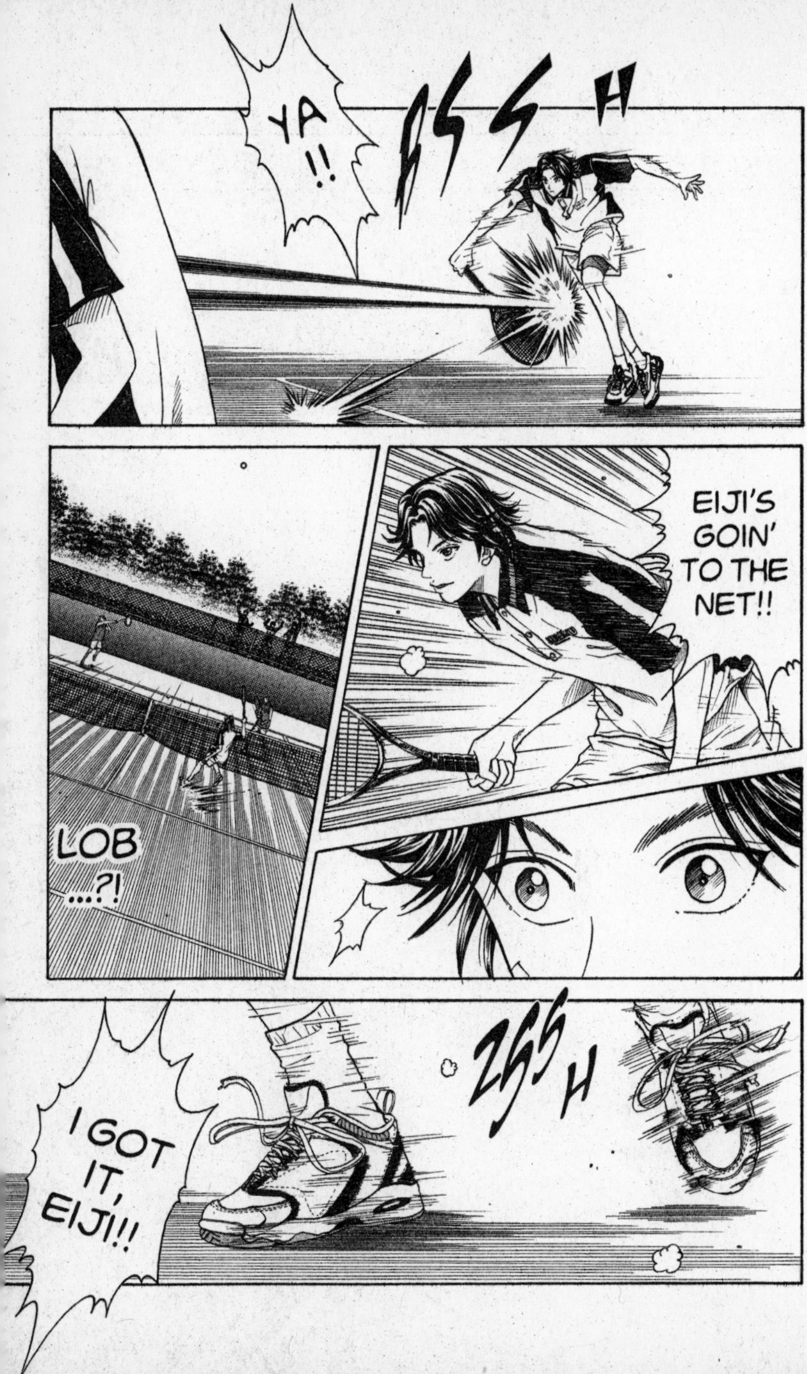
BSSH
YA!!
EIJI'S GOIN' TO THE NET!!
LOB ...?!
ZSSH
I GOT IT, EIJI!!

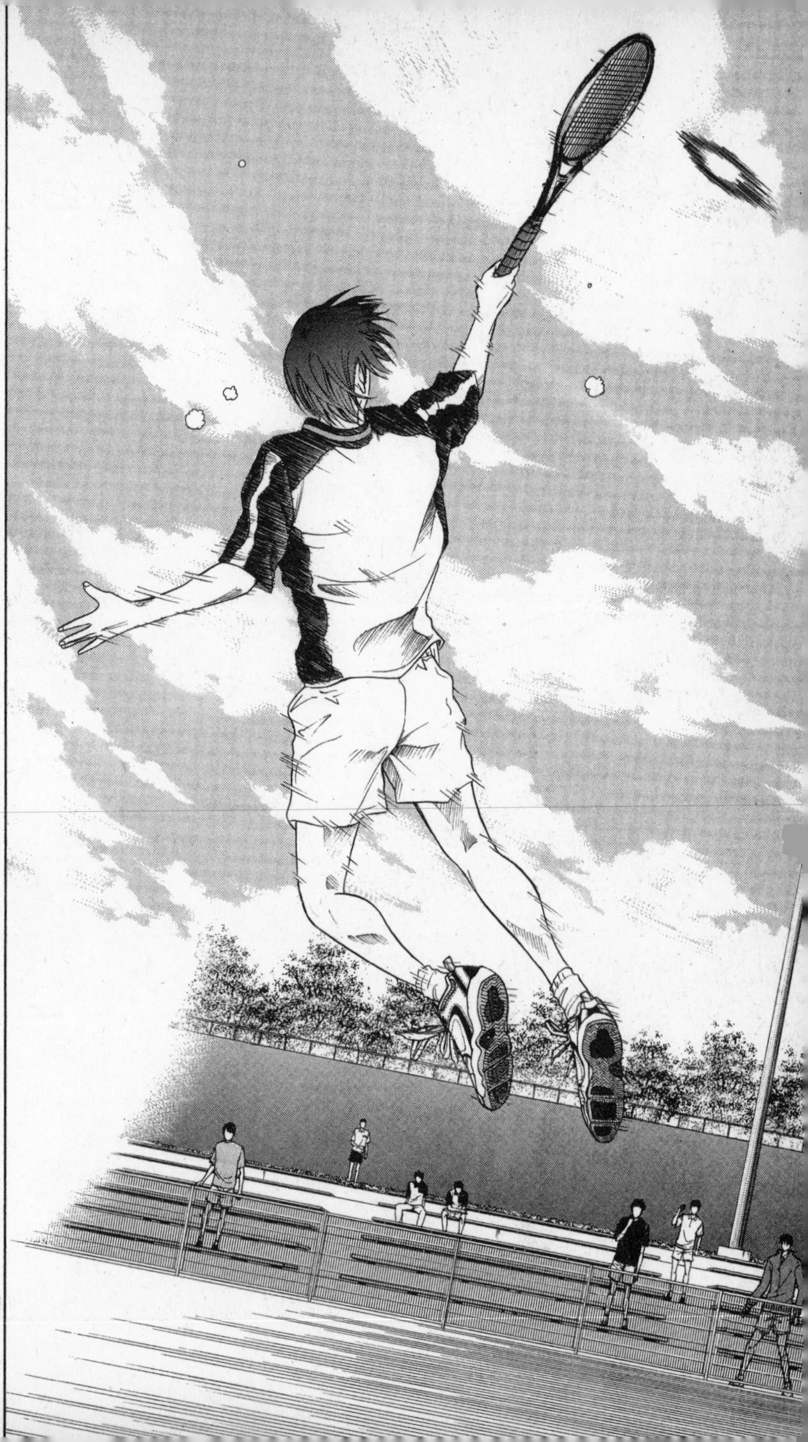

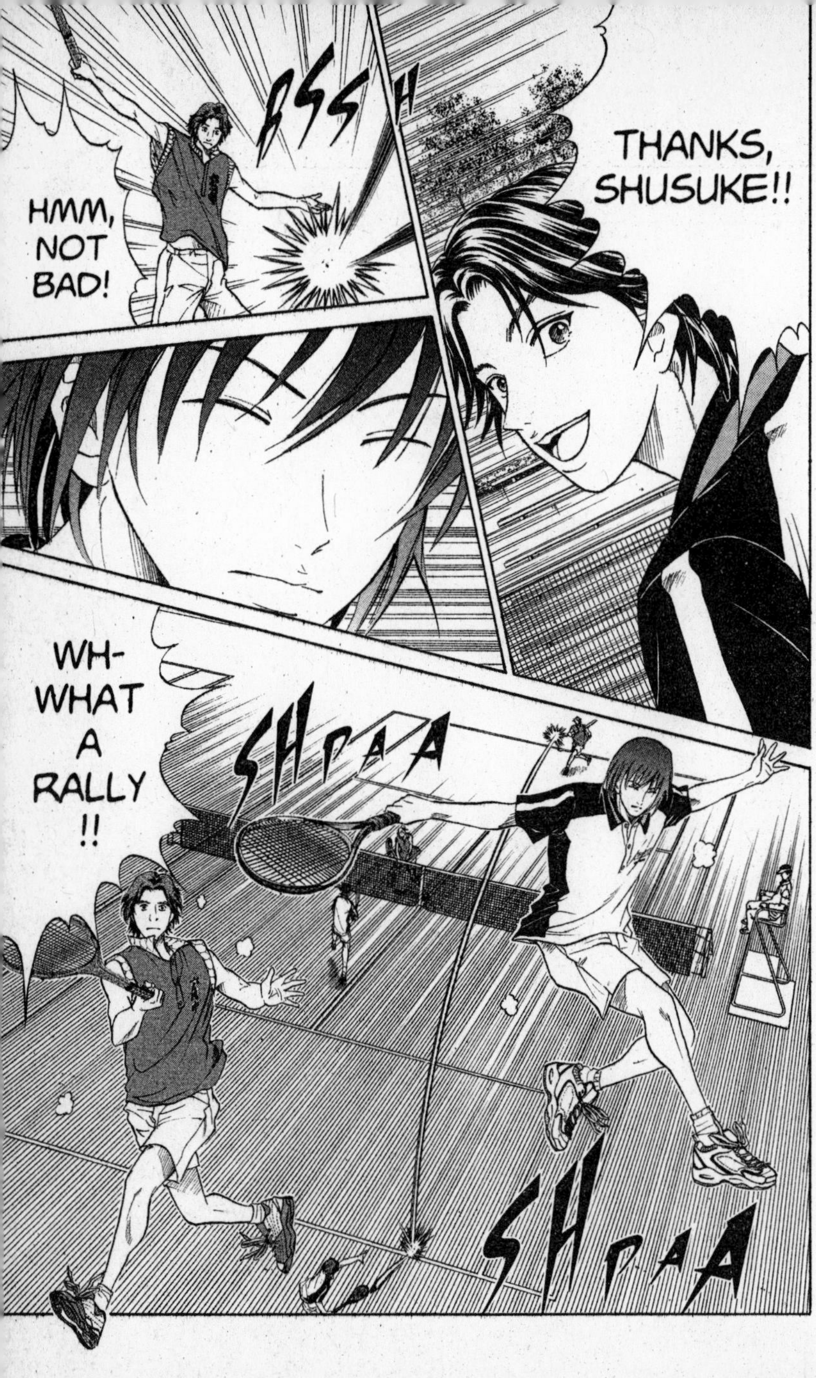
THANKS, SHUSUKE!!
BSSH
HMM, NOT BAD!
SHPAA
WH-WHAT A RALLY!!
SHPAA

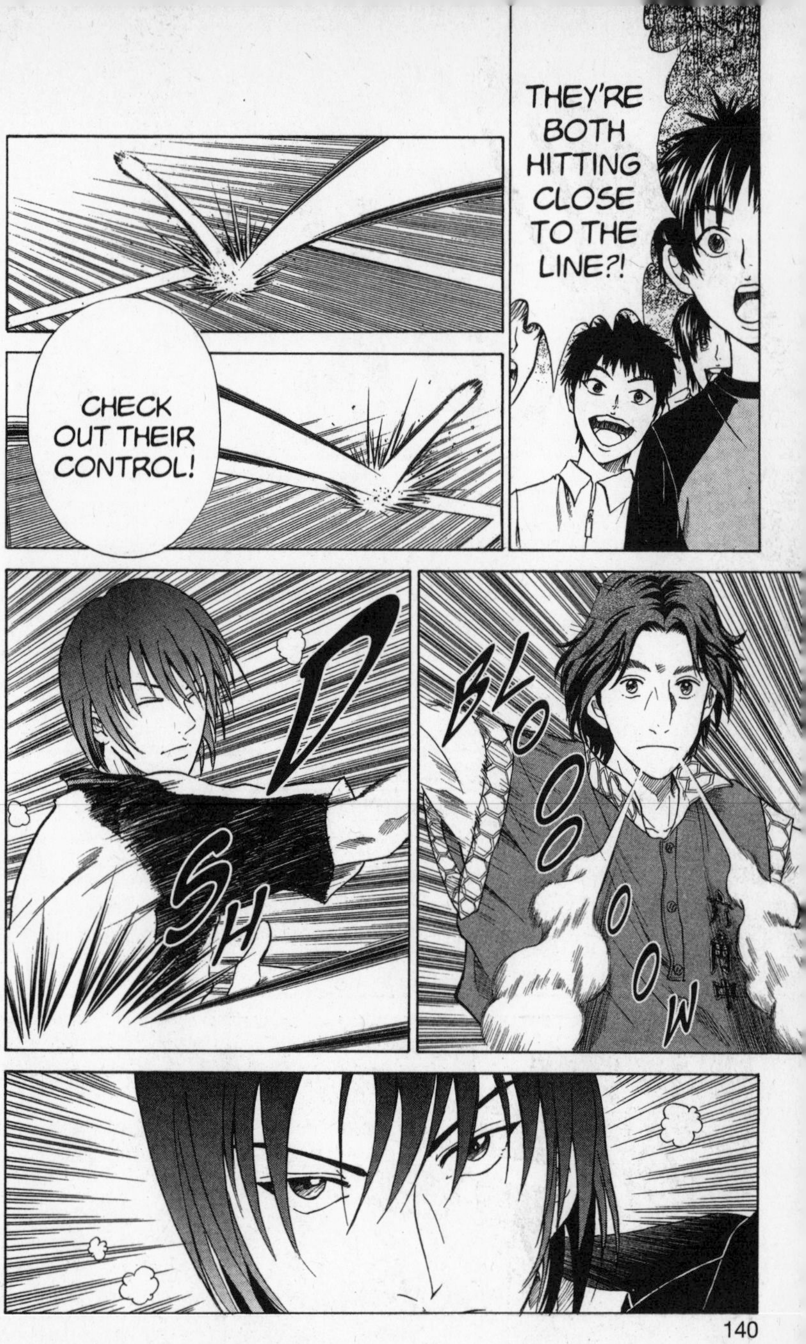
THEY'RE BOTH HITTING CLOSE TO THE LINE?!
CHECK OUT THEIR CONTROL!
BLOOOOOOOW
D
SH

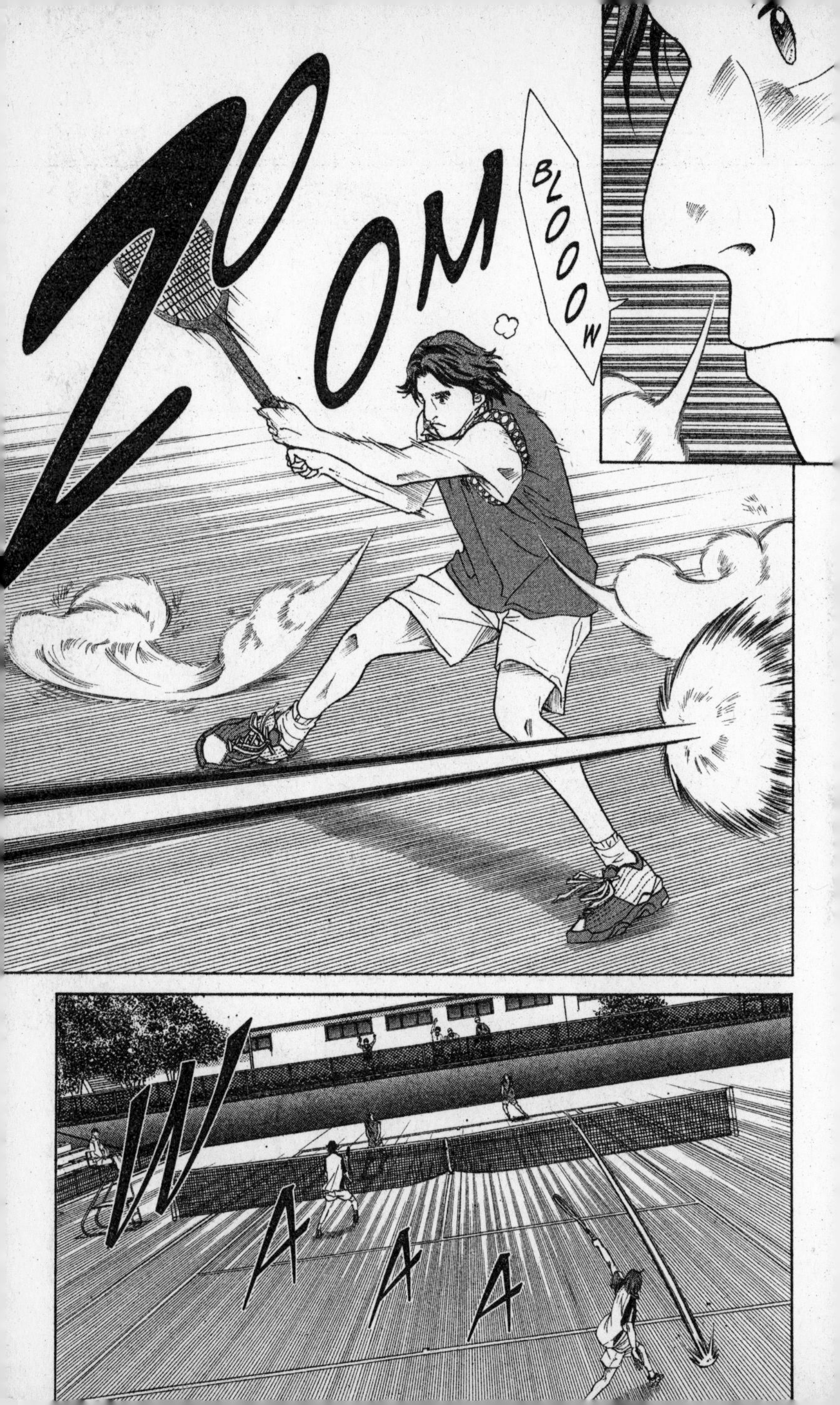
BLOOOOW
ZOOM
WAAA

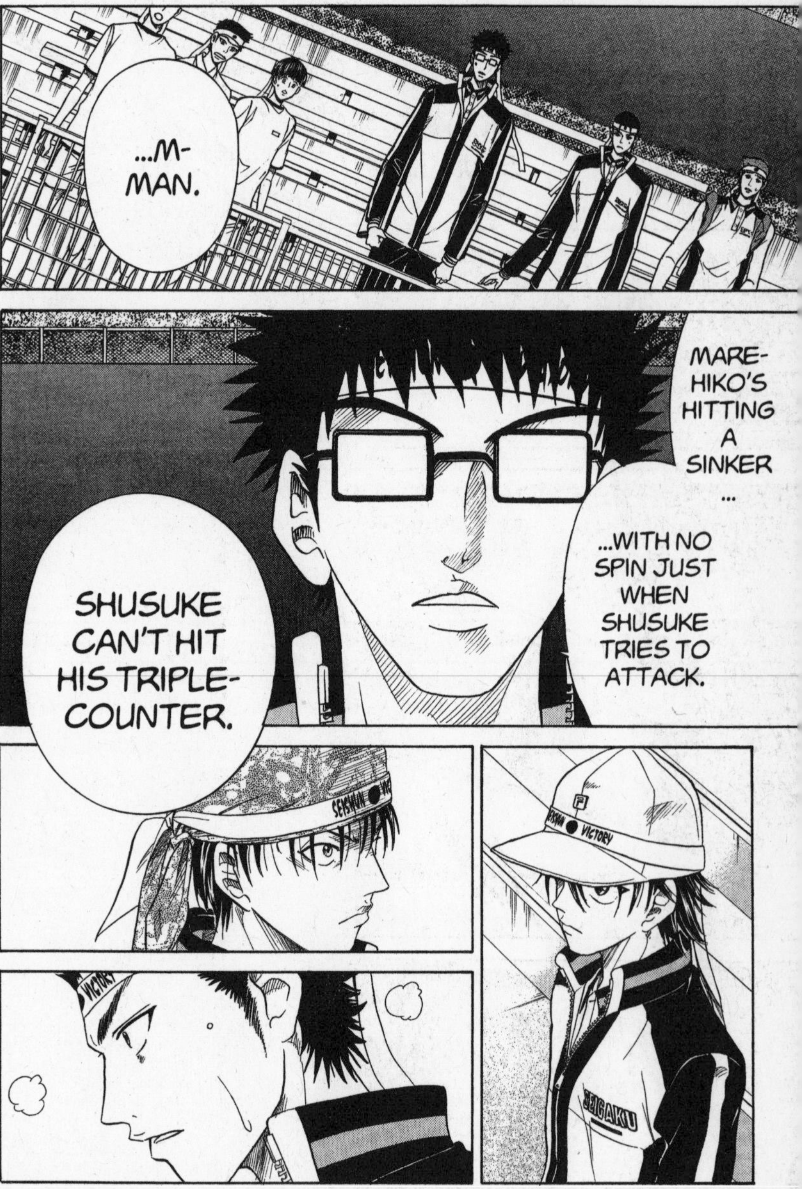
...M-MAN.
MARE-HIKO'S HITTING A SINKER ...
...WITH NO SPIN JUST WHEN SHUSUKE TRIES TO ATTACK.
SHUSUKE CAN'T HIT HIS TRIPLE-COUNTER.

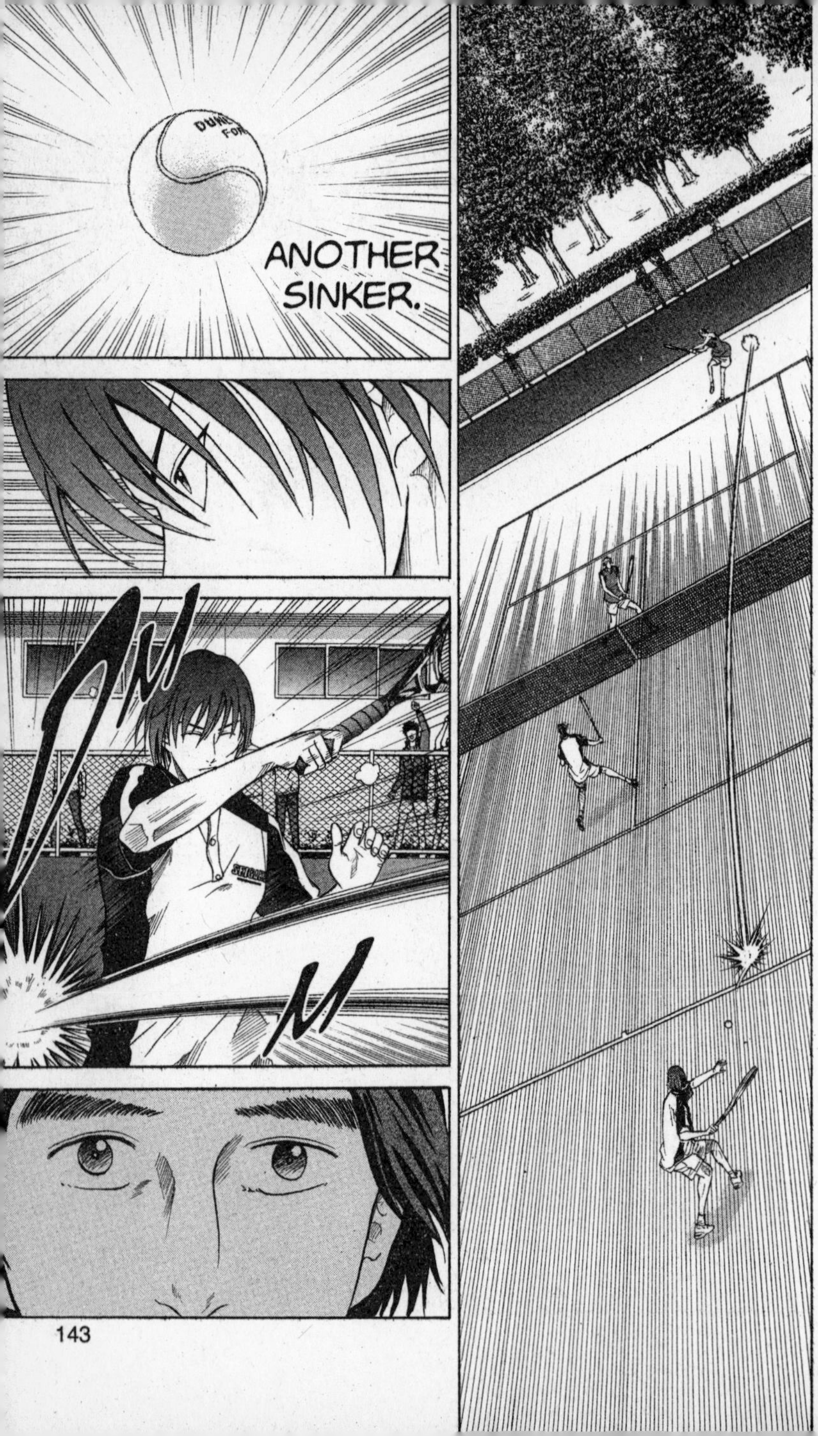
ANOTHER SINKER.
VM
M

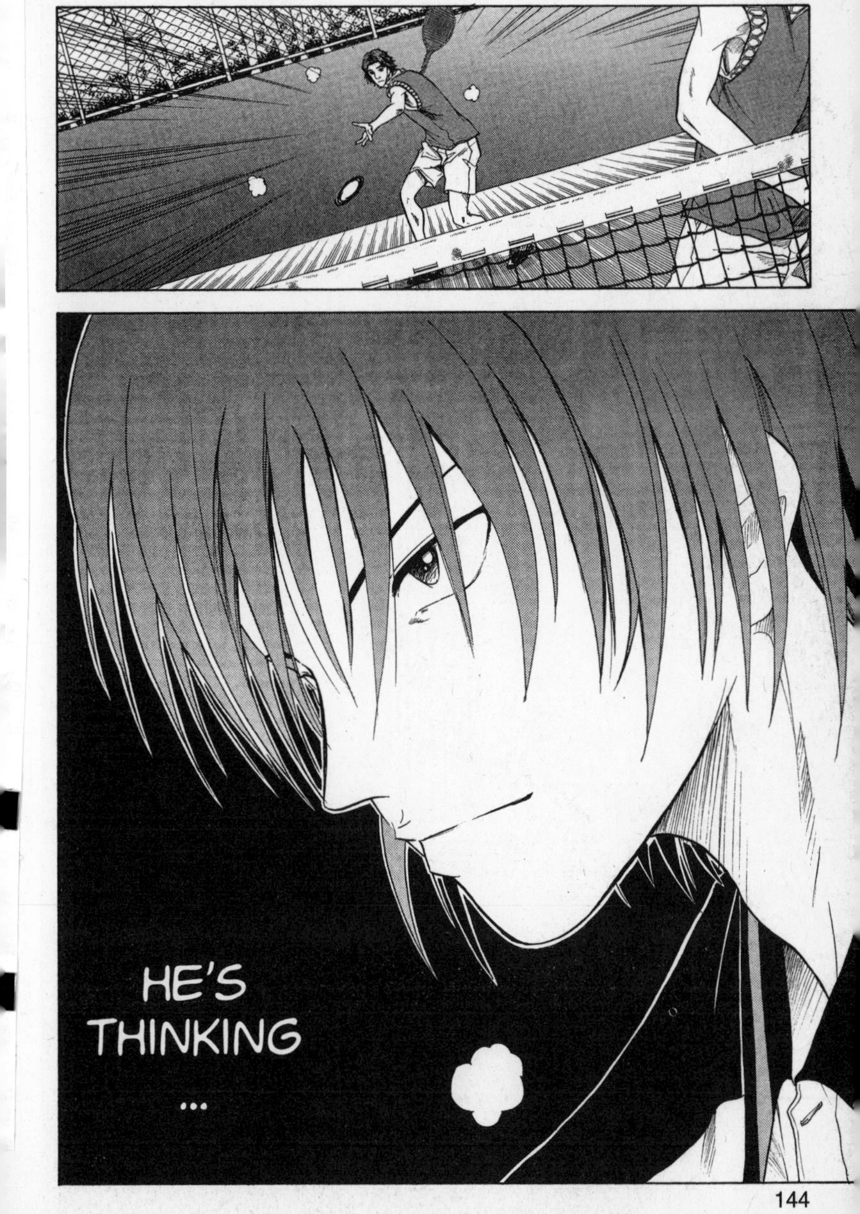
HE'S THINKING
...

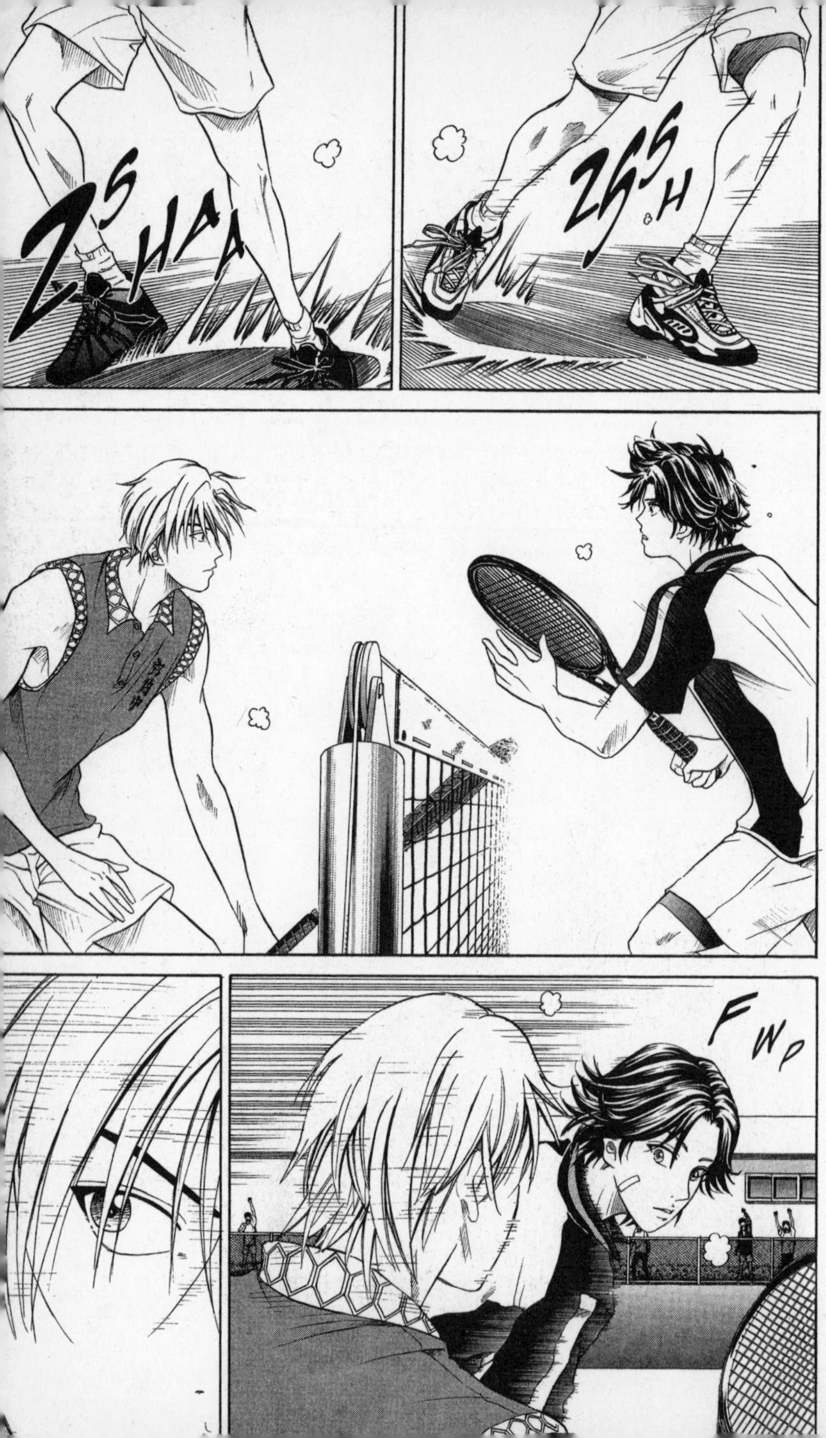
ZSSH
ZSHAA
FWP

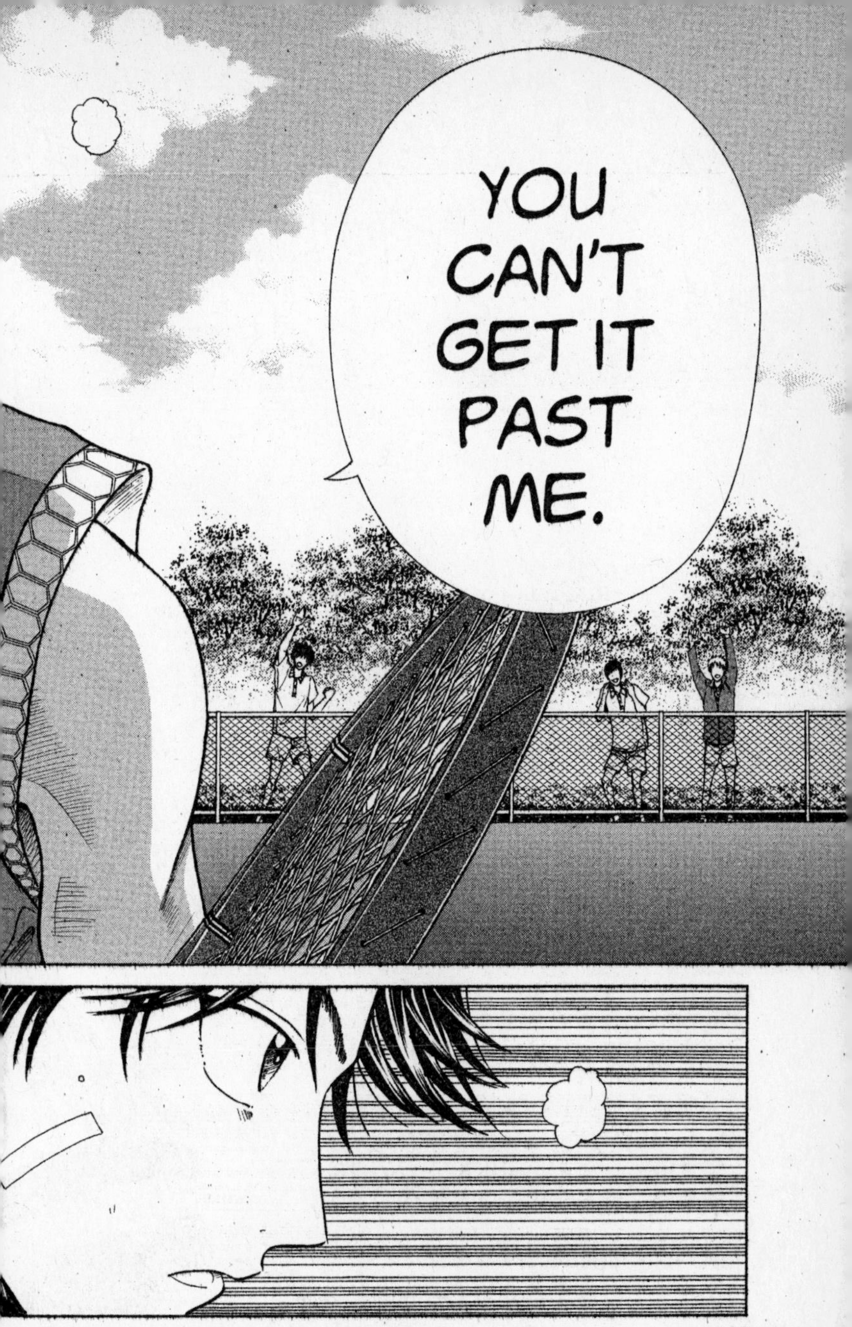
YOU CAN'T GET IT PAST ME.

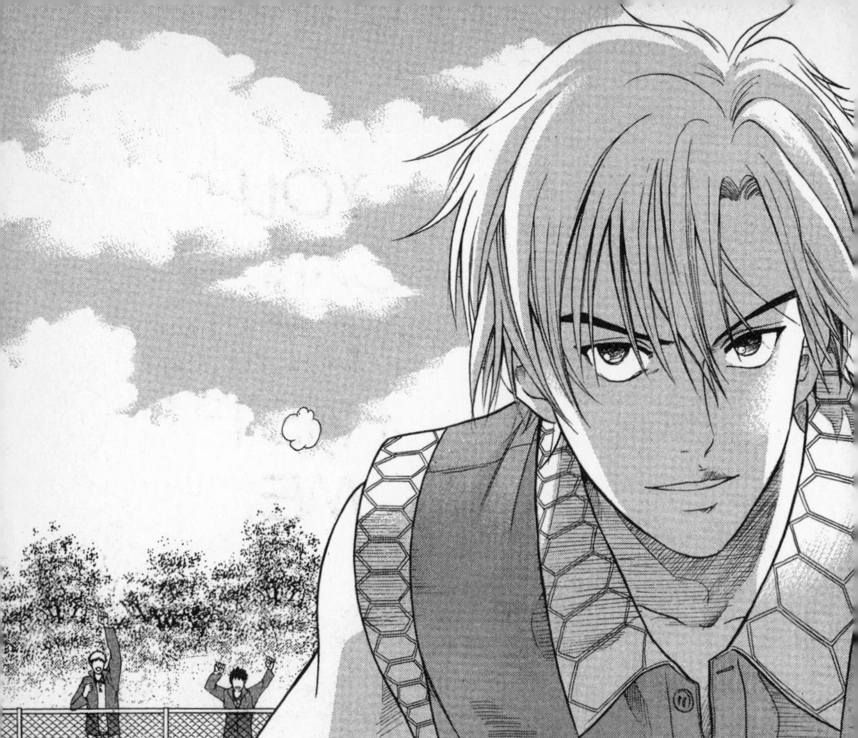
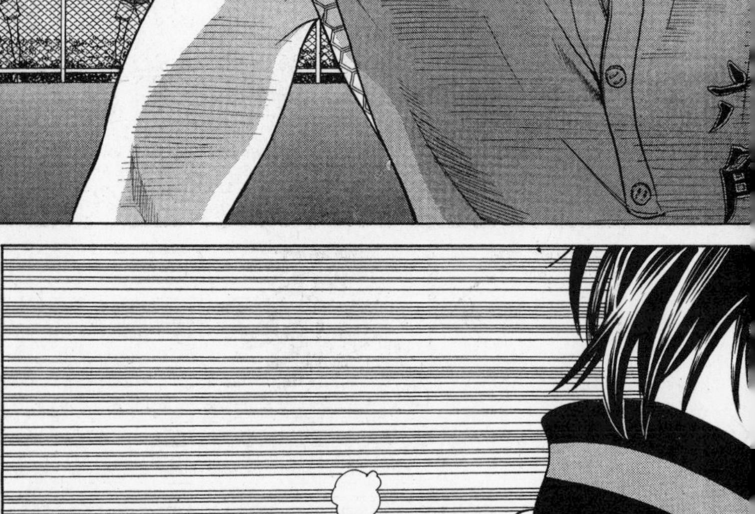

テニスの王子様

THE PRINCE OF TENNIS™

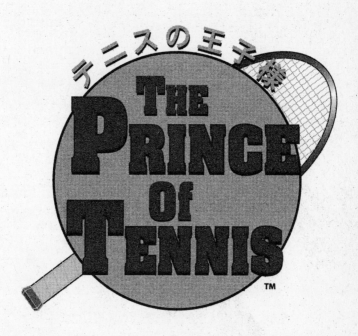

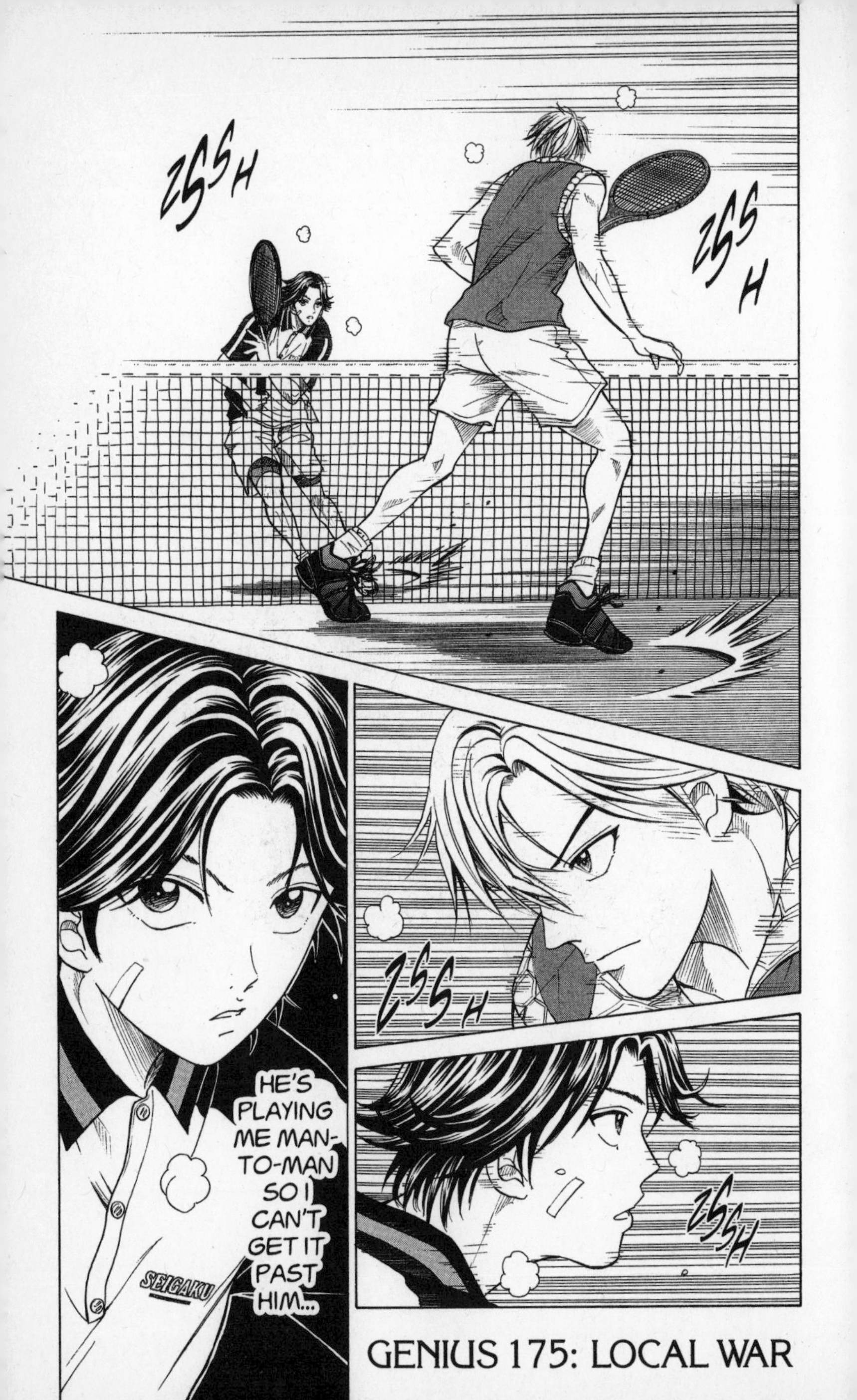
ZSSH
ZSSH
ZSSH
HE'S PLAYING ME MAN-TO-MAN SO I CAN'T GET IT PAST HIM...
SEIGAKU
ZSSH

# GENIUS 175: LOCAL WAR

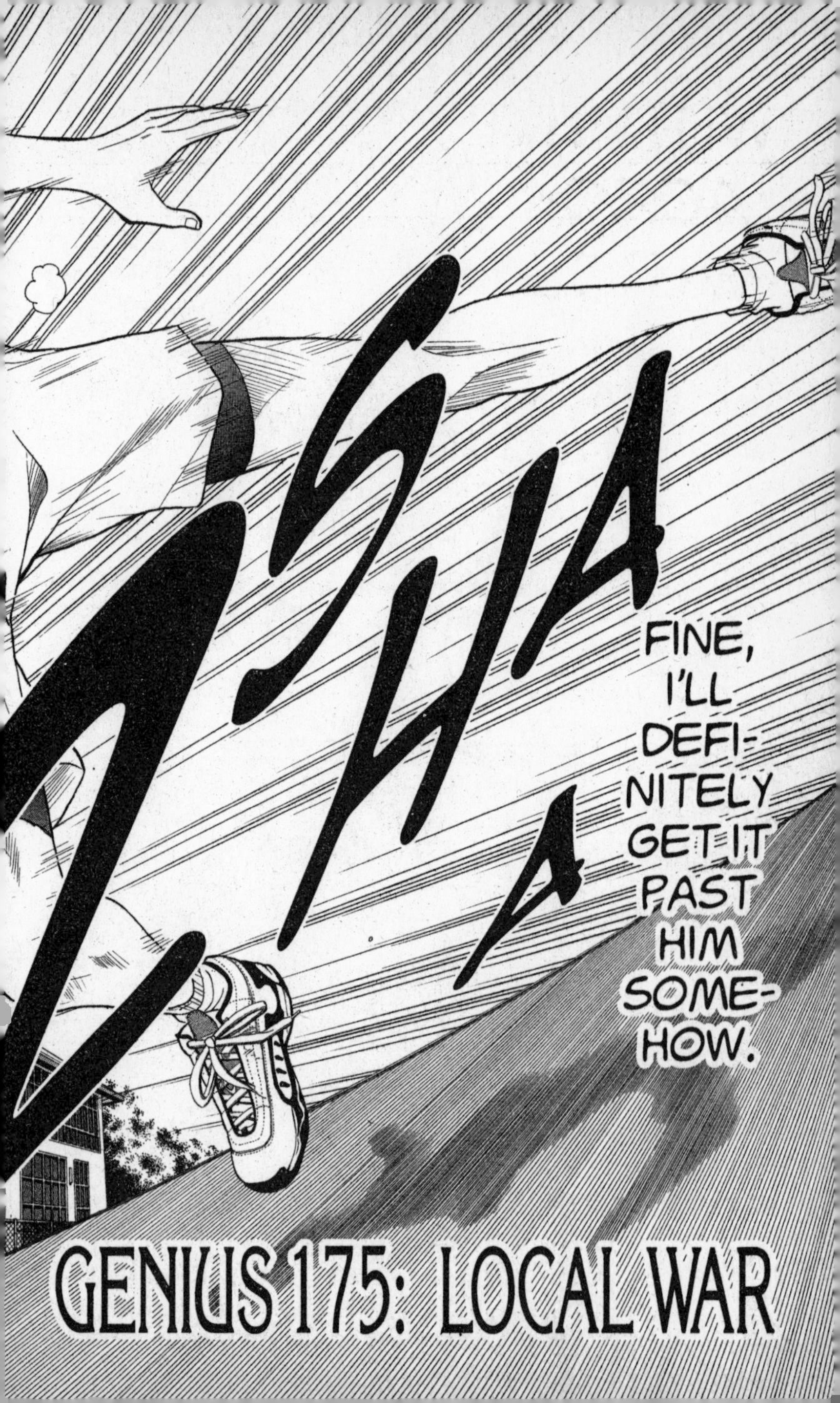
FINE, I'LL DEFI- NITELY GET IT PAST HIM SOME- HOW.

# GENIUS 175: LOCAL WAR

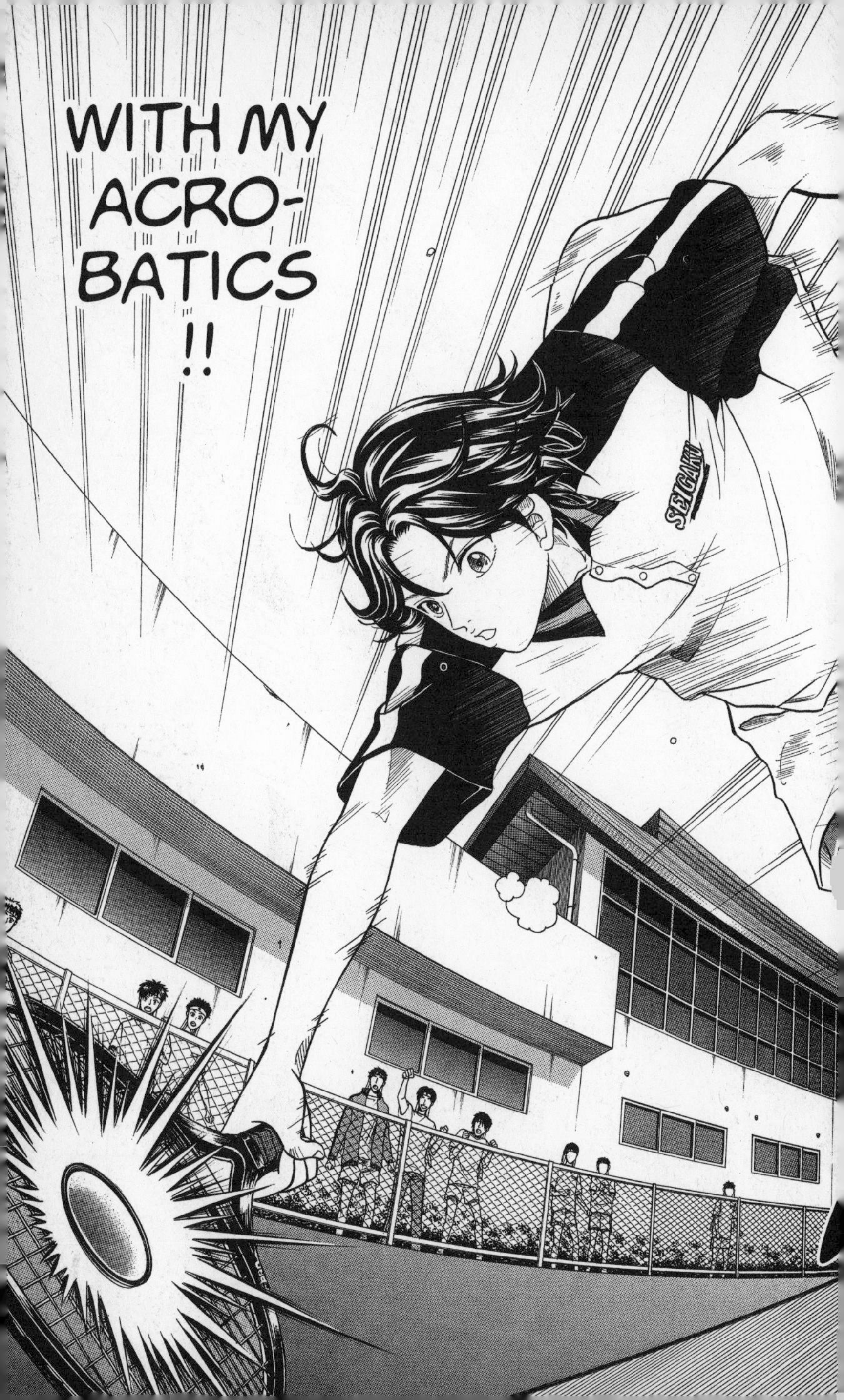
WITH MY ACRO-BATICS !!
SEIGAKU

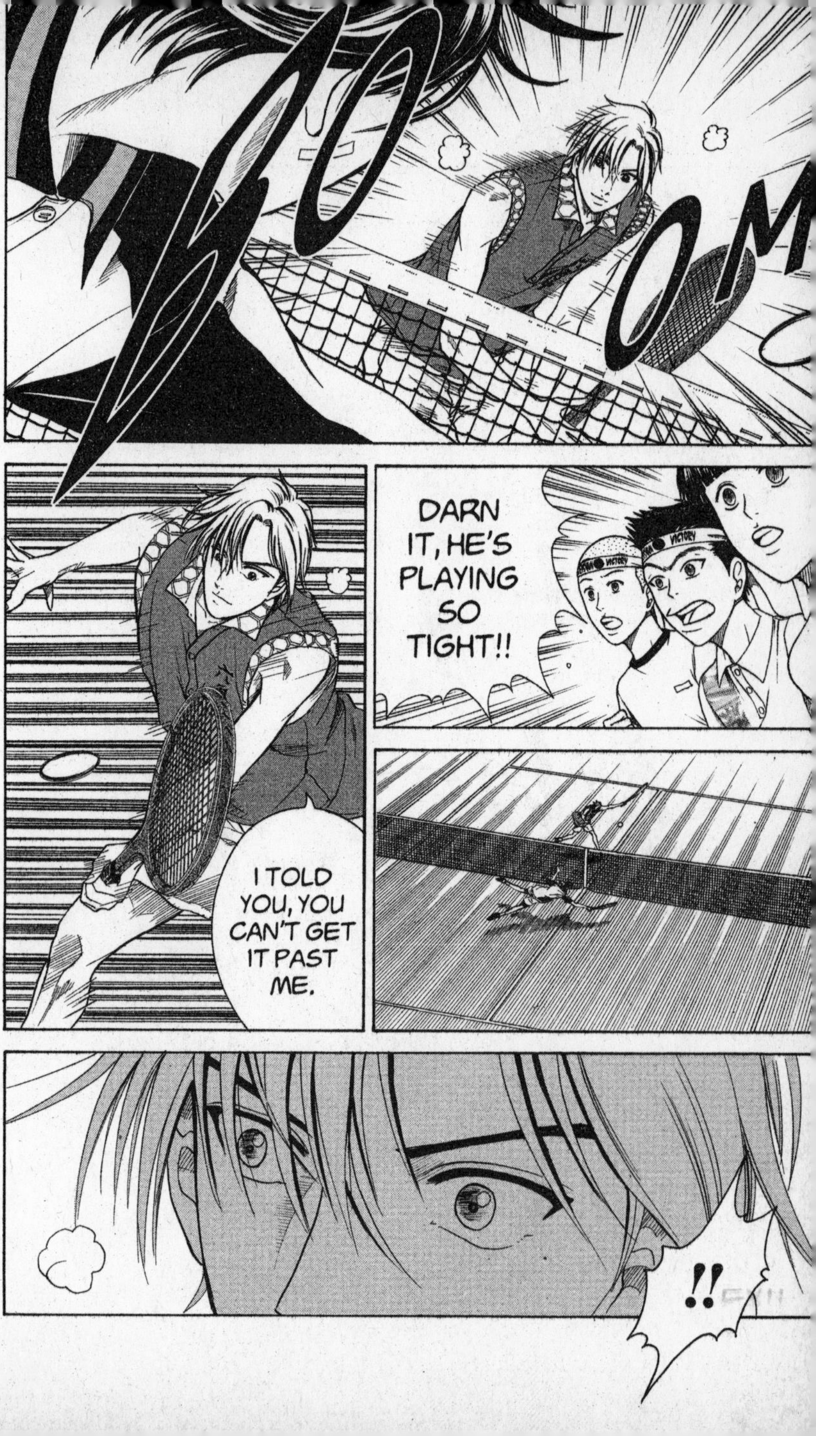
VOOM
DARN IT, HE'S PLAYING SO TIGHT!!
I TOLD YOU, YOU CAN'T GET IT PAST ME.
!!

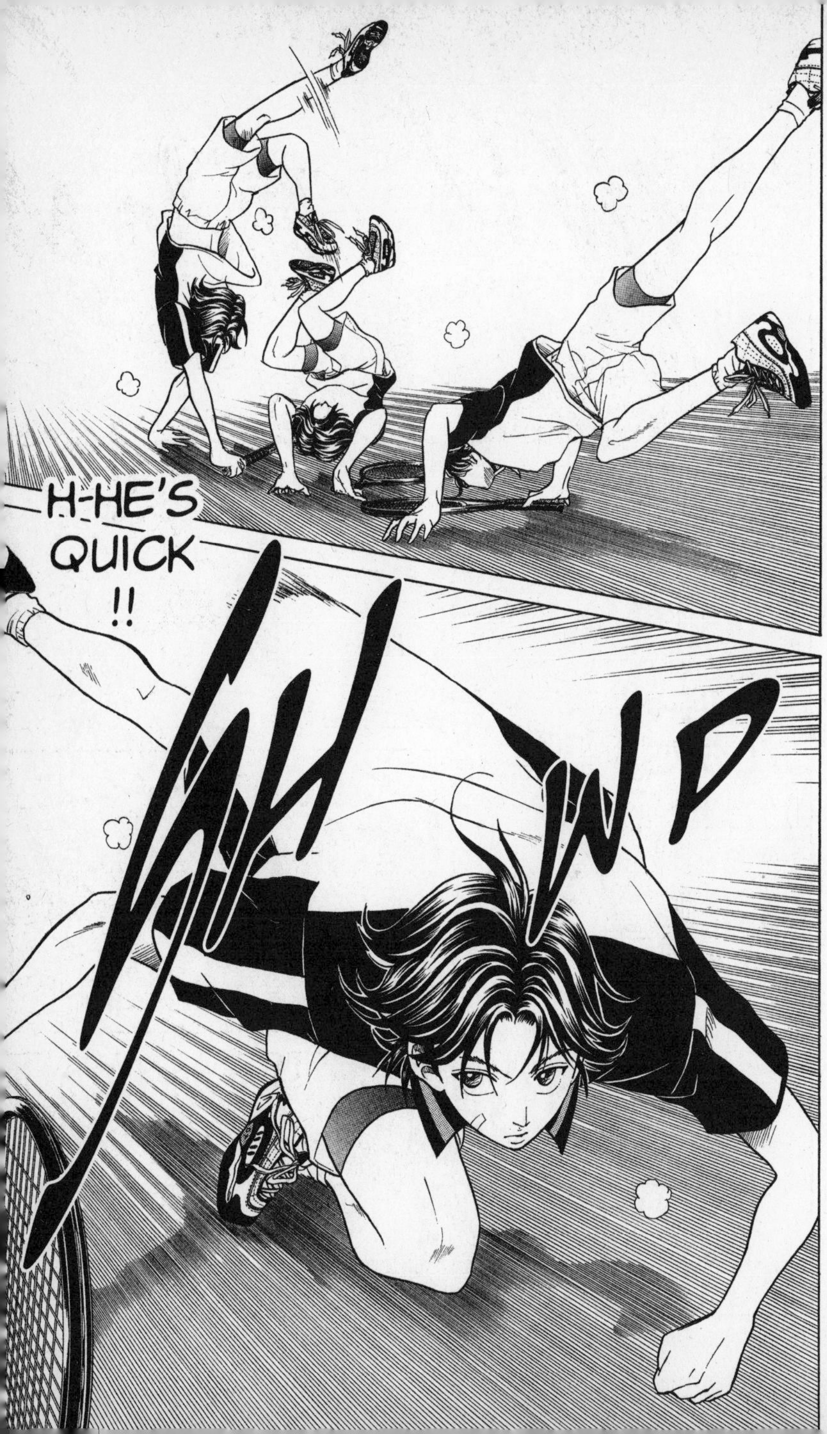
H-HE'S QUICK !!

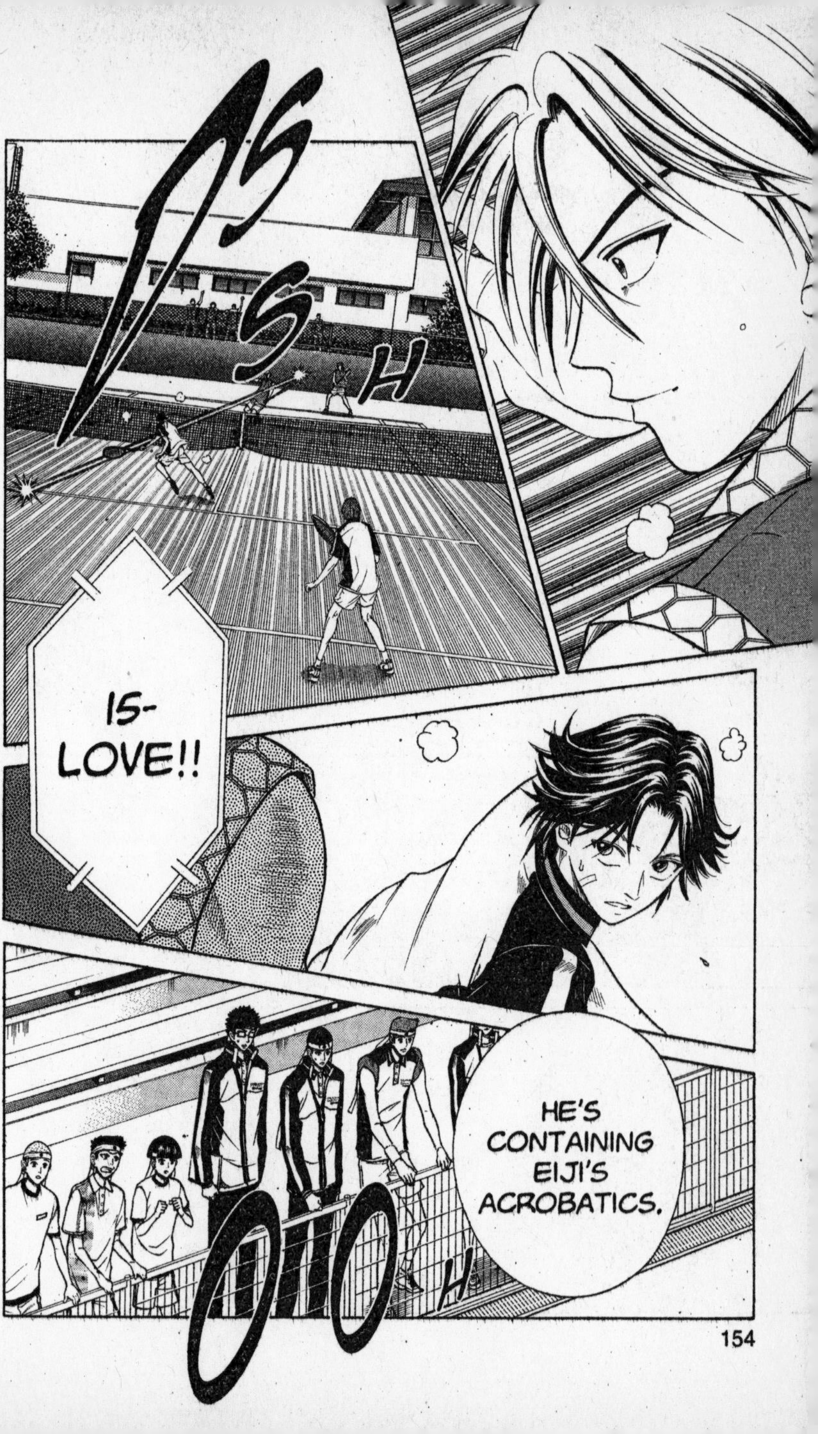
SHH
15-LOVE!!
HE'S CONTAINING EIJI'S ACROBATICS.
CLINCH

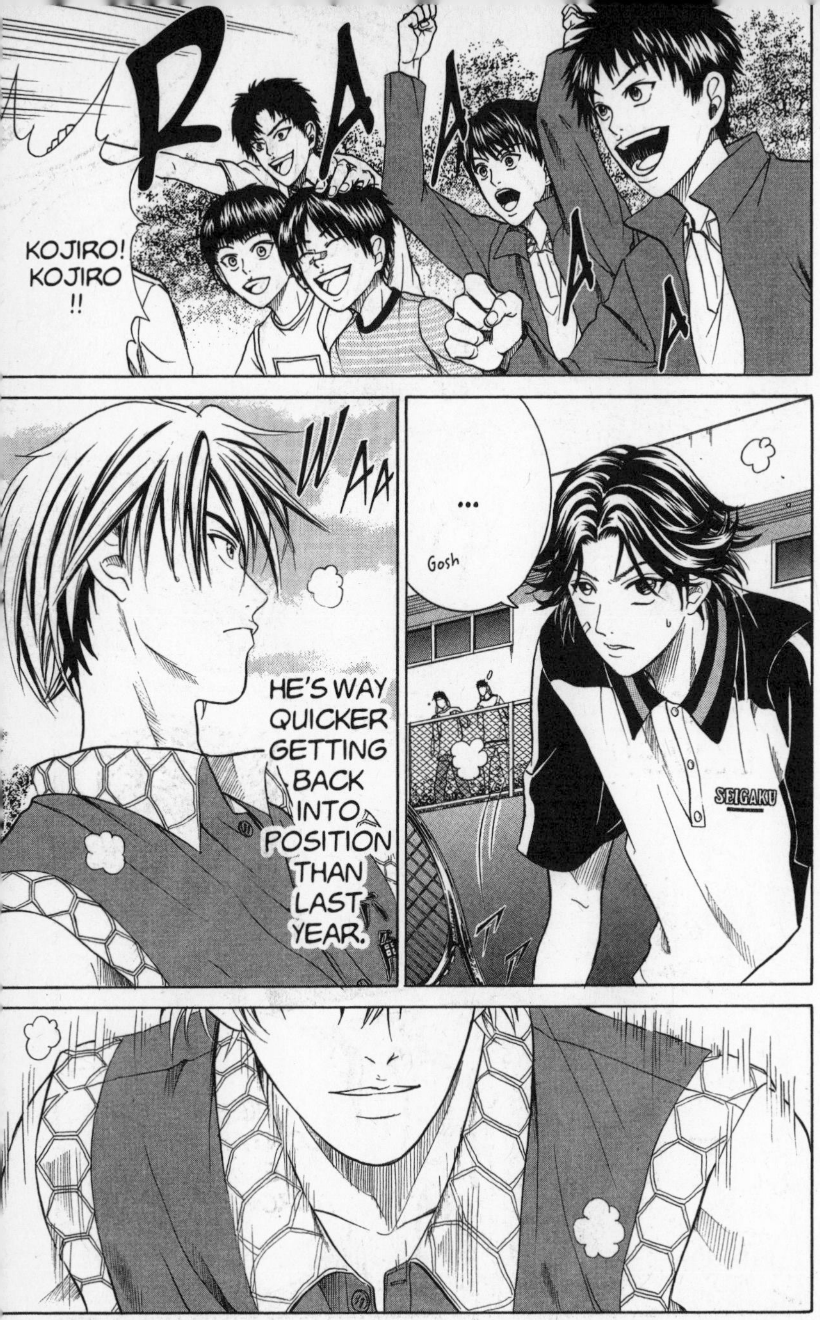
RAAAAA
KOJIRO! KOJIRO !!
...
Gosh
WAA
HE'S WAY QUICKER GETTING BACK INTO POSITION THAN LAST YEAR.
SEIGAKU

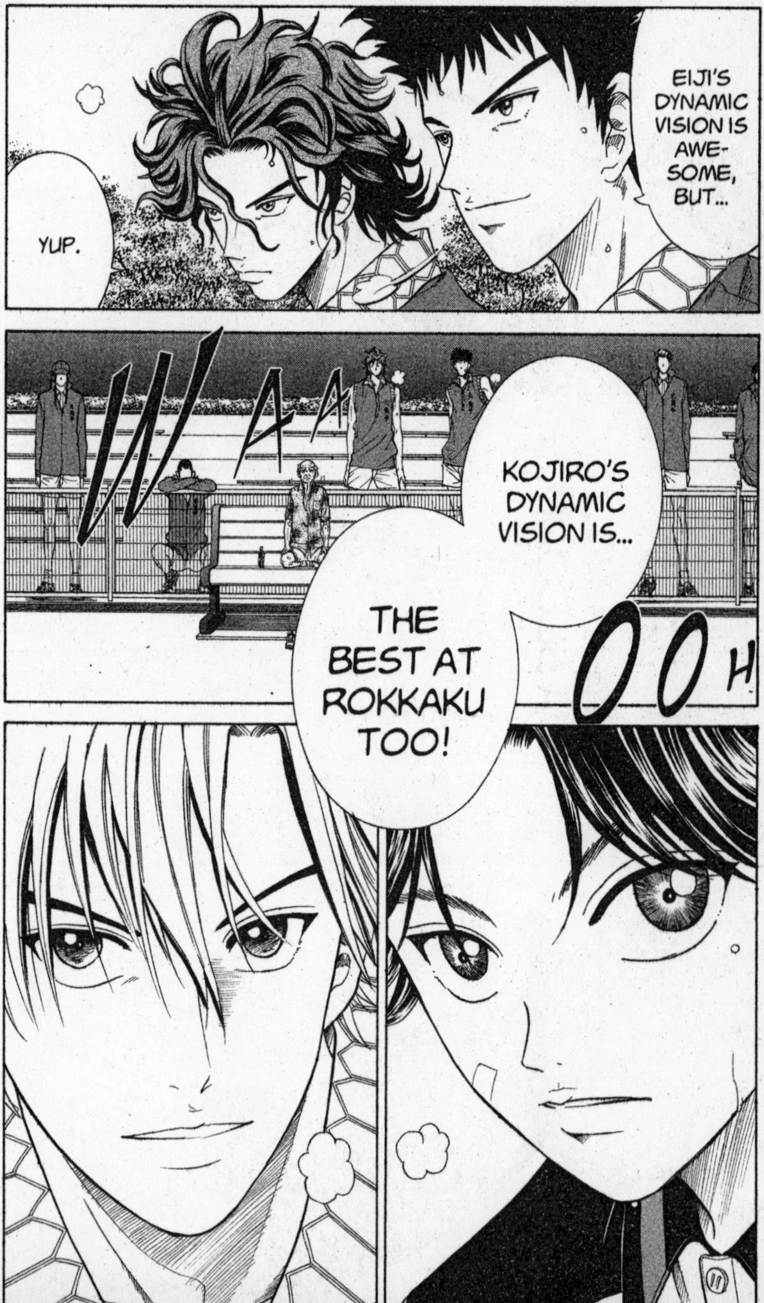
EIJI'S DYNAMIC VISION IS AWE-SOME, BUT...
YUP.
KOJIRO'S DYNAMIC VISION IS...
THE BEST AT ROKKAKU TOO!
WAAOOH

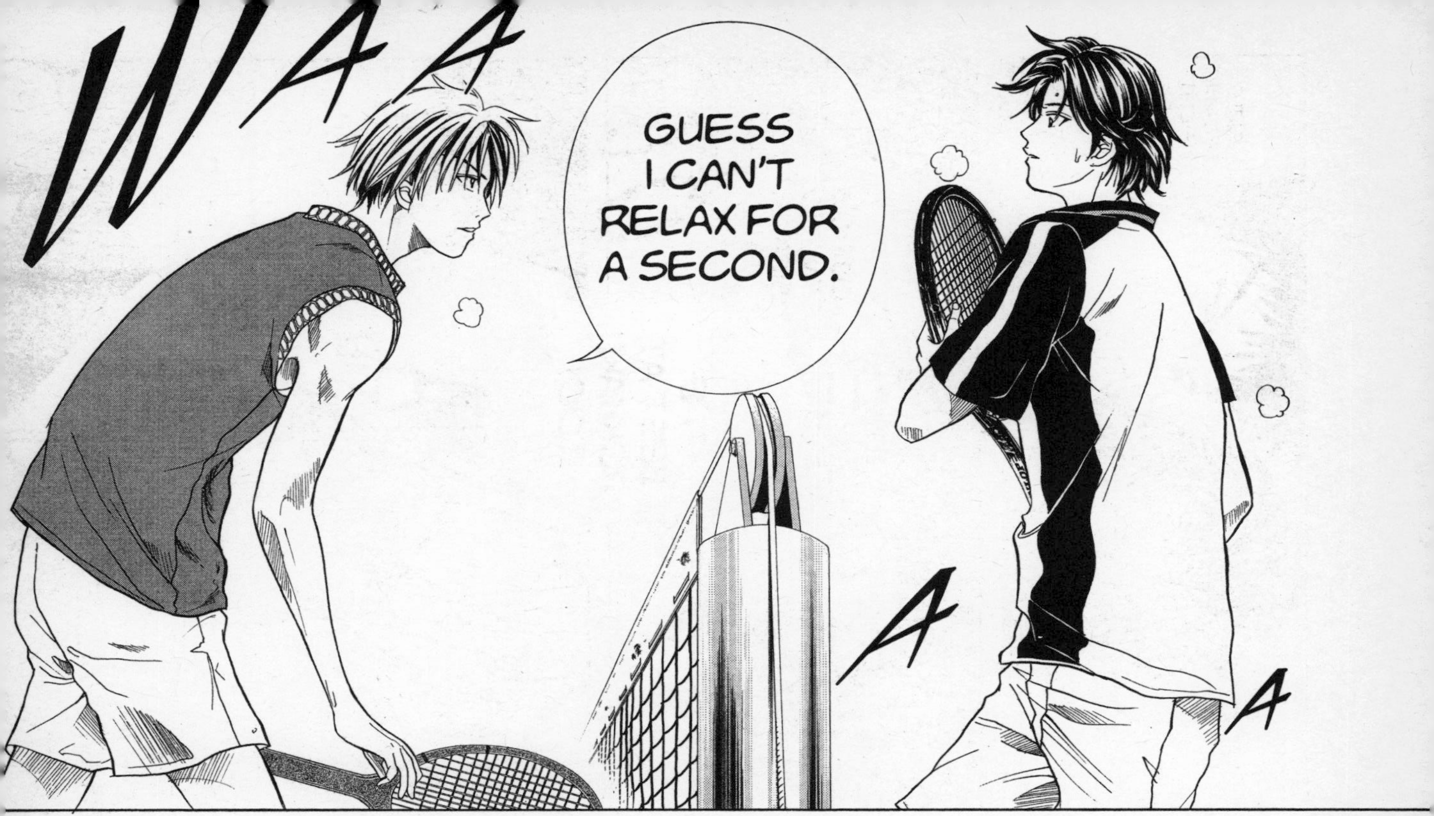

GUESS I CAN'T RELAX FOR A SECOND.
WAAAA

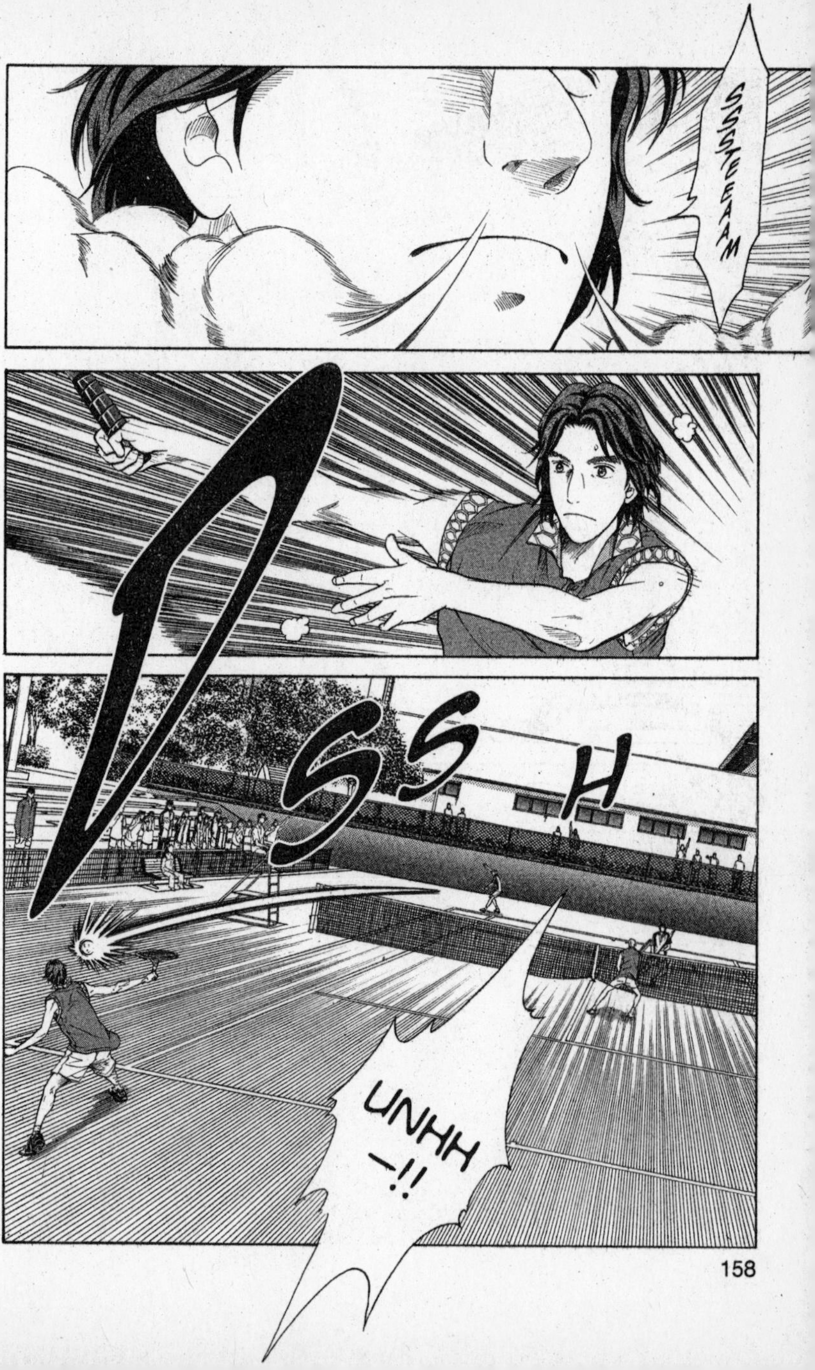
SSSTEAAM
VSSH
UNHH
—!!

READ THIS WAY

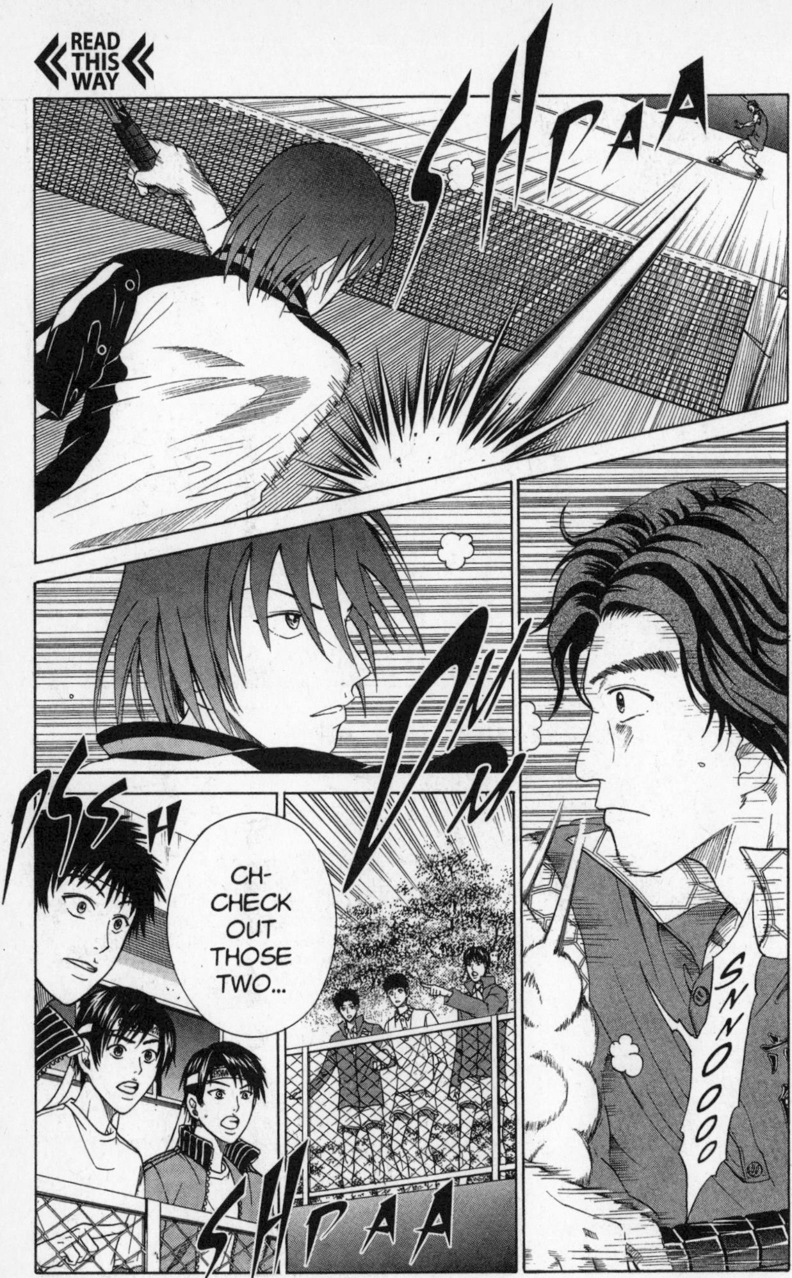
SHRAA
SNNOOOOO
PSSH
CH-CHECK OUT THOSE TWO...
SHRAA

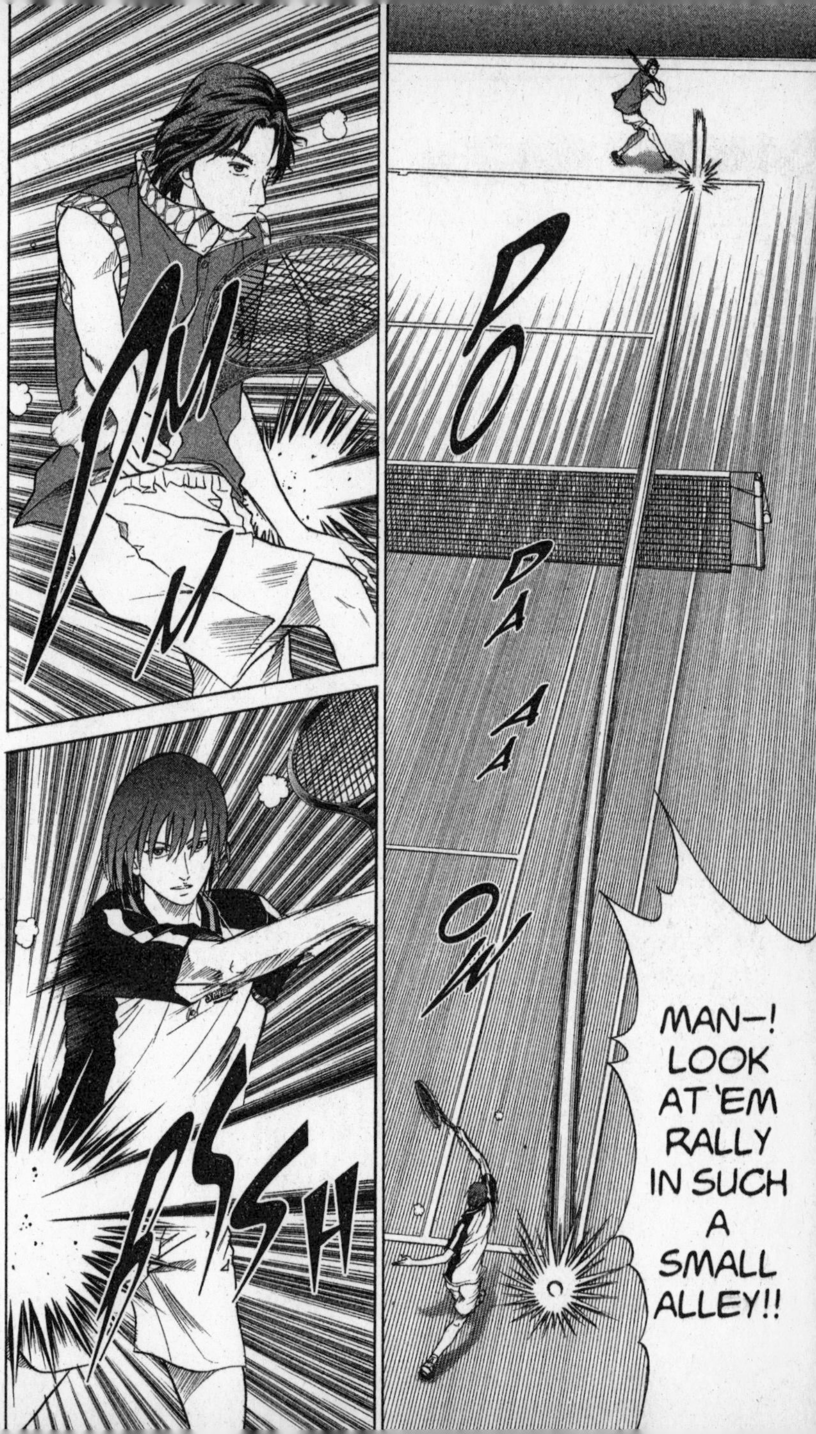
MAN-! LOOK AT 'EM RALLY IN SUCH A SMALL ALLEY!!
KSSH

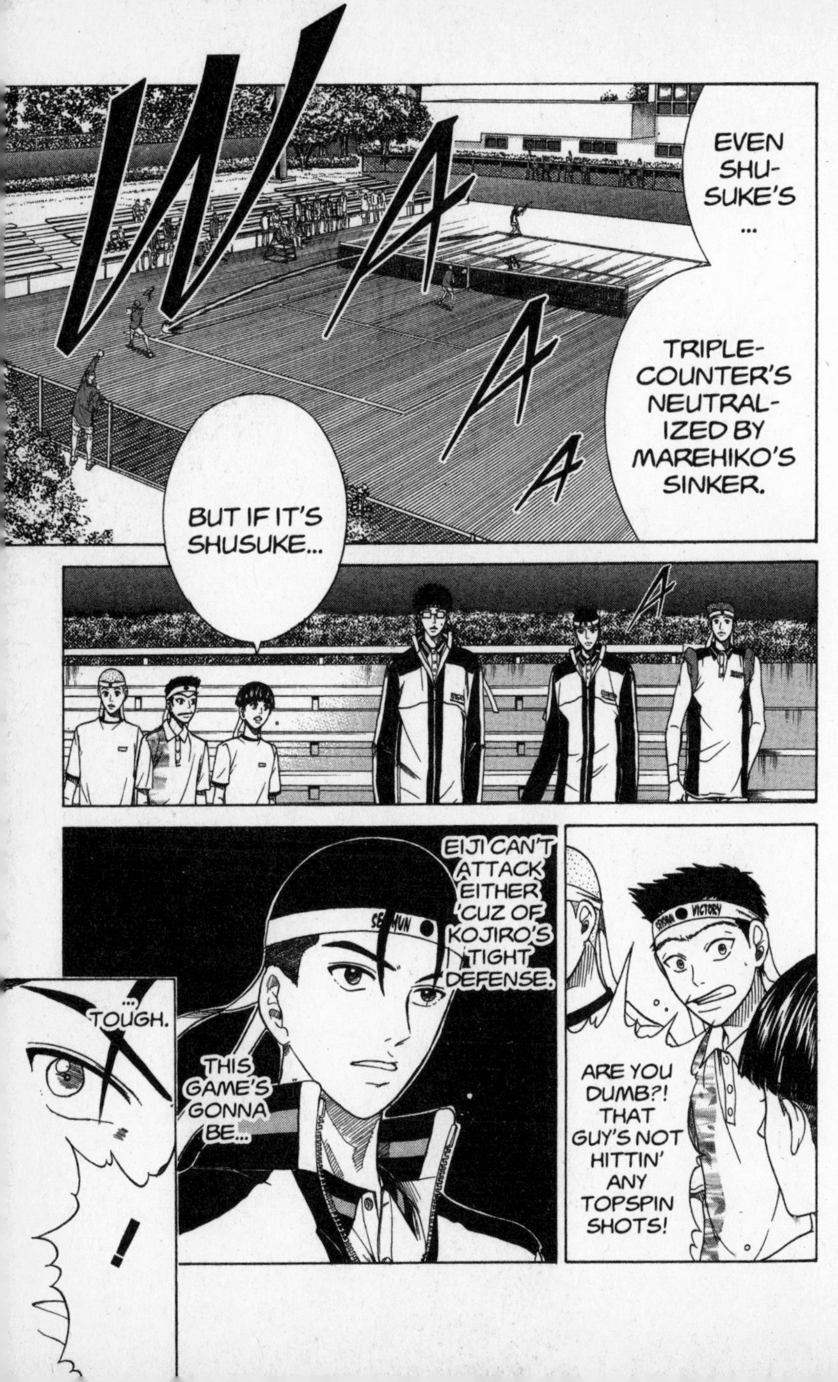
WAAAA
EVEN SHUSUKE'S ...
TRIPLE-COUNTER'S NEUTRAL-IZED BY MAREHIKO'S SINKER.
BUT IF IT'S SHUSUKE...
A
ARE YOU DUMB?! THAT GUY'S NOT HITTIN' ANY TOPSPIN SHOTS!
EIJI CAN'T ATTACK EITHER 'CUZ OF KOJIRO'S TIGHT DEFENSE.
THIS GAME'S GONNA BE...
... TOUGH.
!

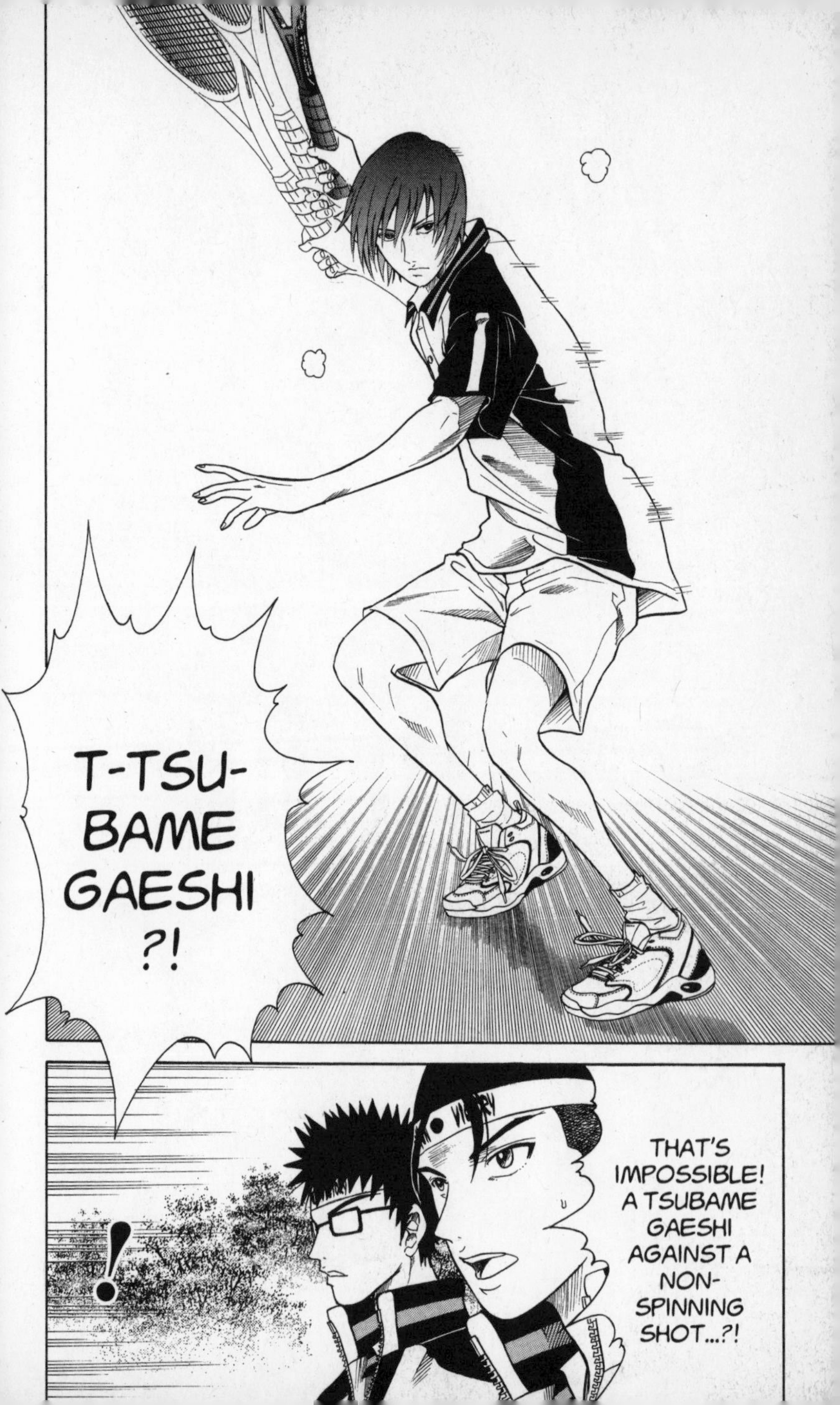
T-TSU-BAME GAESHI ?!
THAT'S IMPOSSIBLE! A TSUBAME GAESHI AGAINST A NON-SPINNING SHOT...?!
!

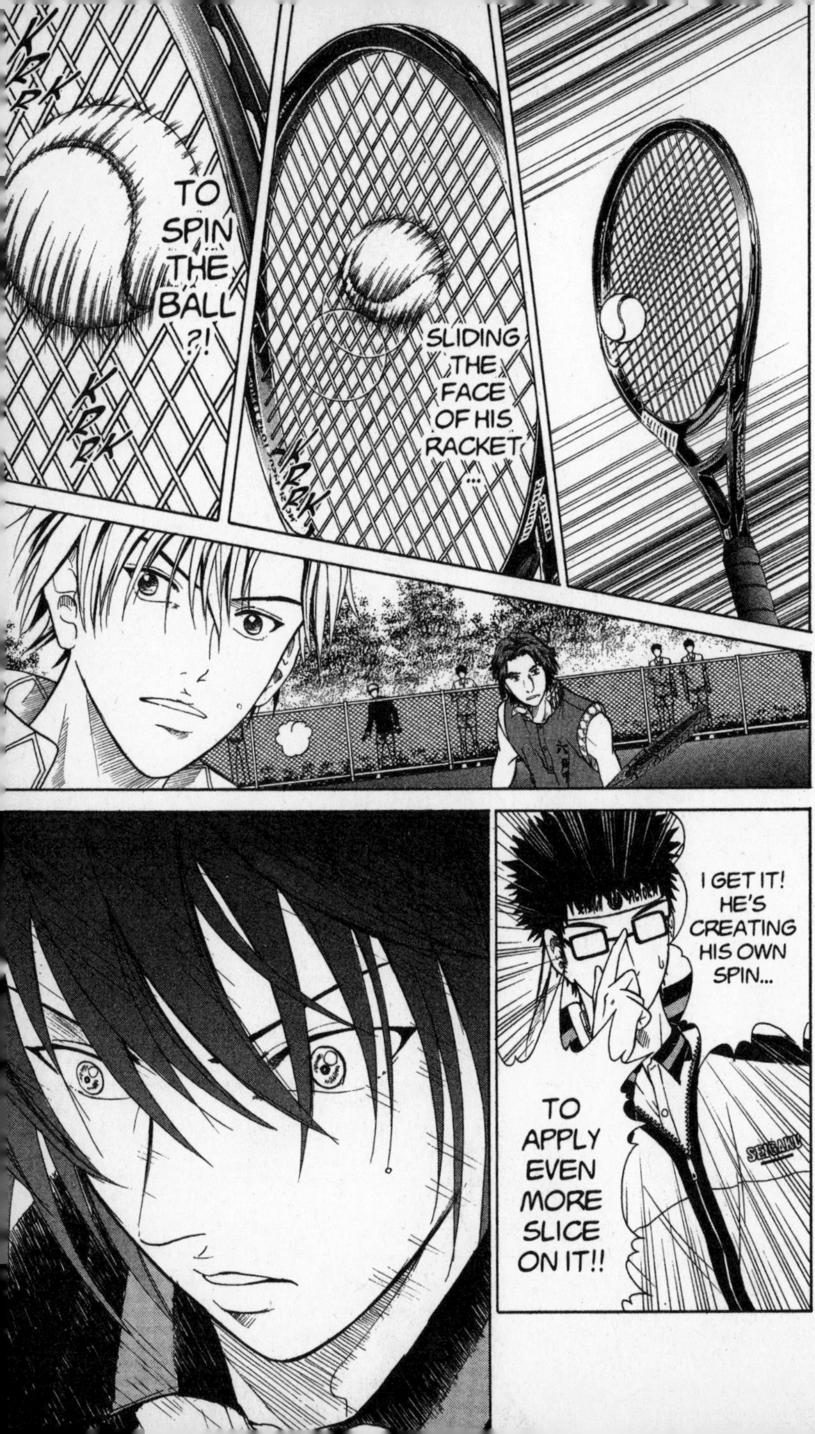
SLIDING THE FACE OF HIS RACKET...
KRRK
TO SPIN THE BALL?!
KRRK
KRRK
I GET IT! HE'S CREATING HIS OWN SPIN...
TO APPLY EVEN MORE SLICE ON IT!!
SEIGAKU

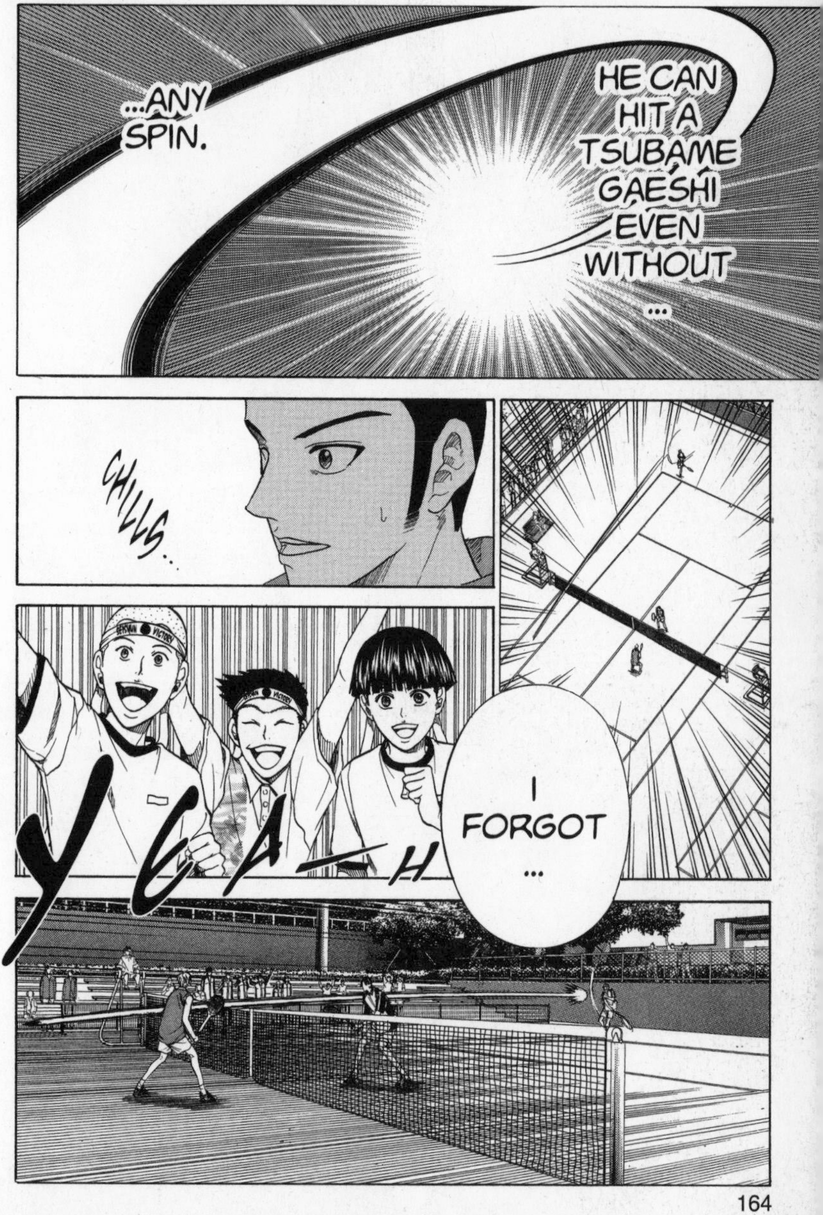
HE CAN HIT A TSUBAME GAESHI EVEN WITHOUT ...
...ANY SPIN.
CHILLS...
I FORGOT ...
YEA—H

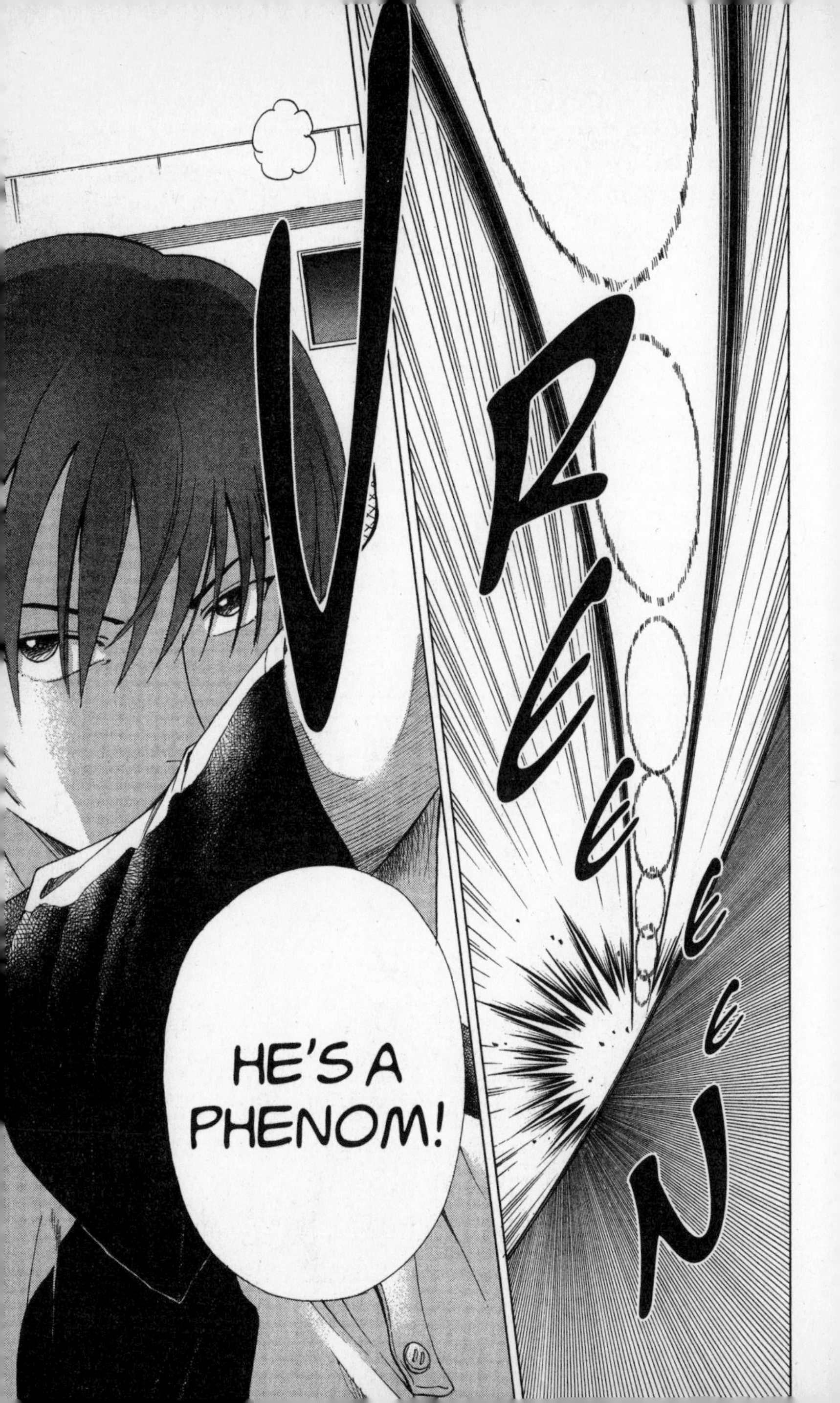
HE'S A PHENOM!

Thank you for reading *The Prince of Tennis*, volume 20.

Congratulations—we finally reached volume 20!! I'm so happy and thankful we've been able to bring *The Prince of Tennis* this far. Thank you!! And as a way to express my appreciation, let's do it!! Volume 20.5!! Fanbook number 2. Yay—Yay—!!

To tell you the truth, I was determined not to put out a second Fanbook. I put together 10.5 with that in mind. I wanted to make something you'd be glad you bought. I changed things around just before the deadline and included a story, drew a new color story. I put in a lot of hard work. It was the first project brought to me after my then-editor told me *The Prince of Tennis* would never become an anime, so I remember working feverishly on it. And when it became a huge success, I'm sure the Fanbook fad it created in WJ is fresh in your minds (laugh).

Anyway, warm messages like "I can't wait for volume 20.5", "Please put out 20.5", "Please make a Fanbook centered around the other schools," never stopped over the past two years. And you all waited patiently. Give yourselves a round of applause—!!

I hate betraying your hopes. We are currently making Fanbook 20.5 that's centered around the other schools. (It'll go on sale in December simultaneously with volume 20.) I hope all of you participate in the projects. We'll begin taking requests from the Weekly Shonen Jump going on sale in September. Now that I've decided to do it, I'll give it everything I have. Let's make another Fanbook together!!

Please continue supporting *The Prince of Tennis* and Ryoma. I'll see you next volume.

Send fan letters to: The Prince of Tennis, Takeshi Konomi c/o VIZ Media, LLC P.O. Box 77010 San Francisco, CA 94107

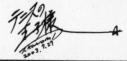

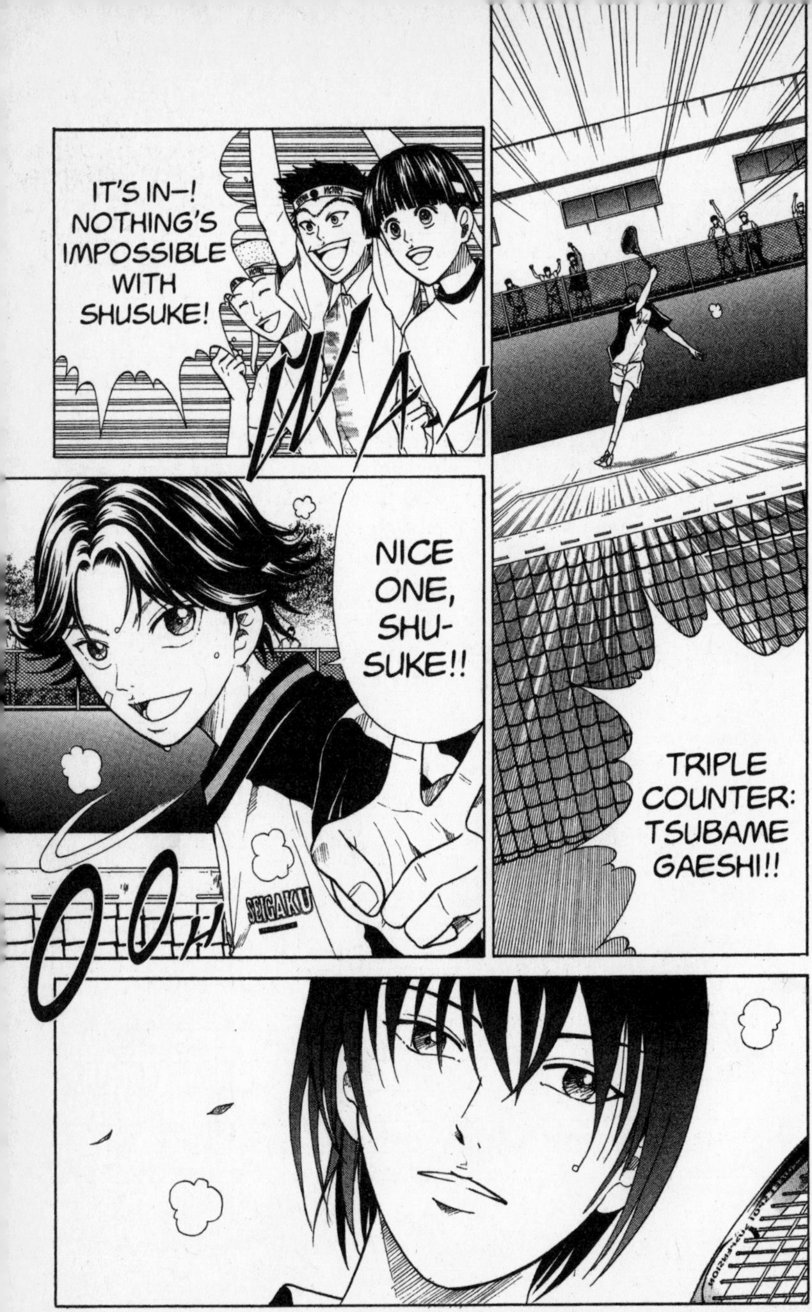
TRIPLE COUNTER: TSUBAME GAESHI!!
IT'S IN—! NOTHING'S IMPOSSIBLE WITH SHUSUKE!
WAA
NICE ONE, SHU-SUKE!!
OOH
SEIGAKU



# GENIUS 176: RETURNED IT...

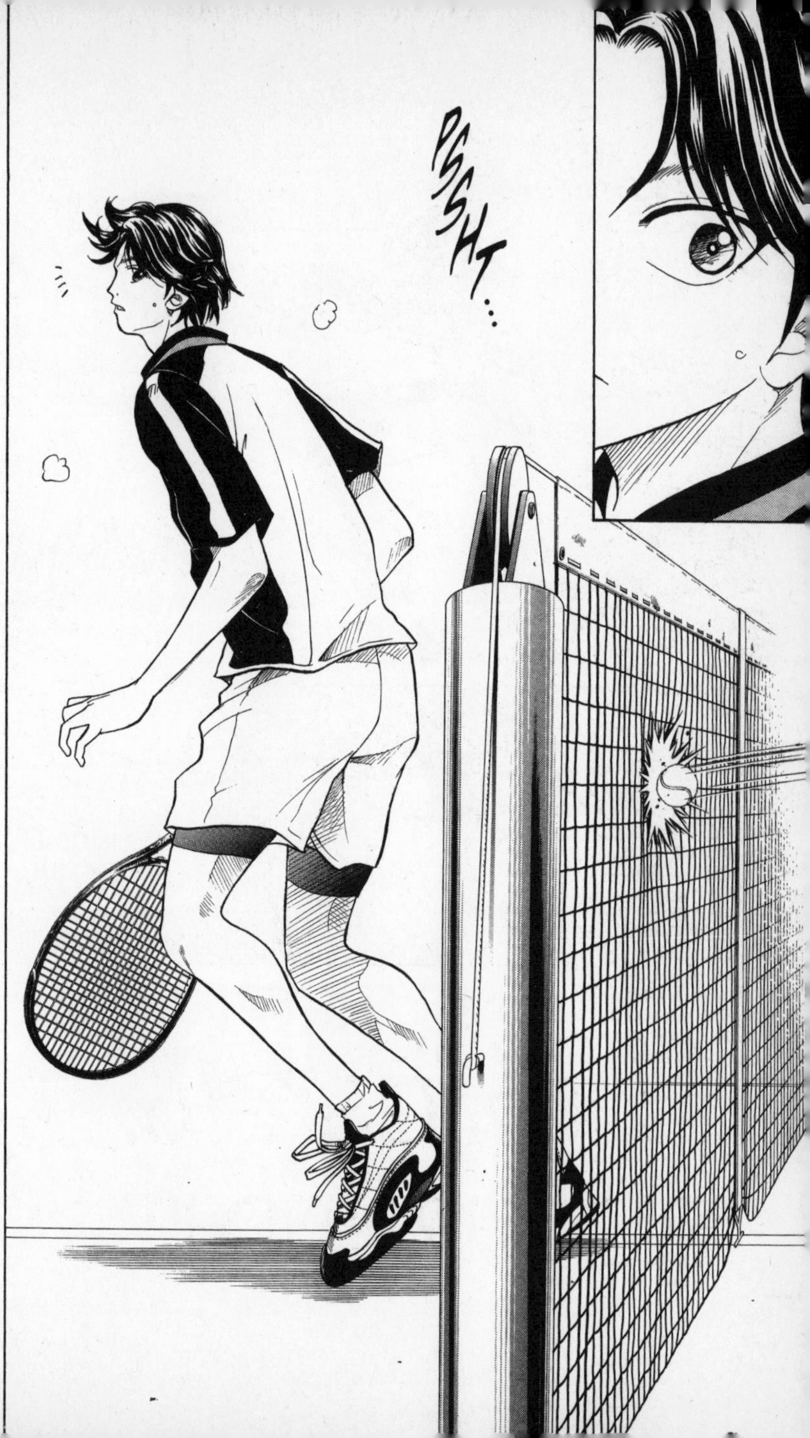
PSSHT...

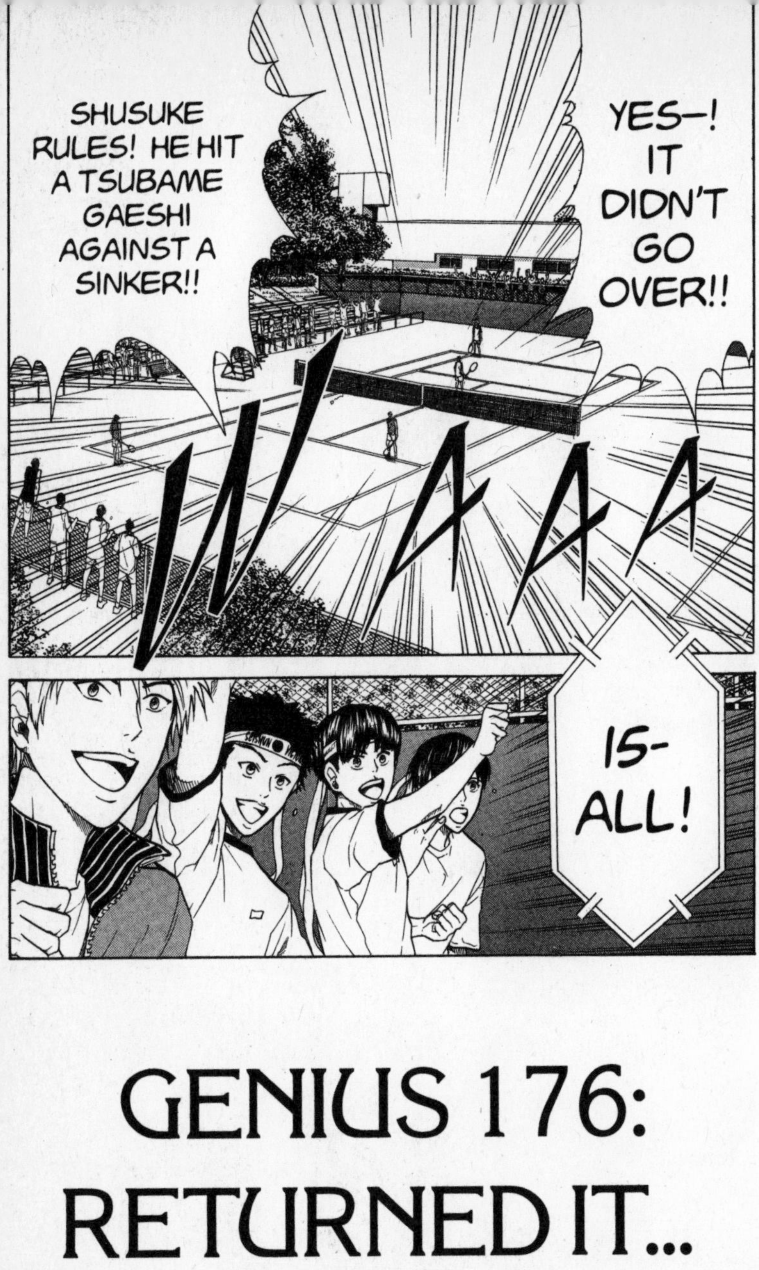
YES—! IT DIDN'T GO OVER!!
SHUSUKE RULES! HE HIT A TSUBAME GAESHI AGAINST A SINKER!!
WAAAA
15-ALL!

# GENIUS 176: RETURNED IT...

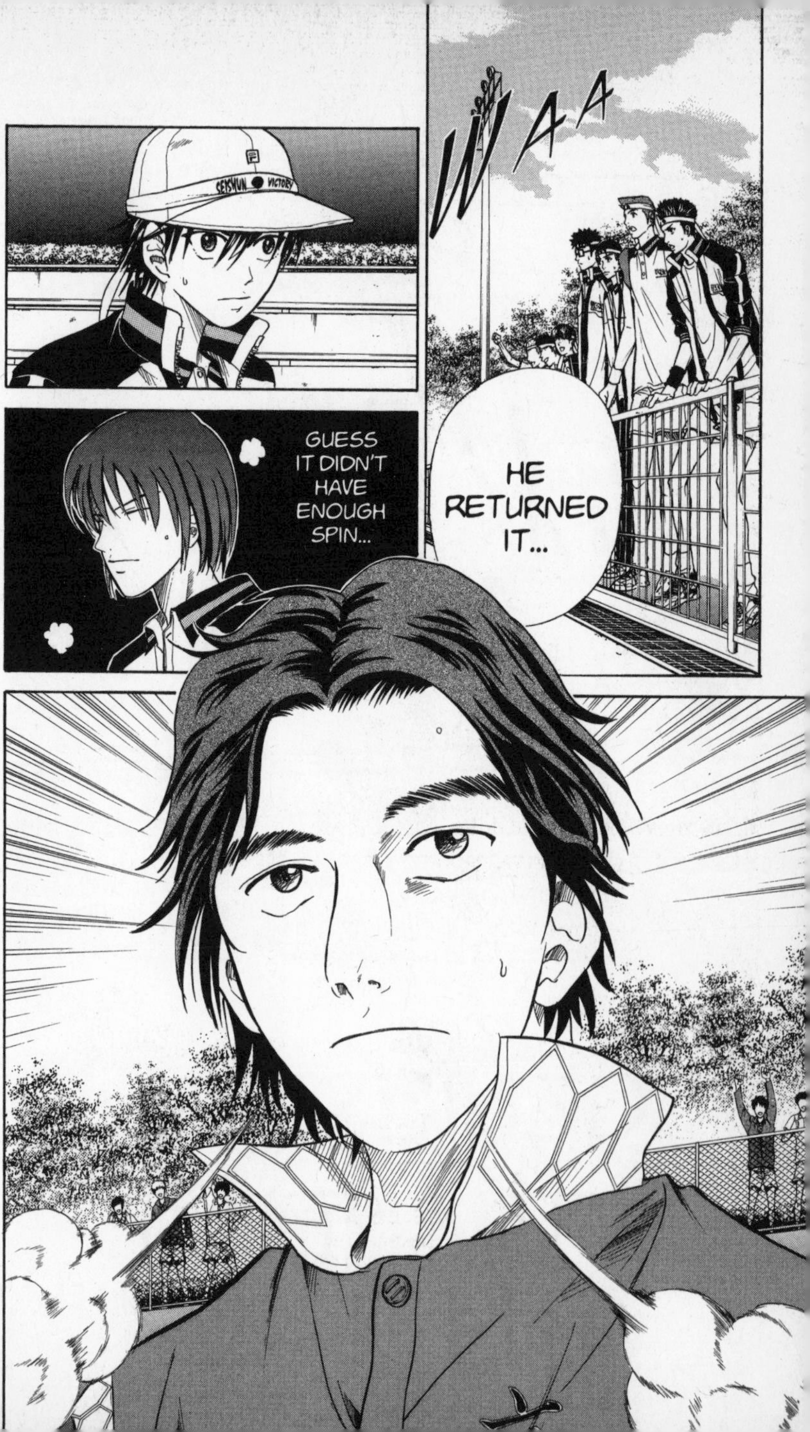
WAA
HE RETURNED IT...
GUESS IT DIDN'T HAVE ENOUGH SPIN...

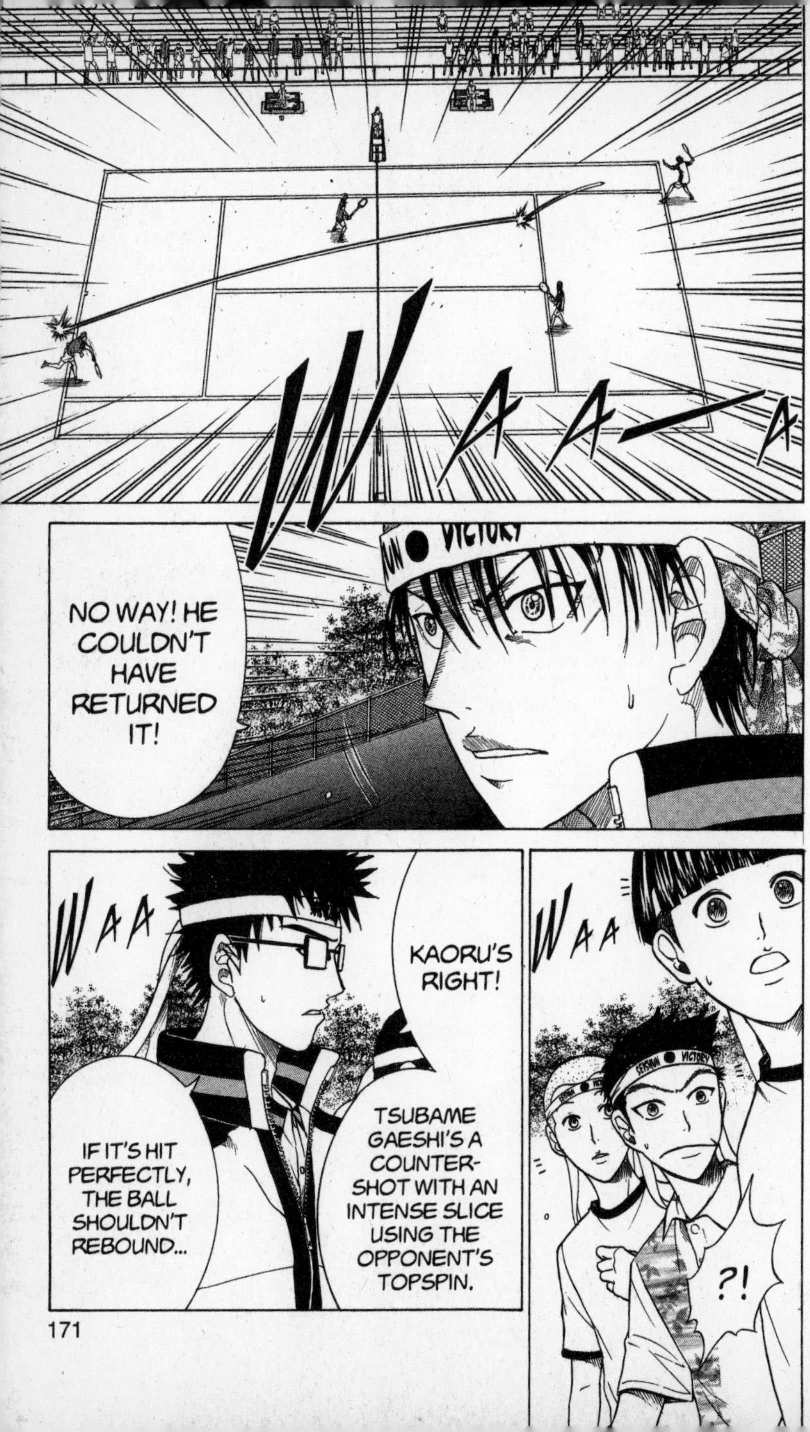
WAA—A
NO WAY! HE COULDN'T HAVE RETURNED IT!
WAA
?!
KAORU'S RIGHT!
WAA
TSUBAME GAESHI'S A COUNTER-SHOT WITH AN INTENSE SLICE USING THE OPPONENT'S TOPSPIN.
IF IT'S HIT PERFECTLY, THE BALL SHOULDN'T REBOUND...

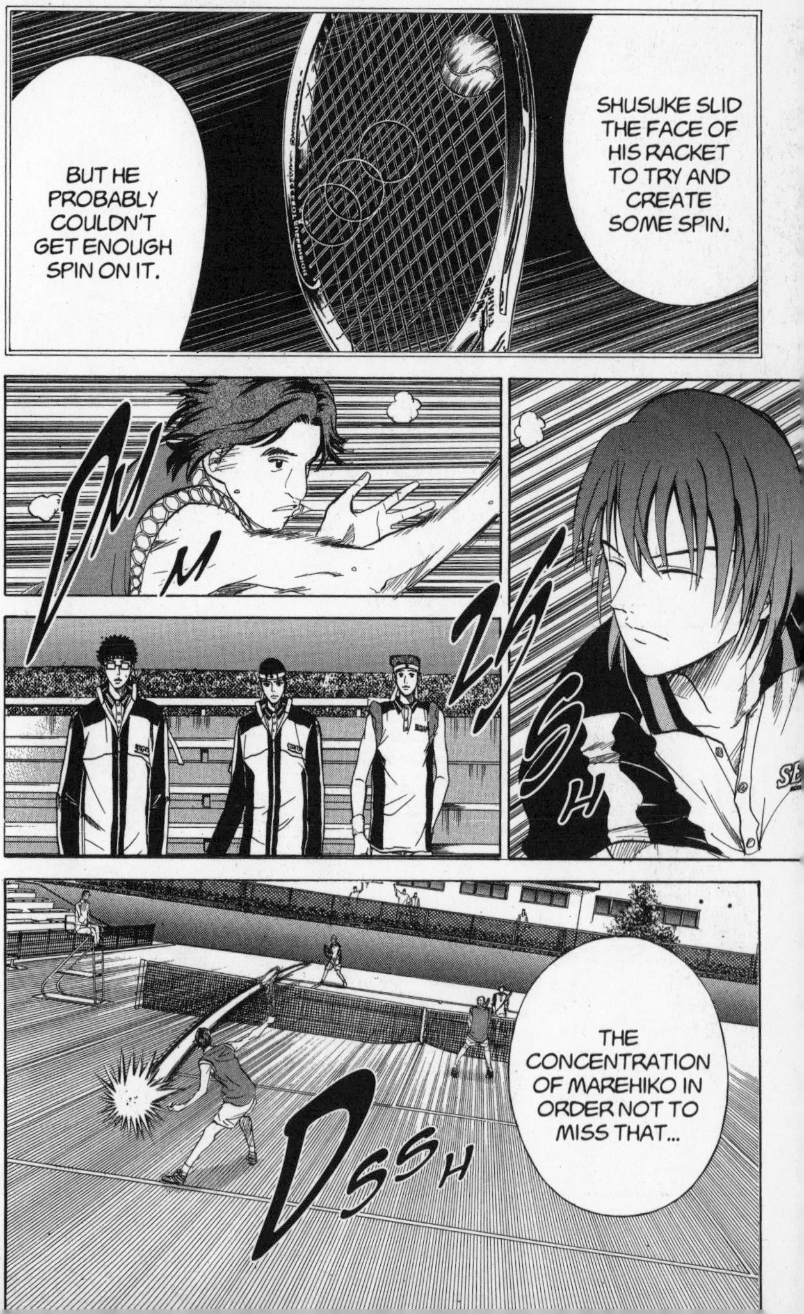
SHUSUKE SLID THE FACE OF HIS RACKET TO TRY AND CREATE SOME SPIN.
BUT HE PROBABLY COULDN'T GET ENOUGH SPIN ON IT.
ZSSH
THE CONCENTRATION OF MAREHIKO IN ORDER NOT TO MISS THAT...
DSSH

READ THIS WAY

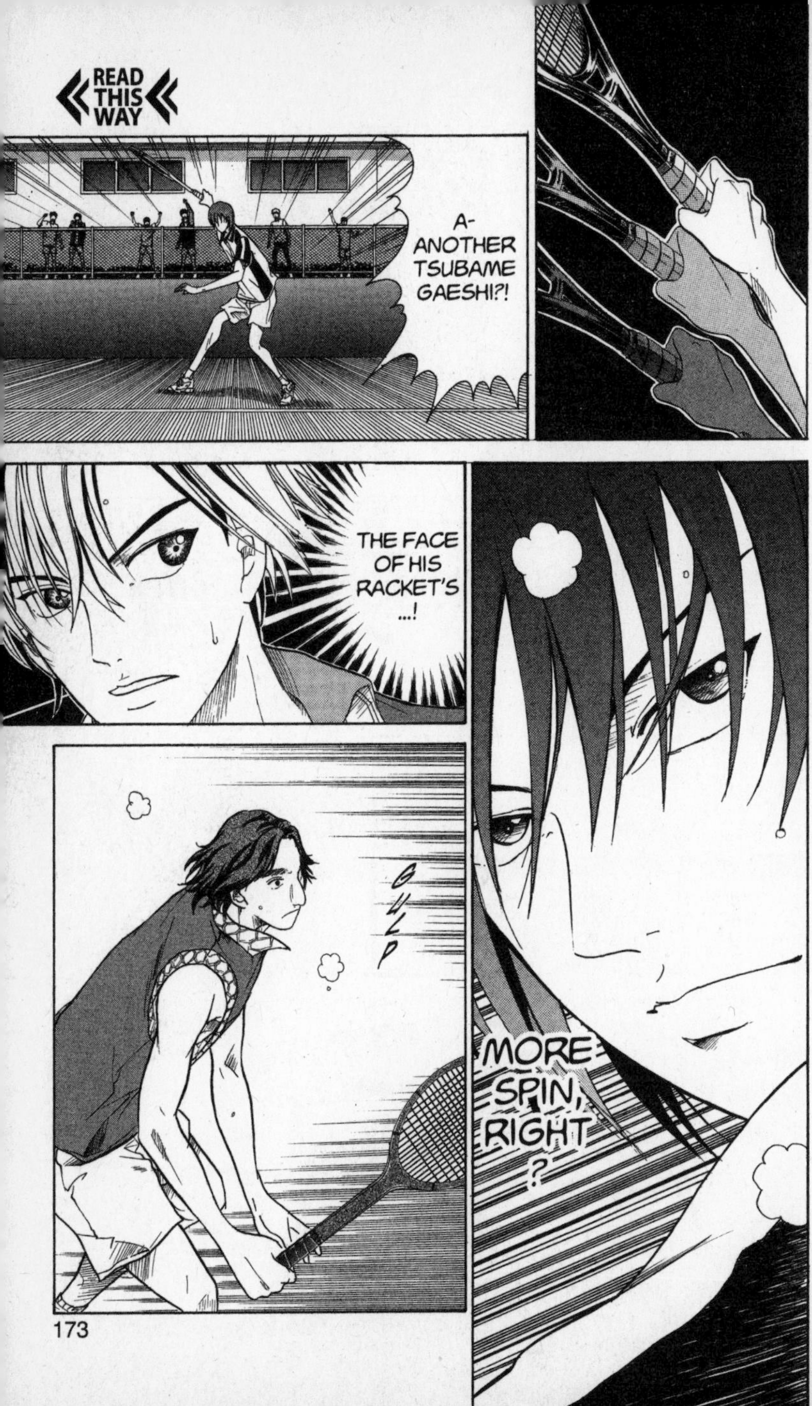
A- ANOTHER TSUBAME GAESHI?!
MORE SPIN, RIGHT?
THE FACE OF HIS RACKET'S ...!
GULP

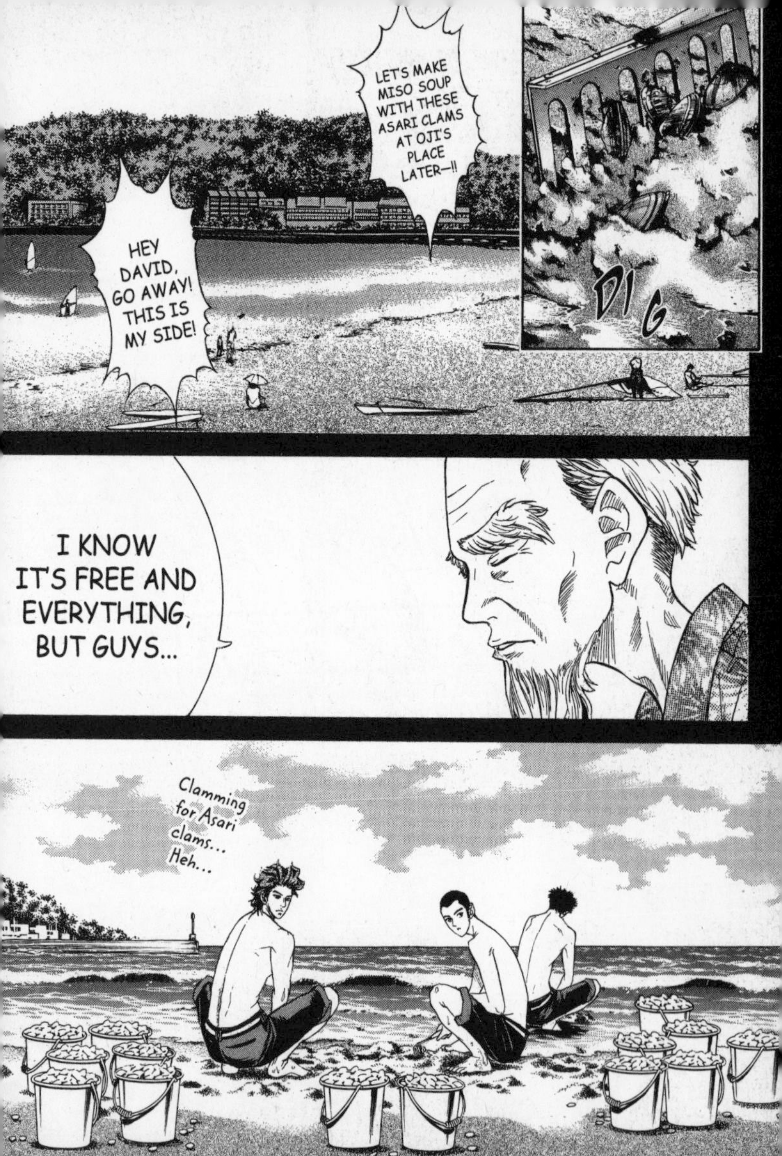
DIG
LET'S MAKE MISO SOUP WITH THESE ASARI CLAMS AT OJI'S PLACE LATER—!!
HEY DAVID, GO AWAY! THIS IS MY SIDE!
I KNOW IT'S FREE AND EVERYTHING, BUT GUYS...
Clamming for Asari clams... Heh...

READ THIS WAY

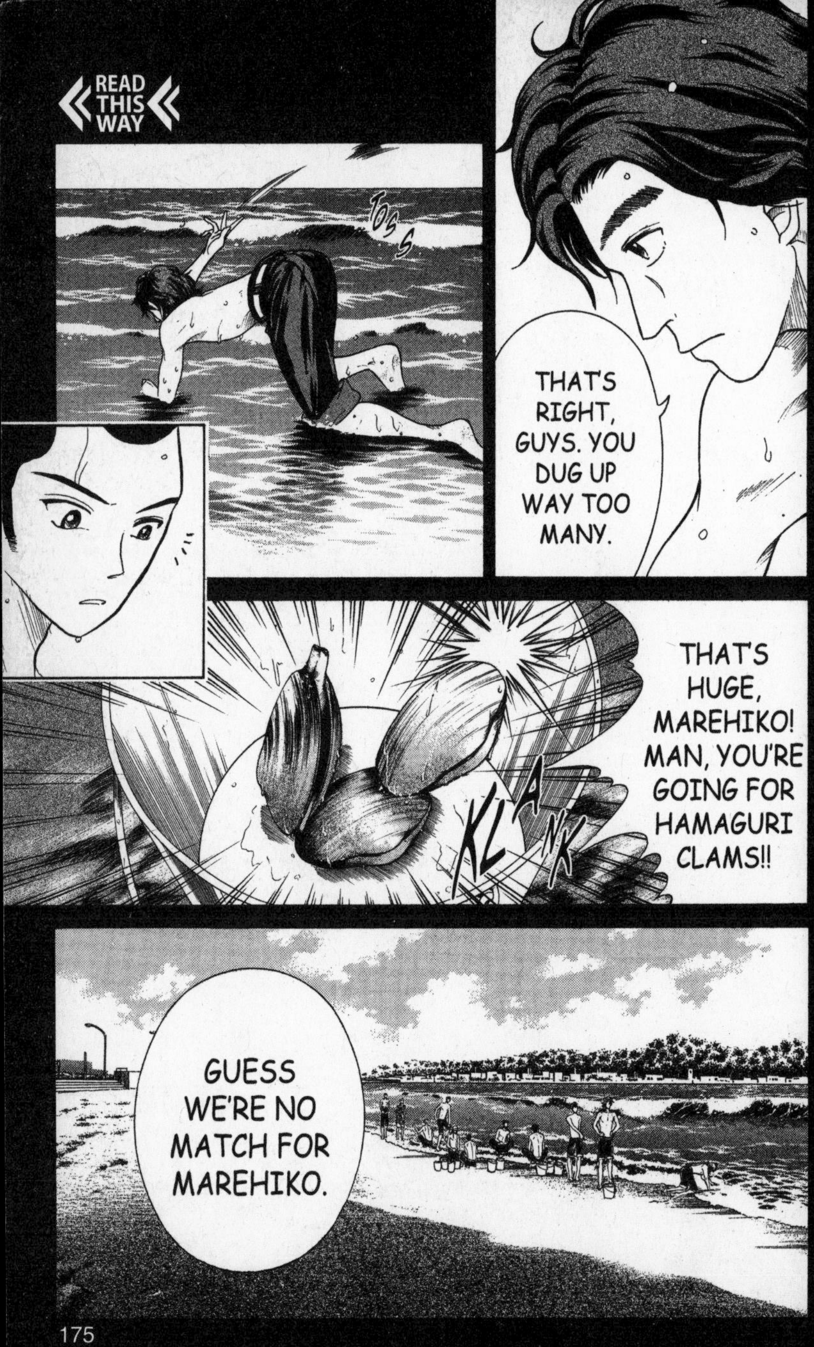
THAT'S RIGHT, GUYS. YOU DUG UP WAY TOO MANY.
TOSS
THAT'S HUGE, MAREHIKO! MAN, YOU'RE GOING FOR HAMAGURI CLAMS!!
KLANK
GUESS WE'RE NO MATCH FOR MAREHIKO.

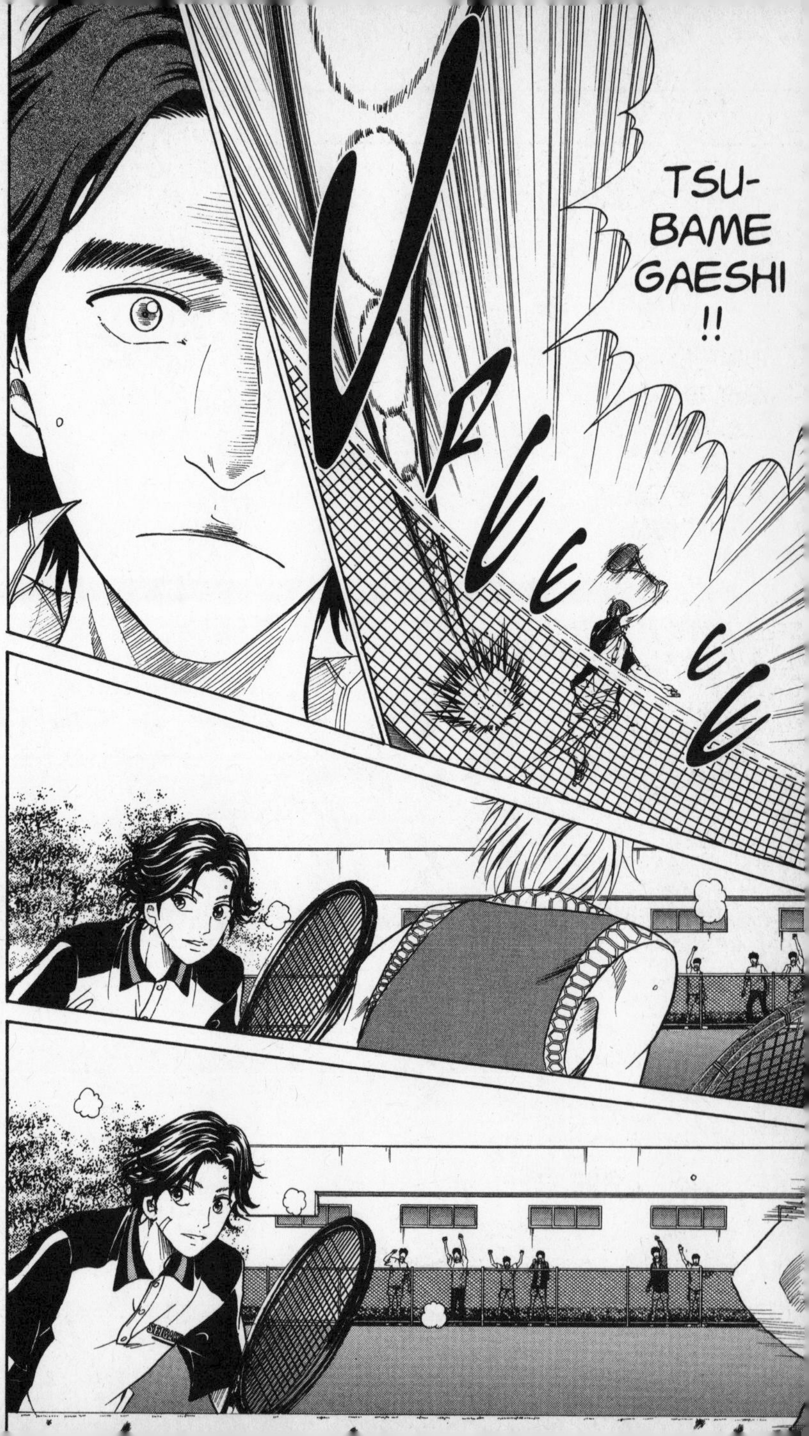
TSU-
BAME
GAESHI
!!

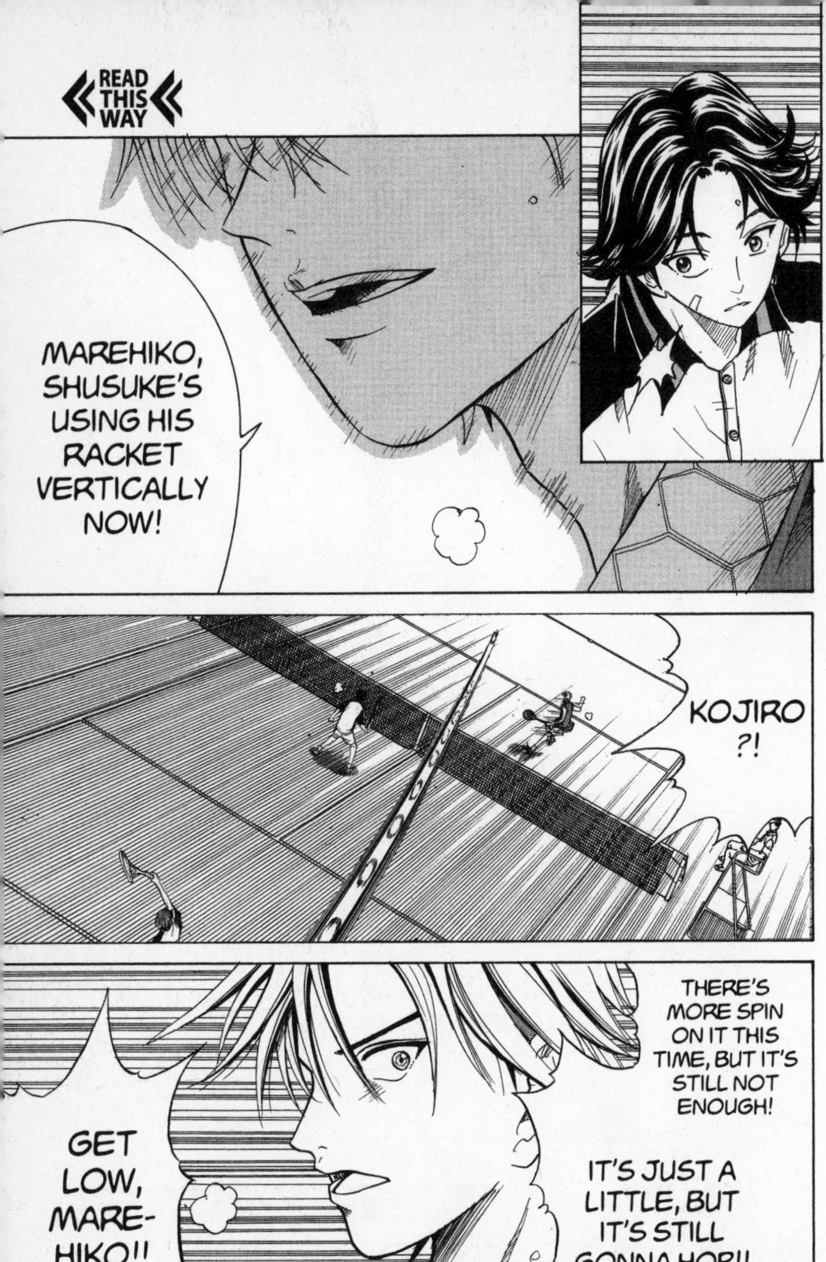
READ THIS WAY
MAREHIKO, SHUSUKE'S USING HIS RACKET VERTICALLY NOW!
KOJIRO ?!
THERE'S MORE SPIN ON IT THIS TIME, BUT IT'S STILL NOT ENOUGH!
IT'S JUST A LITTLE, BUT IT'S STILL GONNA HOP!!
GET LOW, MARE-HIKO!!

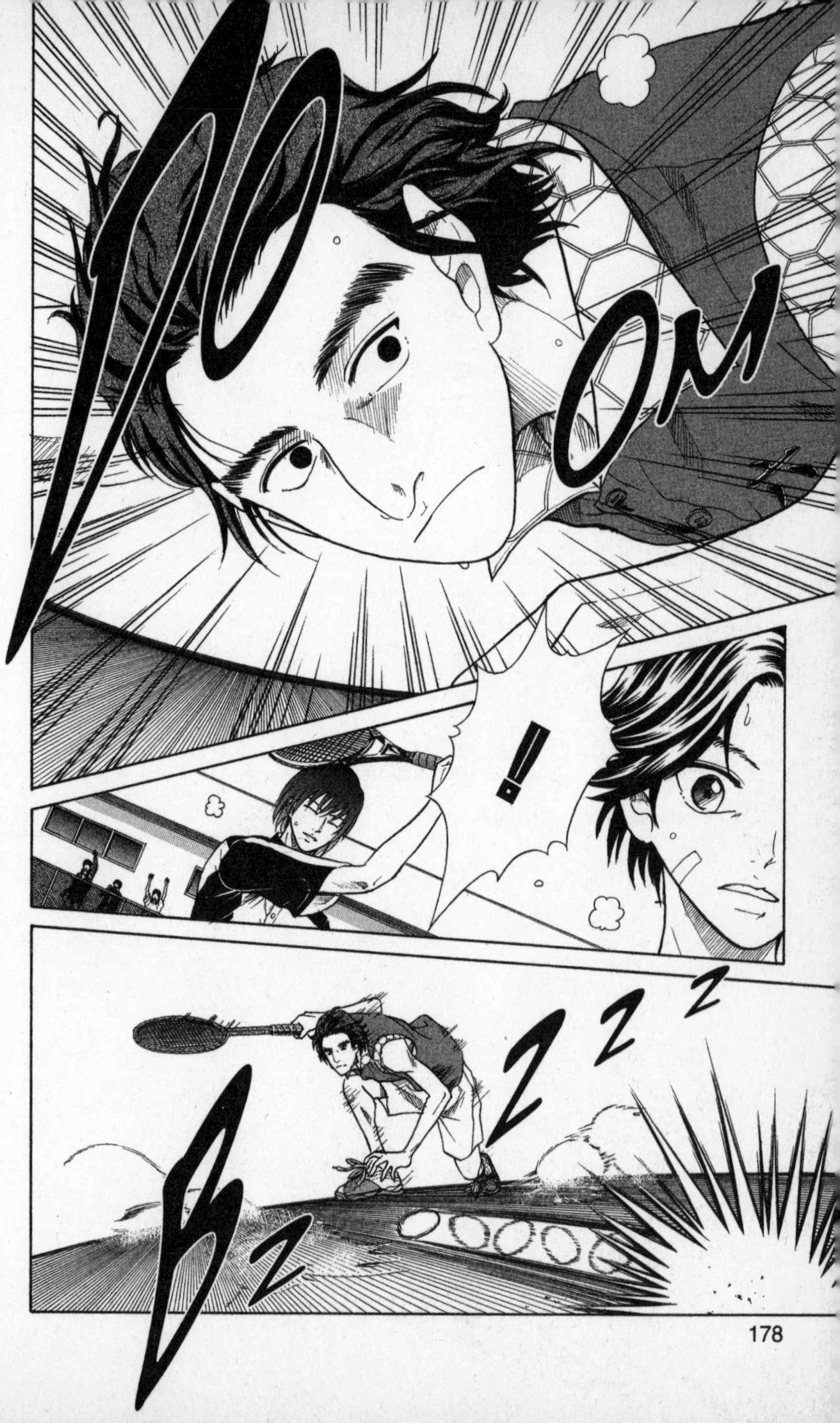
VOOOM
!
BZZZZZ

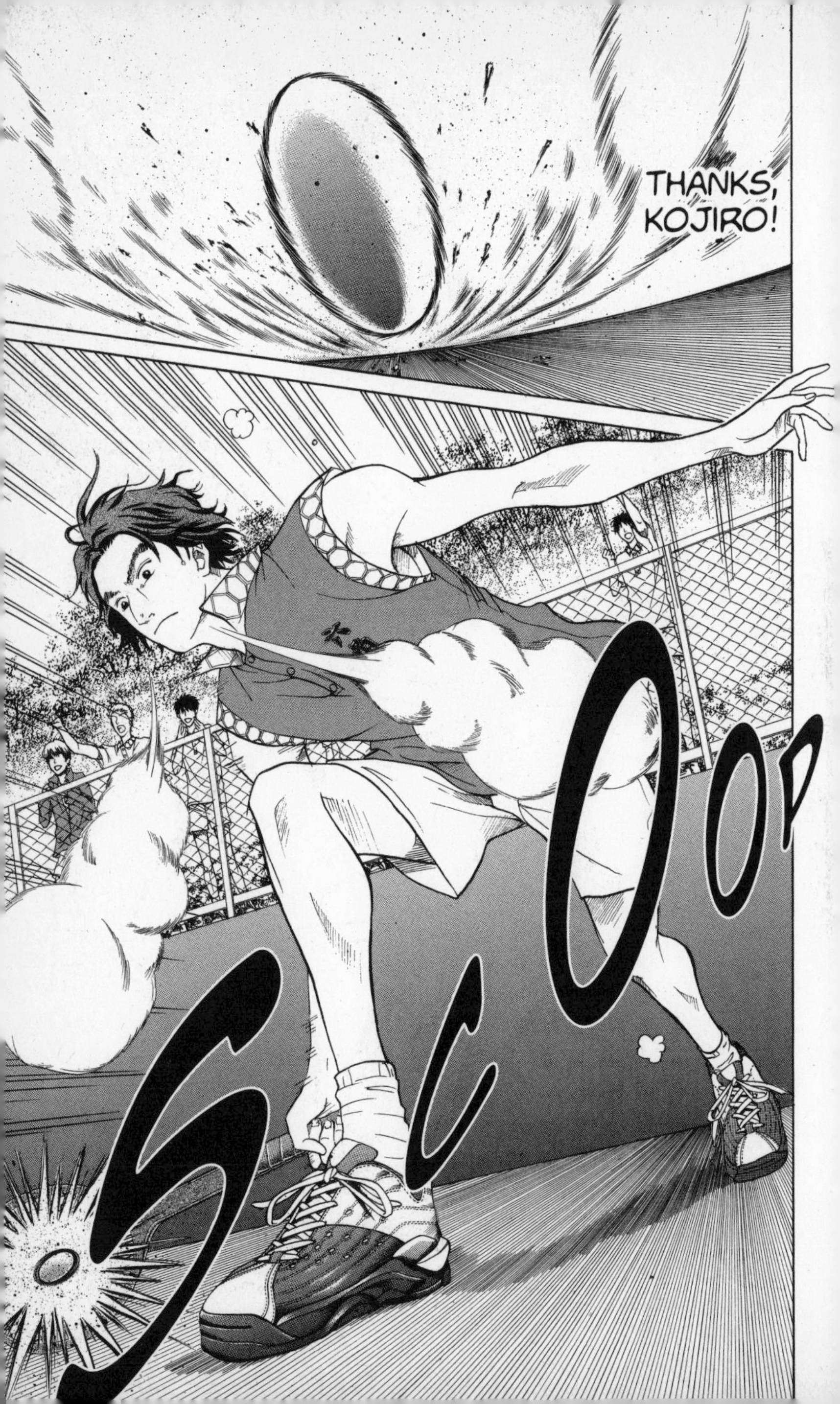
THANKS, KOJIRO!
SCOOP

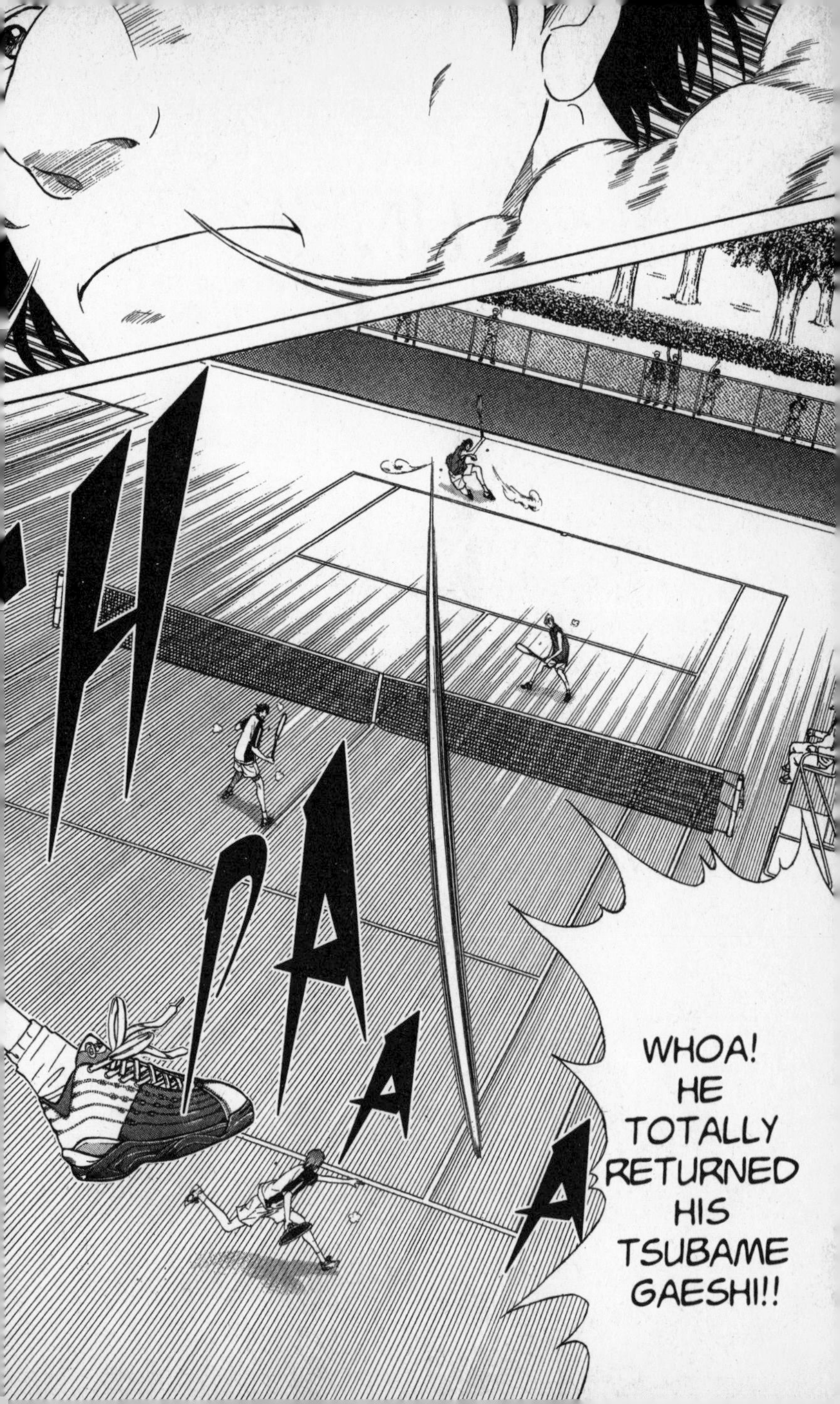
WHOA! HE TOTALLY RETURNED HIS TSUBAME GAESHI!!

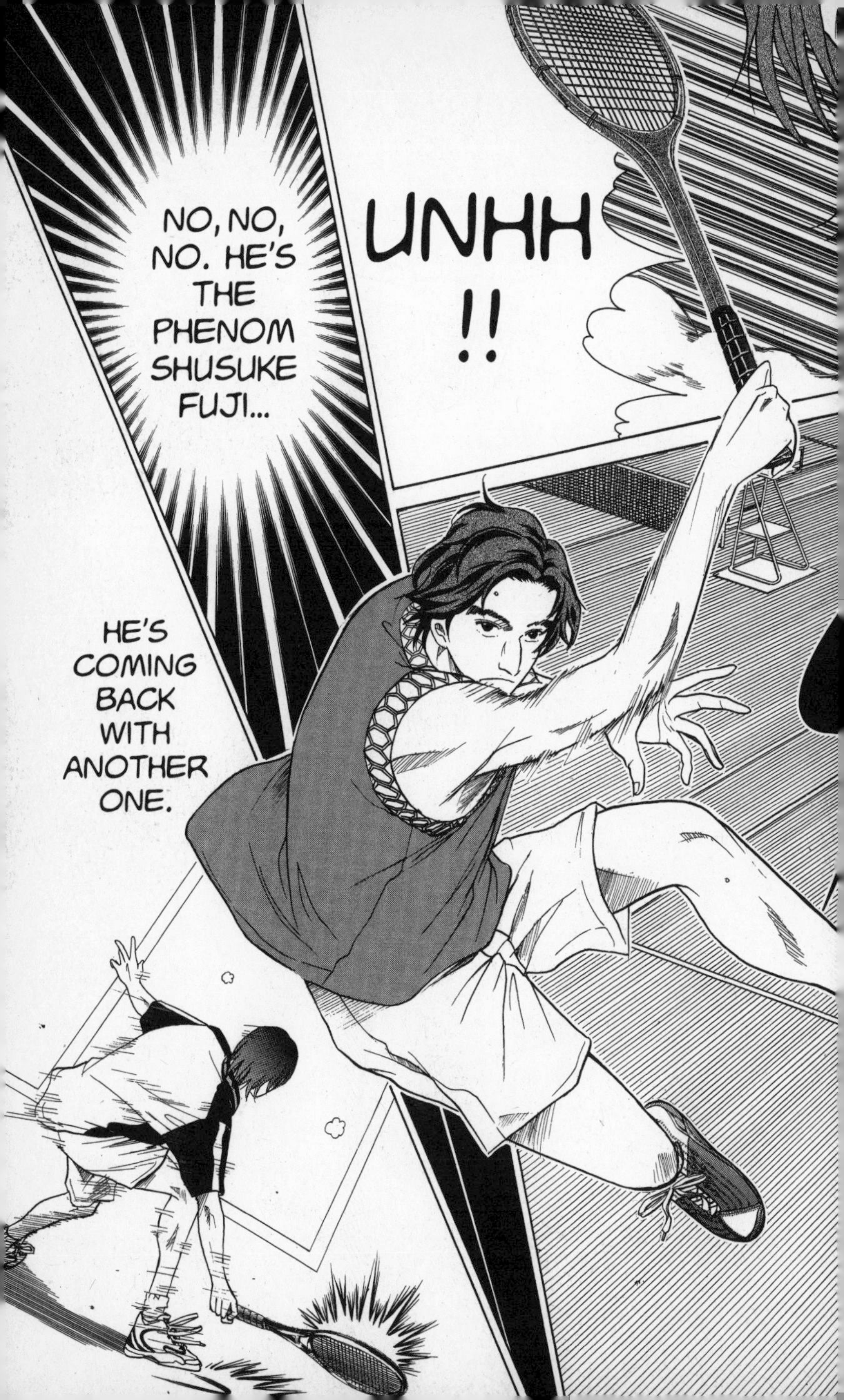
UNHH !!
NO, NO, NO. HE'S THE PHENOM SHUSUKE FUJI...
HE'S COMING BACK WITH ANOTHER ONE.

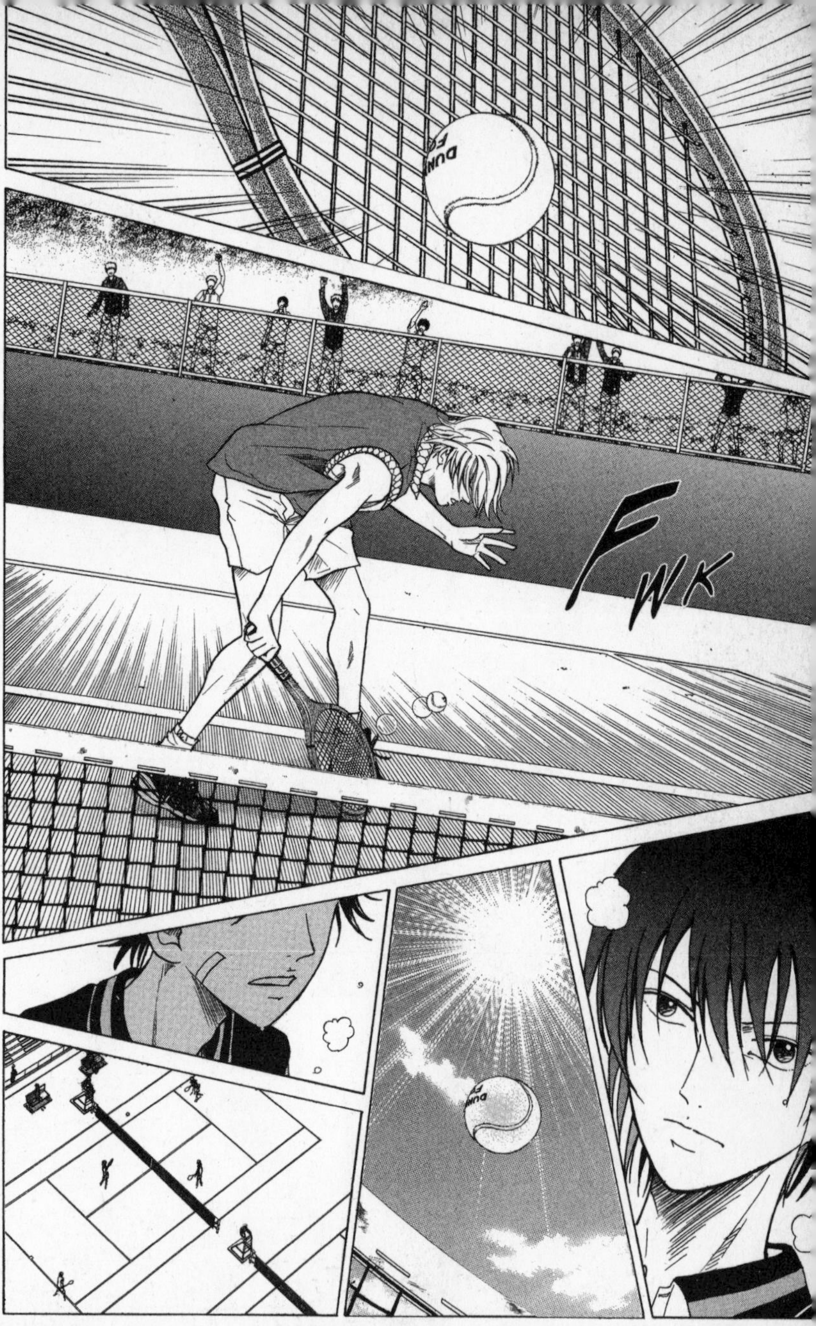
FWK

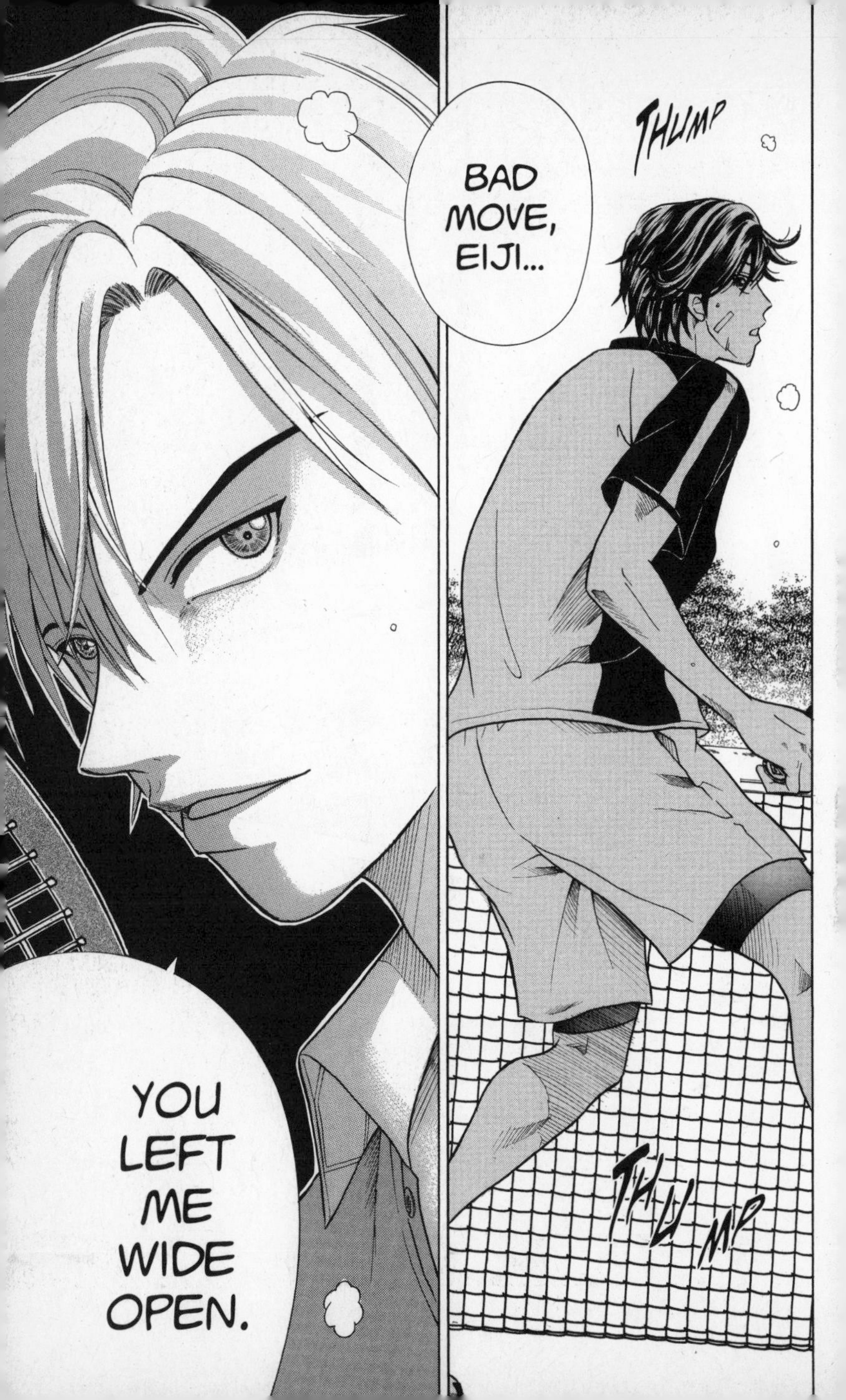
THUMP
BAD MOVE, EIJI...
THUMP
YOU LEFT ME WIDE OPEN.

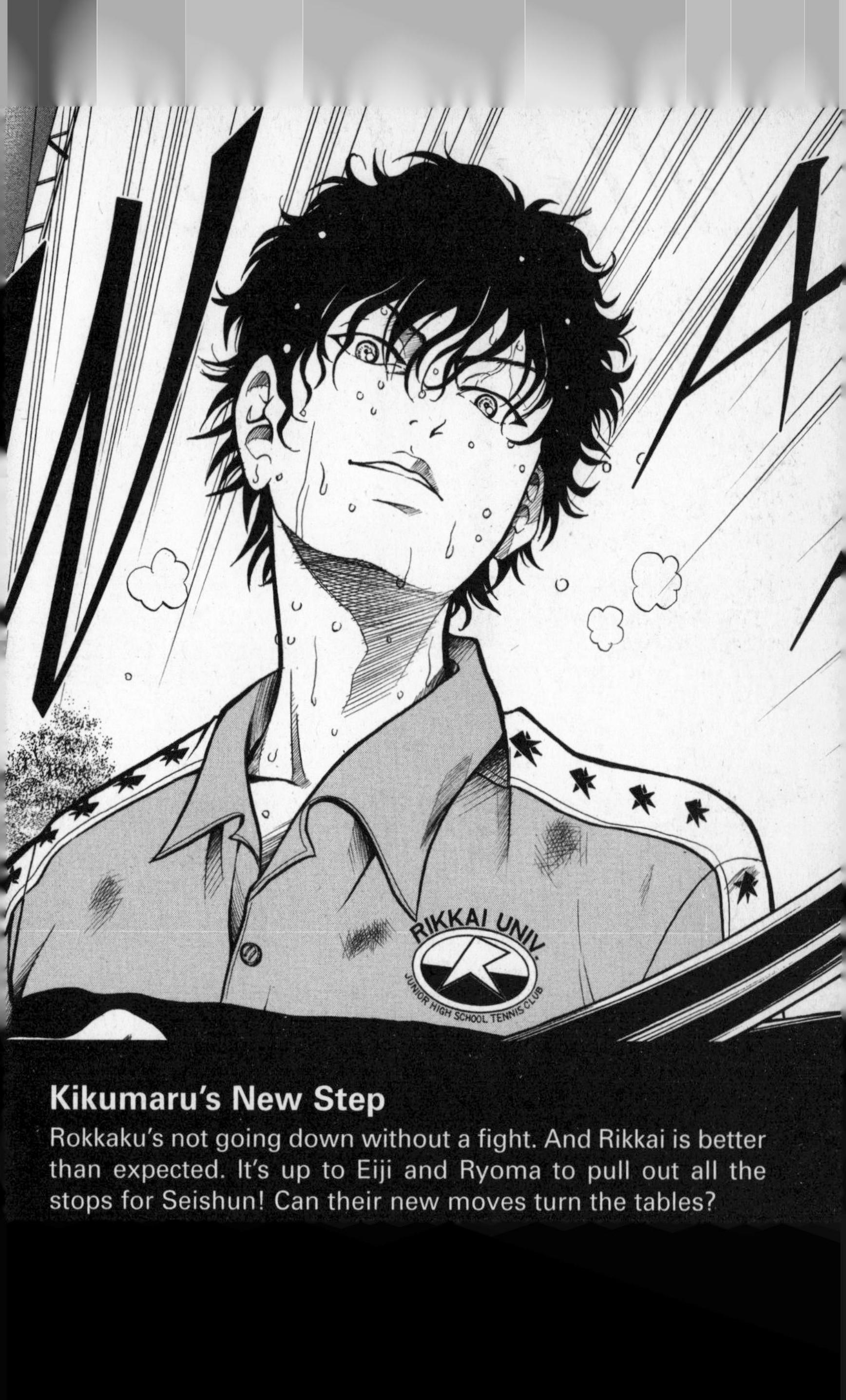
RIKKAI UNIV.
JUNIOR HIGH SCHOOL TENNIS CLUB

## Kikumaru's New Step

Rokkaku's not going down without a fight. And Rikkai is better than expected. It's up to Eiji and Ryoma to pull out all the stops for Seishun! Can their new moves turn the tables?

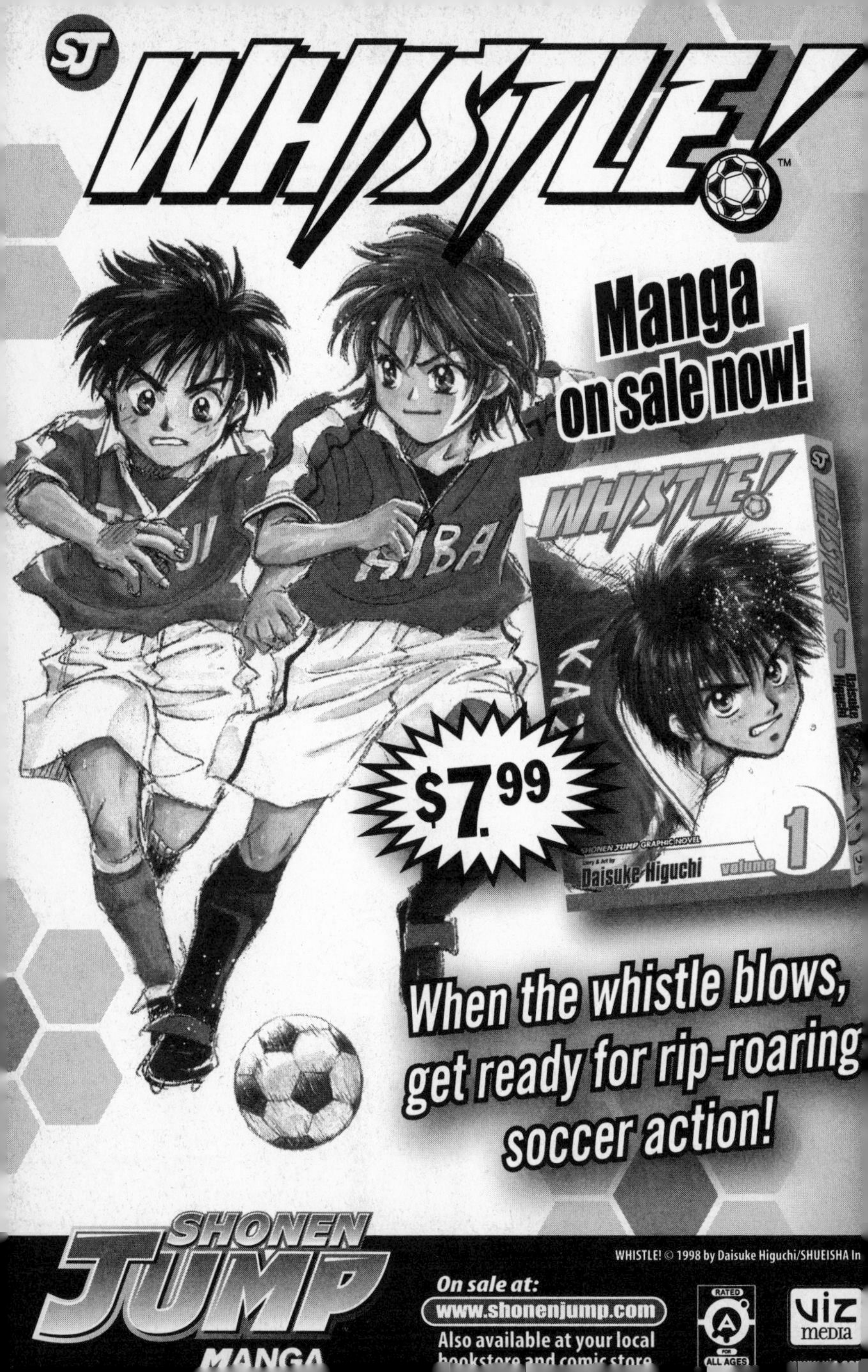

SJ
WHISTLE!™
Manga on sale now!
WHISTLE!
SHONEN JUMP GRAPHIC NOVEL
Daisuke Higuchi
volume 1
$7.99
When the whistle blows, get ready for rip-roaring soccer action!
SHONEN JUMP MANGA
WHISTLE! © 1998 by Daisuke Higuchi/SHUEISHA In
On sale at:
www.shonenjump.com
Also available at your local bookstore and comic store
RATED A FOR ALL AGES
VIZ media

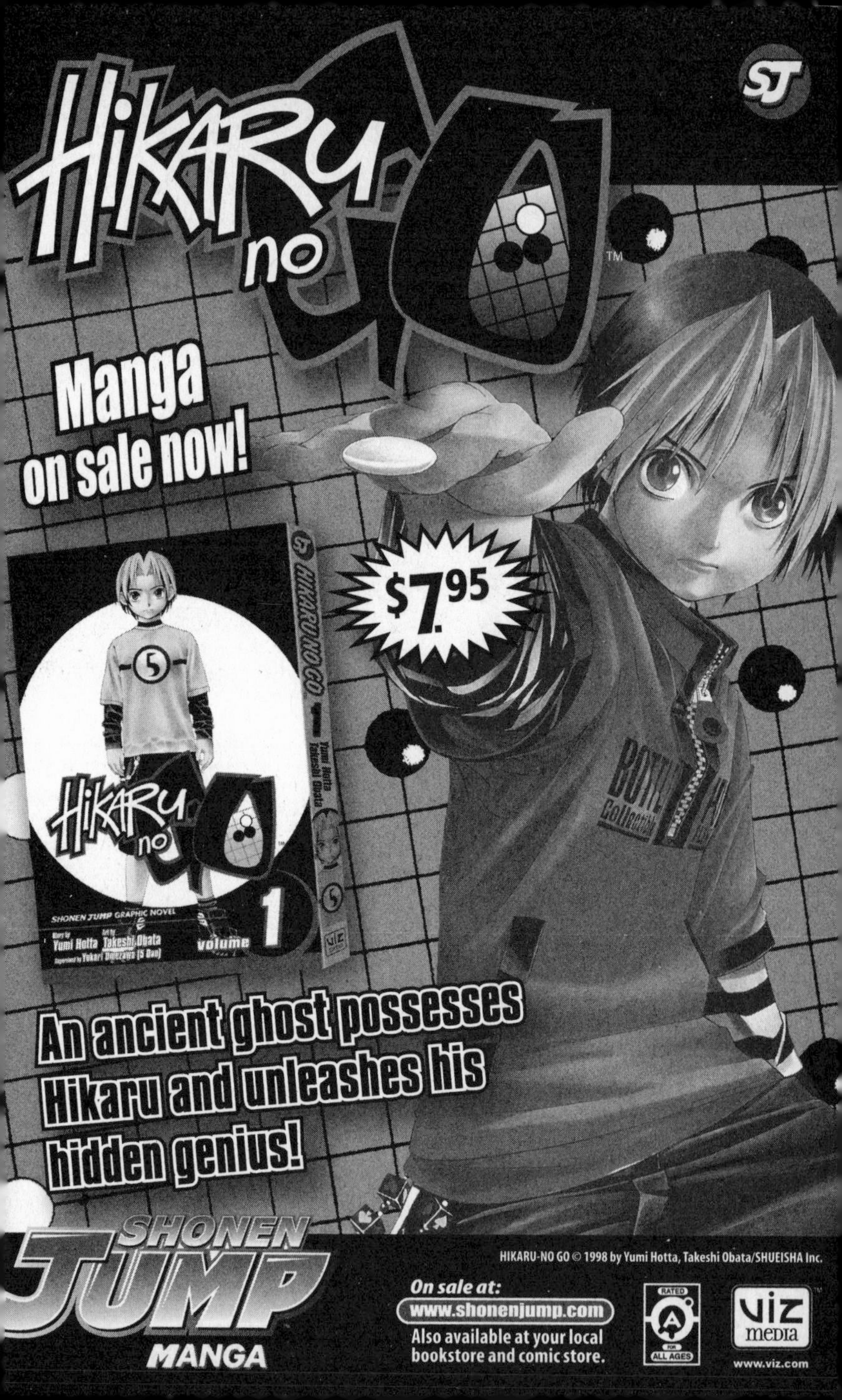

HIKARU no GO™
Manga on sale now!
$7.95
SJ HIKARU NO GO 1 Yumi Hotta Takeshi Obata
SHONEN JUMP GRAPHIC NOVEL
Story by Yumi Hotta Art by Takeshi Obata
Supervised by Yukari Umezawa (5 Dan)
volume 1
An ancient ghost possesses Hikaru and unleashes his hidden genius!
SHONEN JUMP MANGA
HIKARU-NO GO © 1998 by Yumi Hotta, Takeshi Obata/SHUEISHA Inc.
On sale at:
www.shonenjump.com
Also available at your local bookstore and comic store.
RATED A FOR ALL AGES
VIZ media
www.viz.com

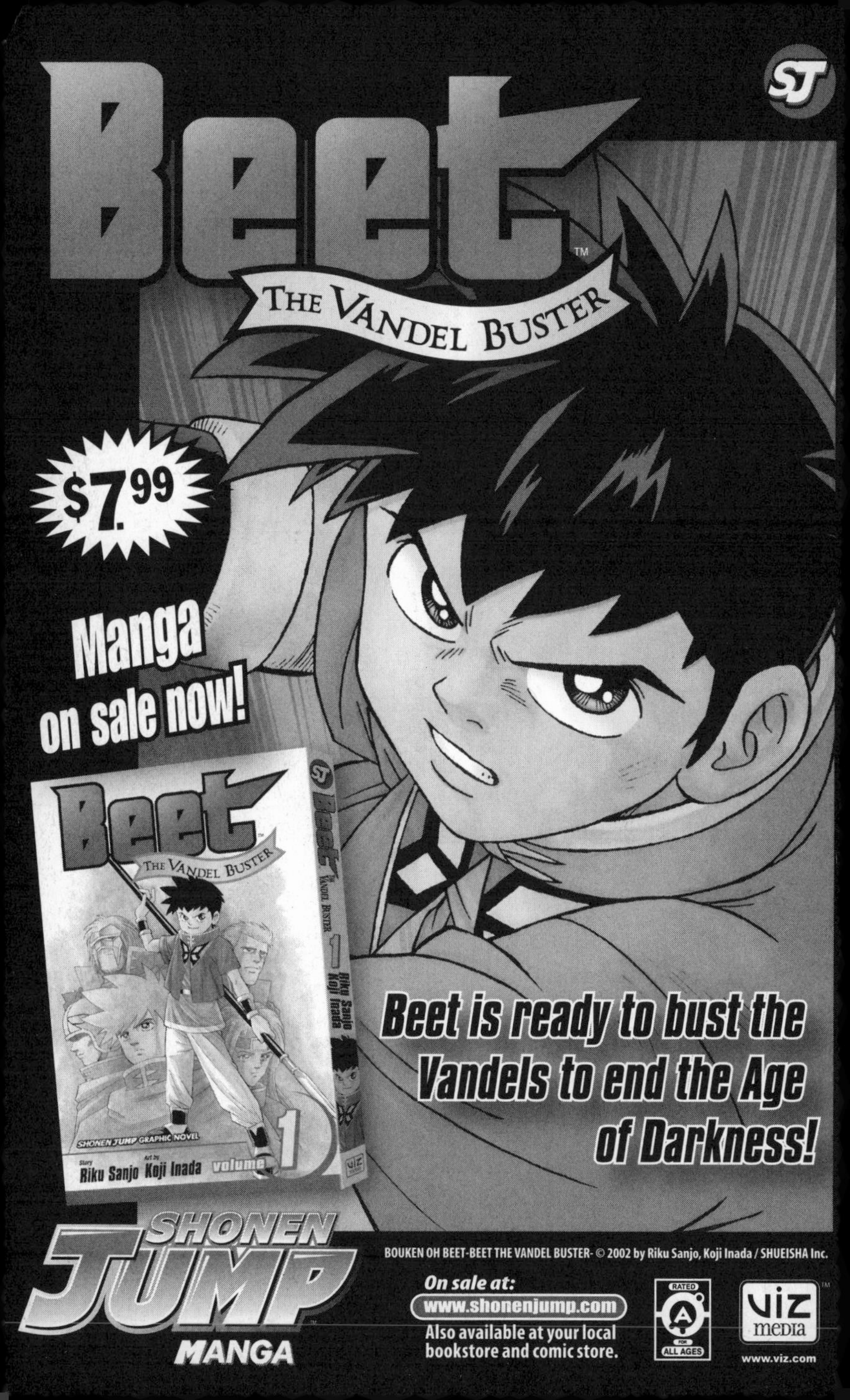

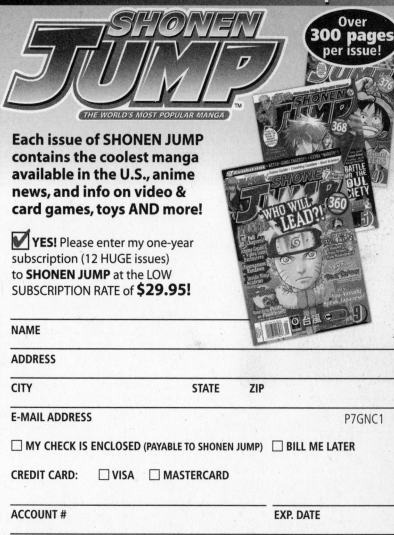